Humanitarian Intervention

Also by Aidan Hehir

Humanitarian Intervention After Kosovo: Iraq, Darfur and the Record of Global Civil Society

State-Building: Theory and Practice (co-edited with Neil Robinson)

Humanitarian Intervention

An Introduction

Aidan Hehir

palgrave
macmillan

First published 2010 by
PALGRAVE MACMILLAN

Palgrave Macmillan in the UK is an imprint of Macmillan Publishers Limited, registered in England, company number 785998, of Houndmills, Basingstoke, Hampshire RG21 6XS.

Palgrave Macmillan in the US is a division of St Martin's Press LLC, 175 Fifth Avenue, New York, NY 10010.

Palgrave Macmillan is the global academic imprint of the above companies and has companies and representatives throughout the world.

Palgrave® and Macmillan® are registered trademarks in the United States, the United Kingdom, Europe and other countries.

ISBN-13: 978–0–230–22030–0   hardback
ISBN-13: 978–0–230–22031–7   paperback

This book is printed on paper suitable for recycling and made from fully managed and sustained forest sources. Logging, pulping and manufacturing processes are expected to conform to the environmental regulations of the country of origin.

A catalogue record for this book is available from the British Library.

A catalog record for this book is available from the Library of Congress.

10 9 8 7 6 5 4 3 2 1
19 18 17 16 15 14 13 12 11 10

Printed and bound in China

For Sarah, Esmé, Elsie and Iris and . . . no more!

Contents

List of Boxes

Abbreviations

AMIS	African Union Mission in Darfur
AU	African Union
CCPDC	Carnegie Commission on Preventing Deadly Conflict
CDR	Coalition pour la Defense de la Republique
DIIA	Danish Institute of International Affairs
DPKO	UN Department of Peacekeeping Operations
ECOMOG	Economic Community of West African States Monitoring Group
FRY	Federal Republic of Yugoslavia
HRW	Human Rights Watch
ICC	International Criminal Court
ICED	International Commission of Enquiry on Darfur
ICISS	International Commission on Intervention and State Sovereignty
ICJ	International Court of Justice
ICRC	International Committee of the Red Cross
IICK	Independent International Commission on Kosovo
IMF	International Monetary Fund
IPA	International Peace Academy
IR	International Relations
JEM	Justice and Equality Movement
KLA	Kosovo Liberation Army
MNRD	Mouvement Revolutionnaire National pour le Developpement
MSF	Médecins Sans Frontières
NATO	North Atlantic Treaty Organisation
NGO	Non governmental organization
NSS	National Security Strategy of the United States
OIC	Organisation for Islamic Conference
PNAC	Project for a New American Century
R2P	Responsibility to Protect
RPF	Rwandan Patriotic Front
SFRY	Socialist Federal Republic of Yugoslavia
SLA	Sudanese Liberation Army
UK	United Kingdom
UN	United Nations
UNAMIR	UN Assistance Mission for Rwanda
UNHCR	UN High Commissioner for Refuges
UNMOVIC	United Nations Monitoring, Verification and Inspection Commission
US	United States of America
WMD	Weapon of mass destruction

Acknowledgements

Thanks firstly to Steven Kennedy at Palgrave Macmillan who encouraged me to write this book and provided excellent advice throughout. Nicholas Wheeler's input and suggestions were also invaluable and I thank him enormously for his time and input. Many others provided helpful advice and I would like to thank in particular Ian Bache, John Hobson, Tony Payne, James Gow and Patricia Hogwood.

Thanks also to everyone at the (new and improved!) Department of Politics and International Relations at the University of Westminster, in particular, Liza Griffin, Paulina Tambakaki, Simon Joss, David Chandler, Tom Moore, Giovanni Navarria and Rob MacMaster.

It was a pleasure to teach the final year undergraduate students in 2007-08 and their enthusiasm inspired me to continue with this book. Thanks also to Richard Smittenaar whose excellent dissertation was particularly useful for the conclusion to this book. Thanks also to Tom Gregory and his (far from embarrassing) work on 'The Ego and His Own'.

I would also like to thank Frank Black, Conor Barry, Polly Jean Harvey, Kyra, Chris, Mary, Elliot, Joe, Adam, Lauren, Dawn Carter, Aki Kaurismäki and the makers of calpol.

As ever thanks to my family, George, Niamh, Paul, Hazel, Jay, Nial, Rita, Ashling, Aran, Katie, Hannah, Emily, Chris, Lola Bee, Sue, Lucy, and especially my mother, Mary.

Finally, the biggest thanks go to my girls, Esmé, Elsie and Iris, and my wife Sarah. Nothing is worth doing if it's not for ye . . .

Introduction

Humanitarian Intervention in Contemporary International Relations

Humanitarian intervention generates intensely divisive debate within academia, between policy makers and amongst the general public. Humanitarian intervention is relevant to academics and students studying international relations (IR), philosophy, political theory, security studies, international law and peace studies. It is an issue that directly impacts on the agenda of states, non-governmental organizations (NGOs) and international organizations from NATO to the United Nations, and the African Union to the Arab League. It also, most importantly, affects ordinary people; those suffering ethnic cleansing, civil war and genocide, and those moved by these scenes of human anguish who cry out for something to be done.

In the post-Cold War era, debates about humanitarian intervention have become more frequent, more heated and more public, and the issue has moved to the very centre of the international political agenda. This book provides a comprehensive overview of the key concepts central to this debate, an analysis of the major sources of controversy, and an exploration of key case studies which highlight the practical manifestation of these issues. It is designed to act as a key source and guide for students, practitioners and the general reader.

The first section in this introduction comprises an examination of the evolution and nature of the contemporary debate, highlighting the key events and themes that have propelled humanitarian intervention to the forefront of IR. The second section provides an overview of the structure of this book and a guide on how to use its information to undertake further research in this area.

The contemporary debate

The contemporary controversy surrounding humanitarian intervention is not a uniquely modern phenomenon; humanitarian intervention has long been a divisive issue. While the terms of the debate may have altered, the actors may

1

have changed and the international context may be radically different, the question, 'Should external actors intervene on behalf of suffering people, and if so, how?' has been posed, in some form, for centuries if not millennia.

Accepting this, however, the issue did become more focused and problematic as international society organized itself into a community of sovereign states in the 17th century (see Chapter 3). The very idea of sovereignty implies inviolability, and the primacy of the principle of non-intervention in international relations. As international law increased both its scope and remit from the 19th century on, with sovereignty at its core, the status of humanitarian intervention became more ambiguous and contentious (see Chapter 5). Humanitarian intervention necessarily challenges the statist bias in IR and international law, and as states have assumed more formal legal powers and entitlements, the tension between the rights of states and the rights of the individuals within them has increased.

This tension has become especially keen in the post-Cold War era. With the implosion of the Soviet Union and the new primacy of the liberal democratic state, three themes emerged which impacted on and enlivened the issue of humanitarian intervention. They are discussed in the following sections.

(1) The end of history *(ideological shift)*

The end of the Cold War was famously heralded by Francis Fukuyama as 'the end of history'. Fukuyama was of course not suggesting that nothing of note would ever happen again; rather he argued that the collapse of communism signalled 'the end point of mankind's ideological evolution and the universalization of Western liberal democracy as the final form of human government' (1992, p.3). The issues of concern for future generations would centre on improving the functioning of liberal democracy, and crucially for the humanitarian intervention debate, spreading this model across the globe.

During the 1990s the eastward expansion of the European Union and NATO, the sharp turn towards capitalism in China and the increased willingness of the developing world and Russia to implement structural adjustment programmes at the behest of the World Bank and International Monetary Fund (IMF) were all cited as evidence of a universal appetite for the proliferation of liberal democracy and a general acceptance of the primacy of the liberal state model. The events of 11 September 2001 demonstrated, however, that there were some who rejected these changes during the 1990s, although these predominantly non-state actors were largely confined to the shadowy periphery at the time.

As capitalism spread, so too did democracy, as the core group of democratic states, loosely termed 'the West', increasingly tied financial aid and political support to democratic reform. Liberal democracies espoused a commitment to the centrality of human rights in their foreign policy, and therefore the internal character of states became an international issue (Chandler, 2002, pp.1–20). Acceptance into the democratic club was conditional on adherence to notions of individual inviolability and basic standards of human welfare. Those states that refused to reform their domestic system in line with the liberal ideal were increasingly portrayed as 'failed' or 'rogue' states and cast as international pariahs. Therefore, in contrast to the Cold War where the defining aspect of a state's relationship with the West was its disposition towards the Soviet Union, in the post-Cold War era this changed and the domestic dynamics within a state became, at least rhetorically, the seminal factor in determining its relationship with the West.

Antonio Cassese notes that human rights are 'subversive' and 'destined to foster tension and conflict among States' (2005, p.375). The increased focus on human rights certainly heightened international tension in the post-Cold War era; sovereignty became an increasingly contested concept as states subjected to criticism for their record on human rights sought to reject what they described as 'interference' and even 'neo-colonialism'. The West increasingly began to argue that a state's legal entitlements should reflect its adherence to human rights norms – the idea of 'conditional sovereignty' – and this generated a divisive international debate (see Chapter 6). The logical consequences of the march of liberalism were increased tensions between ostensibly liberal and illiberal states, and occasionally, the determination that particular instances of human rights violations had to be stopped by external military action or 'humanitarian intervention'.

The rise of the 'international community' (structural shift)

A second catalyst for the rise in the contemporary relevance of humanitarian intervention was the structural changes caused by the end of the Cold War. During the Cold War the world was divided between the East and the West, with the Soviet Union and the United States leading their respective spheres of influence. This was commonly referred to as a bipolar world order. When communism collapsed the United States stood as the sole remaining superpower, and we entered the so-called unipolar era.

While this fundamental structural change was considered by some observers to be both temporary and inherently dangerous (Layne, 1993; Mearsheimer, 1990), others considered that the new structure would have positive consequences for international justice and facilitate the promotion of human rights (Shaw, 1994, p.155). The rationale behind this perspective was that the new international order would be less polarized, and hence cooperation between states against rogue human rights violators would be more feasible than during the era of great-power competition. This cooperation would, it was argued, enable the United Nations (UN) to finally fulfil its mandate and take a more proactive role in international relations. The UN-sanctioned action against Iraq in 1991 seemed to confirm these hopes.

Throughout the 1990s people looked to the 'international community' more and more to solve the pressing issues of the day, and the United Nations in particular was called upon to extend its influence. This led to a dramatic increase in the number of UN-mandated peacekeeping operations, and interventions sanctioned by the Security Council under Chapter VII of the UN Charter (see Chapter 5). Additionally the internationalization of previously domestic issues led to significant developments in international law. The International Criminal Tribunal for the former Yugoslavia (ICTY) was established in 1993, and similar tribunals were later established in Rwanda, Sierra Leone, Cambodia and East Timor. The most notable consequence of this process occurred in 1998 when the General Assembly voted to establish the International Criminal Court, with unprecedented powers to prosecute individuals for genocide, war crimes, crimes against humanity and crimes of aggression.

The internationalization of human rights had two major effects. First, it ensured that the domestic human rights record of states became a legitimate issue for discussion at the international level. Previously, during the Cold War, adherence to human rights was essentially deemed a domestic concern, and strange as it may now seem, the dominant perspective within the discipline of IR was that human rights was not an appropriate issue for research (Lu, 2006, pp.5–6). Second, it raised expectations about the capacity of the 'international community' to solve intra-state humanitarian crises both within the West and indeed amongst those suffering at the hands of repressive governments (Kuperman, 2003). Since 1945 extensive human rights legislation had been codified in international law, although the suffocating effects of the Cold War negated the enforcement of these laws. With international cooperation now more feasible, the world was said to be entering an era of enforcement (Robertson, 2002).

Yet while human rights became a central issue in IR and expectations were raised about the capacity of the international community, and especially the United Nations, to enforce these rights, a number of situations demonstrated that the new international order was neither able nor indeed willing to act whenever egregious human rights violations occurred. The violence in the Balkans in the early 1990s, and most influentially the genocide in Rwanda in 1994, graphically illustrated the ongoing limitations in human rights enforcement. The international mood had changed, however, and whereas during the Cold War inaction in the face of human rights abuses was often lamented as a tragic but unalterable reality, in the 1990s tolerance for such reasoning declined. The rise of liberalism, as discussed in the preceding section, coupled with the heightened awareness of humanitarian crises caused by the internationalization of human rights and the communication revolution (see the following section), raised expectations, and the demand for action led to the emergence of a conviction that unilateral humanitarian intervention could be legitimate. Many argued that progressive liberal states should not desist from intervening to protect people from their own governments simply because one of the permanent five (P5) members of the Security Council vetoed such action. NATO's intervention in Kosovo in 1999 (see Chapter 11) was indicative of this perspective, and propelled the issue of unilateral humanitarian intervention to the top of the international agenda; the invasion of Iraq in 2003 ensured that it stayed there (see Chapter 12).

Globalization and the communication revolution *(technological shift)*

The process of globalization did not begin only when the Cold War ended, but the spread of capitalism which followed the collapse of communism certainly facilitated its acceleration. Open borders, free trade and competition are central to capitalism, and as these principles spread around the world they had significant implications for global communication.

First, increased competition led to an acceleration in technological innovation in the communication sector, leading to advances in satellite communication, the rapid growth of the internet and a greater ability to broadcast live from around the world. Increased global trade means that events in one part of the world have implications for businesses thousands of miles away. Hence, interest in global events increased due to accelerated economic interdependence. Additionally the 1990s saw a great increase in sources of information, as new radio and television channels emerged in competition with state-owned media. As the audiences for media sources grew, so did the need to broadcast 24 hours a day to appeal to global audiences in different time zones. With a greater number of channels broadcasting for a longer amount of time, the need for news stories grew, and reporters were sent across the globe to feed this growing appetite.

Human suffering, macabre as it may seem, generates keen public interest, and thus news reports from crisis areas are a virtual guarantee of high audience ratings. Live 'on the spot' reporting has the benefit of immediacy, but arguably at the expense of context and background; faced with scenes of carnage and death, reporters parachuted into trouble spots were accused of focusing on the emotive tales of suffering and making ill-founded determinations that X was an aggressor and Y a victim so as to enable audiences to engage quickly with what was happening (Kuperman, 2003). These simple narratives were certainly comprehensible to foreign audiences but often obscured the true causes of conflict. Thus the term 'the CNN effect' was coined to describe the new influence of the media on public opinion; presented with an obvious 'bad guy' and a 'helpless victim', people saw these crises as resolvable if an external force intervened to stop the aggressor from attacking the victim (Hammond, 2002, p.176). The growth of advocacy journalism in the 1990s witnessed the explicit commitment amongst certain journalists to take sides and proffer policy proposals. Thus the superficial presentation of the dynamics of a conflict, and the explicit support afforded to one party to a conflict, shaped public opinion, and led audiences to conclude that the solution was humanitarian intervention.

An additional problematic feature of the rise in influence of the media was that, as the International Commission on Intervention and State Sovereignty (ICISS) cautioned, many conflicts in inaccessible or unattractive parts of the world went unreported, and thus the media reportage often 'skew[ed] the response of the international community in an inconsistent and undisciplined manner' (2001, pp.5–6).

In tandem with the communication revolution, the number of NGOs increased exponentially during the 1990s, particularly in the first half of the decade (Anheier, Glasius and Kaldor, 2001). A great number of these NGOs were committed to highlighting human rights abuses and raising public awareness so that this would generate domestic pressure for action within Western states. The rapid proliferation of humanitarian NGOs and the increased capacity of the global media had reciprocal benefits: the NGOs exploited the new media, especially the internet, to disseminate their work, while the media used the reports of these NGOs as a source of information and news, thereby spreading the findings of these NGOs.

The result, therefore, was that in the post-Cold War era 'public opinion is better informed (the CNN effect) about geographically remote conflicts, and less tolerant therefore of inactivity on the part of their own governments' (Moxon-Browne, 1998, p.192). Situations in 'unimportant' parts of the world, such as those in Kosovo and Somalia, which became matters for domestic debate within Western states in the 1990s, in contrast to the Cold War era, therefore owed much to the communication revolution and the proselytizing of NGOs.

In summary then, we can see that the coincidence of three dynamics – one ideological, one structural and one technological – unique to the post-Cold War era contrived to propel humanitarian intervention to the top of the international political agenda. While there is much evidence to support this view, it is of course not universally accepted. Certain observers argue that the increased focus on human rights and appetite for intervention had a more nefarious genesis, namely the attempt to further empower Western states by legitimizing intervention through the invention of a new foreign policy rationale which legitimized the armaments industry in the absence of communism and created a conceptual distinction between the civilized core and the barbarous hinterland (Chandler, 2000a; Chomsky, 1999, Orford, 2003). The contested nature of arguably every aspect of humanitarian intervention is, however, one of the reasons that this is such a fascinating subject.

Using this book

This book has three parts. Part I focuses on the foundational concepts central to, and the theoretical basis for, humanitarian intervention. Part II examines the key sources of controversy which have generated the most heated discussion. Part III provides an overview of the history of humanitarian intervention and empirical insights into key case studies in the post-Cold War era which have brought together the concepts and controversies noted in Parts I and II.

This book is an introduction to humanitarian intervention, and while I have highlighted as many different perspectives on this issue as possible, what follows is not exhaustive. It is simply not feasible to examine the entire spectrum of perspectives on humanitarian intervention, and although this book is possibly more comprehensive than any other, it is not definitive. Additionally there are many more case studies which have influenced the trajectory of this debate than the four focused on in Part III.

My intention in each chapter is to provide the reader with an insight into differing perspectives on each issue. This book is not designed to support any one viewpoint or privilege a particular school of thought, and consciously aims to provoke the reader's interest by raising more questions than it answers. Understanding humanitarian intervention is not possible by simply accumulating facts, as there are very few uncontested 'facts' as such. The key to engaging with this issue is to read widely, engage with different perspectives and form an opinion based on your accumulated knowledge.

The bibliography lists all the sources used in this book, and following the usual convention there are extensive references throughout each chapter which can be used as a guide to certain perspectives and insights. There are myriad journal articles on this issue, and a number of academic journals are particularly rich sources of information (see Box I.1).

Each chapter has a Further Reading section which highlights literature specifically relevant to the chapter. This is not a definitive list, and the references in each chapter should be the primary source of guidance to relevant literature. Many academics specialize in humanitarian intervention, and their lists of publications, usually available through their university websites, should be explored. Box I.2 lists a number of scholars whose work is particularly apposite, although there are many more active in this field. (Apologies to those not listed!)

The questions at the end of each chapter should ideally be answered without referring back to the text of the chapter in which they appear. It is not imperative that these questions be answered immediately; they are indicative of the type of questions asked when discussing the issues raised in the chapter, and therefore should be referred back to when more research is undertaken.

Box I.1　Some key journals on humanitarian intervention

American Journal of International Law
American Political Science Review
Civil Wars
Ethics
Ethics and International Affairs
European Journal of International Law
European Journal of International Relations
Foreign Affairs
Global Governance
Global Society
Human Rights Law Review
International Affairs
International Journal of Human Rights
International Political Science Review
International Peacekeeping
International Relations
Journal of International Law and International Relations
Journal of Intervention and State Building
Journal of Peace Research
Journal of Social Philosophy
Millennium
New Perspectives Quarterly
Philosophy and Public Affairs
Political Studies
Security Dialogue
Survival
Third World Quarterly
World Politics

Box I.2　Some key authors on humanitarian intervention

Daniele Archibugi
Mohammed Ayoob
Alex Bellamy
Ken Booth
Chris Brown
Ian Brownlie
Alan Buchanan
Michael Byers
Richard Caplan
Antonio Cassese
David Chandler
Simon Chesterman
Jean Cohen
Neta Crawford
Alex de Waal
Timothy Dunne

Richard Falk
Tom Farer
Stanley Hoffmann
J. L. Holzgrefe
Robert Jackson
Mary Kaldor
Robert O. Keohane
Alan Kuperman
Anthony Lang
Andrew Linklater
Mahmood Mamdani
Richard Miller
Justin Morris
Terry Nardin
Anne Orford
Oliver Ramsbotham

Nicholas Rengger
Oliver Richmond
Adam Roberts
Gerry Simpson
Karen E. Smith
Michael Smith
Jane Stromseth
Fernando Tesón
Ramesh Thakur
Michael Walzer
Thomas Weiss
Jennifer Welsh
Nicholas Wheeler
Paul Williams
Tom Woodhouse

Part I

Concepts and Conceptions

Chapter 1

What is 'Humanitarian Intervention'?

One of the dominant controversies of our time is the question, 'What is to be done when a state is unwilling or unable to halt a humanitarian crisis within its territory?' Images and accounts of disaster often generate impassioned calls to 'do something' amongst observers, and reignite the debate regarding the rights and responsibilities that states, and the international community, have to alleviate suffering abroad. 'Humanitarian intervention' is an issue of uniquely broad interest which continues to be debated in the international arena, within academia and in the popular media. While there is general consensus as to the importance of humanitarian intervention, it is also one of the most divisive issues in contemporary international relations.

Ideally, an investigation into the controversy surrounding humanitarian intervention and its impact on international relations would start with a definition of humanitarian intervention. Central to the controversy surrounding humanitarian intervention, however, is that the very meaning of the term is itself controversial. As Anthony Lang notes,

> The contention over the meaning of . . . 'humanitarian intervention' suggests both the difficulty and importance of definitions. In fact, in trying to define this particular term, two issues arise. First, there is no clearly defined understanding of the term. Second, any definition contains within it certain normative assumptions. (2003, p.2)

The term is also used widely in legal, political and philosophical literature, and the definition employed tends to reflect the field of the analyst. Humanitarian intervention is not, of course, unique in this respect; many terms employed in the social sciences, from 'terrorism' to 'sovereignty', evidence similar definitional controversies, and one could plausibly argue that all key concepts in politics are, to some degree, 'essentially contested'. Despite the acknowledged difficulty in determining precisely what 'humanitarian intervention' is, many have, for reasons of expediency, employed the term with a stated degree of caution. A number of definitions have been offered (see Box 1.2), and through an analysis of these definitions a composite definition can be formed which, although it might itself be contentious, at least narrows the parameters of the debate. This is the aim of this chapter.

11

This chapter comprises two sections. The first narrows the scope for ambiguity by outlining what humanitarian intervention is *not*, through differentiating 'humanitarian intervention' from both 'humanitarian action' and 'strategic military intervention'. The second section highlights those aspects of humanitarian intervention that impact on its definition. This section focuses on, in turn, the status of the parties involved, the question of consent, the means employed, the motives, and the issue of legality. These issues are examined here in terms purely of their impact on the formulation of a *definition* of humanitarian intervention, not on the process of evaluating the *legitimacy* of a given intervention.

'Humanitarian intervention', 'humanitarian action' and 'military action'

Central to the definitional difficulty, as Lang's earlier quote notes, is the word 'humanitarian'. As we shall explore in greater detail in this chapter, the use of an essentially positive adjective – humanitarian – to describe an intervention largely determines the parameters within which the evaluation of this intervention can proceed. An intervening party that declares its actions to be 'humanitarian' is explicitly attempting to legitimize these actions as non-partisan and moral, and hence inherently justified, rather than selfish and strategic, and hence necessarily contentious. Therefore, in a similar way to branding an act of violence 'terrorism', the term 'humanitarian intervention' carries intrinsic normative assumptions. Hence, the application of this term elevates any discourse beyond pure description, making it both subjective and contentious. In this respect the statement, 'In March 2003 the USA launched a military intervention against Iraq' constitutes a neutral description of Operation Iraqi Freedom, whereas 'In March 2003 the USA launched a humanitarian intervention into Iraq' is necessarily evaluative and subjective. As the International Commission on Intervention and State Sovereignty (ICISS) stated, '[the] use in this context of an inherently approving word like "humanitarian" tends to prejudge the very question in issue – that is whether the intervention is in fact defensible' (2001, p. 9).

One of the key distinctions which must initially be drawn is between 'humanitarian intervention' and 'humanitarian action'. 'Humanitarianism' and 'humanitarian action' are terms widely used among aid workers and non-governmental organizations (NGOs). In this context the term 'humanitarian' is used to denote an altruistic, apolitical concern for human welfare. Cornelio Sommaruga, President of the International Committee of the Red Cross (ICRC), outlined this distinction in an address to the UN General Assembly in 1992:

humanitarian endeavor and political action must go their separate ways if the neutrality and impartiality of humanitarian work is not to be jeopardized . . . it is dangerous to link humanitarian activities aimed at meeting the needs of victims of a conflict with political measures designed to bring about the settlement of the dispute between the parties. (Lu, 2006, p.44)

The ICISS avoided using the term 'humanitarian intervention' in its 2001 report partly because of the opposition expressed by humanitarian agencies towards the militarization of the word 'humanitarian' (2001, p.9). Kofi Annan's address to a symposium organized by the International Peace Academy (IPA) in 2000 is particularly illustrative of this desire to separate humanitarian action from military intervention. Annan, noting the widespread confusion about the meaning of the term 'humanitarian intervention', called for the preservation of the specific role of humanitarianism:

[We must] get right away from using the term 'humanitarian' to describe military operations. . . . military intervention should not . . . in my view, be confused with humanitarian action. Otherwise, we will find ourselves using phrases like 'humanitarian bombing' and people will soon get very cynical about the whole idea. (Annan, 2000)

Despite Annan's plea the term 'humanitarian intervention' continues to be used widely, and the cynicism he foresaw has indeed become a feature of this debate.

Traditionally humanitarian organizations adopted an apolitical stance, refusing to engage with questions of right or wrong, focusing instead on humanitarian need and relief. In recent times, however, the avowal of neutrality has been challenged by so-called 'new humanitarians' who reject the traditional approach. As Fiona Fox notes, 'New humanitarian aid provision is overtly political, embracing a politically conscious aid strategy which, it is argued, can positively impact on the politics of a conflict or post-conflict situation' (2002, p. 19). This clash between 'traditional' and 'new' humanitarianism is exemplified by the different strategies employed by the ICRC and Médecins Sans Frontières (MSF), a group established by activists frustrated by the ICRC's neutrality and refusal to publicly condemn human rights violators (see Box 1.1). MSF is one of a number of humanitarian organizations that have begun to increasingly focus on 'human rights' rather than 'human needs', thereby necessarily adopting a political strategy.

These new humanitarians have at times been amongst the most vocal supporters of military intervention. Bernard Kouchner, founding member of MSF, has consistently championed the merits of external intervention. He was a particularly vocal supporter of NATO's intervention in Kosovo

Box 1.1 Médecins Sans Frontières

According to its website, MSF 'was founded in 1971 as the first nongovernmental organization to both provide emergency medical assistance and bear witness publicly to the plight of the people it assists. A private nonprofit association, MSF is an international network with sections in 19 countries' (MSF, 2007). MSF has a stated commitment to 'intervene in any country or crisis is based solely on an independent assessment of people's needs – not on political, economic, or religious interests. MSF does not take sides or intervene according to the demands of governments or warring parties' (MSF, 2007). It also, however, publicly condemns offending regimes and seeks to pressurize states and international organizations to take certain action – including military interventions – against these states.

In 1999 MSF was awarded the Nobel Peace Prize. On accepting the award James Orbinski stated:

> Silence has long been confused with neutrality, and has been presented as a necessary condition for humanitarian action. From the beginning MSF was created in opposition to this assumption. We are not sure that words can always save lives, but we know that silence can certainly kill. Chandler, 2002, p. 31)

in 1999 and later supported the overthrow of Saddam Hussein in 2003, albeit with certain provisos (Kouchner, 1999; Sciolino, 2007). Similarly, Human Rights Watch (HRW), in its *World Report 2000*, endorsed the interventions in both Kosovo and East Timor in the previous year and offered a very favourable analysis of the 'international community's ... new willingness to deploy troops to stop crimes against humanity'. HRW urged this trend to continue and heralded 'a new era for the human rights movement' (HRW, 2000).

Thus while humanitarian organizations have been critical of the use of 'humanitarian' as an adjective to describe military intervention, many have adopted an approach that necessarily weakens the distinction between humanitarian action and humanitarian intervention, with groups engaged in the former often overtly calling for the latter. This has been criticized by certain observers who see the blurring of the distinction between military action and humanitarian intervention through the human rights discourse as compromising traditional humanitarian principles (Chandler, 2002, pp. 21–53). Many argue that the neutrality of humanitarian organizations has been key to their success, and the new dispensation risks the merging of humanitarianism and Western foreign policy, which would necessarily compromise the status of these groups and potentially make them targets in those conflicts where they have explicitly taken a partisan position (Weiss, 1999).

Humanitarian intervention is additionally different from what may be described as strategic military intervention. The UN Charter is clear about the prohibition of the use of force in international relations. This principle finds its clearest expression in Article 2.4: 'All members shall refrain in their international relations from the threat or use of force against the territorial integrity or political independence of any state, or in any other manner inconsistent with the Purposes of the United Nations.' While the use of force is therefore clearly outlawed, certain exceptions to this rule do exist.

Article 51 of the UN Charter permits the use of force in self-defence. Chapter VII of the Charter also permits the use of force, but unlike Article 51, action taken under Chapter VII must receive prior approval from the Security Council (this is dealt with further in Chapter 5). Under Article 51 states are permitted to employ military force when they have been attacked, although the precise meaning of self-defence has become a particularly contentious issue since the launch of the 'War on Terror' in 2001 (Dinstein, 2005; Gow, 2005; Hehir, 2008c). The use of force in response to Iraq's invasion of Kuwait in August 1990 was sanctioned by UN Security Council Resolution 660 and constituted a manifestation of collective self-defence (Dinstein, 2005, pp. 273–7). The stated basis for the intervention was therefore not humanitarian but political. States need not advance any humanitarian rationale for the use of force if acting in self-defence. In fact, as Chapter 5 will demonstrate, humanitarian intervention is widely considered illegal and hence the trend has been for states to offer a legal justification based on Article 51 for instances of military intervention rather than a humanitarian justification, even when the latter was the more obvious impetus. A military intervention can thus be legal and legitimate without being humanitarian.

While the US-led intervention in Kuwait constituted a legal intervention sanctioned by the United Nations, many illegal military interventions and actions have evidenced a similar lack of an expressed humanitarian motivation. A military intervention is judged illegal if it transgresses international law, regardless of whether the aggressors advanced humanitarian motives or whether, if humanitarian motives were advanced, these motives were accepted as genuine.

Lassa Oppenheim's classic definition of war – 'a contention between two or more states through their armed forces, for the purpose of overpowering each other and imposing such conditions of peace as the victor pleases' (2006, p. 202) – makes no mention of humanitarianism. It is clear, therefore, that a military intervention need not be a humanitarian intervention, though a humanitarian intervention is widely considered necessarily to constitute a form of military intervention. Of course, the issue becomes more complex when states declare their military actions to be motivated by humanitarianism but these claims are not accepted by the wider international community. Infamously, Hitler portrayed Germany's invasion of

Czechoslovakia in 1939 as a humanitarian intervention, though few accepted his claims. In recent years the US-led invasion of Iraq has ignited controversy precisely because of the largely, though not exclusively, *ex post facto* humanitarian justifications offered (see Chapter 12). The issue thus becomes a matter of determining the legitimacy of the claims made, and this is the focus of Chapter 5. Of course, before the legitimacy of a putative humanitarian intervention can be determined it is necessary to determine a basic definition of 'humanitarian intervention'. It is to this task that we now turn.

Features of humanitarian intervention

Now that we have determined that humanitarian intervention is different from 'humanitarian action' and 'strategic military intervention', the following section will focus on those features routinely, though not uniformly, identified as fundamental to 'humanitarian intervention'. Box 1.2 provides a number of definitions of humanitarian intervention which form the basis for the analysis that follows.

The status of the parties involved

In the first instance definitions generally insist that the intervener is a third party to the conflict. J. L Holzgrefe's definition refers to states undertaking action 'aimed at preventing or ending widespread and grave violations of the fundamental human rights of individuals other than its own citizens' (2005, p. 18). Many of the other definitions listed similarly focus on interventions where the subjects whose suffering has prompted the intervention are not citizens of the intervening state. In this respect we can see that there appears to be some consensus over the relationship between the intervening actor and those in distress. Yet Holzgrefe provides the example of Richard Baxter as a counter to this consensus. Baxter's definition, unusually, describes action taken 'for the protection from death or grave injury of nationals of the acting state' (Holzgrefe, 2005, p. 18).

The precise status and composition of the intervening actor is quite ambiguous; few definitions explicitly identify the intervening actor. They offer instead a broad list of potential interveners, such as John Vincent's 'a state, a group within a state, a group of states or an international organization' (Vincent, 1974, p. 13). This aspect of the definition – the precise nature of the intervener – is therefore seemingly of minor importance. Provided that the intervening party is not based within the state where the crisis is taking place, the identity and composition of this party – be it a substate, state or trans-state actor – is not deemed significant, at least to the definition of humanitarian intervention, though it is of some legal importance.

Box 1.2 Definitions of humanitarian intervention

.the proportionate transboundary help, provided by governments to individuals in another state who are being denied basic human rights and who themselves would be rationally willing to revolt against their oppressors. (Tesón, 1998, p. 1)

the threat or use of force across state borders by a state (or group of states) aimed at preventing or ending widespread and grave violations of the fundamental human rights of individuals other than its own citizens, without the permission of the state within whose territory force is applied. (Holzgrefe, 2005, p. 18)

action taken against a state or its leaders, without its or their consent, for purposes which are claimed to be humanitarian or protective ... including all forms of preventive measures, and coercive intervention measures – sanctions and criminal prosecutions – falling short of military intervention. (ICISS, 2001, p. 8)

a short-term use of armed force by a government ... for the protection from death or grave injury of nationals of the acting state ... by their removal from the territory of the foreign state. (Baxter, in Holzgrefe, 2005, p. 18)

coercive interference in the internal affairs of a state, involving the use of armed force, with the purposes of addressing massive human rights violations or preventing widespread human suffering, (Welsh, 2006a, p. 3)

the threat or use of armed force by a state, a belligerent community, or an international organization, with the object of protecting human rights. (Brownlie, 1974, p. 217)

[When] the 'international community' ... intervene[s] in the domestic affairs of one of its members for humanitarian reasons, which can provisionally be defined as 'primarily in the interests of the local inhabitants. (Brown, 2006, p. 135)

Activity undertaken by a state, a group within a state, a group of states or an international organization which interferes coercively in the domestic affairs of another state. It is a discrete event having a beginning and an end, and it is aimed at the authority structure of the target state. It is not necessarily lawful or unlawful, but it does break a conventional pattern of international relations. (Vincent, 1974, p. 13)

coercive action by one or more states involving the use of armed force in another state without the consent of its authorities, and with the purpose of preventing widespread suffering or death among the inhabitants. (Roberts, 2002, p. 5)

The question of consent

Definitions invariably identify humanitarian intervention as an act undertaken without the consent of the host state. States experiencing humanitarian crises can appeal, and have appealed, to the international community for help, resulting in many cases in the deployment of international troops, such as the establishment of the UN Mission in Sierra Leone in October 1999.

Jennifer Welsh's definition, however, does not stipulate 'non-consent'. This is because she claims that '"non-consent" is in practice very difficult to maintain – particularly when consent is ambiguous or coerced' (2006, p. 3). Indeed, while the Federal Republic of Yugoslavia (FRY) clearly did not consent to NATO's intervention in 1999, technically Indonesia did consent to the deployment of an Australian-led force in East Timor in September 1999. The nature of Indonesia's 'consent' does support Welsh's concerns given that extensive international pressure was brought to bear on the government of B. J. Habibie and the consent eventually given was, to a large degree, a function of coercion (Wheeler and Dunne, 2001). While the question of coerced consent is a valid one, it is nevertheless clear that the majority view assumes consent to be absent.

The means

The focus of this second section of the chapter is not on the debate surrounding the legitimacy of any given intervention, but rather on identifying those features that generally feature in definitions of humanitarian intervention. Therefore, the focus here on the means employed relates only to how they have been conceived in various definitions, rather than the more controversial issue of how the means impact on the perceived legitimacy of any given intervention (see Chapter 8).

Definitions of humanitarian intervention generally emphasize military means as a central component, as evidenced by Iain Brownlie's 'the threat or use of armed force', a formula emulated by many others (1974, p.217). As with the previous features analysed, however, there are definitions that do not conform to this view. Fernando Tesón's definition stresses that the means must be 'proportionate . . . including forcible', thereby suggesting that non-forcible intervention may still qualify as a humanitarian intervention (1998, p.1). David Scheffer explicitly emphasizes peaceful means, referring to 'non-forcible methods, namely intervention undertaken without military force' (Holzgrefe, 2005, p.18).

Perspectives on the issue of means are linked to the question of consent; an emphasis on non-consent will naturally encourage a focus on coercive means, and vice versa. In a literal sense, of course, humanitarian organizations such as Oxfam and Save the Children engage in humanitarian interventions insofar as they intervene in a state for humanitarian purposes.

This activity has not, however, been the cause of the controversy surrounding 'humanitarian intervention', and as stated earlier, one of the clearest differences between 'humanitarian intervention' and the work of Oxfam and others is the use of force. Generally, therefore, the popular conception of 'humanitarian intervention' involves the use of force, if only to facilitate the narrowing of the parameters of the debate.

The motives

Whether an intervention must be inspired by humanitarian motives to qualify as a 'humanitarian intervention' is a highly contentious issue, which is dealt with in detail in Chapter 8. It is clear, however, that many definitions do emphasize humanitarian motivations. While Adam Roberts indicatively states that the purpose must be 'preventing widespread suffering or death among the inhabitants' (2002, p.5), others have gone further, stressing that the intervention must be motivated solely by altruism and the intervening party must have no interests involved (Miller, 2000a, p.54). This would appear to be an unreasonably onerous requirement. Thomas Weiss notes that 'Motives behind humanitarian interventions are almost invariably mixed', and this, he argues, does not fundamentally undermine an intervention (2007, p.7). Chris Brown's requirement that the intervention be 'primarily in the interests of the local inhabitants' possibly best reflects opinion on this aspect of the debate (2006, p.135).

Nicholas Wheeler, however, does not place significant importance on the motives behind an intervention, and focuses instead solely on the outcome (2002, p. 38). While this view is endorsed by others, it is a minority position, with most definitions including at least some reference to humanitarian motives. Of course, an individual's perspective on this aspect of the definition of humanitarian intervention will have significant implications on their judgement regarding the legitimacy of a given intervention.

The issue of legality

One of the primary sources of controversy surrounding humanitarian intervention is its legal status. While there is some disagreement over whether humanitarian intervention is legal, the majority of legal scholars consider it to be illegal at present. This, however, does not necessarily have implications for the legitimacy of an intervention; NATO's intervention in Kosovo in 1999 was judged by the Independent International Commission on Kosovo (IICK) to have been 'illegal but legitimate' (2000, p.4).

The definitions in Box 1.2 evidence little reference to legality, and those that do mention it are ambivalent. When we examine the definitions provided it is clear that many refer to coercive acts undertaken without the consent of the host state. Given that non-consent implies a breach of sovereignty, and as discussed earlier, such action is prohibited under international law, these acts are by definition illegal as they do not constitute acts of self-defence. If international law is mentioned in definitions it is only to assert that it is not integral to whether a particular act constitutes a humanitarian intervention. In this respect the question of legality has little real impact on the definition of humanitarian intervention.

Conclusion

As Alex Bellamy notes, 'almost every aspect of humanitarian intervention is contested' (2006b, p. 202), and hence defining humanitarian intervention is understandably contentious and difficult. The difficulty that surrounds the definition of the term derives largely from the normative assumptions inherent in the word 'humanitarian'. In this sense, the use of this subjective adjective necessarily complicates the formation of an objective definition, given that the word 'humanitarian', to a large extent, constitutes a positive value judgment. Catherine Lu suggests that the term should be abandoned in favor of 'label[ing] interventions in terms of the substantive activities that define them'. In this way NATO's Operation Allied Force would simply be described as a 'military intervention' (Lu, 2006, p.139). Similarly Antonio Cassese avoids the use of the term 'humanitarian intervention', preferring the more legally descriptive 'forcible countermeasures to prevent crimes against humanity' (1999, p.29).

These are valid concerns, yet while attempts have been made to change the terms of the discourse, most notably by the ICISS, 'humanitarian intervention' remains an oft used, though possibly misused, term. This is unlikely to change given how embedded the term has become in the public and academic lexicon. The pragmatic approach, therefore, is to conform to the prevailing discourse, accept that the term will continue to be used, and try to clarify its distinctive features. To this end, for the sake of further enquiry and based on the above analysis of existing definitions, the following definition constitutes the type of act to which all subsequent uses of the term 'humanitarian intervention' in this book refer:

> Military action taken by a state, group of states or non-state actor, in the territory of another state, without that state's consent, which is justified, to some significant extent, by a humanitarian concern for the citizens of the host state.

This composite definition is clearly not a legal definition, nor is it without contention, but it serves to differentiate 'humanitarian intervention' from 'humanitarian action' and 'strategic military intervention', and thus significantly narrows the parameters of enquiry. The legality, morality, legitimacy and broader implications of such an action for international relations and international law remain outstanding, and these issues constitute the remaining focus of this book.

Questions

- Does the term 'humanitarian intervention' carry intrinsic normative assumptions?
- How can we distinguish 'humanitarian intervention' from 'humanitarian action'?
- How does 'humanitarian intervention' differ from 'strategic military intervention'?
- Based on existing definitions, what are the key features of humanitarian intervention?
- Is 'humanitarian intervention' a useful term or is it inherently flawed?

Further reading

Bellamy, A. and Wheeler, N (2008) 'Humanitarian intervention in world politics' in J. Baylis and S. Smith (eds), *The Globalization of World Politics* (Oxford: Oxford University Press).

Chesterman, S. (2002) *Just War or Just Peace?* (Oxford: Oxford University Press); Chapter 1.

Dinstein, Y. (2005) *War, Aggression and Self-Defence* (Cambridge: Cambridge University Press); Chapter 3.

Holzgrefe, J. L. and Keohane, R. (eds) (2005) *Humanitarian Intervention: Ethical, Legal and Political Dilemmas* (Cambridge: Cambridge University Press); Chapter 1.

Lang, A. (ed.) (2003) *Just Intervention* (Washington DC: Georgetown University Press); Chapter 1.

Welsh, J. (ed.) (2006) *Humanitarian Intervention and International Relations* (Oxford: Oxford University Press); Chapter 1.

Wheeler, N. (2002) *Saving Strangers* (Oxford: Oxford University Press); Chapter 1

Woodhouse, T. and Ramsbotham, O. (1996) *Humanitarian Intervention in Contemporary Conflict* (London: Polity); Chapter 1.

Useful websites

International Commission on Intervention and State Sovereignty (2001) *The Responsibility to Protect*, http://www.iciss.ca/pdf/Commission-Report.pdf

Sherman, J. (rapporteur), 'Humanitarian Action: A Symposium Summary', International Peace Academy, International Policy Conference, 20 November, 2000, http://www.ciaonet.org/wps/shj04/

Simons, P. C. 'Humanitarian intervention: a review of literature', Ploughshares Working Paper 01-2, http://ploughshares.ca/libraries/WorkingPapers/wp012.html

Chapter 2

The Just War Tradition

The contemporary debate on humanitarian intervention focuses on the question of when it is right – or just – to use force. It is unsurprising therefore, that those engaged in this debate have drawn upon the rich philosophical lineage of the Just War tradition. The extent to which the contemporary debate employs the language of the tradition is clear; the tradition's key criteria – just cause, right authority, last resort and proportional means – are the central foci of the modern discourse and have been employed by both proponents and opponents of various interventions.

Humanity's propensity to engage in warfare is an obvious feature of our history. This tendency has catalyzed many moral and legal texts seeking to variously critique, restrain and justify the resort to force (Evans, 2005, p.1). In response to the prevalence of war certain religious and moral theories have espoused pacifism, the absolute prohibition of force. Conversely some 'realist' perspectives view war as an inevitable aspect of human existence which defies moral appraisal (see Chapter 4). As Chris Brown notes, 'neither position sees a moral problem associated with the use of military force; force is either unproblematically wrong (pacifism) or simply morally unproblematic (realism)' (2006, p.100). The question of whether a war can be 'just' therefore excludes realists and pacifists. Just War theorists do not endorse or promote violence, however. Rather it is with great reluctance that many have advanced the position that under certain extreme circumstances the use of force is permissible. The tradition represents an attempt, therefore, to delineate these circumstances, and constitutes 'a two-thousand-year old conversation about the legitimacy of war' (Bellamy, 2006b, p.2).

This chapter is divided into three sections. The first section outlines the key tenets of the tradition and the widely proffered, though controversial, tripartite division of the tradition's principles. The second section traces the evolution of the tradition, outlining the key thinkers, events and themes that have shaped its tenets and contemporary form. The final section addresses the contemporary status of the tradition and the manner in which it has often come to be used controversially as a checklist legitimizing intervention.

The central tenets

The Just War tradition comprises many disparate influences and there are significant differences between its key proponents. Thus as A. J. Coates argues, 'The unity that is the Just War tradition embraces many formulations that content one with another and that defy uniform classification' (2006, p.59). The diversity inherent in the Just War tradition does not undermine its status as a 'tradition', however, as traditions, according to Nicholas Rengger, 'can have many roots . . . traditions as I understand them do not have an essence or a central core' (2002, p. 362). The now commonly used term, 'Just War theory', is perhaps less applicable, however; O'Donovan asserts that the Just War tradition is neither a theory nor is it about just wars, but that it is rather a 'proposal for doing justice in the theatre of war' (Rengger, 2005, p.152).

It is important to outline initially what the Just War tradition is not. The impetus behind the Just War tradition was to create a means by which war could be evaluated, not a means to justify war. The key theorists associated with this tradition conceived of war as always a lamentable occurrence which could sometimes be justified *in extremis*. The fact that certain wars could be judged as justifiable did not constitute an endorsement of a war, but rather an acknowledgement that 'there are some wrongs that are worse than the wrong of war itself' (Bellamy, 2006b, p.3).

There are many sub-traditions with very different philosophical orientations and ideological dispositions. These sub-traditions are united, according to Alex Bellamy, by three common factors. First is a shared concern that the recourse to war should be limited and the manner in which it is fought constrained. Second is a common origin in Western traditions of theological, legal and philosophical thought. Third, the thinkers involved endorse a common set of rules governing the decision to wage war and the manner in which it is fought, although 'they differ in both their interpretations of the rules and the relative weight they attach to them' (Bellamy, 2006b, p.4).

In relation to the third commonality mentioned, there is, Robert Myers notes, 'little argument about the criteria', and the basic template is clear (1996, p.118). The tenets of the Just War tradition are invariably divided into two categories of criteria: those governing the resort to force (*jus ad bellum*) and those governing conduct during war (*jus in bello*). A third category concerning justice after war (*jus post bellum*) has more recently been added (Orend, 2000). Rengger rejects the idea of creating a third category, however, arguing that this is already implicit in the tradition (2005, p.154). Thus the judgment of war undertaken through this framework comprises an assessment of the motives, the methods and the post-conflict policies pursued by the intervening actors. Each of the three sections contains a series of related criteria as outlined in Box 2.1.

Box 2.1   The Just War criteria

Jus ad bellum
1 Right intention: Those using force must be motivated to do so by just rather than expedient intentions.
2 Just cause: Force must only be used to correct or prevent a grave injustice.
3 Proportionality of ends: The anticipated benefits of using force must outweigh the injustice being addressed.
4 Last resort: Force should only be used after all peaceful means have been exhausted or are clearly not viable.
5 Likelihood of success: Force must only be used if there is a strong likelihood of military victory.
6 Right authority: Only recognized public authorities have the right to authorize the use of force.
7 Proper declaration: The resort to force must be publicly declared and publicly justified.

Jus in bello
1 Discrimination: Force must only be directed against aggressors and never against civilians or non-combatants.
2 Proportionality: The force used should be the minimum necessary to achieve victory and proportionate to the original aggression.
3 Just conduct: All national and international laws governing the use of force must be obeyed in the course of the military action.

Jus post bellum
1 Just peace: The final settlement should be publicly declared, reasonable and fair.
2 Proportionality: The aim of the settlement should be to confirm those rights initially violated.
3 Discrimination: The settlement should discriminate between the leaders, the military and the civilians of that group held responsible for the violence.
4 Responsibility: Aggressors, on both sides, must be punished in a fair and accountable manner.
5 Compensation: Innocent victims, on all sides, must be compensated for their losses.

The very idea of dividing the tenets of the tradition in this way is rejected by some, who see this as having led to the erroneous separation of *jus ad bellum* from *jus in bello* and the encouragement of a 'checklist' approach in the contemporary era (O'Donovan, 2003, p.15; Rengger, 2005, p.153).

The major criticisms and controversies surrounding the utility and application of the Just War tradition are explored in the final section of this chapter. The next section outlines key influences on the evolution of the tradition.

The evolution of the Just War tradition

It is not possible to chart the evolution of the Just War tradition comprehensively here. The tradition spans over 2000 years of history, has been influenced by a great many thinkers and events, and does not constitute a continuous line of like-minded philosophers working in relay. Rather it comprises 'different streams of thought' which intermittently interweave, collide and separate (Bellamy, 2006b, p.7). This section seeks only to identify the contribution of certain influential thinkers and highlight the context in which they wrote (see Box 2.2).

The tradition has been strongly influenced by religious thinking and Christianity in particular; James Turner Johnston describes it as 'the collected consensus of the Christian culture of the West on the justified use of force, set squarely within the normative consensus on the purpose of political power' (2005, p. 14). It would be wrong however, to conceive of the tradition as inherently Christian or even religious, especially in its later phases (Donnelly, 1989, p.60; Boyle, 2006, p.31). Evidence from across the non-Western world shows that the ethics of war have been debated, in some

---

Box 2.2 Key texts in the Just War tradition

Cicero (106 BC–43 BC): *De officiis*, 44 BC.
St Ambrose (337–397): *De officiis*, 388–390.
St Augustine (354–430): *The City of God*, 413–418.
Gratian of Bologna (birth/death unknown – c. mid-12th century): *Decretum*, 1140.
St Aquinas (1224–1274): *Summa Theologiae*, 1265–1274.
Francisco de Vitoria (1492–1546): *On the American Indians*, 1539.
Alberico Gentili (1552–1608): *On the Law of War*, 1589.
Hugo Grotius (1583–1645): *On the Law of War and Peace*, 1625.
Samuel von Pufendorf (1632–1694): *On The Law of Nature and Nations*, 1672.
Emerich de Vattel (1714–1767): *The Law of Nations*, 1758.
Immanuel Kant (1724–1804): *Perpetual Peace*, 1795.
Francis Lieber (1798–1872): *General Orders No. 100*, 1863.
Michael Walzer (1935–): *Just and Unjust Wars*, 1977.

form, for millennia (Christopher, 2004, pp.9–11; Nardin, 1998). Rengger, however, accepts that the tradition does have a clear Christian and Western foundation but argues that this is unproblematic as it does not preclude its prescriptions from having universal applicability (2002, p.326).

The oft-quoted progenitor of the Just War tradition is St Augustine of Hippo (354–430), although the tradition's lineage can be traced back further; the work of the Roman statesman and philosopher Cicero (106 BC–43 BC) was of particular influence on Augustine (Bellamy, 2006b, pp.19–20). Before the fourth century AD the Christian church avowed an outright prohibition on the use of force in keeping with Jesus' instruction, 'If someone slaps you on the right cheek, turn and offer him your left'. Jesus taught that life on earth was but a transitory phase where one's behaviour would determine one's status in the infinite afterlife (Evans, 2005, p.2). Hence death was not to be feared as much as sin, leading to the idealization of sacrifice and martyrdom. The dominant posthumous interpretation of Jesus' teachings emphasized his pacifism and rejected the idea that war could ever be 'just' (Elshtain, 1992, p.44).

During Augustine's time, however, this principle became increasingly untenable. The adherence to pacifism amongst Christians, epitomized by the stoic sacrifices in the Colosseum at Rome, certainly derived from a strict reading of Jesus' commandments but was also inspired by the belief in the imminent second coming (Johnson, 1987, pp.14–17). By the end of the second century AD, however, belief in the return of Christ had waned, there were many Christians in the Roman army and the Church had begun to find an accommodation with the Empire. Thus, the timing of Augustine's work has led to speculation about the motivation behind the changes wrought by his theory. Augustine wrote at a time when the Roman Empire was under constant threat. Rome was eventually sacked by the Visigoths in 411 and Augustine's own city, Hippo in North Africa, faced the threat of invasion throughout his time there, eventually falling to the Vandals the year after he died. The relative order established by Rome was manifestly more attractive to the Church than the prospect of a Europe divided amongst pagan tribes.

In 312 Emperor Constantine converted to Christianity and by the end of the fourth century, Christianity was made the official religion by Emperor Theodosius I. Given the Roman Empire's reliance on military might, the conversion to a pacifist religion was problematic. The creation of a framework for legitimizing warfare was obviously attractive to both Rome and the Church. Mark Evans notes, 'Unsurprisingly, then, it is at this juncture that the Just War tradition is thought to receive its major initial stimulus' (2005, p. 2). According to Myers the Church was determined to cultivate a relationship with the Roman Empire so as to have some protection against the 'barbarians' massing on the Empire's periphery. To facilitate the union the Church 'turned its back on Christ and the new testament, and thus

Christianity' in favour of tales of heroic warriors in the Old Testament and certain creatively interpreted passages of the New Testament (Myers, 1996, pp.120–1). Augustine, however, was critical of the Roman Empire's lust for *dominium* and the false nature of *Pax Romana* (Elshtain, 2003a, p.105).

Augustine, building on the work of St Ambrose (337–397), highlighted certain sections of the Bible and pronouncements made by Jesus which suggested that force, though always regrettable, could be legitimate (Deane, 1963, p.154). He argued that pacifism was neither a divine law nor a reasonable course of action given that earthly life was necessarily fraught with danger and violence;

> Whoever hopes for this so great good [perpetual peace] in this world, and in this earth, his wisdom is but folly. . . . For in the very great mutability of human affairs such great security is never given to any people, that it should not dread invasions hostile to this life. (Augustine, in Deane, 1963, p.155)

Augustine determined that the sin of violence lay not in the act itself but in the motivations behind the act. He argued that force was justified if the intention was just and if the act was ordered by a just ruler. It therefore followed that a soldier carrying out the orders of his ruler was acting justly because it was not he who had decided to kill and he personally took no pleasure in it. War could be justified if waged on four grounds; in self-defence, to collect reparations or reclaim stolen property, if divinely sanctioned, and to maintain religious orthodoxy (Bellamy, 2006b, p.28).

The role of the authority ordering the use of force is of paramount importance in Augustine's schema. The state in itself was neither moral nor good but its utility lay, according to Augustine, in its instrumental value – that of providing the forum for adherence to, and the application of, God's laws. He argued that war could only justifiably be waged by states. This clearly state-centric conception is understandable, however, when one considers that Augustine's religious convictions held that humans can never achieve true justice or righteousness, and that it was God who ultimately rewards and punishes. The temporal abuse of the framework he avows is therefore insignificant given the capacity of God to punish wicked rulers.

In 395 the Roman Empire permanently divided into its Western and Eastern parts, and by 476 the Western Roman Empire had effectively fallen after a defeat to Germanic tribes. The aftermath of Rome's collapse, the so-called 'Dark Ages', witnessed the emergence of many rival groups and widespread violence throughout Europe. This disaggregated order was not a propitious environment in which to preach restraint, and the disposition advocated by Augustine was ignored in favour of a militaristic culture (Johnson, 1987, p.58). Certain groups adopted the iconography of the church and the idea of divinely sanctioned war but ignored the more restrictive elements of Christina thinking (Bainton, 1986, p.103). The Church's attempt to reassert its dominance eventually evolved into the launching of the Crusades, which 'jarringly fused certain Just War ideas with a sanctioning of morally unmitigated violence against unbelievers' (Evans, 2005, p. 3). The siege of Jerusalem in 1099 by Christian crusaders led to the massacre of some 70,000 Muslims, after which Raymond of Aguilers declared, 'It was a just and splendid judgment of God that this place should be filled with the blood of unbelievers' (Bellamy, 2006b, pp.46–7). Augustine's endorsement of divinely sanctioned war had become an abused aspect of his teaching embraced in isolation by warmongering zealots.

Writing during the last years of the Crusades, St Thomas Aquinas (1224–1274) built on the work of Augustine and those related aspects of canon law to produce 'a short, clear statement [which] provided what is probably the classic statement of the traditional just war theory' (Boyle, 2006, p.35). Aquinas did not separate *jus ad bellum* from *jus in bello*, and articulated a view clearly based on the earlier Augustinian perspective. Aquinas rejected the notion of a 'Crusade' and preached a reactive doctrine (Evans, 2005, p. 3).

In the *Summa Theologiae* Aquinas stated that war could be justified only if three conditions were met:

> Firstly, the authority of the ruler at whose command war is to be waged. . . . Secondly, there is required a just cause: that is that those who are attacked for some offence should merit the attack. . . . Thirdly, there is required, on the part of the belligerents, a right intention, by which it is intended that good may be accomplished or evil avoided. (Boucher and Kelly, 2003, p.122)

In terms of proper authority, Aquinas stated that only the head of the state (or polity) can rightfully order war as, uniquely, 'rulers have the right to safeguard that public order against external enemies by using the sword of war' (Finnis, 1998, p.284). Aquinas, like Augustine, argued that private citizens and public officials were bound by different rules (Bellamy, 2006b, p.26). Aquinas did not outline a list of potential just causes, but argued that such a cause would involve a reaction to harm done by others to one's state, including, controversially, punitive action. As Joseph Boyle notes, this punitive element is today rejected both by positive law, and perhaps more relevantly, Catholic doctrine (2006, p.39). With respect to right intention Aquinas draws on Augustine's writing to condemn those who fight for reasons of revenge, hatred or power even if the initial two criteria are met. Self-defence on the part of a state was self-evidently just so long as it was a necessity caused by unprovoked attack (Boucher, 1998, p.198). His doctrine of double effect (see Box 2.3) additionally sanctioned action

Box 2.3 The doctrine of double effect

'Unintended negative consequences are excusable if four conditions are satisfied:

1 The desired end must be good in itself.
2 Only the good effect is intended.
3 The good effect must not be produced by means of the evil effect.
4 The good of the good effect must outweigh the evil of the evil effect (proportionality).'

(Bellamy, 2006b, p.124)

which caused unintended harm provided the intention and the outcome were just and the harm caused was unavoidable and unintended. Aquinas's emphasis on right intention, according to Robert Holmes, 'means that one must intend to promote the good and avoid evil; merely having a just cause and legitimate authority is insufficient' (1992, p.200).

The Western Schism in 1378 divided the Western Christian church and resulted in three separate popes claiming rightful authority. This led to the declaration of crusades against fellow Christians, thus highlighting the subjective nature of 'divinely' sanctioned war. The excesses of the crusades did much to undermine the idea of a divinely sanctioned war, and led to the emergence of 'natural law' as the preferred moral reference point (Evans, 2005, p.3). The universalism ostensibly inherent in natural law enabled the eventual emergence of international law, conceived as a universally applicable positive expression of natural law.

During the 14th and 15th centuries the conduct of war rather than its inception became the dominant focus, with the development of the chivalric code (Bellamy, 2006b, pp.40–4). The 'discovery' of America in the late 15th century and subsequent European colonization led to increased speculation about how the indigenous peoples – routinely described as savages – should be treated and whether the ethics of warfare then ascendant in Europe should be extended to these peoples.

Francisco de Vitoria's (1492–1546) writings are of paramount importance to the evolution to Just War thinking (Bellamy, 2006b, p.50). Natural law, according to Vitoria, could be determined without divine revelation. He believed that objectively a war may be just on one side but that only God could truly tell. He wrote:

> where there is provable ignorance either of fact or of law, the war may be just in itself for the side which has true justice on its side, and also just for the other side, because they wage war in good faith and are

hence excused from sin. Invincible error is a valid excuse in every case. (quoted in Bellamy, 2006b, p.53)

Thus states could not wage a Just War simply because they felt it was just, and Vitoria suggested that the decision to use force should be taken only after wide consultation, including with those who opposed the use of force. According to David Boucher:

> Vitoria implies that the Law of Nations and customary law are to be equated with human positive law, and not with the Natural Law. . . . If Natural Law as a dictate of reason prohibits the killing of the innocent, the Law of Nations as a deduction from this determines who are to be regarded as innocent. (1998, p.200)

Like Augustine and Aquinas, Vitoria argued that citizens should obey their leader and trust their sovereigns. Vitoria believed that all commonwealths had the right to declare war provided they were a 'perfect community' – namely self-sufficient and independent (Boucher, 1998, p.202). Bellamy notes that this, coupled with the argument that just wars were inherently subjective, 'unwittingly paved the way for later realists and legalists' who used this to claim that as just wars were impossible to objectively appraise, it should be assumed that wars waged by sovereigns were just (2006b, p.55).

Vitoria's appraisal of Spain's war on the aboriginals in America contained a provision directly related to the contemporary debate on humanitarian intervention. In outlining permissible grounds for the use of force, he argued that the practice of cannibalism was so contrary to natural law that it was permissible for external forces to intervene to stop it (Boyle, 2006, p.45). Despite his misgivings about Spanish colonialism, therefore, Vitoria believed that there were certain moral grounds for external interference.

The Dutch lawyer Hugo Grotius (1583–1645) is often referred to as the father of international law. His views were shaped by the holy wars of the 17th century – in particular the Thirty Years War (1618–48) – when opposing sides articulated Just War rationales and claimed divine blessing. Grotius rejected the notion of divinely sanctioned wars and wars to enforce religious orthodoxy, and sought to establish a secular natural law basis for the recourse to force. 'Grotius's objective', according to Paul Christopher, 'was to supplant the impotent and corrupt ecclesiastical authority with an external, objective, secular authority that the competing political interests (i.e. nation states) would accept – a corpus of international laws' (2004, p.67).

Grotius believed in the law of nature, but argued that it was not evidenced through the expression of individual will, but rather 'has an objective existence as a criterion of human action' (Boucher, 1998, p. 212). This natural law, Grotius believed, formed the basis of the law of nations. This law he argued, however, was the product of formal agreement between states though it was designed for the good of humanity rather than just the states which created it (ibid., p.213). His criteria for a Just War were self-defence, the punishment of wrongdoers, the enforcement of legal rights, the reparation of injuries and situations when there was no possibility of effective arbitration (Bellamy, 2006b, p.73). After the Treaty of Westphalia (1648) and the development of the modern nation state (see Chapter 3), the nature of 'just' wars evidenced a definite state bias, and 'national interests became increasingly prominent in Just War theory's concept of justice' (Evans, 2005, p.4).

Following Grotius the legalist approach began to dominate. Samuel von Pufendorf (1632–1694), though not dismissive of divine law, sought to orientate the regulation of state conduct and warfare more towards positive law. He believed that law was universally valid and not particular to Christian societies. Emmerich de Vattel (1714–1767), whose contribution to the development of positive international law is profound, sought to codify the notion of sovereign equality and inviolability. Unlike Grotius and Pufendorf he argued that war could not be waged justly on behalf of foreign citizens as this created an easily abused pretext for intervention (Boucher, 1998, p.259). War could only be waged by states on the basis of self-defence to preserve the common good of the state.

Immanuel Kant (1724–1804) was sceptical of the power of natural law and moral persuasion, since states 'are not subject to a common external constraint' (Bellamy, 2006b, p.82). Kant sought to integrate normative perspectives into clear legally binding treaties between states, and was critical of the prescriptions articulated by Grotius, Pufendorf and Vattel which, he argued, had not and could not restrain states as they lacked a legally constituted framework (Boucher, 1998, p.269).

Following the French Revolution (1789), the emphasis on the conduct of states meant that the *jus ad bellum* aspect of the tradition was largely sidelined in favour of an emphasis on the conduct of war, and 'from the late eighteenth century onwards little of importance was written in the tradition until the mid twentieth century' (Rengger, 2002, pp.354–5). Writers such as Hegel, Meinecke and Clausewitz largely dismissed the question of right authority, assuming that states necessarily possessed this right, thus 'the traditional questions of the jus ad bellum [were] largely irrelevant' (ibid., p. 359).

The American jurist Francis Lieber (1798–1872) wrote *General Orders No. 100* during the American Civil War, outlining conventions governing the conduct of armies at war. The 'Lieber Code' laid the foundation for the emergence of laws of war, which became more explicit and international by the end of the 19th century. This codification was contrasted, however, with what Peter Malanczuk describes as 'an almost complete abandonment of the distinction between legal and illegal wars' during the 18th and 19th centuries (2006, p. 307). By the outbreak of the First World War the rules governing the resort to force had lost any real legitimacy, and aggression was routinely legitimized as self-defence; indeed this was the justification offered by Kaiser Wilhelm II for the invasion of Belgium in 1914.

Following the carnage of the First World War the League of Nations was established as an attempt to limit the resort to war. While Articles 10–16 of the League Covenant required all disputes to be submitted to the League before force was used, the League manifestly failed to act as a higher authority than its constituent member-states. The outbreak of the Second World War and the subsequent Cold War led to the intellectual dominance of the realist perspective, which largely dismissed moralizing about war, preferring instead to focus on explaining the interaction of states and the extent to which a balance of power, rather than abstract moral principles or legal doctrine, could limit the outbreak of war (see Chapter 4). Yet, while realism assumed primacy in the post-Second World War era, the evolution of international law evidenced the formal incorporation of many of the Just War tradition's key prescriptions (see Chapter 5).

The contemporary evolution of Just War thinking has been a largely driven by events (Rengger, 2005). Michael Walzer's key modern rendering of the Just War tradition – *Just and Unjust Wars* (1992a) – was written in response to the Vietnam War, and the increase in interest in the tradition in the 1990s was in large part due to the increased exposure afforded to, and incidents of, intra-state crises. Many of the so-called 'new humanitarians' – those concerned with contriving some means by which the suffering of people abroad could be halted – looked to the tradition to justify their advocacy. As the final section of this chapter will demonstrate, however, some argue that the modern usage of the Just War discourse constitutes a misappropriation of the tradition.

Contemporary relevance

The revival of interest in the Just War tradition in the 1990s owed much to those instances of intra-state conflict that challenged both positive international law and the foreign policy preferences of Western states (Hehir, 2008a, pp. 33–52). Interest in the tradition had revived prior to the 1990s, however, when the carnage of the Second World War had led many to invoke the *jus in bello* provisions of the tradition (Rengger, 2002, pp.353–63).

The renaissance in Just War thinking occurred against a backdrop of societal change which was to have significant influence on the contemporary manifestation of the tradition. According to Rengger the new approach to the Just War tradition, in both scholarship and practice, 'disclosed a character very different from that which the Just War tradition had traditionally displayed'. In identifying the catalysts for this change Rengger points to the 'general hostility to war under any circumstances in liberal public cultures', 'a concept of *jus in bello* largely transformed by both legal instantiation and military habituation', and finally 'the effective secularization of the societies in question' (Rengger, 2002, p.358). Jean Elshtain suggests that the modern incarnation of the tradition is based on certain shared principles:

> the current heirs to this way of thinking assume (1) the existence of universal moral dispositions, if not convictions – hence the possibility of a nonrelativist ethic; (2) the need for moral judgments of who/what is aggressor/victim, just/unjust, acceptable/unacceptable, and so on; (3) the potential efficacy of moral appeals and arguments to stay the hand of force (1992, p. 324)

References to the tradition abound in the contemporary discourse. Nicholas Wheeler, in his influential book on humanitarian intervention, *Saving Strangers*, acknowledges that his four criteria for legitimate intervention derive from the Just War tradition (2002, p.34), while Thomas Weiss describes the International Commission on Intervention and State Sovereignty's (ICISS) criteria as a 'modified just war doctrine' (2007, p.106). Tony Blair claimed that NATO's intervention in Kosovo was a 'just war', and his criteria for intervention bear a striking similarity to the Just War tradition's criteria (Blair, 1999).

The two clearest distinctions between modern interpretations of the tradition and its historical antecedents are the contemporary separation of *jus ad bellum* from *jus in bello* and the deemphasizing of the importance of right intention. Indicative of the separation of the two major categories, Walzer argued that if the indiscriminate bombing of German cities was the only way to stop the spread of Nazism, then this violation of *jus in bello* would yield to the greater good of the defeat of Nazism (1992, p.251). This may be a persuasive argument but it is not in accordance with the Just War tradition, which does not permit such selective adherence (Brown, 2006, p.108).

In the contemporary era the concern with motivation has diminished, with many arguing that it is the outcome rather than the intention that determines whether a war is just (Wheeler, 2002, p.38; see Chapter 8). The importance afforded to intention by both Augustine and Aquinas belies their religious conviction, in particular the idea of the soul's progression in the afterlife. The emphasis on intention in Aquinas's doctrine of double effect is clear, but from a consequentialist point of view, it does not make sense to support one action and condemn another because of the intentions of the actors if the outcomes were similar.

As the tradition has increasingly been used as a template for the discussion on the legitimacy of humanitarian intervention, it has been criticized on a number of grounds. The major criticisms are offered below.

Is the tradition universally applicable?

While it is clear that the tradition's evolution evidences a clear progression away from religious dogma, the question of its Christian character remains. Additionally, while the basis for the tradition may have moved from divine law to natural and positive law, overviews of the tradition's key thinkers rarely include non-Western writers. In what sense then does the tradition's obvious Western and Christian foundation preclude its universal application?

It would seem unreasonable to argue that ideas are limited in their applicability to the origin of their initiators. It is additionally not true that Western culture alone has articulated prescriptions on the use of force and just conduct in war. Rengger describes the Just War tradition as 'global', arguing that any tradition is 'part of an ongoing and potentially never-ending conversation in which many different assumptions will take centre stage at various points' (Rengger, 2002, p.362). Hence the dominance of Western Christian voices is conceived as but temporal.

Those who defend the universal applicability of the tradition argue that its basis is natural law, rather than divine law, which, by definition, is applicable to all humanity. Terry Nardin argues that the contemporary variant of natural law – common morality – constitutes a universal code which informs politics and law, though it is often obscured or ignored by dominant politico-legal systems. 'Common morality', he argues, 'is a critical morality possessing wider authority than the moral practices of particular communities (Nardin, 2003, p.18). Thus a belief in the existence of a common morality necessarily enables one to view the Just War tradition as the expression of universal truisms rather than 'any purely particularist and partisan creed' (Evans, 2005, p.8). This argument is persuasive if one accepts the underlying validity of a universal moral code knowable to all. Clearly relativists reject such an idea, and hence argue that the applicability of the Just War tradition is limited.

The tradition is inherently statist

The tradition is criticized for its statist bias and for enabling the issue of just authority to be appropriated by states. The issue stems from the earlier proponents of the thesis – Augustine and Aquinas – who have been accused as having delegated great power to the state in authorizing war. Aquinas, like Augustine, viewed the state as a unit of order for the common good rather than an aggregation of individuals (Boucher and Kelly, 2003, p.113). The state's utility lay in its capacity to promote and facilitate the common good rather than collective individual goods. Individual good was essentially subsumed through the state into the collective good. Aquinas recommended that citizens obey the state in all but the most extreme circumstances, and favoured 'passive disobedience' over revolt (Finnis, 1998, p.290). As with Augustine, the state-centric nature of Aquinas's prescriptions is ultimately explained by his instrumental conception of the state and belief in divine judgment (Canning, 2003, pp.119–20). Individuals acting out of a duty to the state need not necessarily fear that their own state is commanding an unjust act, as the rulers would face divine retribution while the compliant citizens would not be punished for their obedience.

Aquinas suggested that the 'right authority' is the one who has no authority above them. Those who served a master must seek authorization from that person to use force. The nature of just authority central to his schema, however, is somewhat ambiguous. As John Tooke notes, specifying who this authority might be needs 'serious discussion' yet this is lacking in Aquinas' work (1965, p.26). Additionally, Tooke notes that 'the "common good" of which Aquinas wrote and which must be the aim of a just war, was rather a limited good, that of a city or province, and never the international good of all' (1965, p. 27). In his assessment of the implications of this perspective, Holmes notes:

> The net effect is that it is the interests of the state that are paramount and that its laws, so long as they do not directly contravene divine law, should be obeyed unquestioningly. In this one can see the groundwork laid for Hobbes, Machiavelli, Hegel and Treitschke . . . Clausewitz . . . and of 20th century political realists. (1989, p.141)

Thus the delegation of just authority to states, evidenced throughout the tradition's lineage, would appear to have facilitated the widespread abuse of the tradition, especially in the 18th and 19th centuries.

Anthony Coates, however, argues that this modern interpretation of the tradition is 'deficient' and a misreading of the tradition, which overlooks the fact that the question of justice was linked to the idea of just authority and sovereign inviolability. Coates's reading of the tradition suggests that 'the internal constitution and practice of the defending state needs to be taken into account' and that the legitimacy of the use of force 'depends on the moral status of those who use it and those against whom it is used' (2006, pp.63–4). Similarly Rengger argues that the contemporary status of the Just War tradition constitutes a misappropriation of its tenets. He argues that writers such as Johnston and particularly Walzer have portrayed the tradition in a 'state-centric and legalistic' manner and in a form which 'encourages the tendency to think of it in terms of a juristically based calculus' which fails to accurately apply the tradition's conception of right authority (2005, p.151). Walzer focuses on the state, and his analysis proceeds according to the 'legalist paradigm' which he describes as 'the fundamental structure for the moral comprehension of war' (1992a, p. 61). For Walzer the utility of the Just War tradition lies in its capacity to influence international law as, without legal expression, this code is impotent (ibid., p.288). Rengger argues that a correct reading of the tradition demonstrates that while the state may be the right authority in a given context, this should not be assumed (2005, p.152).

Easily abused/who decides?

The most common critique of the tradition is the charge that its tenets are easily abused. According to Myers, 'These principles . . . actually have no meaning, and there are no boundaries to the ways in which they can be manipulated' (1996, p.126). Reinhold Niebuhr argued that the criteria were inherently indeterminate and values such as 'just' could be easily appropriated and misused (Bellamy, 2006b, p.107). The tradition is held to articulate principles in an authoritative vacuum, enabling states to act as their own judge, leading inevitably to highly subjective interpretations of the criteria (Kaplan, 2003, p.130; Buchanan and Keohane, 2004, p.4). The institutionalization of the criteria would, it is argued, provide a means by which the fulfilment of the criteria could be judged objectively and authoritatively. While the many holy wars and crusades undermined the 'divinely sanctioned' aspect of the early writings on the tradition, the move to a secular legal framework based on states did not eliminate the problem of abuse.

In defence of the tradition Evans argues that while there have been many examples of the misuse of Just War rhetoric, such instances cannot be deemed to undermine the utility of the tradition, as all principles can be misused and this in itself is not a viable grounds for rejecting the tradition (2005, p.7). Aggressors may invoke the tradition, but equally opponents of the aggression can hold the aggressors to account according to the criteria (ibid., p.207).

Defenders of the tradition argue that the problem of misuse stems from 'a misunderstanding of the nature of just war thinking itself as essentially a matter of casuistry' (Weigel, 2007, p.23). Rengger criticizes the contemporary usage of the tradition 'where certain boxes . . . are ticked or not ticked and in the end one comes out with the view: yes this was/was not a just war' (2005, p.151). The use of Just War criteria as an apology or excuse for waging war is a misapplication of the theory. The resort to force is never considered 'good' but rather a regrettable action which can potentially be justified if a set of circumstances – outlined by the Just War tradition – arise. The criteria are not, therefore, a checklist designed to facilitate the use of force, but rather a set of restrictive criteria conceived as a means by which the resort to force can be judged, not enabled (Reed and Ryall, 2007, p.1; Evans, 2005, p.7).

Richard Falk is critical of the contemporary moves towards 'the process of validating war by reference to the Just War doctrine'. This process, he asserts, is problematic because substituting the Just War doctrine for legal doctrine raises the issue of authority; it is plausible that exceptional cases may call for laws to be broken but, he wonders, '[is] the danger of relying on legitimacy to overcome the inadequacies of legality a means to assert the primacy of politics and the subordination of law?' (Falk, 2005a, p.43). Evans argues, however that the question of the justness of a war is not dependant on the views of the initiator of the violence but on the objective judgment of others (2005, p.8). The problem with this defence, however, it that while this expands the judgment of a war's justness beyond that of the protagonists, those not directly involved are not necessarily sufficiently dependable judges. Observers may be secretly biased of course but aside from this it cannot be assured that all will be privy to the same information or that this information is correct or complete. This will lead to differing judgments even though the same framework is being applied. Additionally even if it were possible to find two completely neutral observers, present them with exactly the same information and ask them for their view, there is no guarantee that they would reach similar conclusions. The problem is not that judges will reach different conclusion – this happens regularly in legal trials – but rather the implications of a 'split decision' following the application of the Just War framework: what happens next? This has obvious implications for humanitarian intervention and specifically the appraisal of 'illegal but legitimate' acts (see Chapter 5).

Does the just war tradition have any real utility?

The very idea of trying to impose rules on warfare is emphatically rejected by some. General Sherman's famous statement – 'war is hell' – points to a certain militaristic perspective on war derived from a 'win at all costs' mentality which accepts no responsibility for the horrors which war is deemed to inevitably cause. As Myers asks, 'why would anyone want to follow rules that interfere with victory and retribution . . . once they have crossed the dangerous Rubicon of war?' (1996, p.119). This critique assumes that because of the lack of an authoritative international body, states are not by constrained by moral principles, or even international law, and act solely to maximize their national interest. According to Robert Kaplan:

> in a world without a universal arbiter of justice, discussions of wars as 'just' or 'unjust' carry little meaning beyond the intellectual and legal circles in which such discussions take place. States and other entities . . .

will go to war when they decide it is in their interests (strategic, moral, or both), and will, consequently, be unconcerned if others view their aggression as unjust. (2003, p. 130)

Whether the Just War tradition has directly influenced the behaviour of states is thus a contested point. There is clearly evidence that the creation of certain laws of war – such as the Geneva and Hague conventions – owes much to the tradition, and the UN Charter itself contains provisions which can be traced to Just War principles (Evans, 2005, p.5). Of course the creation of legal doctrine and the articulation of moral principles do not necessarily lead to lawful or moral behaviour.

  Bellamy argues that the tradition fulfils two roles; 'It provides a common language that actors can use to legitimize recourse to force and the conduct of war and that others use to evaluate those claims. It can also inhibit actions that cannot be justified' (2006b, p.5). Rengger, however, argues that the tradition is not capable of stopping wars, and he accepts the basic realist premise that war is inevitable. He rejects, however, the attendant realist disavowal of moral judgements about war in favour of the Just War tradition. '[I]t is' he claims, 'in the task of continually holding up the mirror of our considered moral judgments in the context of war that the tradition performs its most important role' (Rengger, 2005, p.160). International law, he argues, often fails to provide guidance and in these situations – such as humanitarian intervention – 'we must surely look to a larger framework in which to embed such judgments' (ibid., p.147). The tradition is thus vaunted as a framework for examining war, not a means to either prevent or facilitate it (Armstrong and Farrell, 2005, p.11). Undoubtedly the tradition serves as a comprehensive framework which enables us to examine the legitimacy of a war or intervention. This normative goal, however, has certainly not been the limit of the tradition's actual usage, and it has undoubtedly been employed to excuse the use of force. One may question the normative idea of a framework of legitimacy on the basis that such a goal is quite a modest return on 2000 years of philosophical enquiry.

Conclusion

The Just War tradition, according to Rengger, 'has retained a remarkable vitality and power well into our own times'. However, he also warns, 'at the opening of the twenty-first century [the tradition] shows some signs of having reached the limit of its elasticity' (Rengger, 2002, pp.353, 361). A cynic may argue that it is precisely the tradition's elasticity and inherently malleable tenets that have facilitated its longevity. Nonetheless, as long as there are wars there will be moral judgements made about war, and in this sense the tradition is unlikely to lose relevance (Evans, 2005, p.203).

The contemporary debate on humanitarian intervention has clearly stimulated a renewed interest in the tradition, and those engaged in this contemporary debate must engage with the Just War literature even if only to substantiate their critique of the role of morality in international relations. Those engaging with the tradition as a tool for understanding the contemporary question of humanitarian intervention must be conscious, however, that the tradition should not be conceived of as a homogeneous theory which can be applied unproblematically to contemporary events. Additionally, the context in which many of its key thinkers wrote was very different from our contemporary context. In isolation the tradition cannot reasonably be said to determine the justness of a particular war. 'What is considered "just"', according to Bellamy, 'depends on the interplay between the tradition's legal sub-tradition (positive law), moral sub-tradition (natural law) and political sub-tradition (realism)' (2006b, p.7). In this sense the tradition is perhaps best seen as a component in a broader framework of legitimacy.

The key sources of contention posed by humanitarian intervention are inherent in the Just War tradition, and much of the contemporary debate on this issue explicitly refers to the tenets of the tradition. While the tradition cannot provide answers to the questions raised by humanitarian intervention, it is an indispensable framework of analysis for this issue, and the historical debates surrounding the tradition's key tenets are highly relevant and informative for scholars engaged in the contemporary debate.

Questions

- Do you consider the criteria outlined in Box 2.1 to be sufficiently comprehensive?
- Does the tradition constitute a Western Christian view of war or does it have universal applicability?
- To what extent has the tradition informed the evolution of international law?
- Has the tradition had any impact on the behaviour of states?
- What would you consider to be the tradition's primary function?

Further reading

Bellamy, A. (2006) *Just Wars: From Cicero to Iraq* (London: Polity); Chapters 1–5.

Christopher, P. (2004) *The Ethics of War and Peace* (Upper Saddle River, N.J.: Prentice Hall); Chapters 1–4.

Evans, M. (ed.) (2005) *Just War Theory: A Reappraisal* (Edinburgh: Edinburgh University Press).

Holmes, R. L. (1989) *On War and Morality* (Princeton, N.J.: Princeton University Press).

Johnson, J. T. (1987) *The Quest for Peace: Three Moral Traditions in Western Cultural History* (Princeton, N.J.: Princeton University Press).

Nardin, T. (ed.) (1998) *The Ethics of War and Peace: Religious and Secular Perspectives* (Princeton, N.J.: Princeton University Press).

O'Donovan, O. (2003) *The Just War Revisited* (Cambridge: Cambridge University Press).

Rengger, N. (2002) 'On the Just War Tradition in the Twenty First Century', *International Affairs*, 78:2, 353–63.

Walzer, M. (2006) *Just and Unjust Wars*, rev. edn (New York: Basic Books).

Chapter 3

The Sovereign State

The controversy surrounding humanitarian intervention centres on the relationship between the state and its citizens. Minimalist conceptions of the state hold that the state must provide its citizens with security from external aggression and ensure that economic activity can thrive. More expansive conceptions hold that the state must provide positive goods such as human rights, education and healthcare. There is therefore broad, albeit shallow, agreement that the state has certain responsibilities towards its citizens. Controversy arises, however, regarding the nature of these responsibilities, and crucially, what should be done by other states if a state violates these responsibilities. This latter point is highly contentious precisely because sovereign inviolability – that is, the right of states to non-intervention – has become a key feature of statehood. To understand the dilemma posed by humanitarian intervention it is therefore necessary to examine the evolution of the sovereign state and engage with the arguments for and against sovereignty.

In 1999 Kofi Annan, then secretary-general of the United Nations, wrote, 'State sovereignty, in its most basic sense is being redefined' (1999b). Annan cited three main challenges to the sovereign state; the process of economic globalization, international cooperation as manifest through international organizations, and the rise of human rights. While there is no doubt that globalization and international institutions have both impacted on the sovereignty of states to a very significant extent, this chapter focuses on Annan's third challenge, as it is the tension between human rights and state sovereignty that has most relevance to the issue of humanitarian intervention.

This chapter's first section outlines the nature of the sovereign state, its history and the legal rights sovereign states currently enjoy. The second section examines the argument that the status of sovereignty has always constituted 'organized hypocrisy'. The final section outlines the critical perspective on sovereignty advanced by the 'new humanitarians' and the counter-position as articulated by those who see sovereignty as both a normative good and a means of preserving international order.

The evolution of the sovereign state

The codification of sovereignty established both the territorial state and contemporary international system (Kratochwil 1995, p.25). Yet,

41

sovereignty has always been a 'contested concept'. According to Lassa Oppenheim:

> there is perhaps no conception the meaning of which is more controversial than that of sovereignty. It is an indisputable fact that this conception, from the moment when it was introduced into political science, until the present day, has never had a meaning which was universally agreed upon. (2006, p. 129)

Clearly sovereignty is worth having but what it entails is unclear. It is a fundamental norm of the international system yet it has been violated consistently since its inception. It is an idea extolled by its supporters as a bulwark against oppression and power politics, yet its critics argue that it in fact facilitates tyranny. In the contemporary era it has come under greater interrogation than perhaps ever before.

Box 3.1 Key dates in the evolution of the modern state

1439	Johannes Gutenberg invents the movable type printing press.
1517	Martin Luther nails his 95 Theses on the Power of Indulgences to the door of the Schlosskirche in Wittenberg.
1555	Peace of Augsburg signed between Ferdinand I and the Schmalkaldic League. Participants agree to respect the principle '*cuius region, eius religio*' (whose region, his religion).
1648	Peace of Westphalia signed to formally end the Thirty Years War.
1700–1804 (circa)	The Enlightenment – an era of profound change in Europe involving governmental consolidation, the growth of nationalism, the diminution of the power of the church and moves towards the recognition of basic civil rights for all citizens.
1807–14	Peninsular War – Napoleon defeats Spain and Portugal, precipitating independence in Latin America.
1815	Congress of Vienna – agreement signed between Great Britain, Prussia, Austria, Russia and France on borders within Europe following the defeat of Napoleon.
1870–1920	Ottoman, Habsburg, Hohenzollern and Romanoff dynasties in Central and Eastern Europe dissolve.
1884–5	Berlin Conference – agreement to regulate the colonization of Africa.
1899 & 1907	Hague Conventions – conferences on international humanitarian law and the laws governing the use of force. In 1907 all Latin American states attend.

⫸

It is not possible to chart the evolution of the modern state comprehensively in this section. The aim is rather to identify the key catalysts for the emergence of the sovereign state so that we can situate sovereignty in a historical context (see Box 3.1). The guide to further reading at the end of this chapter identifies sources which will provide a more complete history of the state.

From the earliest times humans have formed groups, and these groups have invariably involved some power structure and delegation of responsibilities. The adage 'strength in numbers' has clearly influenced the human propensity towards social organization, as it has for many animals. Unlike animals, however, humankind's agricultural ability and resultant capacity to produce surplus goods, plus our seemingly inherent drive to improve our social conditions, led us to engage in economic activity, particularly trade, which catalyzed the development of complex social organizations.

1919	Paris Peace Conference – agreement reached on the formation of the League of Nations including the League of Nations Permanent Mandates Commission.
1926	Imperial Conference – Great Britain acknowledges right of dominions to participate in international society as equal sovereign states.
1945–80	European decolonization – British, French, Spanish, Portuguese, Belgian and Dutch colonies throughout Africa and Asia gain independence.
1970	General Assembly Resolution 2621 – 'Reaffirms the inherent right of colonial peoples to struggle by all necessary means at their disposal against colonial powers which suppress their aspiration for freedom and independence'.
1975	Helsinki Accords – 35 states from East and West sign agreement on security and cooperation. Principles of sovereign inviolability and equality are reaffirmed but states additionally commit themselves to respecting human rights.
1989–92	End of the Cold War – communism collapses precipitating the emergence of new states in Eastern Europe and a rise in intra-state conflict in Africa.
1993	Vienna Declaration and Programme of Action includes 'the solemn commitment of all States to fulfil their obligations to promote universal respect for, and observance and protection of, all human rights and fundamental freedoms for all'.
2001	International Commission on Intervention and State Sovereignty publishes *The Responsibility to Protect*.
2002	International Criminal Court (ICC) established.
2005	World Summit *Outcome Document* endorses certain aspects of *The Responsibility to Protect*.

War, religion and the modern state

The development of the modern state cannot be traced to one particular event or period and constitutes a long evolutionary process. Large political organizations date back 7000 years to the city-states and empires based around the Tigris, Euphrates and Nile (Russett, Starr and Kinsella, 2000, p.47). These entities evidenced many features of today's 'states' but lacked some or all of those key characteristics that we associate with the modern state, namely distinct borders, centralized authority structures, a bureaucracy and a permanent population of 'nationals'.

The period 1450 to 1650 constituted a transition from the old system of feudal entities to the modern sovereign state system. The old system was characterized by overlapping competencies whereby authority was vested in different, often competing, polities and leaders, such as between the Holy Roman Emperor and the Pope. The old system of medieval Christendom was dominated by the power of the Church which necessarily stifled the emergence of individual states. The Church's power, and hence its influence over the composition of political entities, in Europe was undermined by the Reformation (Jackson, 1996, p.51). In the early 16th century Martin Luther challenged the Pope's authority, and his radical ideas quickly spread throughout Central Europe, where distinct Lutheran churches emerged aligned with particular kings and princes who exploited the situation and consolidated their realm. Europe divided into religiously distinct realms, and religious conflict and general disorder followed. By the 17th century territorial units ruled exclusively by one monarch had emerged, and at this point, 'The leading principle of legitimacy ... undoubtedly was *Rex est imperator in regno suo*: the King is Emperor within his own realm' (Jackson 1996, p.51). Religious conflict in Europe culminated in the extremely violent Thirty Years War from 1618–48.

The emergence of the state system was driven by two key factors: capital and coercion (Russett et al., 2000, p. 48). To consolidate their realm monarchs required significant military and economic resources. Economic growth required a centralized bureaucracy capable of collecting taxes, and this necessitated the creation of a coercive force – an army – capable of enforcing compliance. Thus the state can be seen as a function of the quest for economic growth which created a need for centralized control and superior military capability to maintain internal compliance and repel external interference. Without the latter any political entity was liable to be appropriated by foreign powers, hence Charles Tilly's famous statement; 'The state makes war and war makes the state' (1990, p.32). The centrality of military force in the growth of the state in Europe is recognized as a key factor in the eventual global dominance of European powers. Military competition within Europe created strong, internally consolidated political entities. Rivals sought to achieve military preponderance, thus sparking an arms race which spurred economic growth and also, crucially, technological innovation (Russett et al., 2000, p.49).

Westphalia and the nation-state

The consolidation of the principle of sovereignty is regularly dated to 1648 and the 'Treaty of Westphalia', more correctly titled the 'Peace of Westphalia' – the collective term for the Treaties of Munster and Osnabrück. While the Peace of Westphalia was clearly significant in terms of ending the Thirty Years War, its significance has possibly been inflated, as the Peace of Augsburg of 1555 had first established the basic template of sovereign inviolability (Brown, 2006, p.22). Signatories to the Peace of Augsburg agreed to respect the principle *cuius regio, eius religo*; he who rules a region determines its religion. The Peace of Westphalia reaffirmed this principle and, in essence, set in place the framework for the emergence of independent, territorially defined states, thereby ending the possibility of a united European Empire. In each territory there was no longer multiple loyalties and authorities; rather there was loyalty only to one authority specific to that territory, and external interference was prohibited. Westphalia's chief legacy is the creation of this dual aspect of sovereignty, described by Hedley Bull as internal and external sovereignty (2002, p.8).

Internal sovereignty is the capacity of state authorities to rule inside their borders. External sovereignty derives from the acknowledgment by other states of a state's right to independence and inviolability (non-interference). International relations after 1648 thus involved the struggle by states, and indeed separatists, to acquire and/or maintain these dual elements of sovereignty which Westphalia acknowledged as central to the legitimacy of a state. Augsburg and Westphalia imbued the state with historically unprecedented power, and according to Thomas Weiss and Jarat Chopra, 'transferred to nation-states the special godlike features of church authority. Nation states inherited the pedigree of sovereignty and an unassailable position above the law that has since been frozen in the structure of international relations' (Chopra and Weiss, 1992, p.104).

It would be wrong, however, to view the Peace of Westphalia as ushering in an era of respect for sovereign inviolability. While the recognition of the external sovereignty of states meant that no national or international entity could legitimately interfere in the activities of another state, state practice after 1648 was not conducted in accordance with this principle. The concept of sovereignty manifest under the 'Wesphalian System' was a conspicuously contingent norm. Indicatively, from 1648 to 1815 the number of states actually declined as large states forcibly absorbed smaller ones (Bull, 2002, p.17). The 18th and especially the 19th centuries were characterized by the rise of nation-states asserting the *cuius regio, eius religio* principle, yet the more powerful European states systematically ignored the notion of self-determination and sovereign inviolability, especially in their colonial quests through '*terra nullius*' – no man's land (Clapham, 1999, p.522). According to Jean Cohen this legal arrangement, *jus publicum europaeum* (public law of Europe), was a conspicuously contingent norm which paradoxically facilitated colonialism (2004, p.12). The interests of the 'Great Powers' of the 18th and 19th centuries – the United Kingdom, France, Prussia, the Austrian Empire and Russia – were the primary factor in international relations at this time, and certainly of far greater influence than nebulous legal principles regarding sovereignty.

The idea of the 'nation' constituting the only legitimate source of statehood and governmental authority emerged at the end of the 18th century (Anderson, 1991, p.3). A number of factors coalesced to precipitate the rise of nationalism as a force in international relations: the reappraisal of the old religious communities and scientific truisms initiated by the Enlightenment, the development of the printing press in the 15th century and subsequent consolidation of language communities, the 1789 French Revolution and its assertion of the people's right to choose their government, and the rejection of empires as political units. The French Revolution catalysed a general rejection of the idea of the monarch as the embodiment of sovereignty in favour of popular sovereignty. The state was thereafter increasingly portrayed as a servant of the people, who came to be conceived as an organic national group.

The conviction that the nation should have its own state led to the fragmentation of existing political units, particularly empires, and the emergence of new 'nation-states'. Thus, sovereignty became the goal of the aspiring nations of this period, much as it would again during the period of decolonization in the mid-20th century. The idea of self-determination as an inherent right was explicitly articulated following the First World War by US President Woodrow Wilson, though this right was certainly not universally applied. Indeed, Bill Bowring argues that Lenin articulated a more 'consistent and revolutionary' avowal of self-determination which, in contrast to Wilson's, sought to catalyze the wholesale disruption of existing states (2008, p.18). In 1933 at the Seventh International Convention of American States the United States agreed not to interfere in the affairs of Latin American states. The Montevideo Convention articulated a set of criteria for statehood which became and remains the universal standard (see Box 3.2).

The modern state, however, clearly comprises more than the technical trappings outlined in the Montevideo Convention. Central to the existence of the state is what Barry Buzan describes as 'the idea of the state which establishes its legitimacy in the eyes of the people' (1991, pp.66–7). Functional internal sovereignty allows the people to object to the manner in which the state is being run without questioning the very existence of the

Box 3.2 The 1933 Montevideo Convention

Article 1: The state as a person of international law should possess the following qualifications: a) a permanent population; b) a defined territory; c) government; and d) capacity to enter into relations with the other states

Source: Convention on the Rights and Duties of States 1933.

state. The willingness of the citizenry to accede to the state's internal sovereignty is dependent on the state's ability to meet their basic requirements and command their loyalty (Kedourie, 1971, p.12).

The UN Charter

The UN Charter's codification of the sovereign equality of all its members, as detailed in Article 2.1, embedded sovereignty as a universal legal principle. The Charter marked the formal rejection of a hierarchy of states and prohibited the use of force against sovereign equals, except in self-defence. Additionally, Article 2.7 of the Charter prohibits the United Nations itself from interfering in the domestic affairs of its member-states. Many General Assembly resolutions since 1945 have reaffirmed the principle of non-interference, especially as the number of states grew as a result of decolonization. The effect of the codification of sovereign equality in the Charter and subsequent international legislation, in particular the 1960 General Assembly Declaration on the Granting of Independence to Colonial Countries and Peoples, was that 'it no longer made sense to speak of a hierarchical society of states in which rights of membership and participation were granted in proportion to a society's development and capability' (Bain, 2003b, p.66). It must be acknowledged, however, that even after its codification in 1945 sovereignty has not been a consistently respected tenet of international law (see Chapter 5).

The number of states has grown exponentially in the post-Charter era, as reflected in the membership of the United Nations. When the United Nations was established in 1945 it had 51 members; today there are 192. Between 1973 and 1994 UN membership increased by more than one-third, with 28 states joining between 1990 and 1994 alone. The state clearly remains the unit of currency in international relations although, as later sections highlight, the sovereign rights enjoyed by states have been increasingly challenged in the post-Cold War era. Before examining this challenge the next section examines whether the idea of sovereignty has ever been reflected in actual state practice.

Organized hypocrisy?

Sovereignty is a much coveted and protected quality but it is also ambiguous, having many different meanings and manifestations. 'States', according to Sir Arthur Watts 'through their rulers or governments, think of themselves as sovereign. They do not, of course, always know what sovereignty means, but it is clearly worth having and keeping' (2001, p.5). Stephen Krasner identified four ways in which the term has come to be used (1999, pp.9–25). *International legal sovereignty* refers to state practices associated with mutual recognition between territorial entities that have formal judicial independence. *Westphalian sovereignty* refers to a political organization based on the exclusion of external actors from the state's internal authority structures. *Domestic sovereignty* in turn refers to the organization of political authority within the state and the ability of public authorities to exercise effective control within the borders of their own polity. *Interdependence sovereignty* is that ability of public authorities to regulate the flow of information, goods, people, pollutants or capital across the border of their state.

In practice international legal sovereignty and Westphalian sovereignty are the key manifestations of sovereignty. In many cases states lack either or both of the last two forms of sovereignty, but by virtue of possessing international legal sovereignty are considered states. This paradox is particularly apparent in the case of Somalia, which has been without a functioning government since 1991 yet remains legally a state. Additionally while certain states, such as Andorra and Liechtenstein, may possess international legal, domestic and interdependence sovereignty, they are not free from direct external interference and thus lack Westphalian sovereignty. There is an importance distinction therefore between *de facto* and *de jure* states; according to the Montevideo Convention, states must exhibit empirical attributes such as population and effective government, but also juridical attributes, such as borders and independence. A failure to meet the *de facto* attributes, for example the inability to govern effectively, does not necessarily impact on the *de jure* aspect of statehood, and thus Somalia is legally a state, despite the internal turmoil.

Therefore, while by definition sovereign states should have a clearly defined territory, be internationally recognised, autonomous and in control of domestic affairs as Krasner notes, 'only a very few states have possessed all these attributes' (1999, p.220). In legal terms, sovereignty has meant the recognition by the international community of a state's right to exist and the illegality of unsolicited external interference. Krasner shows, however, that in many cases a state's quest for international recognition has paradoxically had the effect of making it less sovereign. He cites the example of states that emerged from the dissolution of the Ottoman Empire in the early 20th century that were willing to cede certain sovereign rights so as to attain international legal recognition (ibid., p. 139). Many ostensibly sovereign states have not been, and are not, economically, militarily or politically autonomous, but are wholly dependent on external support in one or all of these areas (Jackson, 1996, p.2). The absence of certain tenets of sovereignty can be camouflaged, however, by achieving international recognition, which automatically bestows these qualities by implication.

The process of decolonization highlighted the often fictitious nature of sovereignty. According to Robert Jackson, while former colonial states have acquired the legal status of states they are 'primarily juridical' as they lack internal capacity (1996, p.21). Jackson describes this manifestation of sovereignty as 'negative sovereignty', in contrast to positive sovereignty, which means that the state 'also possesses the wherewithal to provide political goods for its citizens' (ibid., pp.28–9). The 'sovereign' state created by 20th-century decolonization is, he argues, a break with the historical evolution of sovereignty, as it created 'states' lacking the *de facto* attributes of statehood and excessively dependent on external support (ibid., p.25). These new states are often characterized by authoritarian regimes with poor human rights records, as the new governments did not emerge from organic political communities but were in many cases imposed by former colonial powers on artificial entities. Some 44 per cent of Africa's internal state borders are straight lines based in many cases on astrological measurements drawn by former colonial powers. Yet in 1964 the Organization of African Unity pledged to respect these arbitrary divisions (Herbst, 1989, pp.673–6). This endorsement of the principle *uti possidetis, ita possideatis* (as you possess, so may you possess) was designed to prevent the eruption of myriad intra and inter-state conflicts which would surely have accrued had it been deemed legitimate to contest African borders (Kum, 1990, p.450).

Thus while decolonization precipitated a great expansion in the number of sovereign states, it is debatable whether these new states were truly sovereign in the Westphalian sense. Additionally, there is some doubt whether this was an inherently positive development given the record of intra-state conflict, oppression and corruption in many former colonies. Of course the fact that these post-independence issues are problematic need not lead us to pine for the return of colonization, but as we examine the proliferation of intra-state crises in the post-Cold War era and the resultant calls for humanitarian intervention, we must acknowledge the role decolonization arguably played in the creation of these unviable entities (Jackson, 1996, pp.23–4).

States possessing international legal sovereignty without Westphalian sovereignty are not unique to former colonies. Bosnia-Herzegovina was recognized as an independent state in 1991 at a time when it demonstrably lacked the trappings of sovereignty (Zaum, 2007, p.33). Since the 1995 Dayton Accords the internationally appointed High Representative has exercised supreme authority in Bosnia-Herzegovina yet Bosnia-Herzegovina is legally a state and a member of the United Nations (Chandler, 2000b). Thus as Dominic Zaum argues, 'recognition as a state and recognition of sovereignty should not be conflated' (2007, p.35). Additionally international financial bodies such as the International Monetary Fund (IMF) and World Bank have imposed many conditions on the provision of monetary aid which compromise the sovereignty of the recipients (Harrison, 2004). Member-states of the European Union have voluntarily agreed to relinquish aspects of their sovereignty by ceding key competencies to Brussels. Thus, it is clear that sovereignty can be compromised in many ways and forms without officially being rescinded.

Sovereignty is less a rigid amalgam of specific tenets but rather, as Chopra and Weiss describe it, 'a quality of a fact' (1992, p.103). Hence 'sovereign states' may evidence significant dependence upon, or susceptibility to, external forces. The significant aspect of juridical sovereignty, however, is the fact that it derives from recognition by the international community of a state's right to exist, and thus the prohibition on unsolicited external interference. This at least imbues the state with an international legal identity which brings with it the right, though not the guarantee, of inviolability. In those states where Westphalian sovereignty is manifestly lacking, such as Bosnia-Herzegovina and post-2003 Iraq, it could be argued that the involvement of foreign powers is accepted by these states, unlike 19th-century colonialism. It is debatable, however, whether it is inherently contradictory to exercise free will and choose servitude (Bain, 2007).

According to Krasner, 'the principles associated with both Westphalian and international legal sovereignty have always been violated' (1999, p.24). The key factor is the interests of states and the relative distribution of power, not 'taken-for-granted practices derived from some overarching institutional structures or deeply embedded generative grammars' (ibid., p. 9). Krasner's critique of sovereignty, however, is challenged by Chris Brown, who argues that the currency of the concept imposes significant restraints on the behaviour of states and does have real influence. When states violate the sovereignty of others they have had to 'explain how their behaviour can be understood in terms of rules [on sovereignty]'. They proffer these explanations, he argues:

> not as Krasner suggests, as a matter of hypocrisy, but because failure to do so, would, as it were, end the 'game', and, at the same time, end their capacity to claim the status of sovereign since this status only exists by virtue of the existence of international society. (Brown, 2006, p.36)

Certainly all states have an interest in upholding the generic legal rights of states, and in this sense the legal status of sovereignty has some impact, albeit modest.

The actual role played by sovereignty in international relations is manifestly different from its normative precepts. Clearly sovereignty has many meanings, is not uniformly manifest and is regularly violated. The next section outlines the extent to which sovereignty has been increasingly challenged in the post-Cold War era by the rise of human rights.

Challenging the sovereign state in the contemporary era

Following the end of the Cold War, intra-state wars became the primary manifestation of global conflict. The domestic and international constraints imposed by the Cold War superpower standoff had marginalized or suppressed many internal disputes. The implosion of the Soviet Union, and the fall of communism generally, lifted these constraints as Moscow no longer propped up communist regimes and the US interest in previously strategically important states waned. 'The end of the Cold War,' according to Francis Fukuyama, 'left a band of weak or failed states stretching from North Africa through the Balkans and the Middle East to South Asia' (2006, p.2). Within many of these 'failed' and 'weak' states 'new wars' broke out which, 'involve[d] a blurring of the distinctions between war, organized crime and large scale violations of human rights' (Kaldor, 1999, pp.1–2).

The rise of human rights

The scale of human rights violations caused by these intra-state conflicts generated international attention and in many cases caused popular outrage. Increased economic interdependence caused by globalization meant that intra-state conflicts, with their potential to provoke regional crises, impacted on Western foreign investment and domestic markets, and risked causing 'epidemics of regional disorders', thereby generating international economic instability in addition to political and social disruption (Hoffmann, 2003, p.23). Thus intra-state conflicts came to be seen as the greatest threat to international stability; the 1994 UN Commission on Global Governance warned: '[While] war between states is not extinct, in the years ahead the world is likely to be troubled primarily by eruptions of violence within countries' (1995, p.81).

The increasingly globalized media and the rapid proliferation of humanitarian non-governmental organizations (NGOs) alerted Western publics to certain conflicts and their humanitarian consequences. The question posed by the *Wall Street Journal*, 'At what point do so-called sovereign governments forfeit their sovereignty through their own despicable acts?' (1992) soon came to encapsulate much of the political debate during the 1990s.

Codified international law regarding sovereign inviolability provided an answer that many felt was unconscionable (Robertson, 2002, p.428). International law on sovereignty was increasingly perceived as outdated, and hence action to alleviate suffering could be illegal but morally legitimate (Kouchner, 1999).

In light of the violence in the Balkans and the genocide in Rwanda (see Chapter 10), a consensus developed that a state's sovereignty should not shield it from external military intervention in cases where it 'brutalises its own people' (Chatterjee and Scheid, 2003, p.5). The tenets of sovereignty, therefore, came to be regarded as barriers to the preservation of human rights, and there began a 'revolution against unfettered sovereignty' (Hoffmann, 2003, p.22). Sovereignty became construed as creating artificial barriers to integration which had become sources of dissonance and contestation (Booth, 2001, p.65; Held, 1995, p.268). Advocates of proactive humanitarianism increasingly focused on the ostensibly anachronistic and immoral aspects of sovereignty (Gow, 1997, p.155). Sovereignty was deemed to 'reward tyrants' and increasingly portrayed as enabling states to oppress, torture and murder their citizens (Tesón, 1996, p. 342). The universality of human rights and the primacy of human security thus combined to challenge the basis of the existing system, and specifically the rights enjoyed by states. Andrew Linklater identified the aim of the human rights movement as 'Transcending state sovereignty' (1998, p.109).

Many argued that states' sovereign rights were dependent on their human rights record (Robertson, 2002, p.372). The principle of sovereign equality thus gave way to a conception of a sovereignty hierarchy. While this perspective found no ready manifestation in positive law, this illegality was often dismissed as an outdated aspect of international law which required reform.

Defending the sovereign state

While those critical of sovereignty within the human rights community base their critique on ethical principles, those who defend sovereignty are not necessarily proponents of power and order, averse to the idea of human rights. Supporters of an alteration in the nature of sovereignty argue that such change is necessary for the good of the global community. Yet, Michael Byers and Simon Chesterman argue that powerful states have an interest in changing the principle of sovereignty, as it 'operates, in a multitude of contexts, to constrain the law-making influence of the powerful' (2003, p.194). While sovereignty has clearly been misused by tyrants, the need to disregard human rights for benevolent reasons has equally been misused historically.

'Throughout history', John Herz wrote, 'that unit which affords protection and security to human beings has tended to become the basic political unit' (1957, p.474). In this sense the evolution of sovereignty has much to do with the capacity of the state to protect groups from external aggression. While the notion of the state as an organic expression of national consciousness inflates its genesis (Bloom, 1990, p.60), the capacity of the tenets of sovereignty, as defined by the UN Charter, to prohibit external interference constituted a major attraction for those determined to extricate themselves from colonialism, as evidenced by the seminal ten-point *Declaration on World Peace and Cooperation* agreed at the Bandung Conference of 1955 (see Box 3.3). The codification of sovereign equality and inviolability in the UN Charter has thus been conceived as a progressive development insofar as it constituted a means by which entitlements, previously almost exclusively enjoyed by Western powers, were universalized. Indicatively, in an address to the General Assembly, Abdelaziz Bouteflika, president of the African Union, described sovereignty as 'our final defense against the rules of an unjust world' (Weiss, 2007, p.16).

The prohibition on external interference was a reaction against the historical trend whereby powerful states used military aggression against

---

Box 3.3 'Declaration on World Peace and Cooperation', 1955 Bandung Conference

1   Respect for fundamental human rights and for the purposes and principles of the charter of the United Nations.
2   Respect for the sovereignty and territorial integrity of all nations.
3   Recognition of the equality of all races and of the equality of all nations large and small.
4   Abstention from intervention or interference in the internal affairs of another country.
5   Respect for the right of each nation to defend itself, singly or collectively, in conformity with the charter of the United Nations.
6   (a) Abstention from the use of arrangements of collective defence to serve any particular interests of the big powers.
    (b) Abstention by any country from exerting pressures on other countries.
7   Refraining from acts or threats of aggression or the use of force against the territorial integrity or political independence of any country.
8   Settlement of all international disputes by peaceful means, such as negotiation, conciliation, arbitration or judicial settlement as well as other peaceful means of the parties own choice, in conformity with the charter of the united nations.
9   Promotion of mutual interests and cooperation.
10 Respect for justice and international obligations.

weaker states or those peoples ostensibly languishing in '*terra nullius*'. Frequently this aggression was presented as emancipatory and progressive – the so-called 'white man's burden' – rather than purely self-interested, hence the latter-day suspicion evident in the developing world towards the 'humanitarian imperative' cited by Western states. According to Bull, the fear of external interference and the determination to maintain the principle of sovereign inviolability as championed by many former colonies is understandable given that this enables these states to 'effectively to combat the foreign domination to which they were subjected when they lacked these rights (1984a, p.6). The prohibition on external interference thus derives from the normative notion that citizens within states should be free to determine their own political system. In this sense, 'restraints to intervention', as noted by Anthony Lang, '[should not] be seen as evil attempts to block the efforts of good humanitarians. Rather, the restraints of sovereignty and the structures of international law that support those restraints serve a moral purpose: the promotion of a community inside clearly defined borders' (2003, p.2).

The idea of sovereignty as a right conditional on meeting certain criteria, such as human rights, rather than a legal tenet enjoyed by all states, constitutes 'proportionate equality' (Bain, 2003b, p.63). The conceptualization of international society as a legal order based on proportionate rather than sovereign equality, as stipulated by positive law, would clearly create a hierarchy of states. This is actively championed by certain observers; Michael Glennon has defended the right of 'enlightened states' to abandon the UN Charter's codification of sovereign equality and inviolability (1999, p.2). According to Glennon these enlightened states naturally act in pursuit of international justice, and he concludes, 'If power is used to do justice, law will follow' (1999, p.7). Richard Falk, however, rejects this argument on the grounds that it is similar to the arguments proffered in favour of the civilizing effects of colonialism. As Falk suggests, 'It seems unavoidable to wonder whether Glennon's use of "enlightened" is not a late 20th century updating of the now unfashionable "civilized"' (2004, p.41).

The framework of international law established by the UN Charter, with sovereign equality at its centre, can be viewed as comprising legal codes designed to militate the capacity of powerful states to influence weaker states, a so-called 'equalitarian regime' (Reus-Smit, 2005, p.71). States are clearly not equal in many respects, but international law has sought to emulate pluralist, democratic ideals by fashioning a regime based on the internationalization of 'one man one vote'. A state's international legal rights are thus not dependent on its economic or military capacity, political composition or culture. The advance of positive law and sovereign equality derived from a rejection of the 'natural law' approach to international relations prevalent in the 18th and early 19th century. The conflation of power – be it economic, military or cultural – and legal rights was characteristic of this era of colonialism, when states legitimised their actions as benevolent (see Chapter 5). A potential consequence of this challenge is the 'legitimisation of a new more divisive international framework based on economic and military power' (Chandler 2002, p.136). Thus the pluralist ideal of inter-state relations and rule formation is fundamentally threatened by the regression from sovereign equality.

Sovereignty, it is argued, promotes order and stability in the international system. While it may not necessarily be compatible with certain expansive conceptions of human rights, it at least provides a basis which facilitates non-violent international interaction and even cooperation. According to Gene Lyons and Michael Mastanduno, the emergence of the principle of sovereignty and its widespread acceptance, led to the development of four major political institutions which enabled international order to be preserved (1995, p.8). First, a balance of power developed in Europe that prevented the rise of an overly dominant state. Second, rules of behaviour gradually became codified in international law, and while a distinct and accepted set of laws for international relations did not immediately emerge, certain state practices were generally accepted as either unlawful or standard custom. Third, the acceptance of sovereignty led to the frequent convening of international conferences to settle major disputes which might otherwise have descended into inter-state conflict. Finally, accepted diplomatic practices and procedures for state-level contact evolved as a result of the greater acceptance of the right of other independent states to exist.

As discussed in this chapter's first section, prior to the signing of the UN Charter the recognition of sovereignty was contingent on the whims of the powerful, and were thus less a legal right than a function of power and/or patronage. Without sovereignty enshrined as the legal foundation for international relations, states acted without significant external constraint and relied on more nebulous grounds for their actions, such as natural law. As Alex Bellamy notes, 'Positive international law . . . derived as a response to the endemic abuse of natural law' (2004, p.141). A system based on natural law is, he states, 'often a more disorderly international society with a much higher incidence of war' (ibid., p.132). Thus the historical evidence suggests that in the absence of positive law, warfare increases, particularly when certain states believe themselves to have exclusive rights to act in the interests of humanity. As Bull notes, 'Particular states or groups of states that set themselves up as the authoritative judges of the world common good, in disregard of the views of others, are in fact a menace to international order, and thus to effective action in that field' (1984a, p.12).

States buoyed by an inflated conception of their own benevolence have historically been the cause of much violence. This clearly has significant implications for the contemporary debate on humanitarian intervention and the idea of 'illegal but legitimate' intervention, whereby certain states act as self-appointed guardians of the common good (see Chapter 5).

Aggressive states have, however, proved unwilling to respect the notion of sovereign equality and inviolability even after the signing of the UN Charter. The occasional breach of the Charter's rules on sovereignty need not, however, be taken as evidence of the wholesale ineffectiveness and impotence of the concept or international law generally. According to Chesterman and Byers, the UN framework contributed to the prevention of a major international conflagration and also operated as an international forum for debate (1999). The capacity of the United Nations can therefore be seen as a positive derived from the rejection of subjective natural law and great power diplomacy in favour of positive international law based on sovereign equality. Undermining this framework through evoking claims of 'conditional sovereignty' and 'illegal but legitimate' interventionism potentially risks compromising the achievement of the positives that have accrued from the framework's establishment and proliferation. The proliferation of standards or criteria to which states must adhere to qualify as sovereign risks destabilizing the system through an unanticipated increase in purportedly benevolent interventionism (Vincent, 1986, p.117).

Many have argued that it is incorrect to conceptualize sovereignty as imbuing the state with the power to do whatever it wants internally. While sovereign inviolability clearly prohibits external interference it does not necessarily separate the individual state from the international system. Sovereignty is better understood as relative – dependent on certain external factors. 'It is relative', according to Gerry Simpson, 'in that this form of sovereignty must constantly treat with the sovereignty of other states.' It is also relative, he notes, in so far as it is 'constrained by the existence of international law itself' (Simpson, 2004, p.41). This is a view similar to that of Bull who, despite a fundamental endorsement of sovereignty, did not conceptualize sovereignty as synonymous with absolute isolation or complete internal autonomy (1984a, pp.11–12).

The wholly negative image of the system founded on sovereignty – 'a quagmire of infighting among nations and groups wholly unable to settle pressing collective issues' (Held, 1995, p.268) – is therefore deemed an exaggeration. Jean Cohen notes that for critics, sovereignty signifies 'a claim to power unrestrained by law and a bulwark against legal, political, and military action necessary to enforce human rights'. She contends, however, that 'the discourse of sovereignty involves normative principles and symbolic meanings worth preserving' (2004, pp.12–13). The arguments presented by many of sovereignty's critics can only be sustained by presenting an absolutist conception of sovereignty which, Cohen maintains, 'has long since been abandoned' (ibid., p. 13). The image of sovereignty presented by its opponents is, therefore, very often a caricature. As Chapter 4 demonstrates, there are few who champion a notion of sovereignty that imbues states with the right to do whatever they please internally.

Additionally it is debatable whether sovereignty is the primary barrier to a more humane world order. Those instances in the 1990s that sparked the greatest moral outcry, the Rwandan genocide in 1994 and the massacre at Srebrenica in 1995, led many to call for a change in the status of sovereignty. It is unclear, however, what influence sovereignty exercised in both these cases. Calls for a diminution of sovereignty in light of these incidents would make sense only if external actors did not intervene because they did not want to break international law. This, however, was not the case. The ineffective response of the international community to both instances arguably derived from a lack of interest and will on behalf of those with the capacity to intervene rather than any commitment to international law (See Gow, 1997; Bellamy, 2002; Chesterman, 2003).

Conclusion

During the 1990s sovereignty came under sustained criticism from those who believed in the necessity of humanitarian intervention. Those supportive of maintaining sovereign inviolability were accused of being 'complicit in human rights violations' (Linklater, 2000) and recalcitrant 'resisters to change' who 'sponsor a limited and almost irrelevant discussion' (Gow, 2005, p.122).

By the end of the decade Thomas Pangle and Peter Ahrensdorf wrote, 'The nation-state is today weaker than it has been since 1815, and arguably weaker than it has ever been since its first form was established in the Treaty of Westphalia in 1648' (1999, p.3). Supporters of humanitarian intervention welcomed this diminution of sovereignty in favour of conditional sovereignty whereby a state's sovereign rights were dependent on its human rights record. The more extreme manifestation of this view held that the West, by virtue of its superior humanitarian record, had a duty to engage in 'a new kind of imperialism, one acceptable to a world of human rights and cosmopolitan values' (Cooper, 2002). The asymmetry between Western states and the rest of the international community was legitimized on the basis that the West was a progressive force in international affairs.

For others, however, the diminution of sovereignty constitutes a regression to the pre-Charter era of great power domination. The danger, according to Chesterman, is that the gradual dismantling of the existing restraints on the use of force will make the international security once again reliant 'on the eirenic munificence of the modern Great Power(s)' (2002, p.236). The negative image of sovereignty, and indeed its supporters, often presented by human rights advocates is thus misleading. Sovereignty is not inherently negative nor has it been created and sustained to facilitate exploitation and the consolidation of power. Equally, however (as is dealt with in Chapters 4 and 5), it would be wrong to view sovereignty as either a legal norm consistently respected since 1945 or a principle inherently subversive of power (Orford, 2003; Simpson, 2004).

The paradox of sovereignty is that while helping to protect states from external interference, the sovereign-state system has additionally meant that states are not subject to international moral requirements because of their autonomous status (Held, 1995, p.79). While few proponents of sovereignty advocate a system based on the absolute autonomy of states, in many cases governments within states have articulated just such a defence in response to international pressure to halt domestic oppression.

Factors other than human rights have challenged the status of sovereignty in the modern era, and clearly the confluence of these many pressures makes it unlikely that the normative rendering of sovereignty espoused during the period of decolonization can be sustained. Of course, sovereignty has proven to be a remarkably resilient feature of international relations, and while its present political and legal manifestation may alter, support for a system based on sovereign states of some kind is still dominant. In offering an explanation for this, Brown suggests that as sovereignty has become the dominant means of organizing the world a '"lock-in' effect" has developed whereby the status quo is maintained because 'the costs of changing it are prohibitively high' (2006, p.39). The next chapter explores theoretical perspectives on the place of human rights in the relationship between the state and its citizens, and the broader issue of what rights and responsibilities the international community has to maintain standards within sovereign states.

Questions

- What were the key events and catalysts for the emergence of the sovereign state?
- To what extent did the Peace of Westphalia alter international relations?
- Is Stephen Krasner correct to claim that sovereignty is 'organized hypocrisy'?
- In what way has the rise of humanitarian advocacy challenged the status of sovereignty in the post Cold War era?
- How persuasive are the arguments in defence of sovereignty?

Further reading

On the rise and nature of the modern state

Anderson, B. (1991) *Imagined Communities: Reflections on the Origin and Spread of Nationalism* (London: Verso).

Anderson, M. S. (1998) *The Origins of the Modern European State System, 1494–1618* (London: Longman).

Beetham, D. (1991) *The Legitimisation of Power* (Basingstoke and New York: Palgrave Macmillan).

Dryzek, J. and Dunleavy, P. (2009) *Theories of the Democratic State* (Basingstoke and New York: Palgrave Macmillan).

Hobson, J. (2000) *The State and International Relations* (Cambridge: Cambridge University Press).

Kennedy, P. (1987) *The Rise and Fall of the Great Powers* (New York: Random House).

Osiander, A. (1994) *The State System of Europe, 1640–1990* (Oxford: Oxford University Press).

Tilly, C. (1990) *Coercion, Capital and European States, A.D. 990–1990* (Oxford: Blackwell).

On sovereignty

Bain, W. (2003) *Between Anarchy and Society* (Oxford: Oxford University Press).

Bickerton, C. Cunliffe, P. and Gourevitch, A. (eds) (2006) *Politics Without Sovereignty: A Critique of Contemporary International Relations* (London: Routledge).

Bull, H. (2002) *The Anarchical Society: A Study of Order in World Politics* (Basingstoke: Palgrave Macmillan and New York: Columbia University Press).

Camilleri, J. A. and Falk, J. (1992) *The End of Sovereignty* (London, Elgar).

Held, D. (1995) *Democracy and the Global Order* (London: Polity).

Jackson, R. (1996) *Quasi-states: Sovereignty, International Relations and the Third World* (Cambridge: Cambridge University Press).

Krasner, S. (1999) *Sovereignty: Organized Hypocrisy* (Princeton, N.J.: Princeton University Press).

Lyons, G. and Mastanduno, M. (eds) (1995) *Beyond Westphalia: State Sovereignty and International Intervention* (Baltimore: Johns Hopkins University Press).

Simpson, G. (2004) *Great Powers and Outlaw States* (Cambridge: Cambridge University Press).

Sovereignty and its Discontents (SAID): BISA working group established as a forum for discussion and debate on the changing nature of state sovereignty and international politics since the end of the Cold War. http://www.said-workshop.org/

Chapter 4

Theoretical Perspectives

The issue of intervention, Martin Wight wrote, 'raises questions of the utmost moral complexity: adherents of every political belief will regard intervention as justified under certain circumstances' (1979a, p.191). The flipside of Wight's observation, of course, is that what one group views as a just intervention another will consider profoundly unjust. Examining International Relations (IR) theory can help us understand why this is the case by enabling us to (broadly) categorize the differing perspectives and draw out those key beliefs that preclude certain individuals and groups from supporting particular interventions or intervention more generally.

Theory is ostensibly a means by which scholars can understand how and why the international system works as it does. Normatively, therefore, it is a politically neutral tool for enquiry and observation based on certain fundamental tenets (see Box 4.1). It is important to note, however, that this perspective on theory has been increasingly challenged in recent years. According to Robert Cox, 'There is no such thing as theory in itself, divorced from a standpoint in time and space. When any theory so represents itself, it is more important to examine it as ideology, and to lay bare its concealed perspective' (1996, p.87). Thus, while the theoretical perspectives examined here are not overtly ideological, with the exception of Marxism, and in the majority of cases are proffered as a neutral academic framework for understanding global affairs, this premise is keenly contested.

Box 4.1 Shared theoretical characteristics of Carr's 'The Twenty Years Crisis' (2001) and Morgenthau's 'Politics Among Nations' (1954)

1 Each developed a broad framework of analysis which distilled the essence of international politics from disparate events
2 Each sought to provide future analysts with the theoretical tools for understanding general patterns underlying seemingly unique episodes
3 Each reflected on the forms of political action which were most appropriate in a realm in which the struggle for power was pre-eminent.

Source: Burchill and Linklater (2005, p.1).

This chapter explores those theories of IR that have most to say about humanitarian intervention: realism, Marxism, liberalism, the English School, cosmopolitanism and post-structuralism. It is important to note that it is impossible to cover the key tenets of each of these theories or even their particular perspective on humanitarian intervention. This chapter seeks only to highlight broad trends and key perspectives, and provide an introduction to the basic presumptions which have led observers to reach certain conclusions about humanitarian intervention. The nuances and heterogeneity of each theory cannot be addressed adequately here, and the categorizations are necessarily broad.

Realism

While we may identify 'statism, survival and self-help' as core beliefs of realism, this tradition has a long history and takes a number of forms (Coicaud and Wheeler, 2008, p.7). Nonetheless, accepting this heterogeneity it is clear that, as Alex Bellamy notes, 'The realist tradition opposes the norm of humanitarian intervention' (2003, p.10).

Realists argue that states do not act on the basis of moral concerns, such as human rights violations abroad, nor are international institutions significant influences on state behaviour (Mearsheimer, 1994). The classical realist perspective articulates a pessimistic view of human nature whereby egoistic passions incline men and women to evil (Boucher, 1998, p.93; Donnelly, 2002, p.86). Thomas Hobbes' widely endorsed rationale for a central authority or 'Leviathan' was that otherwise life would be 'solitary, poore, nasty, brutish, and short' (1968, p.186). In the international system there is no overarching authority to impose order, thus Hobbes argued that 'because there is no Common Power in this world to punish injustice: mutual fear may keep [states] apart for a time, but upon every visible advantage they will invade one another' (Boucher, 1998, pp.145–6). States are trapped in a security dilemma and in a perennial state of tension and fear, and this, rather than the pursuit of international justice, determines their behaviour (Morgenthau, 1954; Wight, 1966b).

In contrast to classical realists, neo-realists put greater emphasis on the influence of international anarchy rather than human nature, claiming that this compels states to adopt a selfish disposition which curtails altruistic action, such as humanitarian intervention (Waltz, 1991, p.29). As the international structure is 'probably unchangeable', international politics is characterized by 'continuity, regularity and repetition' (Layne, 1994, p.11).

In assessing state behaviour realists are guided, Morgenthau claimed, by 'the concept of interest defined in terms of power' (1954, p.5). Power has historically been the primary catalyst for state action, and realism claims to be 'a recognition of the inevitabilities of power politics in an age of sovereign states' (Herz, 1957, p.86). The struggle for power and the struggle for survival are seen as identical, and all other interests are secondary (Spykman, 1942, p.18). Realists assert that law and morality could play a role in the behaviour of states if the nature of the international system was such that states felt bound to a wider community. In the absence of this sense of community, states are compelled to act strategically, not morally, and aim at all time to maximize the national interest and protect their security (Morgenthau, 1951). Therefore, a concern for those suffering abroad does not motivate states to act unless there are national interests involved (see Chapter 8). This does not mean, however, that states should or do behave aggressively at all times, but rather that they aim to consolidate their position and seek equilibrium, or a balance of power (Waltz, 1981).

Hans Morgenthau argued that 'universal moral principles cannot be applied to the actions of states' (1954, p.9), while neo-realists 'do not even bother with morality', disregarding it as an important factor in international relations (Donnelly, 2002, p.107). This rejection of morality clearly has significant implications for humanitarian intervention. Realism assets that morality is not an absolute or universal code, as the Just War tradition suggests (see Chapter 2), and statesmen and women should maintain a situational, case-by-case approach (Rosenthal, 1995, p.xiv). In this respect international issues are dealt with according to prevailing exigencies rather than abstract moral codes (Niebuhr, 1932, p.174). Moral rhetoric is additionally held to invariably shroud more sectional aims, hence E. H. Carr's famous assertion, 'Theories of morality are ... the product of dominant nations or groups of nations' (2001, p.74). Thus it is of no surprise to realists that the currently most powerful group of states – the West – have been most vociferous in advocating human rights and humanitarian intervention (see Chapter 6). Those who claim to be undertaking humanitarian interventions are indicatively accused by Danilo Zolo of engaging in 'an inherently hegemonic and violent undertaking' (1997, p.15). Without an agreed international authority to sanction intervention independently, the question 'who decides?' remains outstanding, leading to subjective determinations on when to intervene derived from narrow considerations of national interest (see Chapter 7).

Certain realists advance a communitarian ethos, stressing the need to respect diversity and promote the equitable interaction of states as a means of preserving order and promoting peaceful coexistence (Chandler, 2004b, p.14). Hence the rights enjoyed by citizens within states are deemed an exclusively internal matter, and a plurality of intra-state human rights regimes is to be expected and respected. Anthony Coates describes this strain of realism as 'the morality of states'. He notes that 'because its main object is to safeguard the autonomy of states, it does so in a form that is too limited to accommodate humanitarian intervention' (Coates, 2006, p.68). Realism, therefore, suggests a clear distinction between the domestic and the international, and the need for a consequent division between the disciplines of politics and IR (Wight, 1966a, p.18). Nonetheless while many modern realists have consciously avoided normative theorizing about domestic politics, many of the historical figures touted as realism's antecedents did in fact discuss these issues at length. Hobbes emphasized the state's duty to provide its citizens with the 'good life' (Jackson, 2006), while Machiavelli's extensive writings on republican constitutionalism have often been overshadowed by his more bellicose prescriptions (Brown, 2006, p.69).

The realist concern with order attributes great utility to the principles of sovereign equality and inviolability, as they limit the extent to which states behave according to subjective considerations of justice and rights (Lyons and Mastanduno 1995, p.8). The extent to which sovereignty is respected, however, derives from the distribution of power, and at any given time the existence of states, and the rights they enjoy, are functions of this prevailing distribution. Sovereignty is often not respected and is, as Stephen Krasner famously stated, 'organized hypocrisy' (1999; see Chapter 5).

The preference for order derived from the pursuit of national interest is described as 'rule consequentialism', whereby if all states limit themselves to specific national interests the community of states will benefit, as inherently disruptive interventionism will be reduced (Welsh, 2006, p.62). Humanitarian intervention necessarily disrupts order, as such action is not a strategic concern and is based on subjective moral judgements (Kissinger, 1992, p.5). Colin Gray argues that humanitarian intervention constitutes a policy which will inevitably antagonize the majority who have an interest in the status quo and ultimately catalyze a backlash against the intervening party by other states (2001). Intra-state conflicts, if left alone, will result in a victory for the powerful group, preserve the natural order derived from disparities in power, and 'enhance the peacemaking potential of war' (Luttwak, 1999, p.36). Thus NATO's intervention in Kosovo in 1999 (see Chapter 11) is criticized as 'a perfect failure' by Michael Mandelbaum on the grounds that it caused instability in the Balkans and antagonized Russia and China (1999). This preference for strategic goals grounded in the national interest and cognizant of the reality of power echoes Carl Schmitt's critique of just wars. Schmitt argued that wars fought for political gain are invariably limited by the strategic goals of the protagonists while just wars, and humanitarian wars in particular, lead to total war because of their inherently expansive goals and moral fervour (1996, p.36).

Action taken to halt or prevent human suffering will create difficulties for the pursuit of a state's national interest, as there are inevitably occasions when, morally unpalatable as it may be, it is necessary to ally with states with dubious human rights records. To intervene in one state on the basis of human rights will expose the intervening state to the charge of hypocrisy, and it is prudent, therefore, to overlook issues such as human rights for the sake of the preservation of alliances (Bandow, 1999).

Realism, despite its expressed adherence to positivism, does have a normative dimension; states do have a moral duty, but it is to prioritize the welfare of their own citizens (Kennan, 1985, p.206; Wight, 1966b, p.128). Thus launching humanitarian interventions for the good of others is a dereliction of duty if the host state has no interests involved and is imperilled by such action (Bellamy, 2003, pp.9–10; see Chapter 8). Indeed, citizens are held to expect their state to act in the national interest and, as David Hendrickson notes with respect to the US intervention in Somalia in 1992, have demonstrated a pronounced unwillingness to accept military casualties when national interests are not involved (1997).

Marxism/critical theory

The Marxist view of international relations is universalist, and events are explained and assessed according to a perceived struggle between the capitalist elite and the oppressed majority, though Marx himself wrote little specifically focused on international relations (Brown, 2006, p.54). Marx believed that colonialism was ultimately beneficial, certainly not because he endorsed the 'white man's burden' argument (see Chapter 3), but because this would accelerate the global transition to capitalism which was a necessary stage on the road to global communism (Marx, 2006). Prior to the outbreak of the First World War Marxists such as Rosa Luxemburg and most notably Lenin began to develop a more critical theory of imperialism, which held that inter-capitalist competition was driving Western states to competitive colonialism which would eventually lead to world war.

Marxists broadly agree with the realist analysis of anarchy but argue that international systemic composition is a product of the conscious design of the dominant economic powers (Cox, 1986). Powerful states have colluded to create a core–periphery dichotomy, and while there is inter-state rivalry among the elite, this is largely negated by the common goal of proliferating capitalist hegemony (Wallerstein, 1974). Marxism, and critical theory more generally, rejects the idea of the international system constituting a set of 'pre-constituted social actors', and criticizes the realist and liberal perspectives for their ahistorical analysis of the international system and inability to foresee future change (Rupert, 2007, p.149). Critical theory, inspired by the Frankfurt School and the writings of Antonio Gramsci, emerged in the 1980s and challenges positivist approaches to IR, seeking instead to act as an emancipatory force (Linklater, 2006).

The system of states is considered a means by which the global economy can flourish to the benefit of certain actors, and hence Marxist IR theory perceives the present legal status of sovereignty (see Chapter 5) as a function of a top-down consolidation of hierarchy rather than a bottom-up evolutionary process (Rosenberg, 1994, p.14). The existing constellation of states is held to be a product of power and oppression, and a social order derived from the dominant class's desire, especially during the Industrial Revolution, to perpetuate its hegemony and domination of the means of production. Preserving sovereign inviolability is not, therefore, the goal of Marxists, as states are considered to be inimical to proletariat solidarity though Marxists do critique intervention as an exercise of power by the strong against the weak. The few genuinely progressive advances in contemporary international law are attributed to the influence of the Soviet Union's promotion of self-determination (Bowring, 2008, pp.10–11).

The Marxist explanation of the unwillingness of states to act morally is similar to that of realism though for different reasons. Humans are not inherently selfish or aggressive but become so because they are shaped by the prevailing societal conditions under capitalism, which engenders greed and selfishness (Boucher, 1998, p.360). This conditioning also occurs in the international system, and thus states behave in singularly self-interested ways so that capitalist exploitation can flourish (Lenin, 1964, pp.26–8). Marxism anticipates that states will be unconcerned about human suffering in other states and will use the pretext of sovereign inviolability to justify this position, but Marxism rejects relativism in favour of sub-state universalism.

The Marxist view differs fundamentally from that of realism in the sense that Marxism is premised on the need to achieve solidarity between the oppressed classes across states and a belief in progressive evolution towards international communism. For Marxists international politics is 'intraclass solidarities combined with interclass war waged both across and within state borders' (Coicaud and Wheeler, 2008, p.10). While Marxists, like realists, consider normative perspectives on international affairs to be inherently partisan, they 'also rely upon an idealist commitment to human welfare that makes the determination of international progress an essential feature of both their scientific explanation and their plan for revolutionary liberation' (ibid.). What Marxist and realist views have in common, Janna Thompson notes, is 'the idea that conflict, injustice, threats of war are embedded in the very structure of relationships in the international world, and that so long as these relationships remain, the peaceful and just world . . . will be impossible to achieve' (1992, p.6).

Marxists argue that humanitarian justifications for intervention hide ulterior motives; for the Marxist, 'Morality is ideology, and thus represents the interests of a class' (Brown, 2002, p.228). Noam Chomsky, indicative of the Marxist approach, argues that the West's increased willingness to undertake 'humanitarian interventions' is part of an escalating Western unilateralism born out of the dramatic extension of Western hegemony in the post-Cold War era. According to Chomsky, 'The right of humanitarian intervention, if it exists, is premised on the good faith of those intervening, and that assumption is based not on their rhetoric but on their record' (1999, p.74). On the basis of what Chomsky sees as the West's history of oppression and violence, the moral argument is implausible.

Western interest in humanitarian intervention, it is claimed, stems from the fact that in the post-Cold War era the leaders of these states 'find themselves without effective economic policies to promote the social justice they claim to serve, but still need a virtuous cause to distinguish themselves from "the right"' (Johnstone, 2000, p.14). Mark Duffield argues 'the strategic complexities of liberal peace ... are part of an already existing system of networked global liberal governance' and thus the spread of liberalism is a means of increasing power (2006, p.258). The linkage between development and security is considered central to the rise in human security and its adoption by the major Western powers (see Chapter 6). Increasingly, however, Duffield and Nicholas Waddell argue, the discourse has shifted away from development towards 'a "harder" version of security which prioritizes homeland livelihood systems and infrastructures' with a view to providing the West with greater security from threats ostensibly emanating from the developing world (2006, p.3). Duffield argues that there has been a marked shift from the prioritization of geopolitics during the Cold War to biopolitics in the contemporary era. This manifests as a concern with the social conditions within the periphery and the 'circulatory terrain of human population'. This shift, Duffield argues, has led to the rehabilitation of 'liberal imperialism ... authored by effective states' (2005, p.144). Human rights have revolutionary potential, but this is denuded when the discourse of human rights is harnessed by the hegemonic powers and expressed in an individualistic as opposed to collective form (Bowring, 2008, p.126).

Marxist analyses of instances of Western intervention highlight this emphasis on power and capitalism. Western interest in humanitarian crises in the 1990s was described as a function of a quest for new markets and the consolidation of Western dominance, and thus driven by 'the American government and business classes, aided and abetted by their European elites' (Mandel, 2003, p.293). The overall aim of humanitarian intervention is 'to be able to punish and reward states that defy the contour of political/ideological order advantageous to the hegemonic state' (Chadda, 2003, p.321). According to Alex Callinicos, 'the real reason' for NATO's intervention in Kosovo was 'the strategic and economic interests of the US and the other Western powers' (2000, p.176), while Ellen Wood described the intervention as part of the 'new imperialism' whereby intervention is directed towards 'ensuring that the forces of the capitalist market prevail in every corner of the world (2000, p.192). In a similar vein, the editorial committee of the Marxist journal *Capital and Class* declared with respect to the 2003 invasion of Iraq, 'Rather than being a humanitarian intervention, the invasion is a brutal act of imperialist aggression' (2003). James Tyner argues that the invasion had nothing to do with humanitarian concerns. but rather constituted a 'militant neoliberal capitalist imperative . . . waged for material gain that – ultimately – would benefit only a select few corporate CEOs, financiers, and bankers' (2006, pp.32–3). Thus the motivation behind humanitarian intervention for Marxists is not human rights but rather the spread of capitalism and the consolidation of the core–periphery dichotomy (Mandani, 2009).

Liberalism

Liberalism holds that man is torn between an innate desire for freedom and a competing desire to live in a society. While man is certainly driven by the quest for personal gain (though not necessarily power), this trait is not inevitably detrimental to human interaction, and can in fact be a catalyst for better societal organization. Thus there is significant scope for contriving rules that benefit the entire society (Keohane and Nye, 1977).

This inherent preference for cooperation over conflict in the pursuit of individual liberty can be transferred to the international realm provided states share certain basic characteristics and hence recognize the utility of cooperation. Thus, in contrast to the realist, and indeed Marxist, analyses, liberalism believes that progressive international cooperation and formal processes of international authority can be developed under certain conditions (see Chapter 7). States that operate according to the principles of free trade will necessarily recognize the benefit of both peaceful interaction and the formal codification of rules to govern trade. Thus according to Immanuel Kant, international trade would lead to a rise in global prosperity especially amongst 'the peace-loving, productive sections of the population', and financial interdependence amongst states would 'make clear to all of them their fundamental community of interests (Burchill, 2005, p.63). Additionally because democratic states are ruled by leaders elected by the people whose preference is for peace, the governments of democratic states are unlikely to be aggressive and 'wars become impossible' (Doyle, 1986, p.1151). This is the basis of the democratic peace theory which holds that democracies do not go to war against other democracies (Levy, 1989, p.88)

Liberalism holds that as the evolution of human society is characterized by progress the current international system is transitory; democracy will gradually spread and the quality of life will increase (Fukuyama, 1992; Howard, 2000, p.31). Unlike Marxists, of course, liberalism seeks to proliferate the Western capitalist system on the grounds that liberal democracy is 'the end point of mankind's ideological evolution' and 'the final form of human government' (Fukuyama, 1992, pp.xi–xii). The fact that there is a correlation between the best political system and the currently most powerful group of states is not a cause of concern for liberals in the way it is for realists and Marxists. Rather than a modern manifestation of the union of power and dominant moral norms, the post-Cold War coincidence between liberal democracy and power is what makes the current systemic configuration so potentially progressive. This desire to see the West spread liberal values has obvious implications for humanitarian intervention, as such action is considered part of the march of human progress and a means by which the global transition to liberal democracy can be facilitated.

Marshall Cohen's perspective is typical of the broad liberal approach to morality; 'It is entirely appropriate,' he argues, 'to judge both a nations and its statesmen's conduct by pertinent moral standards' (Cohen, 1984, p.300). While warning against excessive moralism, Cohen argues that states are duty bound to be concerned about the plight of people resident in other states (ibid., p.324). Michael Walzer dismisses the realist belief that behaving amorally in international relations is excusable on the grounds that there is a systematic bias against such action, and notes:

> If we had all become realists like the Athenian generals or Hobbists in a state of war, there would be an end alike to both morality and hypocrisy. We would simply tell one another brutally and directly, what we wanted to do or have done. But the truth is that one of the things most of us want even in war, is to act or to seem to act morally. (Walzer, 1992a, p.21)

Walzer seeks to bring order *and* justice back to international relations so that statesmen and women can no longer excuse amoral action by taking solace in the realist assertion that international society is irrevocably anarchical. He, like a number of 'institutional liberals', advocates codified international laws which give legal expression to moral norms (1992a, p.288; see Chapter 5 and Conclusion).

Although the state is considered a necessary guarantor of individual liberties, liberalism favours limiting the influence of the state in the 'private' affairs of citizens. Internationally this manifests as an underlying preference for laws and practices that privilege the individual over the state, but unlike cosmopolitanism, not to the extent that the state is fundamentally undermined. Indicatively Marc Weller states that the rise of human rights as an international issue has challenged the fictitious notion that states are international subjects, arguing, 'The state only exists to the extent that the people out of which it is composed have transferred to it the competence to exercise public powers on their behalf' (1999, p.24). The sharp distinction between internal and international as advanced by realism is thus rejected although, as with the normative conception of the domestic system, there is a preference for state autonomy and international pluralism.

The liberal respect for pluralism, however, necessarily encourages the inside/outside distinction on one level, suggesting as it does tolerance for the difference inherent in other states and cultures. There are however limits to this tolerance, and the extension of this privilege to others is in key respects dependent on political and ideological symmetry. Thus, the liberal perspective is often characterized by what Gerry Simpson describes as 'Liberal anti-pluralism', which manifests an intolerance for different regimes and international institutions that do not reflect liberal values (2004, p.280). In this sense there is a clear unwillingness to accept that a state is entitled to inviolability by virtue of being a state; sovereignty is therefore 'conditional' (Gowan, 2003, p.51; see Chapter 6). Non-intervention is described by Fernando Tesón as 'a doctrine of the past' based on relativism and statism (2005a, p.358). Hence, in the post-Cold War era liberals have, somewhat paradoxically, been to the fore in advocating the subversion of the United Nations in cases where humanitarian intervention is deemed necessary, such as in Kosovo in 1999, because of the Security Council's dependence on the assent of non-democracies (see Chapter 7 and Conclusion).

Liberalism does not privilege order, and like Marxism is in fact predicated on the necessity of progressive change and in this sense 'inherently disorderly' (Freedman, 2005, p.101). Liberalism refutes the validity of realism's exclusive concern with order, arguing that 'order without a modicum of justice can only lead to disaster' (Hoffmann, 2003, p.24). The contemporary liberal perspective on intervention, often described as 'liberal internationalism', is at times bellicose and militaristic, stressing the imperative of intervention for the good of humanity (Cooper, 2004). This modern variant of 'disorderly' liberalism is, however, different from older forms. Walzer highlighted John Stuart Mill's classical liberal perspective on intervention and his belief that nations must achieve self-determination without external involvement. Mill did assert, however, that there were three cases when intervention may be permissible. The first is when a state clearly contains two or more separate communities and one is engaged in a struggle for independence. The second is when boundaries have already been crossed and the issue is counter-intervention, and the third, 'when the violation of human rights is so terrible that it makes talk of community or self determination or "arduous struggle" seem cynical and irrelevant' (Walzer, 1992a, p.90). Mill did not, however, give a precise definition of a sufficiently terrible violation of human rights that would warrant intervention, thus leaving the issue open to discretion.

This preference for non-intervention, however, is less apparent in contemporary liberal theory. Interventionism was particularly championed in the wake of the Soviet Union's collapse as the new systemic conditions were seen as enabling greater Western intervention without threatening international war. The West, it is argued, has elevated itself to a new level of consciousness characterized by a rejection of violence and conquest and unencumbered by old-fashioned, legalistic notions of sovereignty (Cooper, 2002). The intervention in Kosovo (see Chapter 11), for example, was 'an action fought for principles . . . to enforce certain minimum values on a state unwilling or unable to accept them' (Cooper, 2004, p.59). Prior to the invasion of Iraq (see Chapter 12), Michael Ignatieff argued that the use of force by progressive liberal states was historically often progressive, noting that 'there are many peoples who owe their freedom to an exercise of American military power'. The choice facing the West in March 2003, Ignatieff claimed, was 'between containing and leaving a tyrant in place and the targeted use of force, which will kill people but free a nation from the tyrant's grip' (Ignatieff, 2003).

The English School

The English School constitutes something of a mid-point between realism and liberalism. International politics is considered to be anarchical, and this forces states to behave in particular ways, but this systemic condition does not preclude the formation of an international society which adheres to mutable shared norms and laws. Hedley Bull notes that a plurality of sovereign states with a limited degree of interaction among them constitutes a system whereas a society is characterized by 'a degree of acceptance of common rules and institutions' (2002, p.225). These societal rules, usually termed norms, 'both constrain and enable actors', thereby limiting the decision-making autonomy of states (Wheeler, 2002, p.6). While these norms may not constitute laws presided over by a judicial system with the power of enforcement analogous to that in domestic systems, they determine a state's international status and its relationship with other states. Nicholas Wheeler argues that realist and Marxist perspectives overlook the extent to which 'the pursuit of international legitimization' binds state actions, noting, 'Even the great powers seek approval from their peers and domestic publics' (2006, p.32). States are not, therefore, conceived of as autonomous actors devoid of external restraint, although the extent to which the force of norms can influence state behaviour has limits. Nonetheless the English School makes both the empirical observation that norms do influence states to a significant extent, and the normative claim that states should be bound by these rules; Chris Brown indicatively assets, 'if diversity entails that states have the right to mistreat their populations, then it is difficult to see why such diversity is to be valued' (1992, p.125).

Within the English School a division exists between the solidarist, or Grotian, view and the pluralists who are closer to de Vattel (Bellamy,

[handwritten margin note: pluralists vs. solidarists in English School]

2005b, p.9). Pluralists stress the importance of the state, arguing that it provides for both order in the international sphere and, depending on the particular internal composition, justice and the protection of human rights domestically (Dunne, 1998, p.100). Individuals enjoy legal rights only to the extent that the state enables them to do so, through the provision of security and domestic legal structures, and thus states are of greater import than individuals. Thus the basic presumption of non-intervention should be maintained (Jackson, 2000).

Solidarists, however, argue that states, though clearly important, are instrumental – a means by which the individual's rights are upheld – and if this normative duty is not fulfilled, 'collective humanitarian intervention' is legitimate in response to 'extreme human suffering' (Wheeler, 1992, p.468). Solidarists argue that international regulation of a state's human rights record is both right and necessary, and a means by which the coherence of the society is upheld (Falk, 2005b). The solidarist view is based on the idea that an international society can coalesce around shared norms and values, and hence the violation of one of these norms – such as respect for human rights – is potentially legitimate grounds for intervention (Wheeler and Dunne, 1998, 2001). Alex Bellamy argues that while pluralists insist that intervention must only take place when the host state consents lest the fundamental rule of the international system be subverted, solidarists by contrast 'claim that the principle of consent is a circumscribed rule with important exceptions in times of massive human suffering' (Bellamy, 2003, p.5). The international society simply could not function if the norms governing intra-state human rights were routinely flouted, and thus intervention is not disruptive, rather it is an occasionally warranted means by which order is in fact restored.

Though Bull is essentially a pluralist, aspects of his work have been highlighted by solidarists to support their perspective. Bull argued that the rule of non-intervention prevailed because unilateral intervention threatened harmony and order within the society of states, although he additionally noted that when an intervention 'expresses the collective will of the society of states' it may not jeopardize international harmony (1984b, p.195). Given that Bull was writing during a period when the international system was arguably more fractured than it is today, it is possible that the contemporary systemic configuration and the greater integration apparent within the West means that this 'collective will of the society of states' may be stronger (Dunne, 1998). Solidarists argue that there is evidence that norms regarding humanitarian intervention have indeed changed; the many human rights treaties signed since 1945 and the emerging consensus that states cannot treat their citizens any way they please are held as examples of the ascendency and increasingly binding power of international human rights norms (Bellamy, 2009b; Greenwood, 1993). The post-Cold War ascendency of these norms is, therefore, indicative of the fluidity of norms and the potential for a 'norm cascade' to force a shift in the prevailing normative rules influencing the behaviour of states (Finnemore and Sikkink, 1998, p. 893). Governments within states might not naturally act morally in pursuing their foreign policy but through pressure exerted from below by the general public – 'the shaming power of humanitarian norms' – they may be compelled to do so (Wheeler, 2006, p.39). Solidarism does not suggest, however, that national interests play no role in the decision whether to intervene, and while humanitarian intervention is morally permissible under certain circumstances, it is not necessarily morally required once these circumstances arise (Wheeler, 2002, p.49).

The pluralist perspective, by contrast, argues that even within an international society states remain the rightful authority on, and guarantor of, human rights. Thus while norms and indeed laws on human rights and intervention exist, they are subjectively interpreted and invariably applied in practice only by powerful states (Bellamy, 2003, p.3). According to Robert Jackson:

> The ethics of human rights have to be fitted into the pluralist framework of international society and cannot sidestep that framework. That is the only operational context within which human beings can be defended in contemporary world politics. Human rights and humanitarianism have no actuality outside that pluralist framework. Solidarism is clearly subordinate to pluralism. (2000, p.289)

Similarly Bull argued that the international society implied by the discourse of universal human rights 'exists only as an ideal, and we court great dangers if we allow ourselves to proceed as if it were a political and social framework already in place' (1984a, p.13). Bull was sceptical of the power of norms and the existence of an international society generally, and argued that if such a society exists it enjoys 'only a precarious foothold' (2002, p.248). Bull stressed that it was untenable to claim that sovereignty can be enjoyed without qualification, but argued that promoting ostensibly 'universal human rights' in a context in which there is no consensus over their meaning or the mechanisms for their enforcement 'carries the danger that it will be subversive of coexistence among states, on which the whole fabric of world order in our times depends'. States that declare themselves to be acting in the common interest for the benefit of all humanity are thus 'a menace to international order, and thus to effective action in that field' (1984a, pp.12–13). This privileging of order over justice in the specific case of humanitarian intervention leads pluralists to espouse what at times appear to be cold-hearted prescriptions. In discussing the crisis in the Balkans, Jackson wrote, 'In my view, the stability of international society, especially the unity of the great powers, is more important, indeed far more important, than minority rights and humanitarian protections in

Yugoslavia or any other country – if we have to choose between the two' (2000, p.291).

While this may appear morally unconscionable it is important to remember that this preference is born from a normative conviction that stability is itself a significant moral good, as it prevents war and destruction. Yet, the prevailing systemic composition has clearly altered, and in the post-Cold War era there is an emerging acceptance amongst pluralists that, at the very least, action taken by the Security Council in response to intra-state humanitarian tragedy now has a strong degree of legitimacy and reflects a limited consensus on humanitarian intervention (Bellamy, 2003, p.12).

Solidarists welcomed NATO's intervention in Kosovo in 1999, with Bellamy asserting that it highlighted 'the extent to which international values and interests have begun to come together during the 1990s' (2002, p.214). While this intervention appeared to affirm the solidarist conception, the 2003 invasion of Iraq highlighted the extent to which the ascendency of the norm of humanitarian intervention facilitated the abuse of humanitarian rhetoric, and arguably the accuracy of the pluralist concern that intervention was inherently destabilizing and likely to be abused by the powerful (Thakur and Sidhu, 2006; Job, 2006).

Cosmopolitanism

Cosmopolitanism believes in a progressive evolution towards a universal order based on common morality. It constitutes a 'break with the assumption of territorially-based political entities' and explicitly disavows statist conceptions of international politics in favour of an agenda predicated on 'the existence of a human community with certain shared rights and obligations' (Kaldor, 1999, pp.115, 147). Catherine Lu argues that realists have overlooked the 'transformative potential' that exists when the barriers between states diminish in importance and the distinction between international and domestic politics is removed (2006, p.50). This merging of the internal and the external has ostensibly accelerated in the contemporary era as states, albeit primarily Western states, have increasingly developed mutually dependent relationships, pooled their sovereignty and contrived new norms on the use of force for humanitarian purposes (Kaldor, 2003, p.17; Levy, Young and Zürn, 1995). Cosmopolitanism asserts that the maintenance of an internal/external distinction is no longer tenable because of the effects of globalization and the general internationalization of post-Cold War inter-state relations (Hayden, 2005, p.91; Held, 2004, p.189; Keane, 2003, pp.4–8). States are no longer the dominant force in the international system and are increasingly constrained by domestic publics, global civil society and transnational organizations such as the European Union (Brown, 2006, p.3; Sørensen, 2001). The international system is therefore considered to be evolving towards a radical new alignment characterized by the diminution of the centrality of the state, increased interdependence, respect for human rights, and perhaps most ambitiously, mechanisms of global governance involving international military capabilities (Woodhouse and Ramsbotham, 2005, p.140).

The cosmopolitan perspective seeks to increase intervention by fashioning a system whereby states are interdependent and the tenets of sovereignty are significantly altered to reflect a preference for human rights. The statist system has encouraged the singular pursuit of national interests and the privileging of order over justice. This has created a world plagued by instability, violence and 'the callous indifference towards the interests of persons beyond (and perhaps even within) the borders of each state' (Hayden, 2005, p.70). Cosmopolitanism argues that the international system of states has created false divisions in the international community and allowed relativist claims of morality to thrive. Given that humanity is not singularly motivated by self-interest, as realists suggest, the projection of this negative (and flawed) diagnosis of motivations onto the international system overlooks the capacity of individuals, and hence states, to act in defence of others (Janzekovic, 2006, p.26). There is, therefore, a need to fundamentally reorganise the international system so as to reflect the underlying universal morality which is humanity's true nature (Küng, 1991, pp.xv–xvi).

Proponents of cosmopolitanism prioritize 'human security' (see Chapter 6) and articulate a trans-state vision of international relations where the individual's rights trump those of the state and thus order and stability amongst states is a secondary concern (Falk, 1995; Kaul, 1995). Andrew Linklater identified the aim of human-centred advocacy as 'Transcending state sovereignty', which he considered 'essential to promoting narratives of increasing cosmopolitanism' (1998, p.109). Humanitarian intervention is therefore conceptualized as 'an act directed towards upholding the non-intervention norm of civil society, which protects an area of freedom for individuals' (Frost, 2001, p.51). Human rights violations are 'legitimate concerns of individual men and women everywhere, communities in all parts of the world, and the society of states as a whole' (Lu, 2006, p.112). Rather than viewing intra-state conflicts as a potential threat that needs to be contained, cosmopolitanism 'would seek to understand the underlying reasons behind human rights conflicts and apply positive measures to solve them' (Archibugi, 2003, p.11).

In addition to this normative defence of humanitarian intervention, trends in the contemporary era have added a practical rationale for increased trans-state humanitarianism. Globalization has undermined state autonomy and fused political, social and cultural interdependence, and therefore humanitarian crises within one state will not be confined to that state. This key supposition mirrors the cosmopolitan maxim proposed in the 18th century by Kant, who held that if the suffering of people abroad were tolerated it would threaten international peace and security because of 'the interconnectedness of the parts that form the whole' (Jackson, 2006, p.30). In stark contrast to realism, therefore, cosmopolitanism argues that increased humanitarian intervention, 'will make for a more peaceful world' (Janzekovic, 2006, p.190).

As the United Nations constitutes 'the creature of an unreconstructed system of sovereign nation states' which promotes 'state interest and militarised power', cosmopolitanism has generally called for an adherence to ostensibly less politicized natural law when dealing with intra-state humanitarian crises (Woodhouse and Ramsbotham, 2005, p.141). Many have compiled lists of criteria that states *should* adhere to for their interventions to be deemed legitimate (see Chapter 2). This attempt to constrain intervention is predicated on the assumption that democracies will intervene only with the endorsement of their domestic populace and global civil society, who can ensure compliance with the criteria (Buchanan and Keohane, 2004, p.19). The emergence of global civil society poses a 'transformative challenge to the customary role of states' (Falk, 1995, p.206) and has, cosmopolitanism holds, transformed the international system to the extent that in no longer makes sense to theorize about a world of self-contained states evolving according to the principle of non-intervention (Farer, 2003, p.146). These groups coordinate international activism which constitutes a 'pervasive, significant, positive influence on the policies of the states' (Hensel, 2004, p.ix). Through the mobilization of NGOs global civil society had become 'a source of constant pressures on the state system' (Shaw, 1994, p.24) and as a consequence of this pressure 'policy makers are more likely to act ... in the interests of the human community' (Kaldor, 2003, p.102). The preference for moral norms is not shared by all cosmopolitanists, however, with Fred Dallmayr arguing that while these norms are progressive they require legal expression and a clear means of consistent and impartial enforcement to be truly effective (2003, p.434).

NATO's intervention in Kosovo was heralded by many cosmopolitanists (Fuller, 1999; Janzekovic, 2006), and though many were highly critical of the lack of coercive military intervention in Darfur (see Chapter 13), the West's engagement with the crisis has been identified as an improvement on the record in Rwanda and a function of international pressure by NGOs (Mayroz, 2008). The United States and United Kingdom's attempts to secure a Security Council resolution prior to the invasion of Iraq is also cited as evidence of the power of international mass movements (Cortright, 2006, p.75).

Post-structuralism

The post-structuralist approach, in so far as a coherent approach exists (Devetak, 2009, p. 183), sees the discipline of IR as part of a wider movement in social thought and seeks to 'unsettle established categories and disconcert the reader' (Brown and Ainley, 2005, p.53). Thus post-structuralist IR scholars have stressed the necessity of an interdisciplinary methodology (Der Derian and Shapiro, 1989).

The theory derives much of its inspiration from Michel Foucault, who argued that power and knowledge are intimately linked, with one implying the other. Using the example of the prison system Foucault suggested that a generic set of assumptions, derived from particular societal power relations, can be identified as underpinning all aspects of society (1991). A dominant discourse or a 'regime of truth' is held to impose critical limits upon our ability to think politically about particular problems faced (Foucault, 1980: p.131). Post-structuralist analyses, therefore, interrogate discourse on a particular theme to highlight the inherent assumptions which perpetuate a particular dominant belief (Malmvig, 2001, p.251). Challenging the prevailing discourse and especially those ideas and institutions presented as axiomatic, Jean Elshtain argues, implies 'a recognition of the ways in which received doctrines ... may lull our critical faculties to sleep, blinding us to the possibilities that lie within our reach' (1992, p.276).

Post-structuralists seek to identify how the primacy of the sovereign state has been maintained by a discourse which overlooks the true evolution of the state and presents state sovereignty as a pre-existing neutral reality (Edkins and Pin-Fat, 1998). Rather than seeing violence as something states are forced to employ in exceptional circumstances by virtue of the international structure or human nature, post-structuralism argues that violence created the state and is central to the system of states. Therefore the periodic eruption of violence between or within states enables states to constitute themselves and is a means by which the state system is perpetuated (Klein, 1994). Attempts to limit violence that advocate the maintenance of the basic system of states, such as the dominant discourse of humanitarian intervention whereby states 'solve' problems in other states, are therefore futile (Campbell, 1994, p.456).

The discourse of 'intervention', as much as it is often represented as a violation of sovereignty, presupposes the existence of sovereignty and therefore helps to reaffirm the idea (Edkins, 2003, p.255; Malmvig, 2001, p.252; Weber, 1995, pp.1–29). Rob Walker argues that despite the often divisive nature of the debate on humanitarian intervention, the dominant opposing positions take the state for granted. The state is conceived as worthy, albeit for differing reasons, and therefore debates about humanitarian intervention since the 1990s have not addressed the real problem – state sovereignty (Walker, 2003, p.280). Humanitarian activism of the sort espoused by global civil society (see Chapter 6) requires the assent of states to undertake interventions, be they military or not, 'and thus rather than challenging state power these actors act as an instrument and rationality of statecraft' (Campbell, 1998b, p.519).

Helle Malmvig argues that the manner in which the discourse of intervention is framed involves a strategy whereby egregious humanitarian violations are portrayed in a way so that 'they constitute the need to do something as evident' and 'work as justifications in and of themselves' (2001, p.257). The popular portrayal of humanitarian crises lacks political analysis and facilitates the idea that the solution can be found in externally coordinated administrative, as opposed to political, action (Edkins, 2000). While these strategies do not necessarily compel intervention they can be used to frame the debate according to 'zero-sum logic' where actors are presented with an exceptional choice between action and inaction, humanitarian intervention or passivity (Malmvig, 2001, p.267). Likewise Jenny Edkins suggests that the discourse presupposes a distinction between 'we' and 'they' which narrows the debate to a focus on 'whether and how "we" should help "them"' (2003, p. 255). While the rhetoric of humanitarian intervention implies a need to 'do something' and 'get involved', David Keen argues that the idea of external involvement occurring only *after* a disaster has erupted is false (2001, p.19). Likewise Anne Orford asserts that the debate about the merits of intervention in Yugoslavia in the 1990s obscured the extent to which the international community 'had itself contributed to the humanitarian crises that had emerged' (2003, p.13).

The discourse of humanitarian intervention reproduces power asymmetries; the West is portrayed as the powerful saviour while the 'other' is cast as the needy victim inhabiting a chaotic distant world (Orford, 2003, pp.83–5). Victims of humanitarian tragedy live in 'an official faraway place' which is 'morally distinct' to the West (O'Tuathail, 1996, p.171). David Campbell, argues that the framing of the international response to the conflict in Bosnia created a conceptual division between 'them' and 'us' whereby the 'other' is represented as lacking the traits that characterize the hegemon and thus the decay in the periphery affirms the good life in the core (1998a). The fate of the 'rescued' other, Patricia Owens claims, is portrayed in a way that 'conform[s] to (usually liberal) sentimental fantasy norms about the "American way of life"'. This discourse means that national myths and the pervading sense of moral benevolence 'appeared upheld and invigorated via representations of these "foreigners"' (Owens, 2004, p.287). Likewise David Kennedy sees the project of the new humanitarians as inspired more by the sense of purpose and self-worth it inspires in the actor than the actual good it does for the 'victim' (2006, p.87). Thus the liberal notion of spreading the good life is in fact a means by which the 'other' is further mystified and the homeland is venerated.

As much as humanitarian intervention suggests a merging of national and international, Orford argues that the discourse serves to reassure the international community that there is a differentiated other, and to locate this other 'somewhere else, outside' (Orford, 2003, p.124). The appropriation of human rights by Western states, it is claimed, has facilitated the image of a barbarous hinterland and a civilized core, and resulted in human rights becoming a means by which the legitimacy of the present order has in fact been bolstered (Douzinas, 2000, p. 129–41). The discourse of humanitarian intervention has therefore stripped human rights of their revolutionary potential.

Conclusion

Explaining the new concern with humanitarian intervention in the post-Cold War era is of significant concern for theorists of IR, and it is clear that consensus is manifestly lacking. By the latter half of the 1990s all major Western states articulated a commitment to 'ethical foreign policies' which seemed to contradict the realist focus on power and the national interest, and appeared to constitute the death knell for realism (Zakaria, 1992). Some have argued that the popular conception of realism purportedly vanquished by recent events is a truncated version of the theory which overlooks its many normative dimensions (Bain, 2006; Molloy, 2006; Williams, 2007). Liberals, cosmopolitanists and solidarists suggest, albeit in differing ways, that this change in foreign policy priorities was the result of humanitarian advocacy whereby academics, human rights organisations and NGOs successfully convinced Western powers to include moral considerations in their foreign relations. Realists, Marxists and post-structuralists by contrast, view the discourse as essentially a rhetorical facade designed to obscure the true power-political motivations.

The utility of examining IR theory when studying humanitarian intervention stems from the capacity of theory to provide a framework for understanding the motivations driving states to behave in certain ways. Whether theory comprises prescriptions as to how states should act, or objective explanations of how states *actually* act is a source of contention. It is increasingly argued that the theorist cannot be seen as an entirely dispassionate observer of international events, and thus all theory is, to some extent, subjective and partisan (Edkins, 2005b, p. 68). This idea that the theorist's personal bias inevitably influences their theoretical beliefs echoes Cox's famous claim, 'Theory is always for someone and for some purpose' (1981, p.128). An individual's view on this perspective on theory necessarily influences their opinion on the utility of theory. Nonetheless, a comprehensive understanding of humanitarian intervention must involve some engagement with theory regardless of the perspective on the accuracy and utility of the various theories here described.

Questions

- What is the function of IR theory?
- Can IR theory ever be truly objective?
- Outline and assess the perspectives of realism, Marxism, liberalism, the English School, cosmopolitanism and post-structuralism on the following issues; the role of morality in international relations; the place of human rights; the relationship between order and justice.

Further reading

Realism

Carr, E. H. (2001) *The Twenty Years Crisis* (Basingstoke and New York: Palgrave Macmillan).

Morgenthau, H. J. (1954) *Politics Among Nations: The Struggle for Power and Peace* (New York: Alfred Knopf).

Niebuhr, R. (1932) *Moral Man and Immoral Society: A Study in Ethics and Politics* (New York: Charles Scribners).

Waltz, K. (1979) *Theory of International Politics* (Toronto: McGraw-Hill).

Williams, M. (2007) *Realism Reconsidered* (Oxford: Oxford University Press).

Marxism and critical theory

Chomsky, N. (1999) *The New Military Humanism: Lessons from Kosovo* (London: Pluto).

Cox, R. (1996) *Approaches to World Order* (Cambridge: Cambridge University Press).

Duffield, M. (2006) *Global Governance and the New Wars: The Merging of Development and Security* (London: Zed).

Mandani, M. (2009) *Saviors and Survivors: Darfur, Politics, and the War on Terror* (London: Pantheon).

Rosenberg, J. (1994) *Empire of Civil Society* (London: Verso).

Liberalism

Cooper, R. (2004) *The Breaking of Nations* (London: Atlantic).

Fukuyama, F. (1992) *The End of History and the Last Man* (New York: Avon).

Holmes, R. L. (1989) *On War and Morality* (Princeton, N.J.: Princeton University Press).

Keohane, R. and Nye, J. (1977) *Power and Interdependence: World Politics in Transition* (Boston, Mass.: Little, Brown).

Walzer, M. (1992) *Just and Unjust Wars* (New York: Basic Books).

The English School

Bull, H. (2002) *The Anarchical Society: A Study of Order in World Politics* (Basingstoke: Palgrave Macmillan and New York: Columbia University Press).

Dunne, T. (1998) *Inventing International Society* (Basingstoke and New York: Palgrave Macmillan).

Vincent, J. (1986) *Human Rights and International Relations* (Cambridge: Cambridge University Press).

Wheeler, N. (2002) *Saving Strangers: Humanitarian Intervention in International Society* (Oxford: Oxford University Press).

Wight, M. (1979) *International Theory: The Three Traditions*, ed. G. Wight and B. Porter (Leicester: Leicester University Press).

Cosmopolitanism

Archibugi, D. (ed.) (2003) *Debating Cosmopolitics* (London: Verso).

Hayden, P. (2005) *Cosmopolitan Global Politics* (Aldershot: Ashgate).

Held, D. (1995) *Democracy and the Global Order* (London: Polity).

Kaldor, M. (2003) *Global Civil Society: An Answer to War* (London: Polity).

Lu, C. (2006) *Just and Unjust Interventions in World Politics: Public and Private* (Basingstoke and New York: Palgrave Macmillan).

Post-structuralism

Campbell, D. (1998) *National Deconstruction: Violence, Identity and Justice in Bosnia* (Minneapolis, Minn.: University of Minnesota Press).

Der Derian, J. and Shapiro, M. J. (eds.) (1989) *International/Intertextual Relations: Postmodern Readings of World Politics* (Lexington, Ky.: Lexington Books).

Douzinas, C. (2000) *The End of Human Rights* (Oxford: Oxford University Press).

Edkins, J. (2005) *Poststructuralism and International Relations: Bringing the Political Back In* (Boulder, Colo.: Lynne Rienner).

Orford, A. (2003) *Reading Humanitarian Intervention* (Cambridge: Cambridge University Press).

Part II

Controversies

Chapter 5

Legality and Legitimacy

One of the most divisive controversies surrounding humanitarian intervention is the tension between natural and positive law. Positive law has developed steadily since the end of the Second World War, and though its effectiveness is debatable, the expansion of its tenets and remit has been marked. The manner in which international law has evolved, specifically with respect to sovereign inviolability and equality, has resulted in the exclusion of humanitarian intervention from the canon of positive law. This illegality has been strongly criticized by humanitarians outraged by what they regard as an amoral, if not immoral, anachronism.

Owing to the nature of some of the humanitarian crises that have occurred in the post-Cold War era, there has emerged a conviction that interventions can be 'illegal but legitimate'. Proponents of positive law suggest that it has developed in response to the endemic abuse of the necessarily nebulous and subjective natural law. Conversely, advocates of natural law assert that its universality and timelessness make it a higher source of guidance than temporal and invariably contrived positive law. The nature of this debate is the focus of this chapter.

This chapter begins by outlining the evolution of international law regarding the use of force, charting its development from the 17th century to the present Charter system. This section also examines the legal status of humanitarian intervention and assesses the various arguments asserting its legality. The second section analyses the rationale behind the 'illegal but legitimate' perspective which holds that, in the case of humanitarian crises, positive law occasionally yields to moral or natural law. This section additionally outlines the counter-argument presented by those opposed to natural law. The final section analyses whether there is a need for legal reform to reconcile the tension between legality and legitimacy highlighted by humanitarian intervention.

The evolution of international law and the legal status of humanitarian intervention

The legal status of humanitarian intervention is a highly contentious issue. On the one hand it would appear that humanitarian intervention is manifestly contrary to codified international law, though as we shall see this is not a universally held view. Yet, even accepting this illegality, the legal pro-scription against humanitarian intervention has increasingly been deemed anachronistic and morally untenable. This aspect of the controversy has meant that humanitarian intervention, more so than any other issue, highlights the tension between international law and morality.

The evolution of international law

The legal status of humanitarian intervention is a function of the evolu-tionary trajectory of international law in the post-First World War era, particularly after the signing of the UN Charter in 1945. The contempo-rary tenets of international law derive from the process of law formation orientated towards defining the rights afforded to states, and the remit of the international institutions established to regulate them. As discussed in Chapter 3, the emergence of the sovereign state in the 17th century led to the gradual development of rules governing relations between these polit-ical entities. While international law expanded in the 18th and 19th cen-turies, the legal system at this time was undermined and abused by the more powerful states and lacked a constitutional base. In the pre-First World War era, 'the dominant powers determined the criteria by which non-European political communities could be admitted to membership of international society, including the degree to which the laws of armed conflict were to apply to the non-European world (Hurrell, 2005, pp. 20–1).

States essentially acted without restraint apart from that derived from domestic considerations and the policies of their rivals and allies (Bellamy, 2006b, p.93). Legal codes certainly existed and states often committed themselves to behave in certain ways, but the malleability of these codes was routinely exploited. For example, it was agreed that self-defence was a permissible basis for the use of force, hence effectively all acts of aggression during this period, including even Germany's invasion of Belgium in 1914, were legitimized as such. Important progress was made with respect to international humanitarian law, however, particularly at the two Hague conventions of 1899 and 1907. War was, nonetheless, in essence consid-ered inevitable, akin to natural disasters; the point of law was to limit its consequences, not its occurrence.

Following the First World War steps were taken to address the resort to force. The Industrial Revolution had imbued modern armies with the capacity to destroy on a historically unprecedented scale, and states now faced the prospect of annihilation. The arms race and the division of Europe into rival pacts prior to the First World War led many to determine that a more developed international forum based on universal legal codes was required. The establishment of the League of Nations in 1919 was the product of this idea, and championed by its proponents as a force for peace. As we know the League was ultimately unable to prevent the re-division of Europe and the outbreak of total war. While the political aspirations of the League manifestly failed, significant developments in international law with long-term implications did occur during the League's existence. The Permanent Court of International Justice was established in 1922, later becoming the International Court of Justice (ICJ) in 1946. The Kellogg–Briand Pact in 1928 constituted a significant renunciation of war as an instrument of foreign policy, and the pact's key provisions were incorporated into key articles in the UN Charter. The normative remit of international law thus expanded to constrain not just the conduct of war but the grounds on which it could legitimately be waged.

As discussed in Chapter 4, the Second World War catalyzed a shift from idealism to realism in IR theory, which largely mirrored international politics during the Cold War. In terms of international law, however, the Second World War accelerated the process of law formation regarding the use of force. The UN Charter constituted an ambitious attempt to constrain the recourse to force, and for the first time codified sovereign equality as the basis of the international legal system. As discussed in Chapter 3, the new legal regime attempted to restrict the use of force through the creation of inviolable states of equal legal status, thereby preventing, at least in legal terms, the overt use of power in international politics. Andrew Hurrell argues that the evolutionary trajectory of international law in the 20th century has been orientated:

> towards a system in which norm creation becomes an increasingly complex and pluralist process, in which ideas of equality become more powerful and pervasive, and in which specific rules come to be understood and interpreted in the light of general legal principles and shared foundational values and as part of an increasingly integrated normative order. (2005, p.18)

The normative goal of pluralist law creation and peaceful inter-state relations could only be realized if the legal subjects of this new regime were afforded equal rights and, crucially, empowered with the right to determine their own fate, hence the need for sovereign equality and inviolability. The impermissibility of humanitarian intervention is thus an arguably involuntary function of this goal.

The establishment of the United Nations and the legal rights granted to states should not be seen, however, as a bottom-up process whereby major powers bowed to pressure exercised by smaller states demanding equality. Gerry Simpson cites the special powers reserved for the permanent five members (P5) of the Security Council as evidence of what he terms 'legalised hegemony' (2004, p.68). Additionally, Anne Orford believes the international legal order has been constructed so as to privilege those militarily and economically powerful states and facilitate domination by the powerful (2003, pp.46–7). Indeed, according to Hedley Bull, 'any historical system of rules will be found to serve the interests of the ruling or dominant elements of the society more adequately than it serves the interests of the others' (2002, p.53). The UN framework was of course constructed by the victorious Allies, who did reserve significant competencies for themselves, some of which still remain, notably the veto powers of the P5. Additionally aside from the evidence of formal hierarchy, actual state practice since 1945 has certainly not evidenced consistent respect for sovereign equality and inviolability. While we can point to the many achievements of international law in terms of the widening and deepening of its remit, the codification of laws and the delimitation of the permissible grounds for the use of force do not in themselves constitute evidence of international law's effectiveness. It remains debatable whether, for all the many impressive advances in international law made since 1945, state behaviour is constrained, to any significant extent, by legal codes. Indicatively, when planning US military strategy following the 11 September 2001 attacks, President Bush declared, 'I don't care what the international lawyers say; we are going to kick some ass' (Coicaud, 2006, p.426). Yet, while international law has been routinely derided as impotent, significant developments in the post-Cold War era, such as the establishment of the International Criminal Court (ICC) and various ad hoc war crimes tribunals, testify to international law's emerging vitality. High-profile violations of international law should not obscure the fact that states obey international law most of the time (Malanczuk, 2006, p.6).

The legal status of humanitarian intervention

The Kellogg–Briand Pact outlawed war as an instrument of state policy except when fought in self-defence or sanctioned by the League of Nations. This principle was incorporated into the UN Charter and finds its clearest expression in Article 2.4 (see Box 5.1). Additionally under Article 2.7 the United Nations itself is prohibited from unsolicited involvement in the domestic affairs of its member-states. Many subsequent treaties, resolutions and statements reaffirmed this principle. Articles 53 and 64 of the 1969 Vienna Convention on the Law of Treaties state that this particular provision is *jus cogens* and therefore accepted by the international community as a principle from which no derogation is permitted. General Assembly Resolution 2131 in 1965 affirmed the Assembly's opposition to all forms of intervention 'for any reason whatsoever', and declares, 'armed intervention is synonymous with aggression'. In 1970 the General Assembly passed Resolution 2625 which reaffirmed the prohibition on 'the threat or use of force against the territorial integrity or political independence of any State'. Clause IV of the Helsinki Accords Final Act of 1975 notes, 'The participating states will respect the territorial integrity of each of the participating states. Accordingly they will refrain from any action . . . against the territorial integrity, political independence, or the unity of any participating state.' The Charter, and supplementary international law, therefore, explicitly recognize the inviolability of the state and outlaws the use of force.

There are two exceptions to the prohibition on the use of force. Article 51 of the UN Charter reads, 'Nothing in the present Charter shall impair the inherent right of individual or collective self defense if an armed attack occurs against a member of the United Nations.' This is premised, however, by the declaration that the use of force in self-defence is only

---

Box 5.1 Key Articles of the UN Charter related to humanitarian intervention

Article 1.1
[The purposes of the United Nations are] To maintain international peace and security, and to that end: to take effective collective measures for the prevention and removal of threats to the peace, and for the suppression of acts of aggression or other breaches of the peace, and to bring about by peaceful means, and in conformity with the principles of justice and international law, adjustment or settlement of international disputes or situations which might lead to a breach of the peace.

Article 2.4
All Members shall refrain in their international relations from the threat or use of force against the territorial integrity or political independence of any state, or in any other manner inconsistent with the Purposes of the United Nations.

Article 2.7
Nothing in the present Charter shall authorize the United Nations to intervene in matters which are essentially within the domestic jurisdiction of any state.

Article 24.1
In order to ensure prompt and effective action by the United Nations, its Members confer on the Security Council primary responsibility for the maintenance of international peace and security, and agree that in carrying out its duties under this responsibility the Security Council acts on their behalf.

Article 39
The Security Council shall determine the existence of any threat to the peace, breach of the peace, or act of aggression and shall make recommendations, or decide what measures shall be taken in accordance with Articles 41 and 42, to maintain or restore international peace and security.

permissible 'until the Security Council has taken measures necessary to maintain international peace and security', and that this right of self-defence 'shall not in any way affect the authority and responsibility of the Security Council'. The ICJ ruled in the 1986 case of *Nicaragua v the United States* that the notion of self-defence should be understood restrictively (Guicherd, 1999, p.21).

The other grounds on which the use of force is permissible are outlined in Chapter VII of the Charter. Article 39 reads:

> The Security Council shall determine the existence of any threat to the peace, breach of the peace, or act of aggression and shall make recommendations, or decide what measures shall be taken in accordance with Articles 41 and 42, to maintain or restore international peace and security.

Article 41 gives the Security Council the power to determine non-military responses to a perceived threat. Article 42 comes into effect if measures taken under Article 41 prove inadequate, and enables the Security Council to sanction more robust measures 'as may be necessary to maintain or restore international peace and security.'

Under Article 24 of the Charter, member-states acknowledge that the Security Council has 'primary responsibility for the maintenance of international peace and security.' The one possible derogation from this rule is the 1950 General Assembly Resolution 377, *Uniting for Peace* (see Box 5.2). This resolution enables the General Assembly to act when the Security Council is unable to sanction action unanimously, or demand a cessation to ongoing military action when there is a threat to international peace and stability. The General Assembly may take up the issue under two conditions. The first is when nine members of the Security Council vote to move the issue to the General Assembly and this vote is immune from the P5 veto. The second is when a majority of UN member-states vote to move the issue to the General Assembly (Krasno and Das, 2008, p.175). The General Assembly can only take the lead on an issue that is not under consideration at the Security Council, but provided this condition is met, technically the General Assembly could sanction a military intervention if two-thirds of its members so agreed.

The procedures outlined in Resolution 377 were first used in 1950 regarding the conflict in Korea, although the first explicit reference to 'Uniting for Peace' occurred during the Suez Canal crises in 1956. However, the ineffectiveness of this principle was evidenced later that year when the General Assembly's declaration that the Soviet Union should discontinue its military action in Hungary was ignored. The Danish Institute of International Affairs (DIIA) found that the *Uniting for Peace* resolution 'Has lost much of its importance [and] is no legal basis for the authorization of humanitarian intervention' (1999, p.61). Additionally moving divisive issues like those posed by humanitarian intervention to the General Assembly is no guarantee that they will be dealt with swiftly. At times use of the *Uniting for Peace* resolution simply created another forum for unproductive rhetoric and division (Krasno and Das, 2008, p.189). Nonetheless, as discussed further in Chapter 6, an increased role for the General Assembly, specifically through the utilization of the *Uniting for Peace* resolution, has been mooted as a possible solution to an impasse at the Security Council (Evans, 2008, p.136; ICISS, 2001, p.53).

Under existing codified international law, therefore, there is no law explicitly sanctioning humanitarian intervention. In its key ruling in the 1949 *Corfu Channel* case the ICJ declared that it could:

> only regard the alleged right of intervention as the manifestation of a policy of force, such as has, in the past, given rise to most serious abuses and as such cannot, whatever be the present defect in international organization, find a place in international law. Intervention . . . would be reserved for the most powerful states and might easily lead to perverting the administration of international justice itself. (DIIA, 1999, p.86)

In its ruling in the 1986 case *Nicaragua v the United States*, the ICJ further declared, 'While the US might form its own appraisal of the situation as to respect for human rights in Nicaragua, the use of force could not be the appropriate method to monitor or ensure such respect' (DIIA, 1999, p.83). In 1986 the UK Foreign Office gave its opinion as to the legal status of humanitarian intervention, which found against its legality, noting, 'the scope of abusing such a right argues strongly against its creation (Holbrook, 2002, pp.140–1). Similarly, the US 1987 Restatement of

---

Box 5.2 'Uniting for Peace': General Assembly Resolution 377, 3 November 1950

'*Resolves* that if the Security Council, because of lack of unanimity of the permanent members, fails to exercise its primary responsibility for the maintenance of international peace and security in any case where there appears to be a threat to the peace, breach of the peace, or act of aggression, the General Assembly shall consider the matter immediately with a view to making appropriate recommendations to Members for collective measures, including in the case of a breach of the peace or act of aggression the use of armed force when necessary, to maintain or restore international peace and security.'

Foreign Relations Law noted, 'Whether a state may intervene with military force in the territory of another state without its consent not to rescue the victims but to prevent or terminate human rights violations, is not agreed or authoritatively determined' (Burton, 1996, p. 428). This apparent consensus on the illegality of humanitarian intervention, however, dissipated in the post-Cold War era.

The provisions of Chapter VII of the Charter have been cited as a possible source of legality. Humanitarian intervention could be sanctioned by the Security Council if intra-state conflicts were deemed a threat to international peace and stability, as increasingly they have been in the post-Cold War era. Security Council Resolution 688 in 1991 declared that the Security Council 'Condemns the repression of the Iraqi civilian population in many parts of Iraq, including most recently in Kurdish populated areas, the consequences of which threaten international peace and security in the region'. Security Council practice in the 1990s reflected the emergence of the view that economic, social, ecological and humanitarian instability were grounds for acting under Chapter VII.

Simon Chesterman, however, notes that Security Council action under Chapter VII during the 1990s was haphazard, leading to 'ambiguous resolutions and conflicting interpretations [of Chapter VII]' (2002, p.5). The sanctioning of action, according to Chesterman, 'depended more upon a coincidence of national interest than on procedural legality' (ibid., p.165). Additionally, it is questionable whether the Security Council has the authority to apply Chapter VII to intra-state crises. According to the DIIA,

> It was hardly the intention of the framers of the Charter that internal conflicts and human rights violations should be regarded as a threat to international peace. There is no evidence that they might have envisaged a competence for the Security Council under Chapter VII to take action to cope with situations of humanitarian emergency within a state resulting from civil war or systematic repression. (1999, p. 62)

Indeed in 1946 the Security Council refused to describe Franco's Spain as a threat under Chapter VII, noting that this Charter provision constituted 'a very sharp instrument' and that care should be taken so that 'this instrument is not blunted or used in any way which would strain the intentions of the Charter or which would not be applicable in all similar cases' (Chesterman, 2002, p.130). The Independent International Commission on Kosovo (IICK) found, 'At present the Charter does not explicitly give the UN Security Council the power to take measures in cases of violations of human rights' (2000, p.196).

Nonetheless, during the 1990s the remit of Chapter VII was stretched to facilitate interventions in situations where the threat to international peace and security was relatively minimal. Following a military coup in 1991 the democratically elected president of Haiti, Jean-Bertrand Aristide, was ousted. The United Nations imposed economic sanctions, which by 1994 were said to have had no effect. In July 1994 the Security Council passed Resolution 940, which determined that the situation in Haiti constituted a threat to international peace and stability, and ordered an intervention to restore the democratically elected President. In practice, as the ongoing situation in many other states attested, non-democratic regimes and benefactors of military coups were not considered to constitute this grave threat in every instance. In addition, in keeping with other uses of Chapter VII during the 1990s, this Security Council ruling was officially deemed an exception. Resolution 940 recognized 'the unique character' of the situation and stated that Haiti's 'extraordinary nature . . . [required] an exceptional response'. Similarly the sanctioning of action in Somalia in 1992 under Chapter VII was premised on it being 'an exceptional response', and the deployment of troops in Rwanda in 1994, through Resolution 929, was described as 'a unique case.' This inconsistent use of Chapter VII has angered many states who accuse the Security Council of hypocrisy (Cassese, 2005, p.347). Interventions sanctioned under Chapter VII have thus clearly become more commonplace but the selective application of this provision has been a cause for concern.

Whether the Security Council has acted in accordance with international law in its use of Chapter VII is a moot point; some have noted that the Security Council is not authorized to interpret the Charter in any way it pleases (White, 2004). Despite these valid concerns about the politicization and legality of Security Council action under Chapter VII, however, an intervention authorized by the Security Council would have a very strong legal case, and interventions authorized by the Security Council have not, historically, been sources of great legal contestation. It is action taken without Security Council authorization – namely unilateral humanitarian intervention – that has proved far more controversial.

Essentially three justifications have been articulated defending the legality of unilateral humanitarian intervention. The first relates to a particular interpretation of Article 2.4 of the UN Charter (see Box 5.1). It is claimed that a true humanitarian intervention would not be directed against 'the territorial integrity or political independence' of the targeted state and would thus not be 'inconsistent with the Purposes of the United Nations' (Tesón, 1998, p.150; Weiss, 2007, p.17). The IICK rejected this argument, noting that 'Charter provisions relating to human rights were left deliberately vague, and were clearly not intended when written to provide a legal rationale for any kind of enforcement, much less a free-standing mandate for military intervention without UN Security Council approval' (2000, p. 168). Chesterman's analysis of the preliminary meetings held to discuss the UN Charter determines that the 'dominant' legal opinion as to the meaning of Article 2.4 holds that it does not provide any scope for humanitarian intervention (2002, p. 53).

Secondly, there is the 'link theory' justification as proffered in particularby Richard Lillich (1967), who argues that, while under Article 24.1 the Security Council has 'primary responsibility for the maintenance of international peace and security', under Article 1.1 UN member-states have a responsibility to maintain international peace and security when the Security Council is unable to carry out its duties in this respect. Under certain circumstances, therefore, the onus is on member-states to act and the prohibition on the use of force as outlined in Article 2.4 is suspended. Geoffrey Robertson similarly argues that Article 2.4 'really means to prohibit any armed attacks which are inconsistent with Charter purposes, and does not necessarily exclude those which are directed to uphold those purposes' (2002, p.434).

In its assessment of the merits of the link theory, the DIIA identified three flaws. Firstly, there is no explicit basis for this rationale outlined in the Charter. Although Article 24.1 states that the Security Council has *primary* rather than *exclusive* responsibility for the maintenance of international peace and security, according to the DIIA, '[This] refers to a subsidiary responsibility of other organs of the UN, notably the General Assembly, but not of the Members states.' Secondly, it is not legally sound to assert that the Charter must be suspended when the Security Council fails to act, as there is no legal basis for this assertion. Thirdly, the prohibition on the use of force is a tenet of customary international law and has evolved independently of the UN Charter, and therefore 'can hardly be conditioned upon the effectiveness of collective security under Chapter VII' (1999, p.82). This view is supported by Thomas Franck and Nigel Rodley, who note that those who drafted the human rights legislation never intended it to be used as a justification for unilateral action. Such action would, in fact, 'bring to a standstill' the very process of defining and codifying human rights (Franck and Rodley, 1973, p.300).

The third justification relates to customary international law. The *Paquete Habana* case (1900) established that in addition to codified doctrines, treaties and court judgments, international law is based on established customary behaviour of states, and this is codified in Article 38 of the Statute of the ICJ. By definition customary law begins with a breach of existing positive law followed by what Cassese describes as 'the fundamental elements constituting custom', namely 'state practice (*usus* or *diuturnitas*) and the corresponding views of states (*opinio juris* or *opinio necessitates*)' (2005, p. 157). In this sense, there may be a legal basis to a principle, such as humanitarian intervention, that has not been formally codified, and states may be considered bound by a customary law even if they have not signed a treaty to that effect. For example, in 1986 the ICJ ruled that the Geneva Convention applied to all states, even those who had not signed it, as it had become part of customary international law.

An analysis of customary international law prior to and since the inception of the Charter, however, suggests that there is no customary international law on humanitarian intervention. In relation to the pre-Charter era, Chesterman's analysis concludes, 'pre-Charter state practice illustrates the paucity of evidence of a general right of humanitarian intervention in customary international law' (2002, pp. 24–5). This view is supported by Franck and Rodley, who argue that the pre-Charter record of intervention does not support the existence of a customary norm (1973, p.285). Citing India's invasion of East Pakistan in 1971, however, they do not discount the possibility that such a norm could emerge, and note that international law is not immutable (ibid., p.303). Therefore, given the lack of any evident norm pre-1945, the only possible legal justification for unilateral humanitarian intervention is that state practice since 1945 has established a customary right of humanitarian intervention.

Fernando Tesón argues that India's intervention in East Pakistan and France's intervention in the Central African Republic in 1979 constituted examples of humanitarian intervention (1988, pp.207,199). He accepts that in both cases the intervening parties did not offer a humanitarian justification for their actions, but he argues that it 'matters little' what states say; the consequences of their actions are the basis upon which any claim of humanitarian intervention can be made (ibid., p. 193). Anthony Arend and Robert Beck's analysis concludes, however, that 'between 1945 and 1990 there were no examples of a genuinely humanitarian intervention', and in addition, during this period there was 'no unambiguous case of state reliance on the right of humanitarian intervention' (1993, p.137). In those cases during this period where the greatest case for a 'humanitarian' justification could have been made, such as India's intervention in East Pakistan in 1971, Vietnam's 1978 intervention in Cambodia and Tanzania's intervention in Uganda in 1979 (see Chapter 9), none of the intervening states relied exclusively on a humanitarian justification. 'Thus', according to Philip Hilpold,

> it can be inferred from these events and reactions that the necessary elements for the formation of a customary rule allowing measures of humanitarian intervention were not only not present but relevant state practice was a thorough confirmation of the rule which excludes the permissibility of such interventions. (2001, p. 445)

It is widely accepted therefore that humanitarian intervention was not a customary norm at the time of NATO's intervention in Kosovo (ICISS, 2001, p.12; Ambos, 1999). Yet the significant international support afforded to NATO in 1999 suggested that Operation Allied Force was 'a potential harbinger of future legality' (Rodley and Cah, 2007, p.278). Nicholas Wheeler similarly notes that the debate on the legitimacy of humanitarian intervention at the United Nations post-Kosovo altered as 'norms had clearly changed', although, he cautions, not to the extent that unilateral humanitarian intervention was widely supported (2002, p.286). An analysis of state practice since 1999 suggests that Operation Allied Force fails to constitute a precedent given that NATO's action failed the two tests outlined by Cassese on customary law formation, namely state practice and the views of states (2005, p.157; Hehir, 2009b). In the aftermath of NATO's intervention the 133 states comprising the G-77 declared, 'We reject the so-called 'right' of humanitarian intervention, which has no legal basis in the United Nations Charter or in the general principles of international law' (2000). Even the states that participated in Operation Allied Force distanced themselves from suggesting that a new norm had been established, and in terms of consistent practice it is relatively clear that similar humanitarian crises have not received the same attention afforded to Kosovo in 1999 (Hehir, 2008a).

On balance it seems fair to conclude that the dominant view on the legal status of unilateral humanitarian intervention is that it is illegal. There has been no fundamental change in either positive or customary international law that can be said conclusively to have legalized such action. This illegal status, however, has become a source of considerable controversy, not least because, as the next section attests, human rights legislation has increased dramatically since 1945 yet this growing legal corpus lacks attendant means of enforcement.

Human rights law

Many human rights treaties have been signed since the UN Charter came into force in October 1945, although the impact of these treaties has been limited. States have demonstrated a willingness publicly to support human rights, increasingly so in the post-Cold War era, but this has not become manifest in an increased adherence to these treaties (Armstrong, Farrell and Lambert, 2007, p.157). Indeed, the proliferation of these expressions of concern for, and commitment to, human rights have not been accompanied by an attendant alteration in the Charter's provisions for dealing with violations of human rights. The result is a large body of both treaty and customary law related to human rights which lacks clear means by which these laws can be enforced. States are subject to scrutiny by UN bodies such as the Human Rights Council (formerly the UN Commission on Human Rights), the Human Rights Committee and the Office of the UN High Commissioner for Human Rights. Compliance with even the supervisory role of these organizations, however, is poor and their enforcement capacity and effectiveness is minimal.

The nature of human rights differentiates this area of international law from the laws governing inter-state relations. As Malgozia Fitzmaurice states, 'Human rights treaties are not contractual in nature and do not create rights and obligations between States on the traditional basis of reciprocity; they establish relationships between States and individuals' (2006, pp. 205–6). States, therefore, may well agree amongst themselves the standards they should uphold domestically, but ultimately the necessarily domestic nature of compliance with these agreements limits the effect the inter-state context of the original treaty can have. Non-compliance with these treaties results in negative consequences only for the domestic citizenry and not other signatories to the treaty. In this respects, as Louis Henkin notes, 'compliance with human rights law . . . is wholly internal' (1990, p.250).

This leads to a key problem with the existing system. The vast corpus of human rights law lacks independent enforcement mechanisms, and the laws are reliant on the Charter's provisions. These provisions, covered under Chapter VII, are essentially ill-suited to being applied to intra-state crises. Even if it is maintained that Chapter VII, imperfect as it is, can be applied to intra-state crises, there remains a key barrier to enforcement, namely the interests of the P5. Unless the P5 agree, no enforcement action can be ordered. An example is provided by the provisions of the 1948 Genocide Convention. Article 8 of the Convention states:

> Any Contracting Party may call upon the competent organs of the United Nations to take such action under the Charter of the United Nations as they consider appropriate for the prevention and suppression of acts of genocide or any of the other acts enumerated in article III.

In practice the 'competent organ' of the United Nations is the Security Council. Thus if states believe that genocide is occurring and wish to stop it, the matter is referred to the Security Council. The crisis in Darfur has been described as genocide by many states, including the United States, and by UN missions to the region. The matter was referred to the Security Council, and while it determined that the situation constituted a threat to international peace and stability, and certain members agreed that the Sudanese government was orchestrating the genocide, no effective action was taken by the P5. (See Chapter 13.) Even if it is widely agreed that genocide is taking place, states do not have the legal right to intervene unilaterally to stop the killing (Dinstein, 2005, pp.72–3).

There is therefore a paradox at the heart of international law regarding human rights. Laws prohibiting certain human rights violations have increasingly been ratified in the post-Second World War era yet the mechanisms for enforcing these laws have failed to evolve, and enforcement remains largely the preserve of the Security Council and the signatories themselves. Frustration at the unwillingness of the Security Council to use the powers at its disposal consistently and swiftly has led to increasing calls for unilateral action, and more fundamentally, the wholesale reform of the international legal system. The following sections examine each of these options in turn.

'Illegal but legitimate'?

Demonstrating the illegality of humanitarian intervention, though not without contention, is relatively unproblematic, and many pro-intervention advocates would readily acknowledge this legal proscription. The major contention surrounding humanitarian intervention does not, however, focus on its legal status. Human rights campaigners argue that the legal proscription is morally untenable and should be violated when humanitarian need is great. NATO's intervention in Kosovo in 1999 dramatically illustrated this controversy and highlighted the gulf between contemporary legal doctrine and evolving conceptions of human rights and ethical state behaviour. The conclusion reached by the IICK – 'the NATO military intervention was illegal but legitimate' – is succinctly illustrative of the central problem (2000, p.4).

The idea that ending suffering is a higher priority than adhering to international law has gained momentum in the post-Cold War era. International law's dependency on the Security Council – itself considered a body of low moral standing – led to the conviction that, as Robertson argued, 'humanitarian intervention cannot be the prerogative of the UN' (2002, p.382). The rejection of the United Nations, and international law generally, demands an alternative source of authority and legitimacy. According to Terry Nardin the basis for regulating humanitarian intervention must be 'common morality' rather than international law, because the latter 'rests on custom and agreement, not moral reasoning' (2003, p.19). This preference for moral reasoning over international law evidences faith in both the objective existence of universal morality and the efficacy of moral norms. As demonstrated in Chapter 2, this embrace of moral or natural law led to renewed interest in the Just War tradition, and many compiled criteria for intervention based on the tradition's central tenets.

The fixation on the legality of an act is seen by some as obscuring the more important question of its moral quality, which is deemed more relevant to determining its legitimacy. In the case of the US-led invasion of Iraq, much of the debate focused on the legality of the intervention. Nicholas Rengger notes,

> what was perhaps oddest, at least to my eye, was that the general discussion both amongst politicians and in the media ... was almost exclusively focused on whether or not then war was 'legal'. At no point

that I am aware of, did anyone seriously discuss the surely related question that even if it was legal, was it morally justified? (2005, p. 145)

It is indeed true that a significant portion of the anti-war movement, particularly those opposed to the war within mainstream political parties such as the Liberal Democrats in the United Kingdom, justified their opposition on the grounds that the intervention was not approved by the Security Council. Many 'anti-war' protestors therefore called for a second UN resolution before the deployment of troops. Yet, as Rengger notes, it is difficult to understand why the assent of the P5 would affect the underlying moral legitimacy of the invasion.

The preference for moral law over positive law clearly has many attractions. International law is certainly deficient in many areas, particularly enforcement, and it is undeniably oriented towards states rather than the people who inhabit them. Moral laws by contrast are human-centred and not restricted by the temporal state system. Additionally many of the more progressive movements and events in human history have been driven by people unwilling to respect the laws of the day. The suffragettes, Gandhi, Martin Luther King and many others consciously rejected their legal systems on moral grounds, and we now generally regard their actions as trailblazing. Additionally international law is not static and *has* demonstrated its capacity to change. Therefore, as Franck notes, 'Even an illegal action, if instrumental in bringing about results widely desired by a community, will not seriously undermine a resilient legal system, one with the elasticity to make allowances for mitigating circumstances' (1999, p.859). Action, such as humanitarian intervention, could thus be deemed illegal but, provided the ethical merits of the action were endorsed by the international community, the intervening party would not be punished. Ian Brownlie, using the example of euthanasia, argues that mitigation is already a feature of domestic law. In certain cases, such as when a father smothers his severely handicapped son, the law has exercised a 'discretion not to prosecute', which means that the principle prohibiting murder remains firm but the punishment takes account of the context of the criminal act (1973, p.146). Humanitarian intervention, therefore, could similarly be justified as an extraordinary remedy to a great wrong (see the Conclusion).

As the first section in this chapter demonstrated, international law has developed in a manner designed to prevent powerful states from arbitrarily using force. The 18th and 19th centuries were eras when, in the absence of legal codes, states claimed to act in accordance with natural law and their own conceptions of morality. The result was colonialism and the subjugation of millions throughout the world. The colonial project was primarily legitimized on the grounds that the 'savages' in Africa, Asia, the Americas, and within Europe in Ireland and the Balkans, required the civilizing presence of their European masters. Central to imperialism was the conviction that 'certain territories and peoples require and beseech domination' (Said, 1993, p.76). As noted in Chapter 3, before the codification of sovereign equality and inviolability there was no legal proscription against imperialism, and while natural law was routinely invoked, the system at this time was disorderly and prone to violence. Rejecting international law in favour of natural, and ostensibly moral, norms therefore risks regressing to this system.

In tandem with the privileging of natural law is the assumption that certain states have more legitimacy to act in certain ways than others by virtue of their superior human rights record. As noted in Chapter 3, this has been manifest as the idea of conditional sovereignty and proportionate equality. Contemporary moves towards recognizing a hierarchy of states, especially manifest in the renewed interest in trusteeship, are, according to William Bain, 'fundamentally irreconcilable with a universal society of sovereign states ordered according to the principle of universal equality' (2003b, p.75). The contemporary shift towards proportionate equality, or 'the formal rehierarcitisation of international society', thus contradicts both the doctrine and direction of positive international law (Reus-Smit 2005, p.72).

Another concern with the pro-morality perspective is the exact nature of the code being championed. The natural law argument outlines the grounds on which states may violate the law to help others but fails to impose enforceable duties to so act. This thus appears to create only a discretionary right or entitlement.

While the risks of a move towards natural law are great, there are limits to the parallels between the era of colonialism and the contemporary discourse of cosmopolitan human rights. As discussed in Chapter 4, cosmopolitan human rights theory not only espouses universal moral norms, it additionally questions the very idea of the sovereign state, and thus, unlike colonialism, does not (generally) act as advocate for a particular state or culture. The debate can thus be seen as a clash between adherents of two codes; those who adhere to 'constitutionalist' principles and those who privilege 'cosmopolitan moralist, rules' (Hurrell, 2005, p.21).

The criticisms made of international law perhaps fail to acknowledge the extent to which it is largely a reflection of prevailing moral norms. Morality informs law, and therefore the ascendency of a moral norm, such as the perceived need to alleviate suffering in foreign lands, need not constitute grounds for rejecting positive law, but rather stands as an argument in favour of amending the law. The existing system therefore may accommodate change, even fundamental change, and act as a means by which emerging ideas are incorporated into a universally legitimate legal structure. Arguably the many positives that have accrued from the strengthening of international law in the past 60 years should not be jeopardized through the abandonment of the core proscription on the unilateral use of force and the basic principle of sovereign equality. It is additionally unlikely that the creation of an 'illegal but legitimate' loophole will meet with widespread international approval given that this kind of action is realistically only available to certain powerful states and their key allies. The legitimacy of such a development is thus questionable.

The need for legal reform

The IICK's conclusion that Operation Allied Force was 'illegal but legitimate' has become an oft-quoted appraisal of NATO's intervention. One aspect of the IICK's report that received less publicity was the corollary, 'Allowing this gap between legality and legitimacy to persist is not healthy' (2000, p.186). The disjuncture between international law and legitimate action exemplified by NATO's action concerned many who argued that reform was required lest international law lose its credibility (ICISS, 2001, p.3). Allowing states to determine independently when force should be used for humanitarian reasons is certainly inherently problematic. According to the UN High-Level Panel on Threats, Challenges and Change, diminishing the UN monopoly on the use of force would fundamentally undermine the authority of the United Nations and cause a chain reaction of unilateral aggression (2004, p.63).

The feasibility of reform

Reforming international law, especially in the highly sensitive areas of the use of force and sovereignty, is far from straightforward. In 1969 the International Law Commission established a sub-committee on the status of humanitarian intervention. The committee examined the potential for drafting a list of criteria for humanitarian intervention which could be incorporated into international law. This process was abandoned in 1976 because the issue 'proved too controversial' and consensus was impossible (DIIA, 1999, p.105). At the World Summit in 2005, states attempted to achieve consensus on new rules regarding the use of force specifically in the areas of self-defence and 'the responsibility to protect' incumbent on all states. The acrimony caused by the invasion of Iraq contributed to the impasse, and the prospects for substantive legal reform remain remote. The final *Outcome Document* did contain two paragraphs related to humanitarian intervention, although concerns remain that little substantive progress was actually made (Bellamy, 2006a; Weiss, 2007, p.117; Wheeler, 2005).

Nonetheless there is some evidence that reform is possible. In its findings the ICISS noted, 'even in states where there was the strongest opposition to infringements on sovereignty, there was a general acceptance that there must be limited exceptions to the non-intervention rule for certain kinds of emergencies' (2001, p.31). This suggests that there is not widespread opposition to the principle of the international community having a role in upholding universally agreed human rights domestically. Indeed, Article 4(h) of the Constitutive Act of the African Union recognizes 'the right of the Union to intervene in a Member State pursuant to a decision of the Assembly in respect of grave circumstances, namely: war crimes, genocide and crimes against humanity'. This provision highlights that, even amongst those states most suspicious of and hostile towards the idea of humanitarian intervention, there is an acceptance that sovereignty does not imbue states with the right of complete domestic impunity.

Potential legal reform

Regardless of the political obstacles, the desirability of reform and the nature of this change remain issues for discussion (Christopher, 2004, p.248). Sir Arthur Watts frames the issue in stark terms:

> There is a choice: the international community must either establish an international force to maintain order, or let states perform that function themselves. The framers of the UN Charter attempted the former, but their good intentions have never really been carried through . . . one is left in practice with self-appointed guardians of the peace. However, that cannot be a satisfactory basis on which to organize a legal order. (2001, p. 10)

Potential reforms range from codifying a right to unilateral humanitarian intervention (Burton, 1996) to the establishment of new international bodies empowered to deploy troops when situations deteriorate to certain levels (Woodhouse and Ramsbotham 2005, p.152; Hehir, 2008a, p.130; Held, 2005, p.25). Additionally there have been arguments in favour of clarifying the grounds on which the Security Council can authorize humanitarian intervention to overcome the problems with the use of Chapter VII as identified. The UN High-Level Panel on Threats, Challenges and Change outlined 'five basic criteria of legitimacy' (see Box 5.3) which they argued should guide the Security Council. The criteria reflect many of the sets of criteria previously articulated, and have obvious parallels with the Just War tradition (see Chapter 2). The UN Panel acknowledged that these criteria did not constitute 'agreed conclusions with push-button predictability', and offered them as a means to 'maximise the possibility of achieving Security Council consensus around when it is appropriate or not to use coercive action' (2004, p.57). The problem, however, is that the Panel's criteria do not address the key problem with respect to the use of force, namely, who decides whether these criteria have been met? (See Chapter 7.) The Security Council will doubtless consider the UN Panel's criteria but these criteria have no obvious power to constrain the Council's

Box 5.3 Five basic criteria of legitimacy

- Seriousness of threat
- Proper purpose
- Last resort
- Proportional means
- Balance of consequences.

Source: UN High-Level Panel on Threats, Challenges and Change (2004, pp.57–8).

deliberations and overcome the central tension between interests and pressing humanitarian need (Hurrell, 2005, p.30).

In addition to the obvious difficulty of ever achieving substantive reform, many oppose establishing a new rule on humanitarian intervention. Oscar Schachter argues that a new law is 'highly undesirable' because it could 'provide a pretext for abusive intervention' (1991, p.126). While this is a widely held view (Stromseth, 2005; Chesterman, 2002, p.231), it has been argued that this potential for abuse is far less damaging to international law than the current status. Jarat Chopra and Thomas Weiss acknowledge the potential for abuse in any new law, but point to the adverse consequence derived from the argument that codification should be avoided;

> Since no definition could be sufficiently comprehensive, it was argued
> . . . that potential aggressors would be able to navigate between provi-
> sions and circumvent the letter of any prohibition. Instead, without any
> defined parameters states found that they did not have to navigate at
> all to contravene the spirit of the prohibition. (1992, p.97)

Thus, viewed in the context of its current status, codifying humanitarian intervention is deemed likely to diminish rather than exacerbate the problem of the misuse of humanitarian justifications for intervention (Burton, 1996, p.422).

Political will or legal obstacles?

While the need for legal reform is often presented as pressing, it is not nec-essarily the solution. If the problem posed by humanitarian intervention was singularly derived from legal restrictions and constitutional inadequa-cies, then clearly relevant reform would be apposite. An examination of the impediments to intervention, however, suggests that they are primarily political rather than legal. States, according to John Mueller, will intervene 'only when their interests seem importantly engaged or where they manage to become self-entrapped' (2005, p.123). If Mueller is correct, and there are strong grounds for endorsing his analysis, then legal reform will not address what Chesterman describes as 'inhumanitarian non-intervention' (2003, p.54). The idea that international law has prevented willing saviours from helping suffering innocents is, Chesterman notes, a misreading of history:

> Implicit in many arguments for a right of humanitarian intervention is the suggestion that international law currently prevents interventions that should take place. This is simply not true. Interventions do not take place because states choose not to undertake them. (2003, p.54)

It is difficult to think of any case where a state wanted to intervene but did not because it would have been illegal to do so. State power and interest, not international law, have therefore been the key variables influencing the decision not to intervene.

Conclusion

According to Cassese, 'the system envisaged in the UN Charter for the maintenance of international peace and security . . . has substantially failed' (2005, p.339). This failure has arguably manifested itself in the various inter-state wars which have occurred since the organization's inception. It is additionally arguable that the United Nations' paralysis in the face of egregious human rights violations perpetrated by states against their own citizens has highlighted the failings inherent in the post-1945 legal system.

As this chapter has noted, international law contains no explicit provision for sanctioning humanitarian intervention. Chapter VII of the UN Charter is the closest approximation to such a code, and has been used increasingly since the end of the Cold War. However, the Security Council's composition, the influence of national interest and the questionable legality of applying Chapter VII to intra-state humanitarian crises have undermined support for Chapter VII. Clearly in certain cases the Security Council has failed to act, and thus, humanitarians argue, this body cannot be relied upon to act when necessary.

Unilateral humanitarian intervention is deeply contentious. While the dominant view is that such action is fundamentally illegal, this has not precluded further discussion. Three responses to this finding of illegality are discernible. First are the counter-claims that there is a legal basis for such action. Second is the claim that law must yield to ethics when it comes to halting massive suffering, and interventions should be judged on their morality rather than their legality. Third is the view that the disjuncture between legality and legitimacy must be addressed. Different legal reforms have been proposed in an effort to address what is considered the shameful spectacle of inertia in the face of human suffering. As we have seen, how-ever, it is debatable whether international law has ever been responsible for inaction. More commonly inaction has been a function of the 'triumph of the lack of will' (Gow, 1997).

The legal status of humanitarian intervention derives from the rights afforded to sovereign states. These rights, as discussed in Chapter 3, are a function of the attempt to mitigate the impact of power in international politics and move beyond the 'might is right' ethos of the 19th century. Facilitating unilateral humanitarian intervention, even if motivated by the desire to 'save strangers', is seen as posing a risk to the 'fragile normative edifice' separating the post-1945 system from that of the 19th century (Chesterman and Byers, 1999). And yet it seems hard to deny that, regard-less the egalitarian motives responsible for the composition of the present system, the current legal framework cannot be deemed effective if atrocities such in Rwanda and Darfur go unchecked. Jean Cohen outlines the choice facing the international community:

> we can either opt for strengthening international law by updating it, making explicit the particular conception of sovereignty on which it is now based and showing that this is compatible with cosmopolitan principles inherent in human rights norms; or we can abandon the principle of sovereign equality and the present rules of international law for the sake of human rights, thus relinquishing an important bar-rier to the proliferation of imperial projects and regional attempts at Grossraum ordering (direct annexation or other forms of control of neighbouring smaller polities) by great powers who invoke (and instrumentalize) cosmopolitan right as they proceed. (2004, p.3)

Tom Farer notes that humanitarian intervention, 'has subsisted on the shadowy periphery of international law' (2003, p.143). It is surely doubtful whether this shadowy periphery can be sustained for much longer.

Questions

- To what extent did the evolution of international law in the 19th and 20th centuries preclude a right of humanitarian intervention?
- What is the basis for suggesting that humanitarian intervention is currently illegal?
- How convincing are the arguments that humanitarian intervention is in fact legal?
- Is legal reform of the status of humanitarian intervention required? What should this legal reform involve?

Further reading

On the evolution and role of international law

Armstrong, D., Farrell, T. and Lambert, H. (2007) *International Law and International Relations* (Cambridge: Cambridge University Press).

Brown, C. (2006) *Sovereignty, Rights and Justice: International Political Theory Today* (London: Polity).

Bull, H. (2002) *The Anarchical Society: A Study of Order in World Politics* (Basingstoke: Palgrave Macmillan and New York: Columbia University Press).

Simpson, G. (2004) *Great Powers and Outlaw States* (Cambridge: Cambridge University Press).

Byers, M. (ed.) (2001) *The Role of International Law in International Politics* (Oxford: Oxford University Press).

On the legal status of humanitarian intervention

Chesterman, S. (2002) *Just War or Just Peace?* (Oxford: Oxford University Press).

Cassese, A. (1999) '*Ex iniuria ius oritur*: Are We Moving Towards International Legitimisation of Forcible Humanitarian Countermeasures in the World Community?', *European Journal of International Law*, 10, 1, 23–30.

Chopra, J. and Weiss, T. (1992) 'Sovereignty is No Longer Sacrosanct', *Ethics and International Affairs*, 6, 95–117.

Danish Institute of International Affairs (DIIA) (1999) *Humanitarian Intervention: Legal and Political Aspects* (Copenhagen: Danish Institute of International Affairs).

Rodley, N. and Cah, B. (2007) 'Kosovo Revisited: Humanitarian Intervention on the Fault Lines of International Law', *Human Rights Law Review*, 7: 2, 275–97.

On the tension between law and morality

Armstrong, D., Farrell, T. and Maiguashca, B. (eds) (2005) *Force and Legitimacy in World Politics* (Cambridge: Cambridge University Press).

Jokic, A. (ed.) (2004) *Lessons of Kosovo: The Dangers of Humanitarian Intervention* (Toronto: Broadview Press).

Lang, A. (ed.) (2003) *Just Intervention* (Washington DC: Georgetown University Press).

Tesón, F. (1998) *Humanitarian Intervention: An Enquiry into Law and Morality* (New York: Transnational).

On codifying humanitarian intervention

Burton, M. (1996) 'Legalising the Sublegal', *Georgetown Law Journal*, 85, 417–54.

Byers, M. and Chesterman, S. (2003) 'Changing the Rules About Rules?' in J. Holzgrefe and R. Keohane (eds), *Humanitarian Intervention: Ethical, Legal and Political Dilemmas* (Cambridge: Cambridge University Press).

Cohen, J. (2004) 'Whose Sovereignty? Empire Versus International Law', *Ethics and International Affairs*, 18:3, 1–24.

Hilpold, P. (2001) 'Humanitarian Intervention: Is There a Need for a Legal Reappraisal?' *European Journal of International Law*, 12:3, 437–67.

Chapter 6

Sovereignty as Responsibility

The responsibility a state has towards its citizens has been one of the dominant themes in political thought. At one end of the ideological spectrum the 'new right' argue that states have minimal responsibilities and should concern themselves only with facilitating the free market, maintaining civil order and defending their borders. At the other extreme communists argue that the state has a responsibility to provide a wide array of social goods including housing, healthcare, education and personal fulfilment. Between these poles there are many differing perspectives, though all agree that states have some responsibilities to their citizens (Brown, 2006, p.2).

This chapter examines the contemporary controversy surrounding state responsibility, focusing in particular on the increasingly discussed idea, 'the responsibility to protect'. The rationale behind the responsibility to protect comprises a dual element; the expression of the responsibilities a state has towards its citizens, and the responsibility the international community has towards citizens in other states.

The next section examines the differing perspectives on state responsibility and the extent to which the rise of human rights has challenged the traditional perspective. This chapter's second section analyses the idea of a 'responsibility to protect' (R2P) as proffered by the International Commission on Intervention and State Sovereignty (ICISS) in 2001. The chief critiques of R2P are examined and assessed in the final section.

State responsibility

The term 'state responsibility' has a different meaning in international law from that of international relations (IR), and refers to the legal responsibilities of states towards other states, and the nature of state responsibility for breaches of international law (see Dixon, 2007, p.242; Crawford and Olleson, 2006, p.451). In terms of IR, the question of state responsibility was until quite recently deemed an exclusively domestic issue. States were considered self-contained entities, and the formal relationship between a state and its citizens was an issue for these actors alone to determine. The responsibility a state had towards its citizens was thus not a topic for discussion within the discipline of IR (Wight, 1966a, p.33). The post-Second World War dominance of realism ensured that the domestic composition of a state was largely removed from the IR agenda (see Chapter 4). This distinction between the domestic and the international has increasingly been challenged in the post-Cold War era, and state responsibility, once the preserve of political theory, is now a key issue in IR.

Traditional approaches to state responsibility

As discussed in Chapter 3, the emergence of the modern state began in the 16th century and accelerated after the Peace of Westphalia in 1648. In the modern era the state has come to be considered a reflection of national consciousness, but this normative union of nation and state really only emerged in the 18th century and flourished after the French Revolution in 1789. The initial impetus for the formation of states had little to do with nationalism and was more a function of the rivalry between monarchs. The system of sovereign states was created to limit the recourse to war, consolidate the realms of the existing hierarchy and facilitate economic growth (see Chapter 3).

With the growth of nationalism after 1789, states began to be conceived as servants of the people rather than institutions to enable the proliferation of monarchical dynasties. The rise of national consciousness necessarily created a sense of community, albeit in most cases 'imagined' (Anderson, 1991), which brought with it heightened expectations about what the state should do for its people. Logically, if a community believes its state to be a servant of the nation, it will expect its institutions to provide certain goods for all members of this nation.

Nation-states, however, are something of a romantic myth (Bloom, 1990, p.60), and even if we accept the existence of strong national homogeneity within many states from the 18th century on, the rights of citizens was not a key concern for many state leaders until the 20th century. Indeed, the emergence of socialism as a political force in the 19th century was a response to the conditions endured by the majority of people, formally disenfranchised from the political system, who suffered from poor housing, inadequate healthcare and oppressive labour practices. The nature of the state's responsibilities to its citizens has been a primary political issue since this period, and remains a key fissure in domestic politics today.

While the nature of the rights afforded to citizens and the state's responsibility to uphold these rights have arguably been primary issues in domestic politics for over 200 years, these issues were largely absent from the IR agenda until recently. The international political issues generated by the formation of the system of sovereign states essentially centred on interstate relations, particularly the laws governing the use of force. The rights of states, therefore, rather than the rights of citizens within states, were the key concern in IR. As Hedley Bull notes, the inability of states to agree on their duties to their citizens led to an agreement amongst states to omit this divisive issue from international law so as to forestall disorder (2002, p.146). Occasionally certain atrocities, or practices such as cannibalism, committed abroad were deemed morally unacceptable, and action was taken, up to and including military intervention. In the majority, if not all, of these cases, however, geopolitical motives were the more pressing concern (see Chapter 9). Certain European states, particularly Great Britain, justified their colonies on the basis that their administration was morally superior and more respectful towards the rights of individuals than the previous indigenous system (Carr, 2001, pp.71–5). This was, of course, debatable to say the least, and in many cases European empires were responsible for extreme brutality.

The nascent international legal system before the First World War was limited to modest constraints on inter-state relations, although international humanitarian law had begun to develop by the end of the 19th century. A small number of states did provide some human rights protection through their constitutions and related domestic legislation, but even where these laws existed there were few effective means of enforcement (Armstrong, Farrell and Lambert, 2007, p.151). During this period, therefore, 'individuals were mere "appendices" of the state to which they belonged, simple pawns in its hands, to be used, protected, or sacrificed according to what State interests dictated' (Cassese, 2005, p.376). What international action was taken to stop domestic oppression was limited to 'remedying particular abuses or on protecting particular minority groups or aliens' (Malanczuk, 2006, p.209).

As discussed in Chapter 5, the humanitarian disaster of the First World War led to a number of significant developments in international law. These were predominately related, however, to inter-state relations. Indeed the Covenant of the League of Nations makes no mention of human rights, although under Article 23(b) members committed to the 'just treatment of the native inhabitants of territories under their control'. The Second World War demonstrated horrifically that more needed to be done to strengthen international law's capacity to limit the recourse to war, and this was reflected in the new international political and legal system created by the UN Charter. However, this dual goal of limiting the recourse to war by strengthening the sovereign inviolability of states and protecting the rights of individuals through human rights legislation became one of the major tensions within the Charter.

State responsibility and the UN Charter

During the drafting of the Charter at the San Francisco Conference (April–June 1945), three groups formed, with different views on the new rules regarding human rights and state responsibility (Cassese, 2005, pp.377–9). The first group comprised mostly Latin American states plus

Australia, New Zealand, India and Norway, and advocated the inclusion of specific obligations to respect human rights. The second group, of major Western powers, opposed the inclusion of any definite obligations regarding human rights and favoured clear proscriptions against the new international organization interfering with 'domestic' affairs (Roberts, 2006, p.72). The third group comprised socialist states which also sought to limit the United Nations' powers, but looked too to bolster the language regarding self-determination and non-discrimination. The outcome of the negotiations constituted a compromise between the last two of these groups, resulting in four key elements within the Charter;

- There were no specific obligations to take action for promotion or protection of human rights.
- The right of self-determination was proclaimed but only as a guiding principle.
- The power of the General Assembly was limited.
- Respect for human rights should only be furthered as a means of safeguarding peace.

As a consequence of this compromise the Charter has struggled to reconcile its provisions on human rights with its proscription against intervention, both multilaterally through the Security Council and (more explicitly) unilaterally by individual states or coalitions of states. While the Charter's Preamble, Article 1 and particularly Article 55 proclaim human rights to be a concern for the United Nations and all its member-states, the proscriptions against intervention in Articles 2.4 and 2.7 seem to override these principles. The Charter contains no provision explicitly sanctioning intervention for the purpose of upholding human rights, and does not specify the human rights that states must uphold. During the course of the drafting of the Charter the French negotiating team proposed the inclusion of a passage authorizing states to intervene in other states without Security Council authorization when 'the clear violation of essential liberties and of human rights constitutes threats capable of compromising peace' (Franck, 2005, p.207). This was rejected by both Western and socialist states.

The Charter thus comprises an uneasy mixture: a prohibition against external interference in the domestic affairs of states, and a commitment to the promotion of human rights. Therefore, as Armstrong and colleagues note, 'it is generally recognized that the legal obligation to respect and observe human rights for all in the UN Charter is too general in provenance' (2007, p.156).

The 1948 Declaration of Human Rights went some way towards clarifying the nature of human rights, but failed to advance any effective enforcement mechanism (Malanczuk, 2006, p.213). The judgments in the Tokyo and Nuremberg trials, however, advanced a prohibition against 'crimes against humanity', applicable to all states in their treatment of both their own citizens and foreigners, which constituted definite progress in the prohibition against intra-state human rights violations (Robertson, 2002, p.203).

The onset of the Cold War limited the possibility of further clarification of what would be done in response to a violation of human rights. The divide between East and West was itself a product of an ideological difference about the responsibilities of states. Consensus was reached, however, on certain issues leading to conventions on genocide (1948), racial discrimination (1965), discrimination against women (1979) and torture (1984). Additionally, significant developments were made in more contentious areas that had traditionally been considered domestic political issues. Todd Landman's statistical analysis finds that since 1945 'there has been an expansion in both the breadth and depth of the [human rights] regime', and he notes that 'an increasingly larger set of human rights has found positive legal expression, while on the other hand a larger number of states have ratified these main instruments' (2005, p.14). Of course, as noted in Chapter 5, the increased codification of human rights did not translate readily into greater respect for, or enforcement of, these rights. In certain cases, most notably the racist regimes in South Africa and Southern Rhodesia, the General Assembly and/or the Security Council condemned the oppressive policies of states towards their own citizens (DIIA, 1999, p.53), but these cases were exceptional. In general while human rights law espoused lofty humanitarian aims, the actual mechanisms of enforcement relied on states. For example in 1970 the ICJ Ruling in the *Barcelona Traction* case stated:

> [There are some rights that] all states can be held to have a legal interest in their protection; they are obligations *erga omnes* . . . such obligation derives, for example, in contemporary international law, from the outlawing of acts of aggression, and of genocide, as also from the principles and rules concerning the basic rights of the human person, including protection from slavery and racial discrimination.

Despite this ruling, international law continued to recognize states as having the primary responsibility for citizens. States could only be bypassed if they failed to provide an effective remedy to the original problem; therefore 'there cannot be a violation of international human rights law unless state authorities fail to provide adequate remedies' (Armstrong et al., 2007, p. 164).

The rise of human security

The end of the Cold War precipitated an upsurge in optimism amongst some over the future of human rights (Shaw, 1994, p.155). The new

systemic conditions were considered to be more conducive to further codification, and perhaps more importantly, increased enforcement of the
existing human rights legislation. The end of the bipolar stand-off which
had suffocated effective human rights enforcement was seen as facilitating
an increased focus on 'human security'.

Mary Kaldor defines human security as 'about the security of individuals
and communities rather than the security of states and it combines both
human rights and human development, freedom from fear and freedom from
want' (2005, p.177). This perspective is informed by a cosmopolitan framework catalyzed and inspired by the end of the Cold War, the effects of globalization, the project of European integration and the increased visibility of
transnational actors (Hutchings, 1999, pp.154–5). Cosmopolitanism constitutes a 'break with the assumption of territorially-based political entities', and
explicitly disavows statist conceptions of international politics in favour of an
agenda predicated on 'the existence of a human community with certain
shared rights and obligations' (Kaldor, 1999, pp. 115, 147). The basic rights
of individuals, regardless of their nationality, were thus increasingly deemed
inviolable and of greater import than the rights of states (Beitz, 1992, p.125).

The cosmopolitan perspective on human security comprises a normative
vision of the responsibilities of states towards their citizens and, significantly, the responsibilities of the international community to citizens in
states that fail to meet these responsibilities. Human rights were thus
deemed an international concern and not the sole jurisdiction of sovereign
states (Linklater, 1998, p.109). In this sense the discourse of cosmopolitanism rejects the international/domestic distinction in both IR theory and
actual state practice as anachronistic and untenable, and seeks greater
international coordination on human rights legislation and enforcement,
and the diminution of the power of the state in respect to the rights of its
own citizens (see Chapter 4).

The idea of 'intervention' presupposes an inside/outside distinction.
'Intervention' occurs when an outside entity intervenes in the internal
affairs of another. In the specific case of humanitarian intervention we are
confronted with a conceptual distinction between the private sphere of the
state and the public domain of the international community (Lu, 2006,
p.4). The guiding premise behind this distinction has been questioned in
relation to humanitarian intervention. Mervyn Frost argues that humanitarian intervention should not, in fact, be considered a violation of the
principle of non-intervention, but rather 'an act directed towards
upholding the non-intervention norm of civil society, which protects an
area of freedom for individuals'. The principle of non-intervention relates
firstly to individuals, and only democratic collectivities of individuals can
be afforded the international right of inviolability (Frost, 2001, p. 51). In
the same vein Kaldor suggests rethinking humanitarian intervention as an
action analogous to domestic police work (2003, pp.134–6).

Box 6.1   Global civil society

Two perspectives exist regarding the origins of global civil society. One view suggests that it has evolved since the mid-19th century, while the second, more prevalent, view sees it as having emerged in the last 30 years as a result of globalization, the spread of Western values and increased communication capacity (Coleman and Wayland, 2006, pp.242–5). Global civil society is not, however, a precise term or a definite actor; while Helmut Anheier, Marlies Glasius and Mary Kaldor describe it as an 'underlying social reality', they acknowledge that it is 'a fuzzy and a contested concept' (2001, p.11).

Central to global civil society has been the emergence of a global human rights network, manifest most clearly in the exponential growth in humanitarian non-governmental organizations (NGOs) in the 1990s. Through the mobilization and influence of NGOs, global civil society constitutes 'a source of constant pressures on the state system' (Shaw, 1994, p.24). According to Kaldor, 'By the end of the 1990s, it could be said that pressure from global civil society had given rise to widespread acceptance of humanitarian norms' (2003, p.132).

Thus great pressure was exerted by advocates of human security to alter the norms governing international relations. Key to the practical application of this pressure was global civil society (see Box 6.1), which aimed to mobilize international humanitarian actors to 'transform state understandings of their national interests, and alter their calculations of the costs and benefits of particular policies' (Keck and Sikkink, 1998, p.203). Domestic and global civil society was envisaged as a means to 'counterbalance the state and . . . prevent it from dominating and atomizing the rest of society' (Gellner, 1994, p.5). Via the so-called 'boomerang effect', citizens in repressive states appeal to global civil society to support their cause and highlight their plight. Subsequent coordinated international activism will compel states to pressurize the offending state into halting its activity (Keck and Sikkink, 1998, pp.9–13). Thus the emergence of global civil society constituted 'the domestication of the international' (Kaldor, 2003, p.78) and a means by which the sovereign rights of states were challenged through normative pressure and humanitarian advocacy. In addition to these normative developments, political changes in the 1990s signalled a fundamental revision of the responsibilities of states.

Political developments in the 1990s

On 5 April 1991 UN Security Council Resolution 688 condemned Iraq for its treatment of the Kurds and Shiites, describing the situation as a threat to international peace and security. While this was an important development, Resolution 688 did not include any provisions for enforcing compliance. As the situation worsened, a coalition of states – the Netherlands, France, the United Kingdom and the United States – launched Operation Provide Comfort, which created 'safe havens' for refugees and imposed no-fly zones over northern, and later southern, Iraq. The coalition justified their intervention as 'consistent' with Resolution 688. This constituted a 'new claim', namely that 'the use of force could be justified to enforce compliance with an existing Security Council Resolution' (Wheeler, 2006, p.34). The actions of the Security Council and the coalition of states in this case indicated a new dispensation which was to be a feature of Security Council deliberation and international action in the 1990s: the Security Council's increased willingness to describe intra-state humanitarian crises as threats to international peace and stability, and an attendant willingness, primarily amongst Western states, to take action – be it multilateral through the United Nations or unilateral through coalitions of the willing – to halt these crises.

In 1991, in his last *Annual Report on the Work of the Organization*, then UN Secretary-General Perez de Cuéllar called for a reinterpretation of the UN Charter's principles on sovereignty and non-interference in domestic affairs, noting 'an irresistible shift in public attitudes towards the belief that the defence of the oppressed in the name of morality should prevail over frontiers and legal documents (Lyons and Mastanduno, 1995, p.2). Building on this idea, Boutros Boutros-Ghali, de Cuéllar's successor, outlined a new agenda for states to reflect the increasingly interdependent world and the new, more propitious systemic conditions,

> The time of absolute and exclusive sovereignty, however, has passed; its theory was never matched by reality. It is the task of leaders of States today to understand this and to find a balance between the needs of good internal governance and the requirements of an ever more interdependent world. (1992, para 17)

In 1993 at the World Conference on Human Rights, all UN member-states adopted the Vienna Declaration and Programme of Action, which declared that 'the promotion and protection of human rights is a matter of priority for the international community'. That same year Francis Deng was appointed as special representative on internally displaced people. In the course of his work Deng argued that sovereign states had a responsibility to protect their neediest citizens. Where a state was unable to fulfil this responsibility, it should accept international support (Deng et al. 1996, p.1). Kofi Annan continued this agenda when he became secretary-general in 1997. In a speech in 1998 he argued that the UN Charter 'was never meant as a license for governments to trample on human rights and human dignity' (Roberts, 2006, p. 86). In a widely cited article in the *Economist* Annan further argued that 'State sovereignty, in its most basic sense, is being refined . . . individual sovereignty – by which I mean the fundamental freedom of each individual, enshrined in the Charter . . . has been enhanced by a renewed and spreading consciousness of individual rights' (1999b, p.49). These and many other developments in the 1990s – not least Security Council action under Chapter VII (see Chapter 5) – marked a trend whereby the state was deemed responsible for the maintenance of basic human rights, and failure to meet this responsibility would result in external sanctions and possibly intervention.

Yet while many declarations by the three UN secretaries-general, Security Council action and international commitments made by states in the 1990s suggested an emerging commitment to, and consensus on, the promotion and protection of human rights, significant disquiet remained amongst many developing states and major regional powers such as China, Russia and India (DIIA, 1999, p.54). This tension came to a head in 1999 when NATO intervened in Kosovo without explicit Security Council approval, although the Council had described the situation as a threat to international peace and security (see Chapter 11). NATO's actions graphically illustrated the conflict between law and morality and the divisions amongst the international community of states over the permissibility of humanitarian intervention. Following the intervention, Kofi Annan asked, 'if humanitarian intervention is, indeed, an unacceptable assault on sovereignty, how should we respond to a Rwanda, to a Srebrenica – to gross and systematic violations of human rights that affect every precept of our common humanity?' (ICISS, 2001, p.vii). The secretary-general called for new thinking on this issue so that a resolution to this perennial problem could be found. This call led to the establishment of the International Commission on Intervention and State Sovereignty (ICISS).

The responsibility to protect

The ICISS began its work in August 2000 and published *The Responsibility to Protect* (R2P) in December 2001. The ICISS, determined that R2P would have a practical application, declared, 'We want no more Rwandas and we believe that the adoption of the proposals in our report is the best way of ensuring that' (2001, p.XIII).

Key tenets

A key aspect of R2P was the attempt to reformulate the terms of the debate surrounding humanitarian intervention. The term 'humanitarian intervention' was deemed inappropriate as it was criticized by humanitarian aid workers and also appeared to prejudice favourably any intervention so described (ICISS, 2001, p. 9). Rather than pose the issue in terms of the rights of intervening states, R2P sought to place the onus on states to meet their responsibilities to their own citizens. Reconceptualizing sovereignty as responsibility has, the ICISS claims, a threefold significance:

> first it implies that the state authorities are responsible for the functions of protecting the safety and lives of citizens and promotion of their welfare. Secondly, it suggests that the national political authorities are responsible to the citizens internally and to the international community through the UN. And thirdly, it means that the agents of state are responsible for their actions. (ICISS, 2001, p.13)

The 'responsibility to protect' therefore resides first with individual states and only secondly with the international community.

R2P employs the concept of 'human security' as the basic framework for its approach (ICISS, 2001, p.15). Building on the 'emerging principle' inherent in this idea, R2P argues that intervention is legitimate when 'major harm to civilians is occurring or imminently apprehended, and the state in question is unable or unwilling to end the harm, or is itself the perpetrator' (ibid., p.16). Intervention does not necessarily imply military intervention, however, and is not considered necessarily limited to action undertaken to stop an ongoing atrocity. Rather, R2P puts forward three aspects to this responsibility; the responsibility to prevent, the responsibility to react and the responsibility to rebuild.

The responsibility to prevent and the responsibility to rebuild are the least contentious aspects of R2P, although they cannot be divorced from the overall argument (Weiss, 2007, p.104). The idea of a 'responsibility to prevent' is that states have a responsibility to ensure that domestic tensions are addressed before they escalate (ICISS, 2001, pp.19–27). Failure by a state to take appropriate or effective preventive measures means the responsibility transfers to the international community. Preventive action by the international community can take the form of sanctions, aid, negotiations, and in extreme cases military intervention. This responsibility also requires creating more effective early warning systems, and implementing measures aimed at tackling the root causes of domestic disquiet, such as economic inequality and political disenfranchisement. The 'responsibility to rebuild' places a responsibility on an intervening state, or states, to contribute to the post-conflict recovery process in the form of monetary aid and political support to ensure a lasting settlement to the original conflict (ibid., pp. 39–45).

The 'responsibility to react' is most related to the central dilemma poised by humanitarian intervention, and is the aspect of R2P that has attracted greatest attention. The ICISS noted that 'above all else' R2P constitutes 'a responsibility to react to situations of compelling need for human protection' (ICISS, 2001, p.29). If a state is either unable or unwilling to meet its responsibility to protect its citizens, the responsibility transfers from the state to the international community.

International intervention to stop human rights abuses need not take the form of military intervention, which is legitimate only in extreme cases (ICISS, 2001, p.29). The ICISS offer six 'Principles for Military Intervention', criteria that must be met for an intervention to be legitimate: right authority, just cause, right intention, last resort, proportional means and reasonable prospects (ibid., p.32). 'Right authority' is clearly the most important criterion given the implications this has for determining whether the other criteria have been met. Reflecting this importance, an entire chapter of R2P is devoted to this question. This issue is here dealt with individually following an overview of the other criteria, and again in greater detail in Chapter 7.

In terms of 'just cause', R2P suggests two thresholds:

> large scale loss of life, actual or apprehended, with genocidal intent or not, which is the product either of deliberate state action, or state neglect or inability to act, or a failed state situation; or large scale 'ethnic cleansing', actual or apprehended, whether carried out by killing, forced expulsion, acts of terror or rape. (ICISS, 2001, p.32)

R2P acknowledges that these thresholds exclude racial discrimination, tyranny and the rescue of foreign nationals, but argues that grave though these are, they do not warrant external intervention (ICISS, 2001, p.34).

By 'right intention' the ICISS suggest that the intervening party must be motivated primarily, though not exclusively, by humanitarian aims (ICISS, 2001, p.36). This is most likely to be achieved if the intervention is multilateral in composition. Regarding 'last resort', R2P advises that every diplomatic and non-military avenue must have been explored, though not necessarily tried, provided there are good grounds for discounting these options (ibid., p.36). On 'proportional means', R2P advises that all interventions must be executed in strict adherence with international humanitarian law and aim to use the minimum degree of force possible. The final criterion – 'reasonable prospects' – advises that interventions should only be undertaken if the action is likely to be successful (ibid., p.37).

Regarding 'right authority', R2P clearly privileges the United Nations, and within the United Nations the Security Council. All those seeking to launch an intervention must seek the Security Council's approval, and R2P warns that attempts to act without explicit UN approval runs the risk of undermining the United Nations and international law generally (ICISS, 2001, p.48). Membership of the United Nations, the ICISS claims, carries an obligation not to use force unilaterally, but also an obligation to use force on behalf of the United Nations if so sanctioned (ibid., p.49). While R2P is clear as to the importance of the Security Council, it additionally acknowledges the problems surrounding this organ's competencies and composition. The unrepresentative nature of the P5 is criticized, as is its lack of accountability to the General Assembly (ibid, p.51). In terms of addressing the biggest issue regarding the Security Council's record on humanitarian intervention – the veto power of the P5 – R2P suggests a 'code of conduct' whereby 'a permanent member, in matters where its vital national interests were not claimed to be involved, would not use its veto to obstruct the passage of what would otherwise be a majority resolution' (ibid., p.51).

If, however, the Security Council does not act when a crisis passes the just cause threshold, R2P suggests a number of alternatives. First, the matter should be taken to the General Assembly, which could employ the powers vested in it through the *Uniting for Peace* resolution (see Chapter 5). While R2P notes that this would not constitute explicit legal sanction, it would provide a significant stamp of legitimacy for any intervention (ICISS, 2001, p. 53). Additionally the ICISS suggest that regional organizations could undertake an intervention and seek to have retrospective legitimacy bestowed on their actions by the Security Council, as happened with the Economic Community of West African States Monitoring Group (ECOMOG) interventions in Liberia in 1992 and Sierra Leone in 1997 (see Chapter 9).

Of course the most obvious alternative, and the one that has caused greatest controversy, is unilateral intervention without any explicit approval from the Security Council or the General Assembly. R2P acknowledges that this is a particularly divisive issue, and accepts that 'it would be impossible to find consensus . . . around any set of proposals for military intervention which acknowledged the validity of any intervention not authorized by the Security Council or General Assembly' (ICISS, 2001, pp.54–5). This impasse on agreed principles, however, means that the central dilemma posed by humanitarian intervention – is it right for states to intervene in other states when they perceive there to be a pressing humanitarian need? – remains unresolved. R2P outlines 'two lessons' which must guide thinking in respect to this dilemma. First it states that in the face of Security Council inaction, 'it is unrealistic to expect that concerned states will rule out other means and forms of action to meet the gravity and urgency of these situations'. Such interventions 'may not be conducted for the right reasons or with the right commitment to the necessary precautionary principles' (ibid., p.55). Second, if action is taken without the Security Council's approval and this action proves successful, 'then this may have enduring serious consequences for the stature and credibility of the UN itself' (ibid., p.55).

Thus R2P constitutes a key statement on humanitarian intervention which aims to embed the idea of sovereignty as responsibility and, crucially, the principle that the international community has a responsibility to act when individual states are unwilling or unable to do so. The final chapter of R2P makes it clear that the principles advanced are intended to have practical application. The next section outlines the international response to R2P.

International reception and the 2005 World Summit

R2P was initially favourably received by Canada, the United Kingdom and Germany, while Argentina, Australia, Colombia, Croatia, New Zealand, Norway, Peru, the Republic of Ireland, Rwanda, South Korea, Sweden and Tanzania all expressed broad support (Bellamy, 2006a, p.151). East Asian countries were 'more cautious' in their response, while perhaps most importantly, the Security Council was quite negative (Macfarlane, Thielking and Weiss, 2004, p.982). In May 2002 the Security Council discussed the tenets of R2P. The United States 'was noticeably unenthusiastic about the debate' while additionally 'there was widespread opinion in the meeting that if new situations emerged . . . the five permanent members and broader Council would lack the political will to deliver troops and would limit themselves to condemnatory resolution' (Welsh, 2006, pp.185, 210). The United States rejected the idea of being bound to commit troops should the R2P threshold be breached, while the Chinese opposed any diminution of the Security Council's monopoly on the legitimization of the use of force, a perspective shared by Russia (Bellamy, 2006a, pp.151–2).

The Non-Aligned Movement rejected the basic premise behind R2P, while the G-77, though it offered no joint position on R2P, suggested amending its provisions to strengthen the principles of territorial integrity and sovereignty (ibid., p. 152). In 2003 the African Union formally replaced the Organization of African Unity, and its Constitutive Act contained provision 4(h) which established 'The right of the Union to intervene in a Member State pursuant to a decision of the Assembly in respect of grave circumstances, namely war crimes, genocide and crimes against humanity'. Thus the African Union appeared to formally adopt the key principle behind R2P. However, the position of the African Union and its members at the 2005 World Summit (see below) undermined the idea that African states had come to endorse the doctrine of R2P (Bellamy, 2006a, pp.157–62).

At the July 2003 Progressive Governments Summit the prime ministers of both Canada and the United Kingdom attempted to include R2P's basic principle in the final communiqué but this was rejected, with Argentina, Chile and Germany being particularly opposed. This marked 'a surprising new kind of hostility among countries that earlier might have been counted among the supporters of the concept (Macfarlane et al., 2004, p.984). The fallout from the invasion of Iraq and the general rhetoric of the Bush administration since 11 September 2001 created a new unwillingness on the part of many Western states to facilitate interventionism, while in the non-Western world any change to the status of sovereignty was viewed with great suspicion. The invasion of Iraq had created a 'poisonous' atmosphere in the General Assembly, and thus the potential for the kind of reform suggested by R2P was greatly reduced (Weiss, 2007, p.125).

In September 2003 Kofi Annan commission a High-Level Panel on Threats, Challenges and Change to examine the United Nations' role in addressing international security concerns. The report recognized the principle that sovereignty and membership of the United Nations brought with it certain responsibilities (2004, p.17). The report further explicitly acknowledged the notion that the international community had a 'responsibility to protect' citizens in other states (2004, p.66). It adopted the just cause thresholds and precautionary principles contained in R2P with some minor amendments (Bellamy, 2006a, p.156). Additionally the report generally advanced a cautious perspective on revising the rules governing the use of force, but did suggest that the Security Council needed to 'enhance its capacity and willingness to act in the face of threats' (2004, p.80). The report 'significantly changed the normative context' within which the debate surrounding R2P had proceeded (Wheeler, 2005, p.99). Kofi Annan welcomed the findings and included the recommendations in his report *In Larger Freedom* (2005a), which he presented to the General Assembly in March 2005.

The 2005 World Summit, held in New York from 14–16 September, marked the 60th anniversary of the United Nations and was billed as the forum where 'the UN must undergo the most sweeping overhaul in its 60-year history' (Annan, 2005b, p.66). Representatives from all of the world's states attended, and engaged in negotiations in an atmosphere clouded by the US-led invasion of Iraq.

Two paragraphs – 138 and 139 (see Box 6.2) – were included in the final *Outcome Document* explicitly endorsing the notion of a responsibility to protect. The fact that this agreement was reached suggests on one level a success on the part of the advocates of R2P. Others have argued, however, that the compromises that secured the inclusion of these paragraphs undermined the essence of the original proposal.

In terms of explaining how the idea of a 'responsibility to protect' came to be included, Bellamy (2006a) suggests that three major concessions were made. First, regarding the question of authority, the idea of the Security Council members agreeing not to use their veto powers – the 'code of conduct' – was jettisoned early in the negotiations. Additionally the notion of legitimate intervention without explicit Security Council approval was 'sidestepped' (ibid., p.155). Second, the just cause threshold included in the *Outcome Document* actually restricted the instances when the Security Council could legitimately intervene. Security Council practice in the 1990s had substantially broadened the Security Council's remit to act (see

Box 6.2 Paragraphs 138 and 139 of the World Summit Outcome Document

138: Each individual State has the responsibility to protect its populations from genocide, war crimes, ethnic cleansing and crimes against humanity. This responsibility entails the prevention of such crimes, including their incitement, through appropriate and necessary means. We accept that responsibility and will act in accordance with it. The international community should, as appropriate, encourage and help States to exercise this responsibility and support the United Nations in establishing an early warning capability.

139: The international community, through the United Nations, also has the responsibility to use appropriate diplomatic, humanitarian and other peaceful means, in accordance with Chapters VI and VIII of the Charter, to help protect populations from genocide, war crimes, ethnic cleansing and crimes against humanity. In this context, we are prepared to take collective action, in a timely and decisive manner, through the Security Council, in accordance with the Charter, including Chapter VII, on a case-by-case basis and in cooperation with relevant regional organizations as appropriate, should peaceful means be inadequate and national authorities manifestly fail to protect their populations from genocide, war crimes, ethnic cleansing and crimes against humanity. We stress the need for the General Assembly to continue consideration of the responsibility to protect populations from genocide, war crimes, ethnic cleansing and crimes against humanity and its implications, bearing in mind the principles of the Charter and international law. We also intend to commit ourselves, as necessary and appropriate, to helping States build capacity to protect their populations from genocide, war crimes, ethnic cleansing and crimes against humanity and to assisting those which are under stress before crises and conflicts break out.

Source: UN General Assembly (2005).

Chapter 5). With authority being once again clearly vested in the Security Council, and the criteria for intervention limited to 'genocide, war crimes, ethnic cleansing and crimes against humanity', the scope for intervention was restricted. Thirdly, while the ICISS stated that the responsibility to protect transferred from the state to the international community when the host state was deemed 'unable or unwilling' to exercise its responsibilities, in the *Outcome Document* this was amended to cases where the host state was guilty of a 'manifest failure' – a semantic change but one that raised the threshold for international action.

Supporters of R2P sought to achieve two things at the World Summit. They wanted the General Assembly to make a commitment to the tenets of the original ICISS document, and they sought to persuade the Security Council to do three things: first, to adopt a resolution committing it to act whenever the just cause thresholds were crossed; second, to submit its decisions to public deliberation about the use of force based on the precautionary principles; and third, for members to agree not to use the veto in cases of humanitarian emergencies where they did not have clear national interests at stake (Bellamy, 2006a, p.153). The two major initiatives proffered by adherents to R2P – securing the P5 endorsement of an obligation to act, and the agreement to remove the veto – were not incorporated into the *Outcome Document*. Additionally the goal of further strengthening the capacity of states to act legitimately outside of the Security Council was unsuccessful, as the endorsement of the basic tenets of R2P was made conditional on the restatement of the Security Council's primacy. The consensus reached was therefore achieved by conceding key aspects of R2P. Thus the *Outcome Document* constituted for some 'a step-backward . . . R2P lite' (Weiss, 2007, p.117).

Challenging the responsibility to protect

The rise in support for a redefinition of sovereignty has been a key feature of post-Cold War international relations. Given the centrality of sovereignty in international politics it is therefore unsurprising that pressure to alter the status of sovereignty has not been greeted with unanimous support. The following sections outline the key objections raised against the new conception.

Specific failings within R2P

Certain observers have noted that there are a number of ambiguities within R2P itself. Both threshold criteria use the term 'large scale' (ICISS, 2001, p.32). The ICISS acknowledged it wished to 'make no attempt to quantify 'large scale' [as this] will not in practice generate major disagreement' (ibid., p. 33). In fact Bellamy argues that this indeterminacy can enable the P5 to block interventions by claiming that the thresholds have not been breached (2006a, pp.148–9). This charge of indeterminacy can be applied to a number of other aspects of R2P: how do we determine that human protection is the 'primary purpose' behind a state's desire to intervene or that the use of force is truly the last resort, given that all alternative means do not have to be attempted so long as there is 'reasonable grounds' for believing that they would not have succeeded? The same, of course, applies to the caution that there must be a 'reasonable chance of success' (ibid., pp.36–7).

R2P's two thresholds for intervention have also been criticized for being too restrictive. Many humanitarian advocates wished to see intervention legitimized if lesser violations of human rights occurred. The thresholds set by R2P are certainly higher than certain cases in the 1990s – particularly Haiti in 1994 – when the Security Council deemed a crisis to be a threat to international peace and stability

The 'code of conduct' suggested for the P5 has also been criticized as inherently nebulous (Hehir, 2008a, pp.121–2). The question of the P5's veto power is central to the controversy surrounding humanitarian intervention, yet the solution advanced by R2P amounts to a non-binding gentleman's agreement which appears to overlook the fact that the national interests of the P5 are invariably involved, and if a case arises where they are not, there is unlikely to be a major problem anyway.

Weiss also criticizes the focus on prevention, arguing that the 'mumbling and stumbling' regarding prevention is a 'superficially attractive but highly unrealistic way to try and pretend that we can finesse the hard issues of what essentially amounts to humanitarian intervention' (2007, p.104). The major issue is, he maintains, the responsibility to react.

A Western idea

The most vociferous champions of the idea of a responsibility to protect are Western, and the rationale underlying the idea is a basic principle of Western liberal democracy. There is scepticism in the developing world over the motivation driving this pressure for change, particularly as the key proponents of R2P are overwhelmingly Western. The 133 states comprising the G-77 have routinely rejected humanitarian intervention, with many members arguing that the focus on human rights is designed to facilitate Western expansion. President of Venezuela Hugo Chavez described R2P as part of a movement whereby 'a few countries try to reinterpret the principles of international law in order to impose new doctrines', and he asked rhetorically, 'Who is going to protect us? Are they going to protect us?' (2005). As noted in Chapter 3, sovereignty is considered by many states in the developing world to be a bulwark against colonialism, and the rhetoric of human rights and 'sovereignty as responsibility' is reminiscent of the arguments proffered by European empires in the 19th century and 'raises the spectre of a return to colonial habits and practices on the part of the major Western powers' (Ayoob, 2002, p.85).

David Chandler argues that the post-Cold War systemic configuration, though favourable to the West and particularly the United States, provided no 'framework which can legitimize and give moral authority to new, more direct forms of Western regulation'. This 'crisis' has led to the assertion of the liberal peace thesis which constitutes 'the convergence of morality and Realpolitik' (Chandler, 2004a, p.75). R2P is part of this liberal peace thesis and thus a means by which the tenets of international law can be manipulated to facilitate the national interest of Western states. Noam Chomsky

similarly discounts the humanitarian rhetoric employed by Western proponents of sovereignty as responsibility as entirely cynical and designed to
erode international law's restrictions (1999, pp.150–7). Christian Reus-
Smit argues that the increased focus on the internal human rights record of
states and attendant desire to determine a state's sovereign rights according
to this record is part of 'the liberal hierarchy thesis' which suggests that liberal democracies should be afforded greater rights under international law
(2005, p.76). Such a realignment of the international system would, he
maintains, be fundamentally at odds with liberal principles and 'a gamble
only for the foolhardy and brave-hearted' (ibid., p.92).

Will lead to increased war and instability

As noted in Chapter 3, many believe that sovereignty, though often violated, has acted as a restraint against great power domination. The norm of
non-intervention and the proscription against inference in the domestic
affairs of other states have, it is claimed, created a more peaceful, orderly
world system. Mohammed Ayoob argues that sovereignty is the foremost
normative structure within existing international society, and he warns that
undermining it 'may lead to either unadulterated anarchy or unmitigated
hegemony or a combination of the two – anarchy within and hegemony
without' (2002, pp.82–3). If we move to a system based on sovereignty as
responsibility, there is the strong likelihood that military interventionism,
be it nefarious or genuinely altruistic, will increase and war will be more
prevalent (Jackson, 2000, p. 291). R2P does not explicitly support intervention without the United Nations' approval but does seem to endorse the
primacy of morality over legal doctrine, and thus the highly contentious
idea of 'illegal but legitimate' intervention.

It is also claimed that the potential increase in violence could also stem
from the actions of not just the militarily powerful but also the militarily
weak. The potential for intervention may well induce certain groups to
provoke their government into using excessive military force in the hope
that the ensuing repression would compel the international community to
intervene to protect the victims of the government's reprisals. An escalation
imperative is thus created predicated on the logic that the greater the
tragedy, the more likely it is that intervention will occur (Kuperman, 2006,
p.19). The problem is thus twofold: first, while the possibility of intervention exists, rebel groups that ordinarily would not have used military force
may do so. Second, once they have attacked the state and provoked a retaliatory attack, there is no guarantee that intervention will take place,
therefore rebels may create and then endure a humanitarian crisis. This,
Kuperman argues, was precisely the strategy employed by the Kosovo
Liberation Army in 1995–9 (2003).

[It's their] responsibility to protect

One consequence of the emergence of R2P not widely predicted by its critics was the extent to which the notion actually facilitated Western *inaction*. States can claim, and have claimed, that in the spirit of R2P, host states have the primary responsibility to deal with intra-state crises and should be left alone to do so. This has been especially obvious with respects to the response to the crisis in Darfur (see Chapter 13). As Bellamy notes in relation to Darfur, '"responsibility to protect" language has now enabled anti-interventionists to legitimize arguments against action by claiming the primary responsibility in certain contested cases still lies with the state and not (yet) with an international body' (2006a, p.33). Indeed, the UK position appears to reflect this: during deliberations on what to do should Sudan fail to abide by Resolution 1556, a senior Foreign Office official stated, 'the best way to deliver security to the people of Darfur is to get those with the primary responsibility for it to do it ... the government of Sudan' (Bellamy, 2005a, p.45). The language used in the majority of Security Council resolutions on Darfur certainly put the onus on the Sudanese government to resolve the crisis despite the United Nations' own investigations charging the Khartoum regime with complicity in the crisis.

As noted in the previous chapter, the adoption of aspects of the responsibility to protect in the *Outcome Document* of the 2005 World Summit was conditional on the removal of any reference to a duty incumbent on states to intervene. In his letter to the president of the General Assembly prior to the World Summit, John Bolton, the Representative of the United States to the United Nations, outlined his country's position on the responsibility to protect:

> we agree that the host state has a responsibility to protect its populations from such atrocities, and we agree in a more general and moral sense that the international community has a responsibility to act when the host state allows such atrocities. But . . . we want to avoid formulations that suggest that the other countries are inheriting the same responsibility that the host state has. (2005)

It is clear, therefore, that the variant of 'responsibility to protect' adopted at the 2005 World Summit did not necessarily make intervention more likely, and actually constituted delineation of responsibility which put the emphasis on the host state rather than the international community. Neither R2P nor the *Outcome Document* proscribe external intervention, but they do not create a duty to undertake such action. The language of R2P can thus be employed by those wishing to avoid intervening and those wishing to block an intervention. Therefore the rhetorical shift from 'humanitarian intervention' to 'the responsibility to protect', described by some as 'ingenious' (Tanguy, 2003, p.142), creates significant scope for states to utilize the new discourse to legitimize both non-intervention and domestic oppression.

Does not address the key problem

It is one thing to assert that sovereignty carries with it a responsibility to protect and that failure to meet this responsibility legitimizes external intervention; it is quite another to create the means by which the latter aspect of this assertion is realized. There is certainly little doubt but that states are today considered to have responsibilities towards their citizens and that there are certain human rights violations which cannot be considered exclusively domestic matters. But we could ask both 'What's new?' and 'So what?'

At the conclusion of the 2005 World Summit Tony Blair declared, 'For the first time at this summit we are agreed that states do not have the right to do what they will within their own borders' (Fisher, 2007, p.109). This is a questionable claim. Since at least the Nuremberg trials in 1945 it has been clear that states could not do whatever they wanted to their own citizens. The concept 'crime against humanity' is formulated in a way that explicitly describes certain actions as affecting more than just the victims themselves, and hence not purely a domestic matter. Many developments during the Cold War, such as the Genocide Convention and the Universal Declaration of Human Rights, outlined the responsibilities states had towards their citizens. Indeed the 1966 International Covenant on Civil and Political Rights committed states to 'respect and to ensure to all individuals within its territory and subject to its jurisdiction the rights recognised in the present Convention, without distinction of any kind'. Thus even before the rise of human security in the post-Cold War era, no state could reasonably claim that it was legally or morally entitled to do whatever it wanted to its own citizens.

What is innovative about R2P was not that it claimed states had responsibilities to their citizens, but that it claimed that in the event that a state failed to meet these responsibilities, the responsibility to protect transferred to the international community. Yet, as innovative as this was, the prescriptions advanced by R2P do not suggest a means by which this latter responsibility can be actualized. R2P does not suggest specific reforms to the Security Council that would force it to act, nor does it support the creation of a new organ – such as a UN police force – that would act whenever humanitarian crises erupted. The end point of R2P is thus seen by some as inherently weak, creating merely a 'discretionary entitlement' (Berman, 2007, p.161). The main obstacle to external intervention historically has not been the legal status of sovereignty but rather the lack of political will. It is debatable where the provisions of R2P, and even less so the World Summit *Outcome Document*, do much to address this key failing. Who decides and who acts remain outstanding questions.

Conclusion

During the 20th century 35 million people died in all civil and international wars; 150 million people were killed by their own governments (Lu, 2006, p.54). Since 1945, inspired by the depravity of the Holocaust, international law has greatly expanded its rules on human rights and codified an increasing number of proscriptions on domestic state behaviour. Yet millions continued to be killed at the hands of their own states and action taken to halt atrocities was inconsistent.

With the end of the Cold War, many hoped that the gap between the tenets of international law and the enforcement of international law would be closed. The new power wielded by Western states, ostensibly those most respectful of human rights, led to great optimism that substantive action could now take place. Tony Blair declared that 'the most pressing foreign policy problem we face is to identify the circumstances in which we should get actively involved in other people's conflicts' (Stromseth, 2005, pp.239–40). Such commitments emboldened those who sought to reorder international relations and international law in favour of human security rather than state security.

With the rise of human security has come the idea of sovereignty as responsibility. Today it seems almost inconceivable that states could claim the right to do whatever they please to the own citizens. Significant disagreement remains about the scope of 'purely domestic matters', but complete inviolability appears an untenable defence. Cassese suggests that there are now five principles on which all states agree (2005, p.398).

- The dignity of the human being is a basic value that every state should try to protect.
- It is necessary to aim at the achievement of fundamental rights of groups and peoples.
- Racial discrimination is universally condemned.
- Large-scale violations are universally condemned.
- The international community can intervene when large-scale violations occur.

It must be acknowledged that while these principles leave much to be clarified they do constitute progress when we consider the situation 100 years ago (Dixon, 2007, p.341). Clearly however, although the state has lost its status as a 'supreme ungovernable entity', this does not mean that the state is no longer the primary actor in international relations. The reaction by the international community of states to R2P and the nature of the 2005 World Summit *Outcome Document* testify to the power of states to reject change that substantially undermines their autonomy.

Between the establishment of the ICISS and the publication of R2P the world had undergone profound change. Some have argued that humanitarian intervention was a victim of the post-11 September 2001 preoccupation with terrorism and self-defence (Welsh, 2006, p.181). Yet the term 'responsibility to protect' is today routinely used and, as evidenced by the crises in Darfur (2003–), Burma (2007) and Zimbabwe (2008), debate about humanitarian intervention continues and the ICISS's report remains a key work on the issue. The idea – central to R2P – of fundamentally altering the international system so that states accept a responsibility to protect citizens suffering egregious human rights abuses in other states is so revolutionary that it is perhaps too early to judge its feasibility. What is fairly certain is that R2P has sparked such a debate about the responsibility of states that this issue is unlikely to ever be considered an exclusively domestic concern, and is likely to remain at the heart of the international relations agenda for some time.

Questions

- Identify the sources of tension between the rights of the individual and the rights of states in the UN Charter.
- In what respects did the rise of 'human security' in the 1990s challenge the traditional view of state responsibility?
- Assess the key tenets of the ICISS report *The Responsibility to Protect* (2001).
- How convincing are the key critiques of R2P?

Further reading

On the responsibility of states to their citizens

Bain, W. (ed.) (2006) *The Empire of Security and the Safety of the People* (London: Routledge).

Jackson, R. (2000) *The Global Covenant: Human Conduct in a World of States* (Oxford: Oxford University Press).

Lyons, G. and Mastanduno, M. (eds) (1995) *Beyond Westphalia: State Sovereignty and International Intervention* (Baltimore: Johns Hopkins University Press).

Robertson, G. (2002) *Crimes Against Humanity* (London: Penguin).

On the 'responsibility to protect'

Bellamy, A. (2009a) *Responsibility to Protect* (London: Polity).

Evan, G. (2008) *The Responsibility to Protect: Ending Mass Atrocity Crimes Once and For All* (Washington DC: Brookings Institution Press).

Weiss, T. (2007) *Humanitarian Intervention* (London: Polity).

Wheeler, N. (2005) 'A Victory for Common Humanity? The Responsibility to Protect after the 2005 World Summit', *Journal of International Law and International Relations*, 2:1, 95–106.

The Responsibility to Protect-Engaging Civil Society: http://www.responsibilityto-protect.org/index.php

The Responsibility to Protect Coalition: http://r2pcoalition.org/component/option, com_frontpage/Itemid,1/

On global civil society and human security

Chandler, D. (2004) *Constructing Global Civil Society: Morality and Power in International Relations* (Basingstoke and New York: Palgrave Macmillan).

Held, D. (1995) *Democracy and the Global Order* (London: Polity).

Kaldor, M. (2003) *Global Civil Society: An Answer to War* (London: Polity).

Keck, M. and Sikkink, K. (1998) *Activists Beyond Borders: Advocacy Networks in International Politics* (Ithaca, N.Y.: Cornell University Press).

Shaw, M. (1994) *Global Civil Society and International Relations* (London: Polity).

The Centre for the Study of Global Governance at the LSE has an extensive online library on global civil society: http://www.lse.ac.uk/Depts/global/researchgcs research.htm

Chapter 7

Who Decides?

Central to controversy surrounding humanitarian intervention is the question of who decides whether a particular situation requires external intervention. It is one thing to formulate basic human rights which states should respect, but it is far more difficult to contrive a universally agreed means to enforce these human rights. Such enforcement requires not just agreement on the thresholds for intervention and the means by which intervention should occur, but also, more problematically, the creation of an authority with the right to determine when these thresholds have been breached and the power to authorize intervention. Despite its centrality to the debate surrounding humanitarian intervention, 'The criterion of legitimate authority,' Anthony Coates notes, 'has become the most neglected of all the criteria that have been traditionally employed in the moral assessment of war' (1997, p.123).

Authority is notably elusive in international politics, and thus the justification of power is more arbitrary and contested in the international arena than it is in domestic political systems. The UN Security Council constitutes an institution with the greatest claim to act as an international authority, but the Council suffers from a perceived lack of legitimacy. Authority without legitimacy is inherently weak, and it is precisely this conundrum that has undermined the Council's capacity to resolve the 'who decides' question.

States routinely reject the authority of the Security Council; former US President George W. Bush outlined his views on the United Nations' authority by declaring, 'We don't really need the United Nation's approval to act. . . . When it comes to our security, we really don't need anyone's permission' (White, 2004, p.660). Additionally states, and many humanitarian NGOs and activists, have criticized the inconsistency and moral bankruptcy of the Council and called for unilateral interventions to address pressing humanitarian need. Yet, many of those who endorsed NATO's actions in 1999 were uncomfortable with the implications of the unilateral use of force. At the time Kofi Annan warned that 'unless the Security Council is restored to its preeminent position as the sole source of legitimacy on the use of force we are on a dangerous path to anarchy' (Hurd, 2007, p.130). These concerns appeared to be confirmed when the US-led coalition invaded Iraq in 2003. The question of authority, often posed starkly as 'who decides?', clearly has implications beyond international law. Chapter 2 noted that the tripartite division of the Just War tradition is not, in itself, especially contentious. Determining whether these sets of criteria have been met, however, is highly contentious, and in the absence of a recognized authority figure, discussion regarding adherence to the criteria is necessarily subjective and potentially interminable.

The first section of this chapter constitutes an assessment of legitimacy, authority and power, highlighting the interdependent nature of these concepts. The second section examines the powers vested in the Security Council, noting the formal limitations on the Council derived from the UN Charter, and the Council's reliance on the assent of states. This chapter's final section analyses alternative sources of authority suggested as a means by which humanitarian intervention can consistently and effectively be executed when the need arises.

Legitimacy, authority, power and rights

As noted in Chapter 6, there is now general agreement among states that sovereignty does not enable a state to treat its citizens any way it pleases. States, particularly in the post-Cold War era, have generally not resisted external intervention on the basis that sovereign inviolability is absolute. Rather they have claimed – albeit often spuriously – that a particular crisis was a domestic concern which they were capable of dealing with. In such situations there is a clash between the state's perception of a particular crisis and that of external actors. This clash derives from differing interpretations of the nature and scale of a crisis rather than from a state claiming an unlimited right to treat its citizens however it pleases and an external perspective countering that certain acts are never justified. For example the Sudanese government has never claimed that it has the right to kill or displace Sudanese citizens in Darfur; rather it has disputed the scale of the crisis and argued that it has not been the cause of the violence (see Chapter 13). In the case of Darfur and many other similar crises, certain actors have called for intervention while others have cautioned against such action. The question of legitimacy arises in this context when we assess whose perspective carries greater weight.

Legitimacy

The term 'legitimacy' is widely used in International Relations (IR), yet it is acknowledged as being an underdeveloped concept (Hurd, 2007, p.1; Wheeler, 2002, p.4). Legitimacy is central to the issue of 'who decides', as the perceived legitimacy of prospective arbiters is a crucial factor in this enquiry. People and states follow rules under three circumstances; coercion, consent and self-interest. Forcing an actor to follow a certain code depends on the utilization, overtly or covertly, of a power asymmetry. Conversely actors voluntarily obey rules if they are convinced of a rule's inherent legitimacy and the legitimacy of the organ that created and enforces this rule (Armstrong and Farrell, 2005, p.5). For example compliance with the law in Chile following Augusto Pinochet's coup in 1973 was, to a large extent, a function of the deployment of the army and the violent oppression of dissent. Compliance with the law in contemporary Norway, however, is a function of the widespread belief in the legitimacy of the Norwegian government and judiciary amongst the general population. Clearly a system of rules is more effective and stable if compliance derives from consent rather than coercion. This consent is ultimately dependent on the perceived legitimacy of the organs which administer the legal system.

Self-interest, however, is another potential motivation for lawful action which does not constitute consent. We may well support a legal regime provided we feel it furthers our interests, but this does not mean we perceive the regime to be legitimate. Such a coincidence between self-interest and lawful action is, however, unlikely to be sustained; while a certain clique in Pinochet's Chile benefited from the laws then enforced, the majority of the population did not. 'Legitimacy therefore,' according to Andrew Hurrell, 'refers to a particular kind of rule-following or obedience, distinguishable from purely self-interested or instrumental behaviour on the one hand, and from straightforward imposed or coercive rule on the other' (2005, p.16).

The perceived legitimacy of a particular institution encourages actors to abide by the rules of that institution even when these rules are inconvenient. Key to this is the sense that the procedures that facilitate the functioning of the legal regime are inclusive and fair. An actor formally involved in the process of decision making is likely to consider the outcome of the process to be legitimate (Cronin and Hurd, 2008, p.8). This applies, crucially, even to those situations where the actor's aims are not realized. The proposal to grant a veto to the permanent five members of the Security Council was strongly opposed by other states during the San Francisco conference on the UN Charter. While the non-permanent members ultimately failed to have this controversial provision removed they nonetheless endorsed the final Charter because, Ian Hurd argues, they were convinced of the procedural correctness of the deliberation process (2007, pp.91–5). Similarly, opposition parties in democracies throughout the world accept the legitimacy of the elected government despite its passing legislation they oppose.

Hurd argues that 'legitimation and internalization of a rule or institution have taken place in states' when three traits are observable. First, citizens treat the rule in question as a necessary part of the strategic landscape for decision making. Second, citizens cease making cost–benefit calculations about the effects of breaking the rule as they consider future behaviours.

Third, citizens use the symbols that derive from the rule or institution as resources (2007, p.79). Whether these traits are observable in terms of the Security Council is discussed later in this chapter. Key to the above is the active incorporation of rules and norms into the behaviour of states. It is not enough, clearly, to acknowledge the legitimacy of an institution and concomitantly act contrary to its rules and procedures.

International politics is characterized by weak authority structures, hence the oft-quoted concept of 'international anarchy' (see Chapter 4). The international institution with greatest claim to act as international authority – the Security Council – suffers from a perceived lack of legitimacy. This derives from a number of issues, not least its composition and inconsistent record of law enforcement. In light of this perceived absence of a legitimate arbiter, some have sought to shift the focus from assessing the legitimacy of the paramount international authority and its judgements to the legitimacy of the act itself. Thus the lack of a universally recognized legitimate authority does not necessarily render the appraisal of the legitimacy of an action impossible.

Alex Bellamy, explicitly drawing on the earlier work of Ian Clark (2005, pp.18–19), notes that there are primarily two ways of understanding legitimacy (2006b, pp.5–7). The first is the substantive approach, which holds that an act is legitimate if it conforms to a particular set of rules. The second is procedural, and this focuses on the manner in which decisions are reached rather than their relationship with a codified set of rules: for example, decisions taken on the basis of consensus. Each perspective is difficult to apply to IR. With respect to the substantive approach, rules require authoritative bodies, and given that the international system is widely regarded as anarchic, this appears to foreclose this process. In terms of the procedural approach, Bellamy states that the present composition of the international system renders this impossible (ibid., p.6). This does not mean that legitimacy is fundamentally elusive, and Bellamy argues that the legitimacy of an act can be deduced by examining what the 'judges and juries' say. Judges are those 'capable of backing up their judgments with material rewards or punishments' while juries 'comprise the rest of world opinion' (ibid., p.6). Bellamy asserts that the claims made by actors can be assessed according to the three subordinate sets of norms: legality, morality and constitutionality. Thus the appraisal of the legitimacy of an act is possible outside of both formal authoritative structures and consensus-based procedures.

There are, however, a number of problems with this approach. First there is clearly enormous scope for disagreement amongst the judges; if we assume that Russia and the United States constitute 'judges capable of backing up their judgments with material rewards', we must accept that it is highly likely that these judges will form different opinions about the legitimacy of a particular action, as was clearly evidenced during the conflict between Russia and Georgia over South Ossetia in August 2008. Given the propensity of these judges to differ so fundamentally, it is unlikely that any clarity will be provided by deferring to their opinion. The powerful global judges will determine their position on a particular case, Bellamy accepts, according to considerations based on natural law, positive law and national interest, with particular emphasis on the latter (2006b, p.128). Second, there something fundamentally problematic about an actor being deemed a judge by virtue of its material power. It is difficult to justify the proposition that a state constitutes a judge of legitimacy because of its capacity to exercise leverage via its large military and/or economic wealth. Finally, as Bellamy acknowledges, global juries will always be less powerful than global judges. International mass movements raise awareness of issues and constitute a source of pressure on the architects of unpopular policies. There is little evidence, however, that such movements have the capacity to 'shame' governments into desisting from unpopular action (Hehir, 2008a, pp.81–4; Bellamy, 2006a, p.150).

Authority and power

If we obey the law because we believe that the governmental and judicial institutions are legitimate, we may say that these particular institutions have authority. If we obey the law solely because we are forced to do so, we may say that the institutions in this case have power but lack authority. Authority implies power, but power does not imply authority. Bruce Cronin and Ian Hurd define authority as 'a relation among actors within a hierarchy in which one group is recognized as having both the right and the competence to make binding decisions for the rest of the community' (2008, p.6). Key to this definition is the focus on right and competence rather than capacity. Following Iraq's invasion of Kuwait in 1990, Saddam Hussein exercised power in Kuwait but he lacked authority in the eyes of both the Kuwaitis and the international community. Authority, therefore, differs from power because of the legitimacy inherent in the former.

As discussed earlier the international system is widely regarded as characterized by the lack of authority. While IR theorists disagree over the extent to which international anarchy impacts on the behaviour of states, the underlying presumption of anarchy is common to the majority of theoretical perspectives (Cronin and Hurd, 2008, p.4). This assumption, however, is challenged by Hurd, who argues that it is based on 'untested premises' and that a form of authority is identifiable in the international arena (2008, p. 24). His analysis resonates with the English School view on the role of norms (see Chapter 4), as he suggests that states, including the P5, invariably justify their actions according to the UN Charter and Security Council resolutions, conduct their foreign policy in accordance with international laws and norms, and seek to utilize the symbols of legitimacy inherent in organs such as the Security Council (2007, p. 187). Hurd does not discount the role played by strategic interests in foreign policy, but challenges the perception of a system devoid of constraint characterized by the singular pursuit of self-interest.

That states seek to justify their acts as lawful is certainly clear (Watts, 2001, p.7). Yet, accepting this, does the desire amongst states to be seen to be acting lawfully translate into a finding that authority does in fact exist in IR? Indeed, Arthur Watts acknowledges that international law is sufficiently malleable to enable states to justify their foreign policy on legal grounds even in extremely dubious cases, because they know legal censure can be ignored, thus highlighting law's inherent weakness (ibid., p.8). Few people in domestic societies wish to be seen as habitual law breakers. Regardless of whether a person desires their peers to perceive them as law abiding, however, compliance with the law is also enforced. Can we identify a similar enforcement mechanism in the international system? It is not at all clear that we can. In this sense while we may accept that state behaviour is shaped by international law, and thus outright anarchy is a misrepresentation, the fact that these rules are not enforced surely undermines the notion that there is authority in international politics. For surely a quality of authority requires not simply that the subjects of the authority believe that authority to have legitimacy, but also that that authority has the power, and indeed the will, to enforce its rules. This casts a shadow over the findings that states justify their actions as being in accordance with international law and specifically seek to have their actions endorsed by the Security Council, for this may be 'little more than high-sounding tokenism' (ibid., p. 8). The desire to seek Security Council approval certainly demonstrates that states attach significant importance to the Council as a legitimate international institution. If, however, states fail to receive the endorsement of the Council and act regardless, then the Council's status as an authority is surely undermined.

An alternative way of looking at international law bridges the gap between authority and anarchy. Armstrong and Farrell argue that international law is best seen 'as a site of legitimation for state action'. The structures of international law such as the Charter, the Security Council and the General Assembly are, they maintain, not analogous to domestic institutions but rather 'political spaces where states engage in normatively bounded deliberation about legitimate action' (2005, p.10). In this respect states seek approval from, and justify their behaviour to, the institutions of international law, especially the Security Council, and their actions are judged by the international community in the light of this deliberation, constrained by the framework of international law. States may choose to disregard the opinion of the international institutions and the community of states, but they will be thereby identified as law breakers more obviously than if the 'site of legitimation' did not exist.

Right or duty?

The controversy surrounding humanitarian intervention derives much of its divisiveness from the question 'Is there a right to intervene?' Whether this is posed in terms of a right of the Security Council or coalitions of the willing to intervene, the nature of this right remains problematic, for how do we understand a 'right'? This question can only be answered by first clarifying the status of the actor. For example, as an individual I have no formal authority. I have the right to own a dog but I am under no obligation to do so. A police officer has the right to ask me to keep my dog on a leash in public places. Additionally, however, because of their status, the police officer also has an obligation to ensure that my dog is on a leash in public places. Legally they are not entitled to choose not to enforce their right in this instance. In the context of humanitarian intervention, then, if we identify that the Security Council has the right to act under Chapter VII of the Charter, to intervene to halt humanitarian atrocities, can we also say that the Security Council actually has an obligation to do so? Similarly, if we seek to identify an alternative source of legitimate authority – namely coalitions of states – can we assume that, failing action by the Security Council, they have a duty to intervene as well as a right? As Franck Berman asks, 'if we are genuinely in the presence of a 'right' . . . where is the correlative obligation, and who has the legal quality to enforce it?' (2007, p.160). The danger is that identifying rights without obligations facilitates selectivity and leads to inconsistency. In this sense the legitimacy of a legal order, and the recognized authority within that order, diminish if the subjects of this order believe that enforcement will occur only when there is a coincidence between the interests and the rights of the authority. There is therefore a need to identify not only that an authority has the right to act, but also that the authority has duties to act, otherwise we are left with an unsatisfactory 'discretionary entitlement' (ibid., p.161).

As will be explored in the final section of this chapter, there are many who argue that the Security Council cannot be the final arbiter when it comes to cases of egregious human rights violations. This argument is necessarily based on morality rather than procedural legality as international law does not permit unilateral humanitarian intervention (see Chapter 5). The moral principle upon which the perspective in favour of action taken without Security Council authorization depends asserts that in the face of human suffering we have a duty – not just a right – to act. The underlying principle is, according to Terry Nardin, 'You shall not stand idly by, whoever you are, if you can provide effective assistance at reasonable cost and without neglecting other duties' (2003, p.21). Thus we are hereby enjoined to act not because we can but because we must. Failure to act is therefore not perceived as unwillingness to exercise one's right but, more seriously, a dereliction of duty (Janzekovic, 2006, p.74).

The question 'who decides?' is thus influenced by our understanding of legitimacy, authority and power and complicated by the need to distinguish between a discretionary entitlement – a right to act – and an obligation – a duty to act. As is explored in the final section of this chapter, states have proved unwilling to assume the latter.

The UN Security Council

We might be forgiven from wondering why the question 'Who decides?' is asked at all; surely it is obvious that the UN Security Council performs this function? Two issues have contrived to undermine the Security Council's status as ultimate international authority. First is the fact that the Council's powers derive from states and the Council is dependent on the assent of states to execute these powers. Second, the Security Council suffers from a poor international perception because of the unrepresentative nature of the P5 and the extent to which the P5 have consistently afforded primacy to political rather than legal considerations. These factors, dealt with in the following sections, have encouraged the formulation of alternative sources of authority, an issue examined in this chapter's final section.

Nature of the Security Council's powers

Under Article 24 of the Charter the Security Council has the 'primary responsibility for the maintenance of international peace and security'. The Council's status as a legal authority is however limited. The Council's powers are exercised in response to breaches of the peace and acts of aggression, and thus 'the powers of the Council are designed primarily to preserve the peace rather than to enforce the law, although these can coincide' (Dixon, 2007, p.7). The Council lacks the authority to 'enforce international law, create binding legal precedents, or legislate new legal norms' (Cronin, 2008, p.61). The Council does not have the power to create law but rather 'simply interprets and applies existing law' (de Brichambaut, 2000, p.275). Resolutions passed by the Security Council are not considered binding law, and are rather material or evidential *sources* of law. Council resolutions are also not indicative of customary law, as the Council is not considered to reflect *opinio juris* – evidence of a general acceptance of a new legal norm (Gowlland-Debbas, 2000, p.300).

The Security Council is formally constrained by the Charter and exercises its power within the framework stipulated therein. The Council's powers, therefore, 'cannot be unlimited' (White, 2004, p.646). In 1948 the International Court of Justice (ICJ) acknowledged the formal constraints upon the Security Council; '[the] political character of an organ cannot release it from the observance of the treaty provisions established by the

Charter when they constitute limitations on its powers or criteria for its judgments' (Gowlland-Debbas, 2000, p.304). More recently in the 1995 *Tadic* case the Appeals Chamber of the International Criminal Tribunal for the Former Yugoslavia (ICTY) declared that the Council must only take action 'within the limits of the Purposes and Principles of the Charter' (*Prosecutor v. Tadic*, p.43). Nonetheless, despite these legal constraints, in reality the Council has acted as the principal interpreter of the Charter's rules and hence its own powers. During the course of the negotiations at San Francisco in 1945 Greece proposed that the ICJ be designated as the sole interpreter of the Charter, but this was rejected. This has meant that in practice 'the Charter is what the principal organs do' (Franck, 2005, p.206).

Regardless of formal limitations the Council is also dependent on its constituent member-states, and as such the Council 'cannot enforce its decisions without the cooperation of others and does not have exclusive jurisdiction over its issue area. In other words the power of states outside the institution matters a great deal' (Voeten, 2008, p.54). Richard Falk notes that there no 'governmental institutions beyond the state that can claim "sovereignty" in the sense of autonomous and ultimate authority to pronounce the law'. The United Nations is, thus, best conceived as a 'club of states' and the role of the Security Council is therefore constrained by this relationship between the United Nations and its members (Falk, 2005a, p.35). This dependence on member states is, of course, most evident in the veto powers of the P5.

Voting at the Security Council is regulated by Article 27 of the Charter; the term 'veto' is not used in the Charter but is implicit in Article 27(3). In practice, while the veto has been deployed by the P5 on many occasions, the threat of the veto has often meant that issues have not even been brought before the Council because a veto was considered inevitable, as was the case in 1999 when NATO did not submit its intervention in Kosovo to a vote. Article 27 stipulates that the veto only applies to non-procedural matters. Determining whether an issue is procedural or not is however itself a non-procedural matter, hence the 'double veto'; a permanent member can veto any attempt to treat an issue as procedural, then veto any proposal on this matter when it is set before the Council as a non-procedural matter (Malanczuk, 2006, p.374). Of course the veto power has additionally ensured that conflicts involving one of the P5 were 'practically excluded from the reach of the Charter's system of collective security' (Dinstein, 2005, p.292).

Action by the Security Council is thus dependent on the assent of states, especially its permanent members. In addition the Council is reliant on states to provide it with military resources when action is authorized. Article 43 of the Charter was intended to provide the United Nations with an organized military force at the Security Council's disposal. This never materialized and thus the Council has not been able to enact Article 42, which enables the Council to *authorize* and *require* the use of force (Dixon, 2007, pp. 330-1). The Council has authorized the use of force at times, such as in response to Iraq's invasion of Kuwait in 1990, but has not as such *required* such action. The Security Council's role in deploying troops during the 1990s was, in many respects, limited to legitimizing action taken by coalitions rather than actively authorizing action itself (Job, 2006, p.63). Articles 45 and 47 outline the scope and structure of the Military Staff Committee which was designed as a means by which the United Nations would have something akin to a standing army, but this entity was a victim of the Cold War and has no significant role (Malanczuk, 2006, p.389).

Council action is thus constrained by the Charter and heavily dependent on states. The P5 have used their veto power to limit the scope of Council action and have consistently adjudicated on matters with political considerations to the fore. Despite the provisions contained in Articles 42 and 43, the Council has avoided any requirement to take action and has not taken steps to empower the Military Staff Committee.

International perception

The veto power and composition of the P5 are today widely criticized. Three of the P5 are members of NATO yet none are from Africa, Latin America or the Middle East. This obviously limits its perceived ability to represent global opinion, and while non-permanent seats increased from six to ten in 1965, this has not resolved the issue of the Council's composition. In 1993 the General Assembly established an 'Open-ended Working Group on the Question of Equitable Representation on and Increase in the Membership of the Security Council'. The work of this group is ongoing although there have been no concrete steps taken to expand Council membership. Via the General Assembly's Millennium Declaration all states pledged 'To intensify our efforts to achieve a comprehensive reform of the Security Council in all its aspects' (UN General Assembly, 2000, para.30). This commitment was followed by more definite proposals in the 2004 report published by the High-Level Panel on Threats, Challenges and Change, which proposed two models for reforming the membership of the Council (see Box 7.1). Kofi Annan's 2005 report – *In Larger Freedom* – endorsed the choice posed by the High-Level Panel, although his recommendation that the Security Council be 'broadly representative of the international community as a whole, as well as of the geopolitical realities of today' constitutes a concession to the influence of power on the Council's composition (2005a, p.42). The 'G4' – Germany, Japan, Brazil and India – have long campaigned for a permanent seat as well as the election of a representative from Africa and the Arab League. Despite significant effort no reforms were agreed at the 2005 World Summit.

Box 7.1 Two models for reforming the UN Security Council

Model A provides for six new permanent seats, with no veto being created, and three new two-year term non-permanent seats, divided among the major regional areas as follows:

Regional area	No. of states	Permanent seats (continuing)	Proposed new permananent seats	Proposed two-year seats (non-renewable)	Total
Africa	53	0	2	4	6
Asia and Pacific	56	1	2	3	6
Europe	47	3	1	2	6
Americas	35	1	1	4	6
Total model A	191	5	6	13	24

Model B provides for no new permanent seats but creates a new category of eight four-year renewable-term seats and one new two-year non-permanent (and non-renewable) seat, divided among the major regional areas as follows:

Regional area	No. of states	Permanent seats (continuing)	Proposed four-year renewable seats	Proposed two-year seats (non-renewable)	Total
Africa	53	0	2	4	6
Asia and Pacific	56	1	2	3	6
Europe	47	3	2	1	6
Americas	35	1	2	3	6
Totals model A	191	5	8	11	24

Source: UN High-Level Panel on Threats, Challenges and Change (2004, pp. 67–8).

In tandem with the obviously unrepresentative nature of the Council is the charge that the Council is undermined by the P5 members' narrow pursuit of their national interests (Rodin, 2002, p.179–80). As was noted in Chapter 5, the Council began to be more active following the end of the Cold War, but action taken by the Council under Chapter VII during the 1990s was inconsistent and motivated by the interests of the P5, especially the United States (Chesterman, 2002, pp.160–2; Graubart, 2008, p.154).

Hurd designed three tests of whether an entity has authority, namely 'Compliance, justificatory discourse and unavoidability' (2008, pp.35–7), and applied these to the Security Council. In terms of compliance with the United Nations, and specifically the Security Council, he notes that there is little evidence that states consistently comply with Council resolutions.

Nonetheless, he argues, absolute compliance with an authority would require 'subordinates who are automatons'. Of greater import is the fact that states feel the need to justify their decisions to the Council and 'frame their behaviours in ways that they believe will bring approval from the institution' (ibid., p.35). This, of course, does not readily imply compliance – and hence Council authority – as such justificatory discourse may well be proffered cynically. Finally he notes that there are signs that the Council has entered into the decision-making calculus of states. The US attempt to gain Council approval for its invasion of Iraq suggests that even powerful states are 'forced to frame their policies around the existence of the Council' (ibid., p.35). Although it is undeniably true that the United States sought Council approval, this is, Hurd admits, not a conclusive indicator of Council authority. He argues that the behaviour of the Great Powers 'suggests that they sometimes approach the Council with the intention of "laundering" their favored policies through the legitimating machine of the Council' (Hurd, 2007, p.129). Indicatively, William Cohen, US Secretary of Defense 1997–2001, described Security Council authorization as 'desirable, not imperative' (Voeten, 2008, p.52). The P5 know that their own contentious polices have a limited chance of avoiding the veto at the Council and so, paradoxically, have a vested interest in downplaying the authority of the very institution they constitute and/or manipulating the resolutions it has previously passed. Indeed, at its Fiftieth Anniversary NATO states announced that they would 'prefer' to act with Security Council backing but 'must not limit themselves to acting only when such a mandate can be agreed' (Caplan, 2000, p.31). Yet as noted earlier three of the five permanent members of the Security Council are members of NATO, and hence NATO was downplaying the importance of an institution that it numerically dominates.

Despite the problems identified above and the prevailing negative image of the Council, there is evidence that people still consider it to be the most legitimate international authority (Cronin and Hurd, 2008, p.15). It is indeed striking that the Council has managed to retain this level of international support although, given the dangers obviously inherent in indiscriminate unilateral action, the Council may well be a beneficiary of the fact that, though deeply flawed, it is the least worst option.

A source of order, not justice

Disappointment with the performance of the Security Council derives from a normative view of the Council's role. It is debatable, however, whether this normative role was ever the guiding rationale behind the establishment of the Council. The idea behind the Security Council, and particularly the special powers of the P5, was that these states were, at least in 1945, the dominant world powers and should have this status reflected in the new legal regime. It was agreed at the Yalta conference among the 'big three' (the United States, United Kingdom and Russia) prior to the San Francisco Conference that the proposed United Nations organization must act in accordance with the wishes of these powers to prevent instability and potentially war. Conflict between the United Nations and one or a number of these states had to be avoided, hence the need for the veto power. In this respect the composition of the Security Council and its mandate had more to do with considerations of order than justice. It is, one could argue, unsurprising that the record of the Security Council evidences a preference for stability and order rather than justice.

Following the Second World War it was perhaps somewhat inevitable that the victorious powers would contrive a new system which served their interests. Political systems are not, many contend, designed by impartial actors based on abstract considerations of justice (Bull, 2002, p.53). Thus in assessing the record of the Security Council we must be realistic about the rationale behind its creation and the interests of those who designed it. Anne Orford criticizes those who imagine that the laws governing the use of force and the architecture of the international legal system are designed to challenge hierarchy and power, asserting that the legal regime was actually designed to facilitate and maintain the prevailing power asymmetry (2003, pp.46–7). Likewise Gerry Simpson challenges what he describes as the 'orthodox approach' (2004, pp.26–37) to the evolution of sovereign equality. While this narrative holds that sovereign equality has emerged as a normative challenge to hierarchy and power, Simpson notes that this 'equality' is fundamentally undermined by what he terms 'legalised hegemony':

> the existence within an international society of a powerful elite of states whose superior status is recognised by minor powers as a political fact giving rise to the existence of certain constitutional privileges, rights and duties and whose relations with each other are defined by adherence to a rough principle of sovereign equality. (Simpson, 2004, p.68)

The powers vested in the P5 are the most obvious manifestation of this phenomenon. Nigel White describes the veto as 'a realist core in an institutionalist framework – a political core in a legal regime' (2004, p.666). Thus the Security Council can be seen in this context to be a means by which the great powers maintain their primacy, and general order is maintained (Gowlland-Debbas, 2000, p.303). Changes in the nature of the powers exercised by the Security Council are therefore not initiated by the subjects of Security Council authority but rather constitute a conscious process designed to facilitate the P5's own agendas. Hence Jonathan Graubart argues that the Security Council's increased willingness to authorize interventions under Chapter VII in the 1990s was a means of 'legitimizing interventions of regional or global powers into the affairs of weaker, mostly Southern states' (2008, p.169). Likewise Vittorio Parsi suggests that the Security Council is itself dominated by the United States and hence Security Council action is a product of US power (2006, p.121).

Alternative authorities

The perceived limitations of the Security Council were manifest emphatically in March 1999 when NATO launched Operation Allied Force. NATO's actions were deemed 'illegal but legitimate' by the Independent International Commission on Kosovo, thereby confirming the gap between law and morality. The intervention appeared to some to confirm the redundancy of the Security Council (Welsh, 2006, p.182).

The lack of Security Council authorization for such an act of ostensible moral worth was deemed of secondary importance by those who, as discussed in Chapter 2, champion moral laws over temporal positive law. This perspective holds that actors need should not be constrained by the prevailing legal system from acting morally. As Terry Nardin argues,

> interventions should be approved by a recognized international authority acting in accordance with reasonably just international laws. But if such an authority does not exist or is substantially unjust or ineffective, either in general or in a given situation, states may act without its approval. Whether the United Nations is a just and effective international authority is a judgment that those contemplating intervention will have to make – and defend. (2003, p.23)

Such an approach does not eliminate the need for an authority *per se*, and alternative authorities to the Security Council have been advanced. Alternatives to the Security Council are examined below, although it is worth noting that there are many who argue that while the Security Council is fundamentally flawed and can thus occasionally legitimately be bypassed, such a situation does not require an alternative authority to the Council. They advocate a position, described as mitigation, whereby the law is broken, and the Council bypassed, but as the cause is just, the intervening party's case is deemed illegal but nonetheless tolerated (see Conclusion).

International morality

Disenchantment with the Council's approach to matters placed before it has led to calls from humanitarian activists to bypass the Council if it fails to discharge its duties (Evans, 2005, p.83). Evans acknowledges that this approach to Security Council authorization is inherently dangerous and potentially facilitates unilateralism of the kind witnessed in 2003 when the United States invaded Iraq. His counter-argument, however, is that the Just War theory comprises more criteria than just right authority, and so any action will be judged on the basis of its adherence to other criteria, and could be condemned on this basis (see Chapter 2). Similarly Alex Bellamy explicitly rejects reformulating positive law, instead advocating a policy orientated towards constructing criteria which will act as constraints on state action. If states abuse the new scope for intervention, global civil society will 'expose the abuse as such, and ... confront the perpetrators with the unjustness of their actions in order to constrain potential abusers through normative pressure at the domestic and international level' (2004, p.134).

Likewise Martha Nussbaum rejects the statist basis of international law. She argues that 'we should give our first moral allegiance to no mere form of government, no temporal power' but rather should pledge allegiance to 'the moral community made up by the humanity of all human beings' (Dallmayr, 2003, p.435). This perspective, central to cosmopolitanism (see Chapter 4), therefore asserts that action should be assessed on moral rather than legal grounds and judged by the international community rather than the unrepresentative and politically motivated P5.

Appeals to international morality are certainly attractive, and there is clearly merit to the suggestion that law is often an imperfect reflection of deeper universal moral norms. It is additionally difficult not to agree that international law as presently organized is deeply flawed (Franck, 2005, p.212). Yet, there are significant problems inherent in this perspective. Firstly, it is debatable whether beyond very broad parameters there is a universal moral code. There is much to suggest that moral pluralism exists, and hence how do we adjudicate between two genuinely different moral arguments? Beyond this obvious difficulty lies a greater problem. As Fred Dallmayr argues:

> Even assuming widespread acceptance of universal norms ... rules do not directly translate into praxis but require careful interpretation and application. At this point eminently political questions arise: who has the right of interpretation? And in cases of conflict: who is entitled to rule between different interpretations? This right or competence cannot simply be left to 'universal' theorists or intellectuals – in the absence of an explicitly political delegation or empowerment. (2003, p.434)

Thus universal agreement on basic moral principles does not necessarily achieve the aim of a consistently responsive, morally conscious international system. It is quite possible even for people who share a set of narrow moral codes to disagree about real-world events, as evidenced by the many differing perspectives within the world's religions. Contriving rules and codes on which all agree does not eliminate the need for some clear means by which disagreements regarding the implementation of these codes are resolved, and thus there is a recognised authority. The underlying dilemma intrinsic to humanitarian intervention is, Anthony Lang maintains, 'not one between amoral politicians and moralistic humanitarians, but one between competing moral claims' (2003, p.2).

Liberal hierarchy thesis

Linked to the idea of reliance on ostensibly universal moral principles is the view that certain states have a greater moral status than others. These states by virtue of their inherent moral legitimacy are championed as arbitrators of global affairs and hence are worthy of formal authority. This necessitates a form of proportionate equality among states, and adherents to this view, Christian Reus-Smit notes, 'advocate the formal rehierarchisation of international society, whereby democratic states would gain special governance rights – particularly with regard to the legitimate use of force and other states would have their categorical rights to self-determination and non-intervention qualified' (2005, p.72).

This 'liberal hierarchy thesis' asserts that liberal democracies are distinguished by characteristics such as their passivity towards one another, their constitutional commitment to the protection of civil and political rights, and their 'comparative moral reliability' (ibid., p.76). Given these characteristics, liberal democracies are the most advanced political actors and thus deserve special rights to adjudicate on international affairs.

There is evidence to suggest that certain prominent figures within Western states, and the United States in particular, adhere to this hierarchical vision. A central tenet of the national mythology of the United States is its ostensible 'manifest destiny' to spearhead progressive global change. Madeleine Albright, secretary of state under President Clinton, described the United States as the 'indispensable nation', and legitimized US leadership on the basis that 'we stand tall and we see further than other countries into the future' (Malone, 2006, p.13). Similarly President Bush justified launching the war on terror on the basis that 'This is the world's fight. This is civilisation's fight,' prosecuted on behalf of all 'civilised nations' (Kinsella, 2005, pp.181–2). As discussed in the concluding chapter, it has been suggested that a formal hierarchy of rights is particularly apposite with respect to humanitarian intervention, and that something akin to a 'concert of democracies' should be imbued with unique powers. The desired evolution of the norm of humanitarian intervention, it is argued, requires that progressive states explicitly usurp existing international law regarding the use of force for the protection of human rights, and ultimately fashion a new norm for others to follow. The liberal hierarchy thesis does not, therefore, advocate the development of a rigid two-tiered system, but rather a temporary hierarchy which will compel others to reform both their domestic system and foreign policy so as to gain advanced rights (Buchanan and Keohane, 2004; Elshtain, 2003b; Ikenberry and Slaughter, 2006, pp.25–6).

Western states are certainly characterized by an adherence to democracy and relatively advanced constitutional commitments to human rights. Nonetheless there is much counter-evidence which suggests that liberal democracies are motivated by self-interest and willing to ignore human rights when this is deemed necessary. The history of Western colonialism, variously legitimized as 'the white man's burden' and *mission civilisatrice*, testifies to how dangerous and easily abused the idea of moral hierarchy can be. Additionally, as noted in Chapter 4, even if states are genuinely motivated by a sense of moral purpose and believe themselves to be a force for good, action taken on this basis is inherently dangerous. Such a view is akin to zealotry and leads to implacable behaviour on the basis that dissent is irrational (Hurrell, 2005, p.25). Thus a sense of inflated moral standing and an attendant belief in one's own legitimacy to rule in defiance of the objections of 'lesser' moral actors threatens the assumption of a dictatorial disposition.

Reform of the Security Council

There is much evidence to suggest that there is widespread consensus on the need for some reform of the present international legal system and specifically the Security Council. This was a key aspect of the Millennium Declaration signed by all the world's states, and has featured in the recommendations of all major commissions into the working of the United Nations since 2000. Specifically in relation to humanitarian intervention it has been suggested that legal reform is required to enable more consistent and efficient enforcement of existing human rights laws (Simma, 1999, p.6), greater clarity regarding those violations of human rights that demand intervention (UN Commission on Global Governance, 1995, p.90) and also, more controversially, to legalize unilateral humanitarian intervention in the event of Security Council inaction (Burton, 1996).

The International Commission on Intervention and State Sovereignty (ICISS) asserted that the problem posed by humanitarian intervention necessitated not finding alternatives to the Security Council but rather initiating reforms to enable the Council to function more efficiently (2001, p.49). The ICISS warned that it was unrealistic to expect that states would not act in the event of Council inaction in the face of a humanitarian tragedy, and that if an intervention was undertaken without Council approval but subsequently deemed legitimate by the international community, this would have 'enduring serious consequences for the stature and credibility of the UN itself' (ibid., p.55). To prevent such a situation the

ICISS recommended that the Council agree a set of guidelines specifying when military intervention should take place, and additionally that the P5 commit to an agreement not to use their veto in matters of humanitarian need when their national interests are not involved.

As noted in Chapter 6, however, this 'code of conduct' for the P5 has been criticized as unrealistic and ultimately weak. At the 2005 World Summit the P5 rejected any proposals which would have limited their powers or their formal monopoly on the authorization of the use of force. Additionally the P5, and the United States in particular, refused to countenance any proposals that would have constrained their capacity to choose when to use force. In a letter to the President of the General Assembly prior to the World Summit, John Bolton suggested amending the section in the draft document regarding the responsibility to protect because 'we note that the Charter has never been interpreted as creating a legal obligation for Security Council members to support enforcement action in various cases involving serious breaches of international peace' (2005). The provisions related to humanitarian intervention in the final *Outcome Document* have done little to address the controversy surrounding who has the authority to take military action, and in effect constitute a reassertion of the status quo (Wheeler, 2005).

Given the failings of the Security Council it has been proposed that greater powers be devolved to the General Assembly. Jean Krasno and Mitushi Das suggest the *Uniting for Peace* provision (see Chapter 5) as a potential alternative to the Security Council. They note that this provision has been long overlooked and become 'essentially useless' (2008, p.186), but argue that it should be reconsidered and strengthened. The Assembly is certainly a more representative body than the Security Council, and has been to the fore in spearheading progressive human rights legislation. Yet, while processes that rely on the opinion of the international community of states are clearly more inclusive than the Security Council, they are not necessarily fairer (Lu, 2006, p.150).

More far-reaching structural legal reform has also been proposed in the form of the creation of a new body for judging the need for military intervention if the Security Council is deadlocked. David Held argues that the United Nations is inherently ineffective and there is a need for 'new bodies at the global level' independent of states (2005, p.25). He states, 'The establishment of an independent assembly of democratic peoples, directly elected by them and accountable to them, is an unavoidable institutional requirement' (ibid., p.273). Similarly Allan Buchanan and Robert O. Keohane have advocated the creation a new body with formal authority comprising 'a coalition of reasonably democratic states' (2004, p.18).

Creating a new body for such authorization, however, potentially flounders on the issue of troops (Wolf, 2005). While a new institution may well authorize an intervention it will have no independent military capacity and will therefore be reliant on states to supply their national forces. This has led to proposals for an international army of some kind (Watts, 2001, p.10). Clearly this would require wholesale reform of the existing system and is highly unlikely to come to pass. The major powers have demonstrated a pronounced unwillingness to countenance the creation of any body with the power to independently authorize force or develop an independent military capability (Thakur and Sidhu, 2006, p.6). In terms of a coalition of democracies, while this would clearly be favourable to the West, and hence highly unlikely to be supported by the developing world, it is not at all clear that Western states have any real appetite for substantive reform (Archibugi 2003, p.8).

More fundamental reform involves transforming the statist structure of both the international system and international law. Tom Woodhouse and Oliver Ramsbotham describe the United Nations as 'the creature of an unreconstructed system of sovereign nation states'. They argue that this present organizing principle is antithetical to human rights and thus reforms which do not address the primacy of the state will have limited impact as they do not reflect 'genuine cosmopolitan values' (Woodhouse and Ramsbotham, 2005, p.141). Such a perspective leads, in effect, towards a world state. This radical idea is widely rejected as undesirable; Kant argued that a universal state will quickly descend into a 'soulless despotism' and 'after crushing the germs of goodness, will finally lapse into anarchy'. David Rodin however rejects this diagnosis, arguing that a world state need not involve a centralized authority with extensive global power. Instead such an entity might comprise 'an extremely minimal form of sovereign power . . . [and] consist solely in the establishment of a world monopoly of military force with a minimal judicial mechanism for the resolution of international and internal disputes' (2002, pp.186–7).

Again this proposal is so radical that it is difficult to imagine how such change could ever evolve. Nonetheless we cannot discount the possibility of a major change to the structure of the international political and legal systems (Thompson 1992, p.94). Today's United Nations, World Bank and International Criminal Court would doubtless have seemed inconceivable to people in the 19th century. Parsi asserts, however, 'to consider a reform of the United Nations that could reduce the power of the United States is pure fantasy' (Parsi, 2006, p.118) and it is difficult to see how substantive change could occur without a seismic event such as a world war or global economic catastrophe that would obliterate the present system and the power asymmetries inherent in it.

Conclusion

To date the question 'who decides' has remained highly controversial, and it seems unlikely that a solution is imminent. This is unsurprising given that creating an international authority with the power to sanction intervention is such a sensitive issue. Yet, since the end of the Cold War, and especially after the genocide in Rwanda in 1994, an unprecedented momentum in favour of reform has been generated and it is therefore of significant concern that no resolution to this issue has been found in this context.

The UN Charter gives the Security Council significant powers but does not outline how the effectiveness of the Council should be measured (Cronin and Hurd, 2008, p.11). Thus, despite near universal agreement that the Council suffers from a legitimacy deficit and is not functioning as it should be, there is no obvious means by which this problem can be resolved (Gowlland-Debbas 2000, p.312). A vicious circle is thus created; the Council's lack of legitimacy continues to impact negatively on its effectiveness, which further erodes its legitimacy.

In an effort to overcome the Council's failings, alternative sources of authority have been championed. Those supportive of the reassertion of the Just War tradition and the application of common morality argue that this provides a universally applicable standard beyond the reach of politically motivated states. It is not clear, however, that the development and utilization of a moral framework such as the Just War tradition constitutes a viable solution to the 'who decides' question (Berman, 2007, p.163). Similarly the idea of empowering liberal democracies with unique rights suffers from the charge of subjectivity; on what objective, empirical basis can this group make a claim to deserve this authority? Such a hierarchy goes against the evolutionary trajectory of international law and is vehemently opposed by the majority of the world's states. It is also potentially very dangerous; this perspective is indicative of what Oliver Richmond describes as 'a liberal and cosmopolitan faith on the part of the interveners in the infallibility of their approach' (2005, p.90). Moral righteousness and zealotry have been the catalysts for some of the more destructive episodes in human history.

If the Security Council continues to be seen as no more than a desirable but discretionary stamp of approval, it is likely to become little more than a 'debating society' (Falk, 2005a, p.42). There are doubtless many who will not lament the demise of the Security Council, and there are few who advance unconditional support for its record and present composition. However, whatever our views on its performance and structure, the possible demise of the Security Council, must be a source of concern given the manifold lack of an obviously better alternative.

Questions

- How can we judge the legitimacy of a particular authority?
- What differentiates authority from power?
- What legal competencies are vested in the Security Council?
- Why does the Security Council suffer from a negative international image?
- Do you believe reform of the Security Council is required? If so what should such reform involve?

Further reading

On the question of legitimate authority

Berman, F. (2007) 'Moral Versus Legal Legitimacy', in C. Reed and D. Ryall (eds), *The Price of Peace* (Cambridge: Cambridge University Press).

Hurd, I. (2007) *After Anarchy: Legitimacy and Power in the United Nations Security Council* (Princeton, N.J.: Princeton University Press).

Hurrell, A. (2005) 'Legitimacy and the Use of Force: Can the Circle be Squared?' in D. Armstrong, T. Farrell and B. Maiguashca (eds), *Force and Legitimacy in World Politics* (Cambridge: Cambridge University Press).

International Commission on Intervention and State Sovereignty (2001) *The Responsibility to Protect* (Ottawa: International Development Research Centre), Chapter 6.

On UN reform

Annan, K. (2005a) *In Larger Freedom: Towards Development, Security and Human Rights for All*, UN document A/59/2005, 21 March [online] http://www.un.org/largerfreedom/ (accessed 2 May 2009).

Burton, M. (1996) 'Legalising the Sublegal', *Georgetown Law Journal*, 85, 417–54.

Chesterman, S. (2002) *Just War or Just Peace?* (Oxford: Oxford University Press), Chapter 6.

Cronin, B. and Hurd, I. (2008) *The UN Security Council and the Politics of International Authority* (London: Routledge).

Falk, R. (2005a) 'Legality and Legitimacy: The Quest for Principled Flexibility and Restraint', in D. Armstrong, T. Farrell and B. Maiguashca (eds), *Force and Legitimacy in World Politics* (Cambridge: Cambridge University Press).

Hehir, A. (2008) *Humanitarian Intervention after Kosovo: Iraq, Darfur and the Record of Global Civil Society* (Basingstoke and New York: Palgrave Macmillan), Chapter 7.

UN High-Level Panel on Threats, Challenges and Change (2004) *A More Secure World: Our Shared Responsibility*, 2 December [online] http://www.un.org/secureworld/report.pdf (accessed 2 May 2009).

Chapter 8

Motives and Means

One of the key areas of contestation in the debate on humanitarian intervention has been the importance of the intervener's motives. The Just War tradition puts a strong emphasis on right intention, but many modern analyses suggest that complete disinterest and purity of motives are unreasonably onerous requirements. They argue that actors will always have mixed motivations, and provided these motivations do not actively contradict humanitarianism they are unproblematic. Others go further, suggesting that motives are, in essence, irrelevant and that an intervention can be considered humanitarian even if the intervening party was motivated purely by self-interest provided the action had positive humanitarian consequences.

Additionally, further controversy surrounds the means employed during a humanitarian intervention. NATO's intervention in Kosovo in 1999 highlighted this dilemma: while certain observers supported the intervention they criticized the manner in which it was executed. There thus exists a tension between those who argue, largely in line with the *jus in bello* thinking outlined in Chapter 2, that the means used must be just, and that the interveners must be prepared to expose themselves to some risk, and those who maintain that a preference for force protection is acceptable.

This chapter begins with an analysis of the question of motives, initially highlighting the normative code presented by adherents to the Just War tradition. This section then proceeds to assess the arguments of those who maintain that the presence of interests is unproblematic or even irrelevant. The second section examines the differing perspectives on the issue of the appropriate means employed during a humanitarian intervention. While both international humanitarian law and the Just War tradition advance clear prohibitions on certain tactics, others maintain that states have a duty to privilege their own soldiers' lives above those of others, and ultimately, 'war is hell'.

Motives

On the day NATO launched air strikes against the Federal Republic of Yugoslavia, President Clinton outlined his motivations for taking action;

> We act to protect thousands of innocent people in Kosovo from a mounting military offensive ... we act to prevent a wider war, to

149

defuse a powder keg at the heart of Europe that has exploded twice before in this century with catastrophic results. By acting now, we are upholding our values. Ending this tragedy is a moral imperative. (Chatterjee and Scheid, 2003, p.6)

Many supported Operation Allied Force because of its purportedly humanitarian intent, but the articulation of a parallel security interest – 'to prevent a wider war' – highlighted that NATO was not motivated purely by the 'moral imperative'. For some this mixture of self-interest and altruism is troubling; would NATO have intervened in the absence of self-interest? We could point to notorious instances of non-intervention, in particular the genocide in Rwanda in 1994, to argue that national interests must be involved before any state will undertake an intervention. Yet, others counter that while some degree of national interest will always be involved, this does not preclude an intervention from being deemed humanitarian. Pure altruism is unrealistic, and an intervention can be described as humanitarian, provided it has positive humanitarian consequences. The following sections explore and analyse these contrasting positions.

The humanitarian imperative

As noted in Chapter 2, the origins of the Just War tradition are invariably traced back to the Christian Saints Ambrose, Augustine and later Aquinas. In contrast to the pacifist position of earlier Christians, these thinkers argued that there were occasions when violence, though always regrettable, was necessary. Amrose argued that Jesus' injunction to 'turn the other cheek' constituted a proscription on the use of force in self-defence, but Jesus did not disapprove of the use of force in defence of others. In fact Ambrose argued that the use of force to protect others was occasionally a duty, stating that 'he who does not keep harm off a friend, if he can, is as much in fault as he who causes it' (Bellamy, 2006b, p.24). Thus, provided the intention is altruistic the use of force is potentially just. This idea influenced Augustine, who stressed that the motivation driving a person to act in a particular way, including the use of force, was a key factor in determining the justness or otherwise of the act, and thus 'restraining men from sin' potentially justified the use of force (Deane, 1963, pp.164–5). Thus, the key concern for Augustine was 'the inward disposition that drove one to war' (Bellamy, 2006b, p. 27).

Aquinas also emphasized the importance of right intention, arguing that we must always intend to do good. Thus for Aquinas, 'merely having a just cause and legitimate authority is insufficient' (Holmes, 1992, p.200). Right intention and just cause are, therefore, separate criteria within the Just War tradition. This has significant implications for the judgment of 'just wars': such an emphasis on right intention potentially precludes certain purportedly 'humanitarian interventions'. If such actions were undertaken for the wrong reasons they would be potentially deemed unjust even if a humanitarian crisis had been occurring prior to, and was subsequently halted by, the intervention. So 'Right intention' as Bellamy states, 'stands at the very heart of the Just War tradition's justifications for killing' (2006b, p.122).

In the contemporary era, and arguably since the Second World War, interventions have invariably been justified, to some extent, as motivated by moral concerns. These justifications have often been spurious or very much secondary to the dominant geopolitical motivation. Some interventions, however, though motivated by self-interest have had positive humanitarian consequences: for example, Vietnam's invasion of Cambodia in 1978 (Wheeler, 2002, pp. 78–110). Those uncomfortable with applying the label 'humanitarian' to such interventions, where the positive humanitarian consequences of the act appear to be coincidental, have sought to distinguish between such action and true 'humanitarian intervention' by focusing on the intention of the intervening party. An essential quality of a humanitarian intervention for some, therefore, must be right intention. According to Miller, humanitarian intervention is 'a form of altruism writ large, a kind of self-sacrificial love' (2000a, p.54). While many of the definitions listed in Chapter 1 (see Box 1.2) refer to humanitarian motives, few ascribe to Miller's high ideal. Frank Berman argues that '[Altruism] is inherent in – or necessarily implied by – the fact that the justification for resorting to force is a humanitarian one' (2007, p.165). He additionally notes, however, that while a necessary component of a humanitarian intervention is that the stated aim of the intervener is humanitarian, such a claim may be cynical and must be objectively judged.

Bhikhu Parekh describes humanitarian intervention as an act 'wholly or primarily guided by the sentiment of humanity, compassion or fellow feeling, and in that sense disinterested' (Wheeler, 2003, p.194). This is a less stringent position on right intention; clearly the intention is important, and it must be at least the primary motivation, but it need not be the only motivation. Similarly to Parekh, the International Commission on Intervention and State Sovereignty (ICISS) argued that 'The primary purpose of the intervention, whatever other motives intervening states may have, must be to halt or avert human suffering' (2001, p.xii). They note that complete disinterestedness may be preferable but caution that 'mixed motives, in international relations as everywhere else, are a fact of life' (ibid., p.36). Nonetheless the primacy of right intention is asserted and thus, according to the ICISS, the ratio of right intention to self-interest must strongly favour the former.

In defence of interests

In contrast to those who argue that motives must be purely or even primarily humanitarian, there are many who assert that the motivations of the intervening party do not undermine the humanitarian aspect of an inter-vention even if there is compelling evidence that considerations of national interests were a major factor in the decision to intervene. Tony Blair's famous Doctrine of the International Community speech in April 1999 outlines the criteria he will assess before making a judgement on whether to intervene (see Box 8.1). As the final criterion makes clear, national interests must be involved before any action is taken.

Chris Brown describes as 'bizarre' the idea 'that actions can only be described as ethical if motives are absolutely pure' (2001, p.23) while according to Michael Walzer, 'Political motivations are always mixed . . . A pure moral will doesn't exist in political life, and it shouldn't be neces-sary to pretend that kind of purity' (2006, p. 26). The nature and centrality of right intention, as proffered by the Just War tradition, are therefore rejected. The fixation with 'pure' motives is seen by some as a distraction from the more important issue. According to Thomas Weiss, 'Looking for parsimony in motives does not really advance the discussion, because not all political motivations are evil. . . . While the ethical humanitarian ratio-nale need not be exclusive or even foremost, it should be explicit and prominent' (2007, p. 7).

Such a perspective rests on the belief that self-interest is not antithetical to moral action. For example, a person attends a fundraising dance in aid of a local homeless charity because they wish to meet their friends and enjoy themselves and because they know that doing so helps homeless people. The fact that this person's motivation for attending the dance was not purely, or even primarily, altruistic does not mean, many would

---

Box 8.1 'Doctrine of the International Community': Speech by UK Prime Minister Tony Blair, 24 April 1999

First, are we sure of our case? War is an imperfect instrument for righting humanitarian distress; but armed force is sometimes the only means of dealing with dictators. Second, have we exhausted all diplomatic options? We should always give peace every chance, as we have in the case of Kosovo. Third, on the basis of a practical assessment of the situation, are there military operations we can sensibly and prudently undertake? Fourth, are we prepared for the long term? . . . having made a commitment we cannot simply walk away once the fight is over. . . . And finally, do we have national interests involved? The mass expulsion of ethnic Albanians from Kosovo demanded the notice of the rest of the world. But it does make a difference that this is taking place in such a combustible part of Europe.
Source: Blair (1999).

argue, that this was not a humane act, as it had positive humanitarian consequences.

A further extension of this logic, however, holds that the motivation need not be altruistic in any way for the act, or intervention, to be deemed humanitarian. Nicholas Wheeler, in contrast to the Just War tradition, discounts right intention from the evaluation of whether a particular use of force qualifies as a humanitarian intervention. He argues that 'if an intervention is motivated by non-humanitarian reasons, it can still count as humanitarian provided that the motives and the means employed do not undermine a positive humanitarian outcome' (2002, p.38). Occasionally the use of force by states for reasons of self-interest, such as self-defence, has had positive humanitarian consequences, he argues, and these can therefore be considered humanitarian interventions. Wheeler points to India's intervention in East Pakistan in 1971, Vietnam's intervention in Cambodia in 1978 and Tanzania's intervention in Uganda in 1979 as evidence. In each case these interventions were acts of self-defence yet all resulted in significant humanitarian benefits (2003, p.195). Wheeler is satisfied if, as in the case of Vietnam's intervention in Cambodia, there is a 'happy – if purely inadvertent – coincidence among motives, means, and a positive humanitarian outcome' (2003, p.197). Similarly Fernando Tesón argues that non-humanitarian motives are not relevant and that the 'true test' is 'whether the intervention has put an end to human rights deprivations' (1998, pp.106–7).

Additionally some argue that self-interest is in fact a necessary component of any successful humanitarian intervention. According to Taylor Seybolt, states motivated to intervene purely by humanitarian concern are likely to withdraw their troops once they sustain casualties, whereas if there is some degree of national interest involved, such difficulties will be tolerated (2007, p.27). The Danish Institute of International Affairs (DIIA) similarly argues that 'states may need more than humanitarian motives to be willing to intervene in a substantial way' (1999, p.111). In fact, some argue that any state articulating a purely altruistic justification for the use of force is likely to meet with domestic opposition. In this sense it may be that justifications asserting some self-interest are in fact a cover for humanitarian justifications (Berman, 2007, p.166). Wheeler and Morris, indeed, argue that Tony Blair was forced to downplay his humanitarian intent in supporting the invasion of Iraq, and that this intent was a far greater influence on his support than he admitted prior to the invasion (2007, p.454).

It would certainly seem too onerous to argue that motivations must be purely altruistic to pass the right intention test. A degree of self-interest is perhaps inevitable, but what about pure self-interest? Returning to the first hypothetical example, the rationale behind hosting charity dances is that people are more likely to give money to charities if they receive something in return for their donation. It is perhaps unproblematic that certain people who attend these functions want to enjoy themselves while they help the homeless. However, it is less clear that acts can be deemed humanitarian if self-interest is the sole motivation. For example, we might wonder at the motivation driving certain celebrities to pay huge sums to attend Elton John's annual 'White Tie and Tiara Ball' to raise money for AIDS research; do they attend because of a genuine desire to support AIDS research, or do they want to enjoy a lavish party and be photographed by the media? Indeed, it could be argued that it would be easier, and more cost-effective, to simply donate the money without the huge expense. If we can be sure that a celebrity, whose fame is on the wane, is motivated to pay to attend this ball purely to achieve publicity and resurrect their career, then can we really describe them as 'charitably minded'?

To assert that uncovering *any* degree of national interest on the part of the intervening state automatically negates any possible humanitarian motivation seems extreme. Yet an exclusive focus on consequences is also problematic. For example, state A discovers that state B has huge oil reserves in its eastern provinces. State A invades state B and occupies these provinces to exploit the oil. The government in state B had previously been involved in a campaign of ethnic cleansing against the minority population of non-nationals in these oil-rich provinces, and this oppression ceases when state A assumes control. In this hypothetical situation, despite the fact that the actions of state A bring an end to ethnic cleansing, can we really describe this use of force as a humanitarian intervention? It would surely be more accurate to describe such action as a military intervention with positive humanitarian consequences. Clearly this is a semantic difference, but if humanitarian intervention is to have any distinct meaning, then motivations must surely be taken into account. Avoiding both extremes – absolute purity of motivation and the outright disregard for motivation – perhaps enables us to come to terms more accurately with the importance of right intention. As Anthony Lang argues, the motivation of the actor cannot be the sole factor analysed when assessing an intervention, but it must at least be one of the factors assessed (2003, p.3).

'He who invokes humanity wants to cheat'

The focus on intention is regarded by many as essentially a redundant exercise. As noted in Chapter 4, the realist and Marxist perspectives assert that the motivations of states are never altruistic, and thus agonizing over the balance between humanitarian intent and self-interest is a waste of time.

President Clinton outlined his intentions in intervening in Kosovo in often emphatically moralistic ways, claiming that the intervention was aimed at 'preventing another holocaust' and halting 'genocide at the heart of Europe' (Jackson, 2000, p.281). Yet Ellen Wood highlights one of Clinton's other statements which points to more selfish intents; 'If we're going to have a strong economic relationship that includes our ability to sell around the world, Europe has got to be a key ... that's what this Kosovo thing is all about.' Wood thus concludes, 'Forget humanitarian motives, this is all about US global hegemony' (2000, p.190). Few supporters of Operation Allied Force argue that NATO was entirely disinterested, and as noted earlier, many are unconcerned about these mixed motivations. For those such as Wood, however, there are always underlying selfish motivations driving states, and it is a question of uncovering these truths. Carl Schmitt's famous maxim, 'He who invokes humanity wants to cheat,' captures the essence of this suspicious, if not cynical, disposition (1996, p.54).

In their analysis of ten cases of intervention, the Research Directorate of the ICISS found 'the rhetoric of humanitarianism had been used most stridently in cases where the humanitarian motive was weakest' (Weiss, 2007, p.37). This is certainly a troubling finding, and clearly adds credence to the notion that there is a difference between states' claimed motivations and their actual motivations. The increased use of humanitarianism as a justification for Western foreign policy and Security Council interventionism in the post-Cold War era is thus seen by some as a cover for geopolitical aims (Graubart, 2008). According to Michael Wesley:

> interventionism gained momentum on the back of an interplay between norms and self-interest that allowed developed states to provide legitimating normative cover for interventions by casting developing states' weaknesses in terms of overarching and supposedly universal and economic, political, humanitarian and security principles. (2006, p.24)

Portraying foreign interventions as humanitarian ostensibly enabled states to justify the use of force in the absence of the 'Soviet threat'. The idea of fighting for human rights has meant, according to Anne Orford, that 'high-violence options . . . [are] . . . now once again marketable to citizens of the USA and other democracies' (2003, p.12).

This of course presupposes that domestic publics are ill-disposed to their states going to war for explicitly selfish reasons. There is much evidence to support this proposition particularly within the West. Even when the United States led a coalition against the Taliban in Afghanistan in response to the 11 September 2001 attacks, the use of force was justified on moral as well as security grounds. We might have assumed that the nature of the atrocities committed against the United States would have enabled the Bush administration to articulate a one-dimensional rationale for the intervention, but interestingly, it was evidently felt that a humanitarian rationale had to be additionally proffered (Hehir, 2008a, pp.57–9). Evidence suggests that the US domestic public is uncomfortable with a foreign policy based purely on self-interest (Cook, 2003, p.146; Wesley, 2006, p.43).

Thus for many the issue of motives is clear: states will only intervene if they have significant interests at stake or if they have no other option but to take action (Mueller, 2005, p.123). Wondering whether humanitarian motivations outweighed self-interest is thus a futile exercise as the latter will always outweigh the former. Humanitarian motivations are seen as either wholly cynical or entirely secondary.

If we expect absolute purity of motives, then clearly there has never been a humanitarian intervention. If we believe that mixed motives are inevitable, this record does not constitute the death of humanitarian intervention. Provided we accept that mixed motivations are inevitable and unproblematic, it is possible to reject the realist/Marxist critique as overly deterministic and empirically unsound. Indeed, why must we assume that all those involved in determining the foreign policy of states are necessarily unconcerned with morality or human rights? It is difficult to accept that upon assuming power, statesmen and stateswomen undergo a highly effective socialization process which filters all altruistic impulses. We can surely accept that those in power afford primacy to the national interest but prioritization need not be a zero sum game. Empirically, can we prove that Tony Blair lied consistently when he claimed that at least part of his reason for supporting the invasion of Iraq was the humanitarian benefits he believed would accrue? We may certainly form our own view about the extent to which this concern for the Iraqi people's freedom outweighed other motivations, but it is not possible to prove that Blair was actively unconcerned about the humanitarian motivations he so emphatically espoused – unless, of course, he admits this himself.

Means

The use of force by states, whether for humanitarian or selfish reasons, constitutes action that necessarily causes destruction and usually death. The laws of war – *jus in bello* – apply to all instances when force is used, but some argue that when force is used for ostensibly just or moral reasons, these rules acquire a unique importance. The Just War tradition comprises both *jus ad bellum* and *jus in bello*, and failure to adhere to the criteria in the latter undermines the justness of the entire intervention (see Chapter 2).

War is, however, conducted by the military rather than the government; while overall responsibility for ordering the use of force lies with the government of a state, the strategy employed is primarily determined by the army. This delegation of competencies, many argue, precludes the notion of a 'humanitarian war' because the intent of the military is always force protection and victory at any cost, hence the maxim *inter arma silent leges* (in the time of war the law is silent). Additionally, governments have demonstrated a pronounced unwillingness to agree to any military strategy that will endanger troops and potentially create domestic mobilization against the war.

'Bombing for humanity'

Attempts to outlaw the use of force are manifest in those tenets of international law that outlaw aggression and generally attempt to minimize the resort to violence. International law, however, does not prohibit the use of force in all circumstances; under Article 51 of the UN Charter states may legitimately use force if attacked, and Chapter VII of the Charter empowers the Security Council to sanction military action (see Chapter 5). The laws governing the use of force emerged in the 18th and 19th centuries when attempts to restrain the recourse to force were essentially abandoned, although restraints on the actual conduct of war were increasingly agreed, if not always honoured (Malanczuk, 2006, p.342). During this period the nature of war differed significantly from the 'total war' which evolved in the late 19th century, resulting in the heavy death toll of both World Wars in the 20th century. Previously wars were fought between armies with relatively little adverse consequences for civilians. Agreements and protocols such as the Lieber Code in 1863 and the three Hague conventions of 1899 sought to establish rules on the conduct of armies, such as the treatment of wounded soldiers and prisoners of war, and the prohibition on the use of certain weapons like gas and, for a time at least, aerial bombing (Laughland, 2002, p.44). International laws governing the permissible means by which states may wage war predate the laws outlawing the resort to force, but nonetheless are arguably the least respected aspect of international law. As Hersch Lauterpacht observes, 'if international law is, in some ways, at the vanishing point of law, the law of war is, perhaps even more conspicuously, at the vanishing point of international law' (1952, p.382).

For some the very idea of killing for human rights is an irreconcilable contradiction. Geoffrey Robertson, describing this as the 'Guernica paradox', asks, 'When can it be right to unleash terror on terrorists, to bomb for human rights, to kill to stop crimes against humanity?' (2002, p.402). As noted in Chapter 2, the Just War tradition argues that force is permissible under certain circumstances. A key aspect of the tradition, however, is those tenets contained within the *jus in bello* framework; discrimination (non-combatants should never be targeted); proportionality (targets should only be destroyed if their military value is greater than the destruction that will accrue); and observance of the laws of war. Implementation of these criteria is influenced by the doctrine of double effect, derived from the writings of Aquinas. This doctrine asserts that harmful consequences of military action can be excused if certain circumstances pertain (see Chapter 2, Box 2.3). Thus even the death of civilians does not fundamentally compromise the justness of a particular instance of the use of force provided the intention was just and the civilians were not deliberately targeted. This does not mean, however, that people can claim that killing civilians was justified for the greater good; Michael Walzer's argument that the destruction of Dresden and other German cities by Allied bombardment was excusable because this hastened the end of Nazism has been criticized as contrary to the Just War tradition because this consequentialist approach is explicitly rejected by the tradition (Brown, 2006, p.108). One may therefore both fight a Just War unjustly and an unjust war justly (MacMahon, 2005).

According to some, those claiming to be engaged in a humanitarian intervention have a greater duty to ensure that they adhere to the laws of war (Janzekovic, 2006, p.109; Hayden, 2005, p.90). The ICISS argues that in the course of a humanitarian intervention international humanitarian laws should be 'strictly' followed, and adds, 'an argument can be made that even higher standards should apply in these cases' (2001, p.37). The ICISS adapts the Just War tradition's *jus in bello* criteria, in outlining the permissible means by which war may be waged:

> The scale, duration and intensity of the planned military intervention should be the minimum necessary to secure the humanitarian objective in question. The means have to be commensurate with the ends, and in line with the magnitude of the original provocation. (2001, p.37)

Therefore, the means employed during a humanitarian intervention are regarded by some as exceptional, and of greater importance in the judgement of the intervention than the means employed during a traditional war. The following sections examine those counter-perspectives that argue that regardless of whether a war is fought for human rights, self-defence or acquisition, certain generic principles of military engagement will always prevail, and thus the means employed 'may not be a pretty sight' (Brown, 2006, p.154).

Force protection

'Countries that champion humanitarian values such as the USA,' according to Robert Jackson, 'are unwilling to risk the lives of their soldiers to defend human rights' (2000, p.289). While this may be something of an exaggeration, given that US troops have been killed during certain ostensibly humanitarian interventions, there is no denying that there is a clear reluctance to send troops abroad for humanitarian missions. Writing in 2000, future Secretary of State Condoleezza Rice stated that while 'there is nothing wrong with doing something which benefits all humanity', this is 'a second order effect' and American foreign policy should be based on the national interest (2000, p.47). During the 2000 US presidential election, candidates Al Gore and George W. Bush both endorsed President Clinton's decision not to send troops to Rwanda in 1994 (Wheeler, 2003, p.192). While Clinton himself has lamented this decision, it seems fair to conclude that presidential candidates, and indeed presidents, do not want to be seen as prepared to endanger the military by fighting wars on behalf of others. Rather, candidates aim to project a conservative vision for the use of force based on national interests.

While this disposition has led to much criticism it is not necessarily immoral, or even amoral, to prioritize the safety of one's own troops. According to Walzer, 'The leaders of states have a right, indeed they have an obligation, to consider the interests of their own people, even when they are acting to help other people' (2002, p.26). Martin Cook argues that individuals enter into a 'military contract' with their state when they join the army which obliges them to take risks and give their lives if necessary. Cook notes, however:

> They do these things on the basis of the implicit promise that the circumstances under which they must act are grounded in political leadership's good faith judgment that the defense of the sovereignty and integrity of the nation (or by careful extension, the nation's vital interests) requires their action. The farther a particular engagement or deployment departs from this clear contractual case, the more difficult it is for political leadership to offer moral and political justification for any killing and especially dying that their military forces experience. (2003, pp.150–1)

Seen from this perspective the unwillingness of Western states to, for example, deploy troops in Rwanda in 1994 or Darfur in 2004 potentially drew on a reasonable appraisal of the likely consequences of such an intervention. The lesson of the US-led intervention in Somalia in 1992 appeared to be that the US domestic public had little appetite for sustaining casualties on behalf of a state thousands of miles away. This led to the so-called 'viet-malia' syndrome, whereby US policy makers, conscious of the effects of the interventions in both Vietnam and Somalia, developed a great reluctance to order troops oversees (Hehir, 2006, p.74).

The United States, though supportive of the idea of humanitarian intervention, has been clearly unwilling to countenance any external control over US troops. Presidential Directive 25 (see Box 8.2), issued five months after the deaths of 19 Rangers in Mogadishu in 1993, emphasizes the preference for independent control and selectivity, and this logic continues to guide US policy, as well as that of arguably the vast majority of states (Cook 2003, p.149). This determination to maintain control over the deployment and use of one's own forces derives in large part from the fact that troop casualties create domestic unease. So long as the state retains command over the

Box 8.2 Presidential Directive 25 (PDD-25), 1994: 'The Clinton Administration's Policy on Reforming Multilateral Peace Operations'

The President retains and will never relinquish command authority over U.S. forces. On a case by case basis, the President will consider placing appropriate U.S. forces under the operational control of a competent UN commander for specific UN operations authorized by the Security Council. The greater the U.S. military role, the less likely it will be that the U.S. will agree to have a UN commander exercise overall operational control over U.S. forces. Any large scale participation of U.S. forces in a major peace enforcement mission that is likely to involve combat should ordinarily be conducted under U.S. command and operational control or through competent regional organizations such as NATO or ad hoc coalition.

Source: Cook (2003, p.147).

deployment of its troops, it can minimize potential domestic uproar. Thus in 1994 the United States was able to pull its troops out of Somalia when public support for the operation plummeted, and during the intervention in Kosovo the United States was able to resist calls for the deployment of ground troops, thereby minimizing potential US casualties.

Therefore given the not necessarily immoral preference for force protection among states, the normative guidelines and international laws governing the means employed during an intervention are likely to be afforded secondary importance. The challenge posed by humanitarian intervention, according to Wheeler, is 'to find a strategy that protects civilians without exposing military personnel to excessive dangers' (2003, p.194).

'War is hell'

Peacekeeping troops are deployed with a mandate to keep the peace and not to kill, but such missions differ fundamentally from humanitarian interventions because they are undertaken with the consent of the host state. Humanitarian interventions by definition are not launched with the approval of the host state, and therefore conflict is inevitable (see Chapter 1). Once we accept that military force is going to be used, we may have to accept that a 'win at all costs' mentality assumes primacy, and the result will be disagreeable (Boucher, 1998, p.62; Myers, 1996, p.119). Carl von Clausewitz, the 19th-century military strategist and historian, argued that 'We can never introduce a modifying principle into the philosophy of war without committing an absurdity' (quoted in Walzer, 1992, p.23), thereby suggesting that once war begins, restraint is impractical (see Box 8.3).

> ## Box 8.3 'the violence and the lethality and the destruction . . .'
>
> The speed and the violence and the lethality and the destruction that is going to occur is beyond anything that you can imagine. If, indeed, you're not going to accept my terms, we need to break this meeting right now. I suggest you go outside, get into your car and ride around the city of Belgrade. Remember it the way it is today. If you force me to go to war against you, Belgrade will never look that way again – never in your life-time, or your children's lifetime. Belgrade and your country will be destroyed if you force me to go to war.
>
> Source: Lieutenant General Michael Short, United States Air Force, commander of the air com-ponent of Operation Allied Force, in negotiations with Yugoslav military officers October 1998 (quoted in Shue, 2003, p.110).

Even though humanitarian intervention is different from self-defence and wars for acquisition, there are certain similarities. A state intervenes with the aim of deploying sufficient military power to force another to behave a certain way. Brown contends, therefore that 'effective humanitarian intervention' constitutes:

> an act of power; it involves taking sides, choosing which of the various parties to support and enforcing one's choice by superior strength. . . . the behavior of the successful intervener may not be particularly attrac-tive, and may indeed involve temporarily contributing to humanitarian distress. (2006, p. 154)

Therefore much as we may wince at the idea of 'bombing for humanity' and implore armies to show particular restraint when engaged in such mis-sions, it is possibly naïve to expect that such considerations will factor in the strategy of intervening forces. This contrast between *jus ad bellum* and *jus in bello* were arguably manifest most emphatically during NATO's intervention in Kosovo in 1999 (see Chapter 11). During Operation Allied Force the UN High Commissioner for Human Rights, Mary Robinson, criticized NATO's methods and, highlighting the general dangers of unilat-eralism, stated that 'NATO remains the sole judge of what is or is not acceptable to bomb' (Roberts, 1999, p.114).

According to George Lucas, humanitarian interventions 'are seriously compromised if the intervening forces themselves deliberately, or even inadvertently, behave unjustly, violate rights, infringe liberty, or destroy the rule of law' (2003, p.77). If we endorse this view, which is indeed embedded in the Just War tradition, then it appears clear that NATO's tac-tics, particularly the strategy of undertaking military action by bombing from 15,000 feet, compromised the purportedly 'humanitarian' nature of their intervention. According to David Rieff, the use of humanitarian rhetoric by NATO during its intervention in Kosovo 'constituted one more demonstration of Napoleon's maxim that in war the moral was to the material as three to one' (2004, pp. 292–3).

Of course, as noted earlier, we could argue that force protection is both a necessity and a duty. As Michael Ignatieff has argued, however, the danger is that this kind of risk-free, or 'virtual', warfare will desensitize the domestic public within the intervening state and increase the propensity to use force (2000, pp. 179–80). What appears to be clear from the example of NATO's operation in Kosovo is that even interventions undertaken for high ideals will be prosecuted according to generic rules of military engagement which appear to afford little consideration to normative moral codes or even international humanitarian law. This is, of course, a troubling finding for anyone supportive of humanitarian intervention.

Conclusion

Despite the protestations of those who disavow the importance of motives, the motivation behind an intervention, particularly a purportedly humanitarian intervention, will inevitably be taken into consideration when people come to judge the merits of a particular instance of the use of force. It seems unrealistic to expect that a putative humanitarian intervention must be motivated purely by altruism. We are thus faced with the problem of trying to determine a means by which we can assess the place of humanitarianism within a hierarchy of motives. We can only do this, of course, if we believe statesmen and stateswomen when they say that they were motivated to some extent by 'moral imperatives'. Clearly realists and Marxists reject this very premise on the basis that morality is not a factor in the foreign policy of states; only national interest prevails, although certain realists argue that the pursuit of the national interest is a moral aspiration (Morgenthau, 1951). Hedley Bull, instinctively sceptical and critical of humanitarian intervention, rejects the idea that asserting the dominance of national interest forecloses all debate about moral intent. This belief in the dominance of national interest, he argues, 'does not even provide a basis for distinguishing moral or ideological considerations in a country's foreign policy from non-moral or non-ideological ones' (2002, p.63). It may be possible that humanitarianism becomes part of the national interest (Pasic and Weiss, 2003, p. 108). We shall doubtless continue to disagree whether the espousal of humanitarian intent in any given case was the 'true' motivation.

Writing in the 19th century Clausewitz claimed that the laws of war are 'almost imperceptible and hardly worth mentioning' (Malanczuk, 2006, p.343). This statement appears to have some ongoing credence given the scale of atrocities and war crimes committed in the period since then. What is perhaps more dispiriting, however, is that this appears to apply even to ostensibly humanitarian interventions. Robertson notes, 'As with modern war of any kind, the result of NATO's bombing [in 1999] was tragedy and terror, the greatest anguish being that much of it was inflicted on the very people that the West had intervened to save' (2002, p.402). States perhaps justifiably retain a pronounced unwillingness to risk their soldiers' lives on behalf of others. Cook argues that until international organizations develop their own military capacity, 'humanitarian intervention and peace-keeping operations will be piecemeal, inconsistent, and dependent on coalitions of the willing. They will be (and morally need to be) risk averse and highly focused on force protection' (2003, p.152).

While the reluctance to put troops in harm's way may appear immoral in light of some of the horrifying humanitarian tragedies that have occurred in the past 20 years alone, it is worth nothing that this reluctance is born in no small part from prudential reasoning, and the sense that domestic publics have a very limited tolerance for casualties and expenditure in the cause of 'saving strangers'. The United States' withdrawal from Somalia in 1994 was, to a large extent, a consequence of the domestic backlash against the deployment following the deaths of 19 troops in October 1993 in Mogadishu (Mayall, 2006, pp. 132–5). It is therefore far from certain that the reluctance to put troops in harm's way is solely a function of unwillingness at the governmental level.

Questions

- Can we expect states to behave in purely altruistic ways in their international affairs?
- Does the presence of some self-interested motivations disqualify an intervention from being described as humanitarian?
- Do states have a duty to always act in the national interest?
- Is 'bombing for humanity' an oxymoron?
- Must states risk their own troops if they are to undertake a humanitarian intervention?

Further reading

Bellamy, A. (2006) *Just Wars: From Cicero to Iraq* (London: Polity), Chapter 6.
Chomsky, N. (1999) *The New Military Humanism: Lessons from Kosovo* (London: Pluto), Chapter 1.
Cook, M. (2003) '"Immaculate War': Constraints on Humanitarian Intervention',

in A. Lang (ed.). *Just Intervention* (Washington DC: Georgetown University Press).

Ignatieff, M. (2000) *Virtual War: Kosovo and Beyond* (New York: Picador), Chapter 8.

International Commission on Intervention and State Sovereignty (ICISS) (2001) *The Responsibility to Protect* (Ottawa: International Development Research Centre), Chapter 4.

Robertson, G. (2002) *Crimes Against Humanity* (London: Penguin), Chapter 11.

Walzer, M. (1992) *Just and Unjust Wars* (New York: Basic Books), Chapters 7 and 8.

Wheeler, N. (2002) *Saving Strangers* (Oxford: Oxford University Press), Chapter 1.

Part III

Cases

Chapter 9

Humanitarian Intervention in History

The resort to war has always been justified by its instigators, although these justifications have not always been based on ethical claims. The attempt to legitimize the use of force on ethical and moral grounds distinguishes 'just wars' from strategic warfare. The Athenians' justification for their invasion of Melos during the Peloponnesian War (431–404 BC) (see Box 9.1) was based solely on what the Athenians considered to be an immutable law of nature; the strong do what they can and the weak suffer what they must. While in the modern era this rationale has rarely been advanced in such emphatic (and honest) terms, realists maintain that the logic of power lies behind all military actions (see Chapter 4).

Whether realists are correct is certainly debatable; what is clear, however, is that at certain times in history states have advanced ethical arguments as justification for military action. The Just War tradition has evolved as an attempt to create a framework for discussion about the legitimate grounds on which force may be used (see Chapter 2). The contemporary debate surrounding humanitarian intervention can, therefore, be seen as the latest manifestation of this attempt to evaluate the ethical claims advanced by states for their use of force.

This chapter provides a (necessarily) brief overview of the history of humanitarian intervention – with a particular focus on the post-Second World War era – building on the more extensive treatment of the evolution

Box 9.1 The Melian dialogue

Our opinion of the gods and our knowledge of men lead us to conclude that it is a general and necessary law of nature to rule whatever one can. This is not a law that we made ourselves, nor were we the first to act upon it when it was made. We found it already in existence, and we shall leave it to exist for ever among those who come after us. We are merely acting in accordance with it, and we know that you or anybody else with the same power as ours would be acting in precisely the same way.

Source: Thucydides (1972, pp. 404–5).

of humanitarian intervention in the chapters in Part I of the book. It identifies the evolution of international attitudes towards humanitarian intervention and provides contextual insight to explain these trends. This chapter demonstrates that in the overwhelming majority of cases, states undertaking purportedly humanitarian interventions have had some significant national interest at stake. Additionally, where there has been no clear national interest there has been no intervention regardless of the scale of the suffering involved.

Humanitarian Intervention: trends and changes

Humanitarian intervention was the primary issue in international relations in the immediate post-Cold War era and, though its pre-eminence has undoubtedly waned in the wake of the 11 September 2001 attacks, it continues to influence the international political agenda. The contemporary currency of this issue, however, should not obscure its historical lineage. Though the actors and international context may well have changed, this issue has been debated for centuries, and if we conceive of humanitarian intervention as derived from the Just War tradition, which many do, then the issue dates back over two millennia (Bellamy, 2006b).

The state and the evolution of humanitarian intervention

The contemporary controversy surrounding humanitarian intervention can only be understood, as Simon Chesterman notes, in the context of the transformation of international law in the 19th century and the emergence of positive legal doctrine, specifically the notion of non-interference (2002, pp.7–8). The term 'humanitarian intervention' was first used by William Edward Hall in 1880, though similar expressions had been employed earlier in the 19th century (Chesterman, 2002, pp. 23–4). Following the expansive codification of international law in the 19th, and especially the 20th, centuries, an act of intervention could not be readily justified according to positive international law unless in self-defence. Hence, interventions were at various times justified as expressions of 'moral norms' or 'natural laws' which ostensibly transcended or preceded legal doctrine. Chapter 5 outlines the evolution and nature of the legal proscriptions against the use of force and how these codes have impacted on the legitimacy of a given intervention.

When people speak of the controversy surrounding humanitarian intervention they therefore speak of the clash between two codes, one legal, the other moral. Questions regarding the morality of war have been posed for thousands of years, but while this Just War tradition certainly informs contemporary debates about humanitarian intervention, Just War thinking is an explicitly moral evaluation of the use of force and one that is not confined to the question of helping those in other states. Humanitarian intervention, therefore, is a controversy derived from the emergence of positive law in the 19th century and especially the codification of sovereign inviolability.

Boxes 9.2 and 9.3 comprise a chronology of key events in the 19th and 20th centuries which have come to form part of the historical narrative of humanitarian intervention. It is important to note, however, that the vast majority of interventions listed are not widely considered to have been genuine humanitarian interventions. Chesterman notes that the examples provided by those authors seeking to claim that humanitarian interventions did occur prior to the UN Charter have had motives retrospectively attributed

---

Box 9.2 A chronology of humanitarian intervention: 1827–1939

1827	Great Britain, France and Russia attack the Ottoman Empire at the Battle of Navarino ostensibly to aid Greek insurgents. British and French motives include a desire to prevent Russia from gaining strategic advantage in the region.
1860–1	France occupies Syria following the deaths of thousands of Maronite Christians. An earlier intervention by Turkey is largely responsible for the eventual end of the oppression.
1877–8	Russia declares war on the Ottoman Empire supposedly to protect Christians in Bosnia, Herzegovina and Bulgaria. Widely believed that the intervention was actually motivated by Russian desire to acquire new territory in the Balkans.
1898	The United States invades Cuba during its war with Spain. Some 200,000 Cubans had died in Spanish concentration camps since 1895. Seen as the closest example to humanitarian intervention in the pre-Charter era.
1900	The United States and Great Britain intervene in China during the Boxer Rebellion ostensibly to protect nationals. Their shared desire to maintain trade links with China is more likely to have been the primary impetus.
1904–17	France, the United States and others call on Turkey to cease oppression of the Armenians. No intervention occurs and one million Armenians are killed.
1913	Bulgaria, Greece and Serbia invade Macedonia ostensibly to protect Christians although few endorse these claims.
1939	Germany invades Czechoslovakia ostensibly to protect the German minority. Hitler's claims of Czech oppression are widely discounted.

Box 9.3 A chronology of humanitarian intervention since the Second World War

1971   India invades West and East Pakistan (Bangladesh) following air strikes launched by the Pakistani government. India also claims to be acting in defence of the people of East Pakistan, one million of whom had been killed by the West Pakistani military in the previous year. Neither the UN Security Council nor the UN General Assembly explicitly support or condemn the intervention.

1978   Following border skirmishes Vietnam invades Cambodia with the support of the United Front for National Salvation of Kampuchea. Pol Pot, responsible for the deaths of a million or more people, is eventually overthrown. Vietnam claims to be acting in self-defence. The Soviet veto blocks a Security Council resolution, supported by the United States, United Kingdom, France and China, condemning Vietnamese 'aggression'.

1979   Tanzania invades Uganda following Uganda's attempted annexation of the Tanzanian province of Kagera. With the support of Ugandan exiles the Tanzanian army overthrows Idi Amin. Neither the Security Council nor the UN General Assembly explicitly support or condemn the intervention.

1991   To enable the provision of humanitarian aid to Kurds in Northern Iraq the United States, United Kingdom and France impose 'No-Fly' zone restrictions on the Iraqi air force and station some 20,000 troops to guard 'safe havens' in the region.

1992   The UN Security Council passes Resolution 794 characterizing the situation in Somalia as a 'threat to international peace and stability' and sanctions the deployment of a US-led military force. Following the deaths of 18 soldiers the United States pulls out in March 1994.

1993–5 In April 1993 the United Nations establishes 'safe areas' around five Bosnian towns. In July 1995 Srebrenica is overrun by Bosnian

⁢⁣⁣⁣➤

to them that were not articulated at the time (2002, p.25). Additionally, Anthony Arend and Robert Beck's analysis of interventions during the Cold War concludes that there were no examples of a genuine humanitarian intervention, nor did any state proffer a legal claim based exclusively on humanitarian justifications (1993, p.137). In the post-Cold War era, however, the record appears less definitive. Since 1991, with the establishment of no-fly zones over Iraq, a number of cases have challenged the preceding historical narrative. The interventions in Somalia (1992) and Kosovo (1999) in particular, have been identified by some as indicative of a new willingness

	Serbs and some 7000 civilians are killed. In August 1995 NATO launches air strikes against the Bosnian Serb military.
1994	Despite extensive media coverage, and pleas from UN officials within Rwanda, 800,000 people are slaughtered by Hutus in 100 days.
1999	NATO launches Operation Allied Force against the Federal Republic of Yugoslavia, claiming to be acting to protect Kosovo's ethnic Albanians. The intervention is neither condoned nor condemned by the UN Security Council and while it is widely supported in the West. China, Russia and the G-77 condemn the action.
1999	Australia leads a UN-mandated force into East Timor to restore order following an referendum on independence. Indonesia consents to the intervention.
2001	The United States launches Operation Enduring Freedom against Afghanistan. Great emphasis is placed on justifying the intervention on humanitarian grounds.
2003	The United States launches Operation Iraqi Freedom, citing the emancipation of Iraq's citizens as one of its goals. As the claims regarding Iraqi weapons of mass destruction prove false, the humanitarian aims are retrospectively inflated.
2003	Government-sponsored militias carry out massacres in Darfur, Sudan. Despite numerous UN reports throughout 2003–04 no intervention takes place. By 2007 the United Nations claims some 450,000 people have died.
2008	Protests by Buddhist monks in Burma are violently repressed by the ruling military junta, leading to calls for external intervention though no action is taken.
2008	President Mugabe of Zimbabwe is accused of initiating the nation-wide oppression of opposition party supporters and activists. Many NGOs call for external intervention although a power-sharing deal brokered by South Africa leads to fragile peace.

to undertake humanitarian interventions. This view is disputed, however, and it is the intensity of this dispute, and the importance of the issues involved, which have propelled humanitarian intervention from the periphery to the very centre of contemporary international relations.

Humanitarian intervention in historical context

The growth of interest in humanitarian intervention in the post-Cold War era is often erroneously portrayed as evidence of an unprecedented disposition amongst states to act morally. In fact states have offered humanitarian justifications for their actions for centuries. Martin Cook notes that the United States 'has always tended to speak in universalizing terms of fighting wars to end all wars, advancing human rights and democratic political order, and opposing tyranny and despotism' (2003, p.146). As discussed in Chapters 3 and 6, the emergence of the modern sovereign state in the 17th century sharpened the humanitarian intervention debate, as clear legal and political distinctions were made between states and individuals. The primacy of non-intervention necessarily contrived against cross-border humanitarian action yet, paradoxically, as the non-intervention norm grew it compelled states undertaking interventions to contrive a humanitarian rationale for their actions.

Colonialism was routinely justified as beneficial to the 'savages' and portrayed as 'the white man's burden' or, in French, *mission civilatrice*. Similarly James Tyner highlights the historical tendency of the United States to justify its expansion in humanitarian terms. Following the annexation of 50 per cent of the territory of Mexico in 1848, President James Polk argued that had these territories remained part of Mexico they would have been 'little value to her or any nation, while as part of our Union they will be productive of vast benefits to the United States, to the commercial world, and the general interests of mankind'. President William McKinley stated on ordering the intervention in the Philippines in 1899, 'We intervene not for conquest. We intervene for humanity's sake [and to] earn the praises of every lover of freedom the world over' (Tyner, 2006, p.35–6).

In the modern era the debate about humanitarian intervention has been shaped by the framework of modern international law established in 1945 with the birth of the United Nations. The horror of the Holocaust catalyzed significant new developments in international law and international organizations designed, at least to some extent, to ensure that egregious intra-state human rights violations could be prevented or at least halted by the international community. The United Nations statement of purposes included a commitment 'to save succeeding generations from the scourge of war' and 'reaffirm faith in fundamental human rights'. Rhetorical support for human rights, however, is one thing; implementing measures to constrain the capacity of states in this regard is quite another. States may well have routinely espoused their support for the idea of human rights, but they have also consistently rejected measures which they deem an infringement of their sovereignty. For example, Antonio Cassese notes that the United States was one of the most vocal proponents for the inclusion of human rights in the Charter. Yet, once this was accepted the United States became one of the more cautious voices during the drafting process, not least because of its racist domestic laws at that time (Cassese, 2005, pp.377–8).

During the Cold War the norm of non-intervention was championed by the many newly independent states that saw sovereign inviolability as a bulwark against external interference. The International Court of Justice (ICJ) ruled on two cases during the Cold War that involved assessing the legality of humanitarian intervention: in both the *Corfu Channel* case in 1949 and *Nicaragua v. United States* in 1986 the ICJ came down in favour of the principle of non-intervention (see Chapter 5). In legal terms, therefore, the principle of non-intervention maintained primacy throughout the Cold War, although the political context was less absolute. While the norm of non-intervention was periodically abused by the rival superpowers, Robert Jackson notes that both the United States and the Soviet Union always sought to justify their interventions to the wider international community as something more than pure *realpolitik* as they 'could not arbitrarily cast the conventional morality of international society aside' (2000, p.254).

Thomas Franck notes that when India invaded East Pakistan in 1971 it claimed to be doing so primarily on the basis of self-defence but it also, though less vocally, justified the intervention as an act of humanity. Despite the fact that it was clear that India's actions had brought an end to a humanitarian crisis and facilitated the eventual independence of Bangladesh, the international community of states overwhelmingly condemned the action. These states, Franck claims, 'felt directly threatened: not by the action itself, which elicited widespread sympathy, but by a precedent that appeared to condone the invasion of a country by a more powerful one' (2005, p.217).

In December 1978 Vietnam invaded Cambodia, bringing an end to the genocidal regime of Pol Pot's Khmer Rouge. Like India in 1971 Vietnam claimed to be acting in self-defence, and attributed the overthrow of the Khmer Rouge to an indigenous uprising. While there was some basis for the self-defence justification, the 'two wars' idea was widely rejected and seen as a means by which the Vietnamese could justify not only taking military action to defend itself but also the more contentious decision to remove Pol Pot's regime (Wheeler, 2002, p.88). Wheeler notes that Vietnam distanced itself from any formal humanitarian justifications, though it did describe the Khmer Rouge regime as 'inhuman' and 'monstrous' (2002, p.88). Vietnam's justifications for its use of force were greeted unfavourably within the United Nations, and for years after the General Assembly continued to recognize the Khmer Rouge as the rightful government of Vietnam, despite the evidence that over a million Cambodians had been killed by the government from 1975–9. Suspicions about Vietnam's motivations and its links to the Soviet Union contributed to the international opprobrium which followed the intervention.

In April 1979 Tanzania invaded Uganda and toppled the regime of Idi Amin. The international community 'responded with mute, but evident, satisfaction' (Franck, 2005, p.219), though there were some dissenting voices (Jackson, 2000, p.259; Wheeler, 2002, pp.122–32). The nature of Amin's regime and the democratic credentials of President Julius Nyerere of Tanzania facilitated this reaction, as did the fact that Tanzania justified its intervention as an act of self-defence – Ugandan forces had indeed invaded Tanzania first – so as to assuage fears that a precedent would be set. This tacit support for Tanzania's actions is evidence of what Adam Roberts describes as the 'trends and disjointed moves [during the Cold War] which pointed, often ambiguously and always controversially, in the direction of accepting the legitimacy of intervention in support of an oppressed and threatened population' (2006, p.80).

Clearly the different reactions to the Vietnamese and Tanzanian actions suggested that the context and the actors involved influenced international reaction to intervention more than the humanitarian consequences of the action. Likewise the United Nations was willing to acquiesce when the Economic Community of West African States Monitoring Group (ECOMOG) militarily intervened in Liberia in 1989 and again in Sierra Leone in 1997, despite the fact that these actions did not have explicit UN authorization at the time they were launched.

As discussed in Chapter 6, many felt that the structural changes wrought by the end of the Cold War provided the context within which humanitarian intervention could become a more established and consistent practice in international relations. The UN-sanctioned action against Iraq's invasion of Kuwait in 1991 and the subsequent intervention to protect the Kurds and Shiites in northern and southern Iraq suggested that this optimism was well founded. Apart from earlier resolutions on Rhodesia and South Africa in 1977, Resolution 688 which sanctioned the collective use of force against Iraq was the first time the Security Council had described a humanitarian crisis as a threat to international peace and stability (Malone, 2006, p.88). The action of the Security Council in this instance, coupled with the deployment of UN-mandated troops to Somalia in 1992, led to further optimism about the future of humanitarian intervention, and as Michael Smith notes, 'from about 1991–1993, there existed a sort of Dudley Do-Right euphoria' (1998, p.66). The Security Council mandated an unprecedented number of interventions under Chapter VII in the 1990s, further suggesting that a new humanitarian dispensation had achieved ascendancy.

The United Nations, to the dismay of many in the developing world, thus appeared to be changing from an organization committed to the principles of non-intervention and the non-use of force into one associated with forceful intervention (Roberts, 2006, p.71). As explored in Chapter 5, however, even these Security Council-mandated actions in the 1990s evidenced a strong correlation between action taken and the national interests of the P5. The intervention in Haiti in 1994, for example, appeared on one level to herald a new intolerance of military coups against democratically elected governments. In fact the United States had an interest in stemming the flow of refugees from Haiti, while China agreed to the operation because the United States promised it support for a World Bank loan (Voeten, 2008, p.51). The response of the international community to the genocide in Rwanda and the ethnic cleansing in the former Yugoslavia also dashed nascent hopes that there was a new will to act to halt suffering. Additionally the United States' retreat from Somalia in 1993 suggested that any commitment that did exist was shallow. Increased interventionism by the Security Council since 1991, Roberts cautions (2006, pp.96–7), has additionally led to a number of 'worrying developments' which have negatively impacted on international peace and security (see Box 9.4) As Roberts' analysis highlights, many developing world states have greeted the increasingly active role of the United Nations with both disappointment and concern.

At the end of the 1990s, however, the intervention by NATO in Kosovo reinvigorated the optimists. Here, it seemed, was a case where states had transcended both their narrow national interests and the restrictive provisions of international law to halt suffering (see Chapter 11). The fact that the intervention was technically illegal but widely seen as legitimate dealt a blow to the system of international law and the credibility of the United

---

Box 9.4 Six 'worrying developments arising from the practice of intervention since 1991'

1 ... the great majority of member states, having long seen the United Nations as an institution in which their sovereignty can be protected, are worried about any doctrine or practice that would challenge that vital UN function.
2 ... states may augment their national armaments to reduce their vulnerability to intervention ...
3 ... there is a risk of the UN building up expectations of its capacity to protect threatened civilians, only to preside once again over another Rwanda.
4 ... actual cases of humanitarian intervention leave the UN having to manage a series of difficult territories.
5 [Disputes over this issue add] to the mutual suspicion among states.
6 ... the governments of many developing countries suspect that the Western powers have down played the economic and social agenda ... because of their preoccupation with the peace and security agenda in general and military interventions in particular.

Source: Roberts (2006, pp.96–7).

Nations itself, as both appeared anachronistic and unacceptably restrictive. According to Jennifer Welsh 'Historians may come to view the Kosovo intervention as the first step on the road to a post Security Council era' (2006, p.182). Operation Allied Force sparked renewed interest in humanitarian intervention and led directly to the International Commission on Intervention and State Sovereignty (ICISS) report *The Responsibility to Protect* (ICISS, 2001), which claimed to constitute a new formulation for the relationship between states, their citizens and the international community (see Chapter 6). This report undoubtedly had, and continues to have, an impact on the humanitarian intervention debate (Bellamy, 2009a; Evans, 2008), though the events of 11 September 2001 displaced this issue from the top of the international political agenda.

In recent years the crisis in Darfur and the invasion of Iraq have further eroded optimism in humanitarian intervention. Many have lamented that Darfur is evidence that nothing has changed since Rwanda, and that state interest remains the primary factor in determining when and where states will intervene (see Chapter 13). Iraq has arguably had much more of a negative impact, increasing scepticism towards any humanitarian claims made by intervening states. It seems clear that the appetite for international military intervention within the United States has dissipated, and the fear of 'another Iraq' is pervasive. According to John Mueller, the United States now suffers from 'the Iraq Syndrome', with the result that 'persecution by [rogue] regimes of their own people will be wistfully tolerated and ignored' (2006, p.189).

Conclusion: assessing the record

Chesterman notes that the cynical invocation of humanitarian concerns is prevalent throughout the history of interventionism; 'the rare cases of intervention that might plausibly be regarded as humanitarian in character have tended to coincide with other motives' (2006, p.163). According to Nicholas Wheeler and Justin Morris:

> in no case have states intervened when there were no vital interests at stake and/or where there were perceived to be high risks to the lives of intervening forces. This produces a pattern of intervention that is highly selective, frequently driven by considerations of national self-interest rather than humanitarian need. It also ensures that when intervention does take place it is widely viewed as morally hypocritical, a rhetorical instrument that rationalizes the projection of force by the powerful. Iraq is only the latest intervention where this long-standing critique can be strongly heard. (2007, p. 448)

In addition to this strong correlation between national interests and the exercise of purportedly 'humanitarian intervention', it is clear that when states do not have national interests at stake, the scale of human suffering has not convinced them to act altruistically. Catherine Lu notes, 'Historically, the society of states has often acted like the drunken friends who desert the scene when violence breaks out' (2006, p.10). The international inaction in the face of both the Armenian genocide in 1915 and the Rwandan genocide in 1994 seem to support this negative appraisal.

Thus the record of humanitarian intervention evidences two trends; first, the presence of a large degree of national interest whenever states have launched a supposedly humanitarian intervention, and second, a marked unwillingness amongst states to intervene when national interests are not at stake regardless of the humanitarian suffering taking place. The following four chapters explore case studies in the post-Cold War era that have significantly influenced the debate on humanitarian intervention and provide qualitative insight into the contemporary difficulties poised by this issue.

Questions

- Is the debate regarding humanitarian intervention a function of the development of the modern state?
- To what extent, if any, has the dynamics of humanitarian intervention changed in the post-Cold War era?
- Can we identify any general trends in the history of humanitarian intervention?

Further reading

Arend, A. and Beck, R. (1993) *International Law and the Use of Force* (London: Routledge).

Bellamy, A. (2006) *Just Wars: From Cicero to Iraq* (London: Polity).

Brown, C. (2006) *Sovereignty, Rights and Justice: International Political Theory Today* (London: Polity).

Chesterman, S. (2002) *Just War or Just Peace?* (Oxford: Oxford University Press).

Danish Institute of International Affairs (DIIA) (1999) *Humanitarian Intervention: Legal and Political Aspects* (Copenhagen: Danish Institute of International Affairs).

International Commission on Intervention and State Sovereignty (ICISS) (2001) *The Responsibility to Protect* (Ottawa: International Development Research Centre).

Jackson, R. (2000) *The Global Covenant: Human Conduct in a World of States* (Oxford: Oxford University Press).

Simpson, G. (2004) *Great Powers and Outlaw States* (Cambridge: Cambridge University Press).

Weiss, T. (2007) *Humanitarian Intervention* (London: Polity).

Wheeler, N. (2002) *Saving Strangers* (Oxford: Oxford University Press).

Chapter 10

Rwanda

The dreadful events that occurred in Rwanda in 1994 changed 'Rwanda', perhaps irrevocably, from the name of a state into a byword for slaughter and international inaction. The failure to act decisively in Rwanda is described by Paul Kennedy as 'the single worst decision the United Nations ever made' (2006, p.103).

Hard as it may now be to believe, in the mid-1980s Rwanda was considered the 'Switzerland of Africa' (Hintjens, 1999, p.244). Economic development was healthy and the inter-ethnic relations, though far from being wholly harmonious, were not a source of major international concern. The decent into organized slaughter was swift, catalyzed by 'the 'moral exclusion' of a category of people, allowing first their 'social death' and then their physical death (Uvin, 1999, p.253). In response to the outbreak of depravity, the international community – particularly the United Nations and Western states – demonstrated a level of both inertia and apathy which continues to shroud their reputations.

This chapter begins by charting the path to the genocide particularly from 1990 onwards, and examines some explanations for the carnage. The second section assesses the differing, though almost universally critical, perspectives on the international response, and analyses the issue of whether more could have been done to either prevent or halt the genocide. The final section assesses the impact Rwanda has had on the evolution of the humanitarian intervention debate, focusing on the proliferation of 'Never Again' commitments, calls for UN reform and finally, the emergence of critical perspectives on the idea of international involvement in intra-state conflicts.

Nature of the crisis

While the disintegration of stability in Rwanda was swift, and the speed of the genocide truly incredible, a number of historical factors – both internal and external – can be identified as having precipitated the carnage in 1994. This section begins with a brief historical overview of the history of Rwanda in the 20th century, and proceeds to examine the main explanations for the genocide advanced since it took place.

179

The evolution of the crisis

Present-day Rwanda was colonized 1898 – becoming part of German East Africa – although the indigenous social and political system largely remained. Following Germany's defeat in the First World War the territory, then named Rwanda-Urandi, was placed under Belgian control and administered from the Belgian Congo. The Belgians infamously based their rule on what they perceived as the existing ethnic hierarchy, thereby privileging the Tutsis over the majority Hutus (Destexhe, 1995, p.38; Gourevitch, 1998, p.55; Melvern, 2004, pp.5–6).

The distinction between Tutsi and Hutu is highly contentious; while the genocide in 1994 is often portrayed as perpetrated by the Hutus against the Tutsis, and this was certainly the rallying cry of the aggressors, there is much to suggest that these distinctions are contrived 'state-enforced political identities' (Mandani, 2001, p.74). In 1933 the Belgians introduced ethnic identity cards which essentially froze the ethnicity of Rwandans and embedded ethnic difference in the political system (Gourevitch, 1998, p.56). Prior to colonial administration the distinction between the Tutsis and Hutus was not deeply embedded; Tutsi and Hutu spoke, and still speak, the same language – Kinyarwanda – intermarriage was frequent and power alternated between the groups without necessarily causing ethnic conflict, although the cattle-owning Tutsis had traditionally been the political elite (Wheeler, 2002, p.210). The Tutsis are often said to be physically distinct, especially in terms of their height, but mixed marriages have ensured that physical characteristics are largely indistinguishable, contrary to what many anthropologists think (Clapham, 1998, p.197; Hintjens, 1999, p.248). Tutsis and Hutus are, according to Alex de Waal, 'different strata of the same group differentiated by occupational and political status' (1994, p.1). Regardless of whatever ambiguity surrounds 'Tutsi' and 'Hutu', these terms had become a feature of life in Rwanda since before independence in 1962 (Uvin, 1999, p.255). Indeed, Peter Uvin argues that the idea amongst scholars that there is no difference between the two is an exaggeration, and a product of a reaction against the extremist Hutu view which incited the slaughter in 1994 (Uvin, 2001, p.77).

In 1959 Hutus rebelled against the Belgian-backed Tutsi administration and some 20,000 people were killed. In 1961 the Belgians left and the Tutsi regime was overthrown. A referendum was held in 1961 and a Hutu-dominated regime came to power under UN supervision, which lasted until 1962 when Rwanda formally became an independent state. In 1963 a Tutsi group launched a failed coup which resulted in widespread violence perpetrated by Hutus against the Tutsis. In 1973 General Juvenal Habyarimana, the minister for defence, led a coup which overthrew the regime of Gregoire Kayibanda and his Parmehutu Party. Habyarimana's supporters in the Mouvement Revolutionnaire National pour le Developpement (MNRD) were predominantly Hutu's from the north of the country who traditionally had less contact with the Tutsis than the Hutus in the south (Wheeler, 2002, p.210). After President Habyarimana came to power discrimination in public office was practised through a quota system, especially in the army (Prunier, 1997, p.49). Uvin agues, however, that the quota system 'served more to maintain the distinctions and allow for social control by the state than to actually discriminate' and that discrimination was not as pronounced in Rwandan civil society (1999, p.258).

Following the overthrow of the government in 1961, thousands of Tutsis fled to Uganda where they formed militias. In 1987 Tutsi refugees in Uganda formed the Rwandan Patriotic Front (RPF) which, like its predecessor, the Rwandanese Alliance for National Unity, sought to both protect Tutsi refugees in Uganda and return to Rwanda to take power. In 1986 the RPF helped Yoweri Museveni to overthrow Uganda's government and thereafter received material support and shelter from his regime.

On 1 October 1990 the RPF, with the support of Uganda, invaded northern Rwanda. France, Zaire and Belgium provided military support to Rwanda, and the invasion was a 'disaster' (Clapham, 1998, p.200). While this initial military foray was unsuccessful it sparked a civil war which favoured the tactics of the RPF. The international community became involved in the situation, and in June 1992 engaged in extensive mediation efforts. The result was the Arusha Accords, proclaimed on 4 August 1993, which formally ended the civil war and established a new power-sharing political structure. The Accords granted a right of return to Tutsi exiles, provided equal representation for the RPF and MNRD, and divided the army so that representation was based on ethnic plurality. On 5 October 1993 the United Nations established the UN Assistance Mission for Rwanda (UNAMIR) which was to oversee the implementation of the Accords.

According to Wheeler two factors compelled President Habyarimana to seek some consolidation with the Tutsis. First, the civil war provoked by the 1990 invasion was a source of ongoing conflict and a drain on national resources. Second, President Habyarimana wanted to reform the country's political structures in line with the conditions of international aid donors. The Accords were a described by some as 'a veritable coup d'etat for the RPF' (Clapham, 1998, p.203). Wheeler argues that 'the peace process was doomed from the outset' as the Arusha Accords were unrealistic and unworkable. The Accords gave power to the smaller political parties at the expense of the extremists, though these groups had control over neither territory nor the armed forces, and little popular support (Wheeler, 2002, pp. 212–14).

As soon as the Accords were signed, extremists within Habyarimana's regime, and even his own family, began killing Tutsis in an effort to scupper the peace process. Members of the Coalition pour la Defense de la Republique (CDR), established in 1992, and the *akuza* – a group of elites including Habyarimana's wife – had been deeply opposed to the peace process and were dismayed by the Arusha Accords. These groups began to organize militias such as the infamous *interhamwe* (those who strand together) and the *impuzamugambi* (the single-minded ones). These militias began as local football clubs and patriotic associations for the unemployed, but also as civil defence units established by the Rwandan government as a supplementary armed force (Melvern, 2004, pp.20–4). Covert plans for genocide, which was referred to as the 'big job' (*akazi gakomeye*) or the 'special work' (*umuganda*), were made as the peace process took place (Hintjens, 1999, p.268).

On 21 October 1993 the president of Burundi – Melchior Ndadaye – was killed in a military coup. As Ndadaye was a Hutu and his killers Tutsis, this strengthened the resolve of the CDR to keep the Tutsis from holding political office, and reinforced the idea that the two communities could not share power. Following Ndadaye's death violence flared in Burundi, and some 200,000 Hutu refugees fled to southern Rwanda. They brought tales of Tutsi oppression, causing widespread fear and panic, which pushed more people towards the Hutu extremists. Wheeler notes that by the time the Arusha Accords were finally signed, there existed 'a chillingly effective organizational structure' which would later implement the genocide (2002, p.212).

Rumours that massive violence was being planned were 'frequent', but Tutsis felt the possibility of coordinated genocide was 'unbelievable' (Hintjens, 1999, p.270). The Carnegie Commission on Preventing Deadly Conflict (CPDC) noted that the group Africa Watch warned in 1993 that Hutu extremists had compiled lists of individuals to be targeted for retribution, and that these were among the first victims the next year (CCPDC, 1997, p.4). On 11 January 1994 Romeo Dallaire, force commander of UNAMIR, cabled the UN Department of Peacekeeping Operations (DPKO) to inform them that he had received intelligence suggesting the militias were planning to kill UN troops and aimed to exterminate 1000 Tutsis every 20 minutes. Dallaire stated that he had been given the location of caches of weapons at sites where the massacres were to take place, and requested permission to seize the weapons. The DPKO refused his request as staff felt this would exceed UNAMIR's mandate and potentially endanger UN troops. Kofi Annan, then head of DPKO, encouraged Dallaire to confront the Rwandan government with the intelligence, which Dallaire did; the Rwandan government, unsurprisingly, denied any knowledge of the plans and promised to investigate. The Security Council itself was not informed of Dallare's warning when it met on 5 April. The Council passed Resolution 909 which commended 'the valuable contribution to peace being made in Rwanda by UNAMIR' and noted that the ceasefire had been respected.

On 6 April 1994 President Habyarimana and President Ntaryamira of Burundi, were killed when their plan was shot down. The perpetrators' identity is unknown although suspicions remain that Hutu extremists, rather than Tutsis, committed the murder. The killings began within hours; road blocks were set up across the country and identity cards were checked. This time-consuming process was superseded by murder on the basis of intelligence, suspicion and hearsay. The mass murder was coordinated by broadcasts from the radio station Radio Television Libre Mille Collines. which encouraged the attackers and passed on intelligence as to where Tutsis were hiding. Moderate Hutus were also killed in their thousands in a horrific orgy of violence. Initially many Tutsis took refugee in churches and other buildings, from where they were able to fend off the poorly armed attackers. By 13 April, however, the Presidential Guard began arriving at these sites. They threw grenades to flush out those hiding, and the militias killed those who fled with machetes and spiked clubs (Kuperman, 2001, pp.15–16). Perhaps 250,000 were killed in the first two weeks which equates to a figure of some 17,500 deaths per day (Kuperman, 2000a, p.98). The death toll for the 100 days of bloodshed ranges from 500,000 to 1,000,000 depending on the methodology used. The Rwandan Ministry for Education conducted a survey which claimed some 1,364,000 had died, a figure described as 'probably too high' (Seybolt, 2007, pp.70–1). In addition to the mass murder there were some 250,000–500,000 rapes (Weiss, 2007, p.62).

The genocide came to an end when the RPF began to overcome the government forces and establish control of Kirgali. The RPF were a more efficient military force and thus able to defeat the numerically superior government forces, who were more concerned with killing civilians than fighting the RPF (Seybolt, 2007, p.71). On 22 June the French intervened in the south-west of the country, creating safe areas into which many thousands of the perpetrators of the genocide fled.

Explaining the genocide

The details of the atrocities committed provides us with a glimpse of the truly cruellest aspects of humanity's capacity for violence (see Box 10.1). Acts of coordinated mass violence such as this are not akin to murder committed in a fit of rage or psychopathic tendencies; rationale people chose to execute this slaughter and mobilized thousands to their cause, and thus, despite the egregious cruelty, it is possible to explain this seemingly irrational act.

While we may be able to explain the path to genocide, there is no single, simple explanation (Hintjens, 1999, p.280). Uvin's review of the literature on the endogenous causes of the genocide highlights three broad explanatory categories (2001, pp.81–5). First is the suggestion that the violence was caused by elite manipulation and the proliferation of racist ideology; the *akuza* in particular are singled out as architects of the violence, driven by a desire to maintain their privileged social and political positions. Uvin

Box 10.1 The horror

The next morning [1 May], at about 10 a.m., twenty-two soldiers returned under the command of Lt. Ildephonse Hategekimana, head of the Ngoma camp. After telling the displaced people that they would be not be killed but would be taken to prison, he called in the civilians to do the killing. A witness who was hidden heard the children crying and the women begging. He heard the 'dull blows, followed by small cries,' which he supposed were the sounds of children being clubbed to death. Then, after an hour, silence. There had been 476 people in the church, 302 of them children. Some victims were taken off to be killed in the nearby woods, a number of the women raped. . . . It rained in the late morning, but when the rain ended in the early afternoon, killers came to finish off the wounded children who were still alive, lying on the grass. As they were clubbing them to death, a vehicle belonging to the Ministry of Health appeared and several officials got out. The killers chatted with them while continuing to club the children on the ground. After the officials left, the killers pillaged the remaining rice stocks of the church as payment for their 'work'.

Source: Des Forges (1999).

suggests, however, that racism was widespread throughout Rwanda, albeit not uniformly so, and thus the elites were 'both manipulative and manipulated' (ibid., p. 81). The second explanation relates to resource scarcity; the sheer weight of numbers created social tension as groups struggled to survive. Indeed, Rwanda had one of Africa's highest population growth rates and the highest population density in Africa for a predominantly rural country. The third category identified by Uvin is the socio-psychological features of perpetrators. These explanations focus on the supposedly obedient nature of the Rwandans and the resultant ability of the elites to order the Hutu masses to commit genocide. Uvin is not convinced by this explanation; 'At the same time that Rwandans are described as obedient and docile; they are also described as distrustful, lying, and dissimulating – features that contradict greatly the former' (ibid., p. 85).

A focus purely on endogenous causes is surely flawed and quite possibly racist. The conflict was often portrayed as a function of 'ancient tribal hatreds'; indicatively John O'Shea of the non-governmental organization (NGO) GOAL stated, 'Two groups are bent on destroying each other . . . the dispute is ethnic. . . . There is out and out hatred between the two groups' (Joras and Schetter, 2004, p. 320). This 'ethnic hatred' explanation was encouraged by the perpetrators themselves, who 'portrayed the situation as one of uncontrollable spontaneous ethnic violence' (de Waal, 1994, p.2). The extremists facilitated that strain of thinking in the international community, and the global media, which opposed intervention on the basis that this was an irrational conflict immune to external council (Melvern, 2004, p.235). The idea of racial difference and ethnic enmity was certainly exploited by the killers, and indeed at times the RPF, but this was no more than a highly effective myth (Hintjens, 1999, p.251; Mueller, 2000, p.42).

In fact a number of external factors, as well as internal developments and trends, contributed to the explosion of violence. The basis of the Tutsi/Hutu distinction owed much to the colonial legacy which cemented this division. Additionally while Rwanda was considered to be a positive economic model in the 1980s, it was heavily dependent on external aid and revenue from coffee. Receipts from coffee fell during 1986–7 from US$14 billion to US$5 billion, and thus Rwanda's debt increased as a result of external factors rather than domestic mismanagement (Hintjens, 1999, p.256). In June 1990 the World Bank and the International Monetary Fund (IMF) forced Rwanda to implement structural adjustment packages which resulted in the currency being devalued by two-thirds. Farming incomes dropped sharply and budget restraints led to healthcare and food shortages. Rather than blame the international financial bodies, the Tutsis were portrayed as the cause of the decline in living standards.

Rwanda was but one of many African states which received support from Western countries during the Cold War despite its lack of democracy. This changed in the early 1990s when 'the international community suddenly rediscovered its attachment to democracy' (Uvin, 1999, p.259). Aid was made conditional on democratization, which forced President Habyarimana to initiate domestic reforms (Collins, 2002, p.160). This angered the Hutu elite and the army, who were opposed to any Tutsi involvement in government, and in an effort to consolidate his constituency, Habyarimana responded to democratization 'by rallying the majority "faithful" against a purported common racial enemy, hoping in this way to prevent regional and class divisions from finding more open political expression' (Hintjens, 1999, p.242). Despite the dubious way Habyarimana and his clique adapted to democracy, France maintained steadfast support for the regime (Kroslak, 2007, pp.99–108). Gerard Prunier notes that France's 'blind commitment' to the Rwandan government had 'catastrophic consequences because as the situation radicalized the Rwandanese leadership kept believing that no matter what it did, French support would always be forthcoming' (1997, p.108). French motivations for supporting Habyarimana against the RPF stemmed in part from a perception that Uganda and the United Kingdom were attempting to displace France's power base in Africa (Clapham, 1998, p.199; Shawcross, 2001, p.106).

Writing on the genocide in Rwanda is often, unsurprisingly, punctuated with moral outrage and highly charged superlatives. Mahmood Mamdani, however, writes of the 'three silences' which also characterize the writing on Rwandan genocide (2001, pp.7–8). The first concerns the history of genocide, whereby many authors 'write as if the Rwandan genocide had no precedent. . . . For Africans it turns into a Rwandan oddity; and for non-Africans the aberration is Africa.' The second silence relates to the perpetrators of the genocide; Mamdani argues that there has been a tendency to ignore the role played by the masses who committed the killings, and a preference for portraying the violence as 'exclusively a state project'. The third silence surrounds the portrayal of the genocide as a function of forces within Rwanda, which ignores the 'regional processes' which contributed to the carnage. Mamdani claims that the genocide was a 'natives' genocide': that is, an act committed by those who had previously been subjugated and victimized, and who saw their task as cleansing their land of a 'threatening alien presence' associated with the former colonial power. It was genocide committed by those who sought to forcibly affirm their power and even, paradoxically, their humanity (2001, p.14).

International response

The international reaction to the genocide has become the main focus of academic enquiry into events in Rwanda in 1994. The international community, in particular Western states and especially the United States, have been strongly criticized for their inaction. This section initially provides an overview of the international response and then assesses the claims that more could have been done to stop the massacre.

International reaction

On 7 April the prime minister of Rwanda, Ms Uwillingiyimana a Hutu, and ten Belgian peacekeepers protecting her were murdered. The intention appears to have been to scare the international contingent in UNAMIR into leaving; the strategy worked. The Belgian government rapidly pulled out all its troops, stating in a letter to the UN secretary-general that UNAMIR was 'pointless' and 'powerless in the face of the worsening situation'. Belgian soldiers faced an 'unacceptable risk . . . making continuation of the Belgian presence impossible' (UN Security Council, 1994). French troops flew into Kirgali to evacuate only foreign nationals, even leaving behind Rwandan staff in the French embassy.

UNAMIR's mandate, as per Resolution 872, was to monitor the ceasefire and the implementation of the Accords rather than engage in peace enforcement. Cognizant of this, Daillaire stated, 'The minute there is a significant ceasefire violation by either side . . . my mandate does not exist here anymore' (Wheeler, 2002, p.214). When the violence erupted and the UN troops themselves became targets, the UN Secretariat and DPKO appear to have decided to extricate UNAMIR before more UN troops were lost in what was claimed to be a civil war. Michael Barnett, a US diplomat at the United Nations at this time, states that while there was 'a brief discussion' about the possibility of UNAMIR intervening to halt the escalating violence, 'I was (and still am) unaware of a single member state who offered their troops for such an operation . . . the Secretariat, who would be responsible for carrying out the mandate, was silent, and silence was widely interpreted as disapproval (1997, p.559).

On 10 April, much to his dismay, Dallaire was told to prepare for withdrawal. According to Alison des Forges, the Hutus saw this as evidence that nothing would be done by the United Nations, and therefore the genocidal government would succeed leading those who initially hesitated to take part in the genocide to take up arms (2000, p.141). Dallaire and his small contingent were left to watch as the carnage unfolded. By 11 April Dallaire recalls his reaction to a cable from the United Nations in New York asking for more information: 'What more could I possibly tell them that I hadn't already described in horrific detail? The odour of death in the hot sun; the flies, maggots, rats and dogs that swarmed to feast on the dead' (Dallaire, 2004a, p.289).

On 20 April 1994 UN secretary-general Boutros Boutros-Ghali outlined three options to the Security Council. The first involved the deployment of thousands more troops under a Chapter VII mandate to force a ceasefire. The second involved scaling UNAMIR down to some 270 troops to engage in negotiations and assist the humanitarian relief operation, while the third option was the complete withdrawal of UNAMIR. Wheeler argues that this proposal was based on an erroneous reading of the violence as the product of a 'tribal war'. He argues that portraying the situation as civil war rather than genocide enabled the United States, France and Britain to legitimize their decision not to intervene (2002, pp.220–21). On 21 April, in what now appears an incredible move, the Security Council, on which ironically Rwanda then sat, voted to reduce UNAMIR to 270 troops. Wheeler argues that there was clearly no way UNAMIR could act effectively under its existing mandate, but this did not mean all UN troops had to be withdrawn; the alternative was 'a change of mandate and the deployment of an effective fighting force' (ibid., p.222).

On 28 and 29 April the Security Council met to discuss the situation. Representatives from the Czech Republic and New Zealand urged the Council to call the situation 'genocide' and initiate more robust action. The secretary-general also urged the Council to reconsider its troop pull-out. On 29 April the International Committee of the Red Cross (ICRC) issued what Linda Melvern describes as 'the most strongly worded statement in its history', outlining the horror of the violence (2004, p.225). The Security Council released a statement which quoted from the Genocide Convention but did not use the word 'genocide'. The Secretariat produced a plan to increase the UNAMIR force to 5000 but according to Barnett this proposal was 'merely symbolic and highly impractical', as these troops would not be deployed for months and no one explained what their role would be (1997, p.560).

On 17 May the Security Council passed Resolution 918 which referred to 'the killings of members of an ethnic group with the intention of destroying such a group in whole or in part'. This Resolution modestly altered UNAMIR's mandate and agreed to increase its number to 5500 troops. According to Simon Chesterman, however, 'intense lobbying by the United States' ensured that the deployment would take place in two phases, with phase one comprising merely 150 unarmed observers and 800 Ghanaian soldiers deployed to secure the airport (2002, p.145). Samantha Power argues that 'staying out of Rwanda was an explicit US policy objective', and she claims the United States '. . . aggressively worked to block the subsequent authorization of UN reinforcements' (2001). Resolution 925 on 8 June noted that 'acts of genocide have occurred in Rwanda' and issued a call for member-states to 'respond promptly' to the secretary-general's request for resources. Logistically this phase II deployment could have taken up to three months to organize.

Then on 18 June France announced that it was willing to launch an intervention to establish a safe area in south-west Rwanda. This came as a significant relief to the United States and the United Kingdom, who were pleased that an intervention was taking place without their involvement (Kroslak, 2007, p.215). On 22 June the Council, somewhat reluctantly given the suspicions about France's motives (see the subsequent section), passed Resolution 929 which sanctioned 'the establishment of a temporary operation under national command'. On the same day Operation Turquoise was launched and 2500 French Foreign Legion troops entered Rwanda. According to Chesterman the main contribution of the French safe areas 'was to save the genocidaires from Tutsi-led retribution' (2002, p.147), while Seybolt claims the Hutus sheltering in the safe areas 'contributed directly to two civil wars in Zaire in 1996 and 1998–2003 that killed more than 3 million people (mostly by disease) and destabilized the entire great lakes region' (2007, p.76). On 22 July the United States, with the support of the United Kingdom, launched Operation Support Hope to provide humanitarian assistance in and around Rwanda. Following the genocide tens of thousands of Hutus were killed in reprisal attacks (Uvin, 2001, p.75).

Could more have been done?

Since the genocide members of the international community, academics and humanitarian NGOs have routinely stated that more could have been done to stop the genocide (see Box 10.2). Dallaire railed against 'inexcusable apathy by the sovereign states that made up the UN that is completely

> ## Box 10.2 5,000 troops . . . 500,000 lives?
>
> The panel generally agreed that early military intervention – within two
> weeks of the initial violence – by a force of 5,000 could have made a signifi-
> cant difference in the level of violence in Rwanda and that there was a
> window of opportunity for the employment of this force during April 7–21,
> 1994. The group acknowledged that such a force would have had to be
> properly trained, equipped, and supported, and possess a mandate from the
> Security Council to enable it to use 'all means necessary' to protect vulner-
> able populations. In Rwanda in 1994, it is likely that 5,000 troops could
> have averted the slaughter of a half-million people.
>
> Source: Carnegie Commission on Preventing Deadly Conflict (1997, p. 6).

beyond comprehensible and moral acceptability' (Shawcross, 2001, p.115).
Prunier describes the international response as a 'mixture of realpolitik,
humanitarian self-satisfaction, half-baked ideology, stale imperialism and
economic blackmail' (1997, p.341). Preventing 'another Rwanda' has
become an oft-used rallying cry uttered to justify international interventions and engagements since. At the time, however, there were those who
claimed that the violence was born from ingrained psychological tribal
forces which could not be stopped (Des Forges, 1999). This perspective has
lost appeal, and few now make these spurious claims.

What then is the basis for the claim that more could have been done?
Key to this view is the fact that international actors were present in
Rwanda prior to the outbreak of the genocide and should have noticed
that plans were afoot. Wheeler notes that the CIA warned that 500,000
would die if the Arusha Accords failed, and that France must have known
that their was an appetite for genocide amongst the many Hutu soldiers
French troops had trained (2002, p.216). France launched Operation
Amaryllis on 8 April to evacuate its staff, military officers and certain
members of Habyarimana's inner circle, including his wife. The French
troops deployed during this operation left on 14 April, and Daniela
Kroslak notes that during this week they witnessed many atrocities and
gathered extensive first-hand information on the true nature of the crisis
(2007, p.176). The evacuation of the French embassy was particularly
swift, and French staff took care to shred all documents within the
building. Kroslak argues, 'It is difficult not to wonder whether the French
government possessed information, owing to its close involvement, that
justified such a reaction' (2007, pp.200–1).

Two days after the Arusha Accords were signed, Belgian intelligence
warned that anger within the army was rife and violence was likely
(Collins, 2002, p.169). Timothy Docking argues that the United States

knew 'from the outset' that Hutus were planning genocide but the Somalia syndrome 'clearly contributed to the administration's failure to act' (2008, pp.215–16) a view shared by Prunier (1997, p.274). The UN 'Independent Inquiry into the Actions of the United Nations During the 1994 Genocide in Rwanda' noted that following the death of Habyaramana the United States, Italy, France and Belgium moved swiftly to evacuate their personnel in a what appears to have been anticipation of an upsurge of violence, yet these states did not share any intelligence with UNAMIR (United Nations, 1999, p.47).

Many point specifically to the cable sent by Dallaire to the DPKO on 11 January which warned that mass killings were being planned. In the cable Dallaire noted that an a 'top level' informant had passed on worrying information:

> Principal aim of Interhamwe in the past was to protect Kigali from RPF. Since UNAMIR mandate he has been ordered to register all Tutsi in Kigali. He suspects it is for their extermination. Example he gave was that in 20 minutes his personnel could kill up to 1000 Tutsis. (Dallaire, 1994)

This cable did not set alarm bells ringing in the DPKO, which refused Dallaire's request to seize weapons caches and did not pass this information to the Security Council. Dallaire claims the return cable from Kofi Annan 'caught me completely off guard', and he notes, 'I was beside myself with frustration' (2004a, p.146). Kofi Annan has since expressed his regret at his decision, further supporting the idea that more could have been done at this juncture (BBC News, 2004). Had UNAMIR begun seizing weapons it would have required more troops and they would likely have acted as a deterrent (Wheeler, 2002, p.218). Wheeler cautions, however, that even if the Security Council had been informed of Dallaire's cable, 'it is not at all certain that this would have encouraged them to send extra troops' (ibid., p.222).

The reluctance to deploy more troops to Rwanda stemmed from the legacy of the deployment in Somalia and the United Nations' own unwillingness to endanger another of its operations. A speculative cable from Dallaire, which today seems eerily prescient but at the time was perhaps one of many warnings dispatched to the DPKO, was unlikely to convince the UN Security Council to radically alter UNIMAR's mandate and increase its troop numbers. Alan Kuperman notes that Dallaire's cable only identified 135 weapons, whereas some 20,000 rifles and 500,000 machetes were eventually used (2000a, p.113). Dallaire also warned in his cable that the intelligence may have been a 'set-up' (Dallaire, 1994). Kuperman argues that Dallaire's expression of concern could only have strengthened the DPKO's caution. This is not a convincing argument, however. Had the cable been the only correspondence between Dallaire and the DPKO then it is plausible that those equivocal aspects of Dallaire's cable highlighted by Kuperman may have convinced the DPKO to reject the request to seize the caches. In fact Dallaire recalls that following Kofi Annan's response forbidding the seizure, he 'made phone call after phone call to New York' explaining the need to carry out the raids (2004a, p.146).

When the killings began, the situation on the ground was confused and information passed to the Security Council by the Secretariat was sketchy. Because the members of the Security Council had little independent information on what was happening, they largely relied on the Secretariat. Human Rights Watch notes, 'the secretary-general's special representative, Roger Booh-Booh minimized both the extent and the organized nature of the slayings', and thus the Security Council was provided with faulty information (Des Forges, 1999). Additionally because many journalists left the country the massacres outside Kirgali were not witnessed, so by 11 April international reports suggested that the killings had stopped or at least slowed down considerably, despite the fact that in rural Rwanda the exact opposite was the case (Kuperman, 2000a, p.102). Prunier notes that because of the 'technical impossibility of catching the killers in the act' there were no television images of the genocide, and this had a major impact because 'in contemporary Western society events not seen on a TV screen do not exist' (1997, p.274).

Nonetheless by the second week of the killings evidence was emerging, not least from UNIMAR's commander, that the violence was a systemic attempt to kill Tutsis. France in particular continued to claim that the violence was a civil war, and called for a ceasefire despite the mounting evidence indicating genocide (Kroslak, 2007, pp.194–9). By late April, representatives of the Czech Republic, Spain, New Zealand and Argentina pressed for more information and looked beyond the Secretariat. The information they received convinced them that genocide was occurring, and they called for more robust action. If these countries of modest international standing and intelligence capability could independently determine that genocide was occurring, then it is surely logical to assume that the P5 could have also done so – or perhaps they did, and decided to ignore the information.

In 1998 President Clinton flew to Rwanda. Although he stayed only a matter of hours and did not leave the airport, his visit was heralded by some as atonement for the US actions in 1994. In his speech Clinton stated:

> We did not act quickly enough after the killing began. . . . We did not immediately call these crimes by their rightful name: genocide. . . . It may seem strange to you here . . . but all over the world there were people like me sitting in offices, day after day after day, who did not fully appreciate the depth and the speed with which you were being engulfed by this unimaginable terror. (quoted in *New York Times*, 1998)

Clinton thus suggested that his administration simply did not know how bad the situation was, the implication being that more would have been done had they known. Kuperman argues that an analysis of UN reports, the reports of leading human rights organizations and international media coverage, including the CIA's Foreign Broadcasting Information Service, indicates that President Clinton could not have known about the genocide until 20 April (2001, p.24). In fact classified documents obtained through a freedom of information request in the United States reveal that the Clinton administration received daily briefings from the CIA. On 23 April a CIA briefing described the situation as genocide, although the Clinton administration refused to use the term publicly until 25 May, when it acknowledged that 'acts of genocide' were occurring. Des Forges described the documents as 'powerful proof that they knew' (Carroll, 2004), while Power claims that the documents 'reveal that the U.S. government knew enough about the genocide early on to save lives, but passed up countless opportunities to intervene' (2001).

Aside from the question about how much was known, there is evidence that intervention after the killings began would not have been as effective as some have claimed. It has been often suggested that a force of 5000 troops could have been deployed to stop the killings. Taylor Seybolt argues, however, that because the killings were carried out with 'lightning speed', early intervention would have saved some tens of thousands of victims but not the majority who died (2007, p.71). Had Dallaire's request on 10 April for 5000 troops been heeded and acted upon, Kuperman states, it would have taken ten days to deploy these troops. By 20 April, however, half the total number of fatalities had already taken place (Kuperman, 2001, pp.84–5). Thus, Kuperman states, 'although some lives could have been saved by intervention at any point during the genocide, even a large force deployed immediately upon recognizing the genocidal intent would have arrived too late to save even half of the ultimate victims' (2001, p.2). Of course 'even half of the ultimate victims' amounts to some 400,000 people, which clearly cannot be dismissed, although it seems clear that once the carnage began, any intervention force would have arrived too late to save the hundreds of thousands killed in the immediate outbreak of violence. The only way the genocide could have been prevented, Kuperman argues, was if UNAMIR been reinforced several months before the outbreak of genocide (2000a, p.116).

The lack of action taken by the international community has led to speculation that certain states, especially France, were causally involved and had a vested interest in the completion of the genocide (Collins, 2002, p.159). Uvin rejects this, noting, 'There are no genius mad-men, collective hysteria, or hidden sinister international complots' (2001, p.97). Nonetheless France's role is open to question. The French had long standing relationship with the Habyarimana regime and were certainly supportive of efforts to defeat the RPF. As the genocide unfolded France acquiesced in the inaction, and despite its strong ties to the country, failed to take a strong lead in pushing for greater action or provide information on events on the ground. As the Rwandan government began to buckle under pressure from the RPF, France suddenly expressed its willingness to intervene in an effort, according to Wheeler, 'to demonstrate to Africa and the rest of the world that France was no paper tiger and that it could project power rapidly on the continent' (2002, p.233). The French force deployed was not equipped for a humanitarian mission and acted more as a traditional blue line around the south-west of the state. Bruce Jones offers three explanations for French action, gained from confidential interviews he conducted with French governmental officials; first, to secure northern Zaire from refugee flows; second, to demonstrate French power to the Security Council; third, to downplay negative domestic criticism (1995, p.231).

Criticism of the international response has been a dominant feature of analyses of the genocide. The Security Council, according to Dallaire, 'floundered in the face of mounting heaps of bodies growing daily' (Shawcross, 2001, p.119). The International Panel of Eminent Personalities of the Organization of African Unity conducted a review which stated:

> There can be not an iota of doubt that the international community knew the following: that something terrible was underway in Rwanda, that serious plans were afoot for even more appalling deeds, that these went far beyond routine thuggery, and that the world never the less stood by and did nothing. That does not mean that the world knew that by 1992 or 1993, genocide was systematically being planned and organized. In fact it seems to us likely that hardly anyone could bring themselves to believe this was the case. (Uvin, 2001, p.91)

With globalization, 24-hour media channels and, not least, a UN peacekeeping force on the ground, it seems incredible that carnage on this scale was somehow kept secret. Refugees who fled Rwanda and the many mutilated bodies that flowed down the River Nyabarongo into Lake Victoria and neighbouring Uganda and Kenya certainly constituted evidence that something terrible was happening (Destexhe, 1995, p.49). It is difficult not to conclude, therefore, that while it was not clear that the situation was as egregious as we now know it was, there was sufficient evidence to warrant a far more robust international response.

Impact on the debate

Books and articles on humanitarian intervention published since 1994 invariably mention the Rwandan genocide as the archetypal case where more could have been done and intervention was warranted. The following sections outline three broad aspects of the impact Rwanda has had on literature on humanitarian intervention since.

Never again!

The refrain 'never again' was uttered in the wake of the Holocaust and catalyzed a raft of human rights legislation (see Chapter 5). The many atrocities committed during the Cold War, in particular the Cambodian massacres in the mid-1970s, undermined the perceived commitment of the international community to the 'never again' refrain, but the genocide in 1994 constituted a uniquely 'staggering indictment' of the 'never again' commitments (Jones, 1995, p.247). While the 1948 Genocide Convention was signed as a means by which the international community could halt such atrocities, the impact of this treaty in 1994 was limited to forcing Western states, and the United States in particular, into contriving ever more imaginative ways to describe the killings without using the 'g word', often provoking ridicule in the process (see Frontline, 2004). As William Schabas notes, this reluctance stemmed from a perception that use of the term triggered an obligation to intervene (2000, p.496).

During the crisis certain world leaders rejected the idea that the international community had an obligation to halt suffering on this scale. President Clinton stated that US troops could not be sent to every trouble spot where Americans were 'offended by human misery', while French President Francois Mitterrand claimed that 'the international community could not act as a global police force and send peacekeepers to all the places where people fight' (Wheeler, 2002, pp.229, 235). Such public disavowals of an obligation to act were far less frequent when the scale of the slaughter was made public (Weiss, 2007, p.99).

In the wake of the genocide, 'never again' once again gained currency. The rights afforded to sovereign states were increasingly questioned (Chatterjee and Scheid, 2003, p.4; Jones, 1995, p.226). Rwanda was one of the 'immediate stimuli' for the International Commission on Intervention and State Sovereignty's (ICISS) report *The Responsibility to Protect* (Weiss, 2007, p.88; see Chapter 6). Indeed, the report opens with the words, 'We want no more Rwandas' (ICISS, 2001, p.XIII). During NATO's intervention in Kosovo UN Secretary-General Kofi Annan stated:

> To those for whom the greatest threat to the future of international order is the use of force in the absence of a Security Council mandate, one might ask – not in the context of Kosovo – but in the context of Rwanda: If, in those dark days and hours leading up to the genocide, a coalition of States had been prepared to act in defence of the Tutsi population, but did not receive prompt Council authorization, should such a coalition have stood aside and allowed the horror to unfold? (1999c)

In October 2001 Tony Blair stated that if something akin to Rwanda happened again, 'we would have a moral duty to act' (Fisher, 2007, p.102).

The barbarity in Rwanda led to a rise in the currency of the 'new wars' thesis, whereby analysts 'stress[ed] the irrational and uncontrollable nature of modern conflicts, alleged to be driven by a dangerous internal dynamic' (Collins, 2002, p.158). Mary Kaldor indicatively wrote about identity politics as the cause of these conflicts (1999, p.8). Such conflicts demanded external intervention, which global civil society could help to bring about by pressurizing recalcitrant governments to take action (see Chapter 6). Indeed, Wheeler argues that the eventual French intervention was a product of domestic pressure within France for action, generated by media and NGO reports. Had global civil society mobilized more effectively, he argues, the Security Council might have been shamed into action (Wheeler, 2002, pp.236–41).

Catherine Lu argues that had the idea of 'sovereignty as responsibility' been touted prior to 1994, the international community would have been legitimately entitled, if not required, to jam the radio stations that helped to coordinate the genocide (2006, p.121). Similarly following the adoption of the idea of a 'responsibility to protect' in the 2005 World Summit *Outcome Document*, the then UK foreign secretary, Jack Straw, claimed that had this provision existed in 1994 thousands of lives could have been saved (Wheeler, 2005, p.96).

Yet while Rwanda sparked great outrage at the immorality of sovereign inviolability, the lack of intervention in 1994 had nothing to do with sovereignty; Wheeler notes that 'the principle of sovereignty was never raised . . . no state tried to defend the UN's stance of non-intervention on the grounds that genocide fell within Rwanda's domestic jurisdiction' (2006, p.36). The intervention in Kosovo in 1999 was routinely justified as atonement for Rwanda (see Chapter 11) yet, as discussed in Chapter 13, the crisis in Darfur in 2003 had more obvious parallels with the situation in Rwanda and a similar record of inaction has been the defining feature of the international response. There is some doubt, therefore, as to whether the outpouring of moral outrage and commitments to act evident since 1994 has had any real impact on the record of humanitarian intervention since.

The need for UN reform

Whenever a humanitarian crisis erupts people look to the United Nations for a solution. As the United Nations has no standing army and is dependent on the will of its member states to act, especially the P5, inaction in the face of tragedy is often not a function of a deficiency within the United Nations despite the criticism it invariable endures. The case of Rwanda in 1994 is different; the United Nations itself, particularly the DPKO and the Secretariat, were culpable of pronounced failings. On 31 May 1994 the secretary-general, Boutros Boutros-Ghali, lamented:

We must all recognise that . . . we have failed in our response to the agony of Rwanda, and thus have acquiesced in the continued loss of human life. Our readiness and capacity for action has been demonstrated to be inadequate at best, and deplorable at worst, owing to the absence of the collective political will. (Holzgrefe, 2005, p.17)

The UN Independent Inquiry into the Actions of the United Nations During the 1994 Genocide in Rwanda found:

The failure by the United Nations to prevent and subsequently to stop the genocide in Rwanda was a failure by the United Nations system as a whole. The fundamental failure was the lack of resources and political commitment devoted to developments in Rwanda and to the United Nations presence there . . . although UNAMIR suffered from a chronic lack of resources and political priority, it must also be said that serious mistakes were made with those resources which were at the disposal of the United Nations. (United Nations, 1999, p.3)

Michael Barnett argues that the UN Secretariat, and particularly the DPKO, failed in its task, which undermined the response of the Security Council. The Secretariat 'thoroughly violated its professional obligations and ethical duties' by suppressing critical information and providing the Security Council with briefings which suggested that the violence was simply a continuation of the civil war (Barnett, 2002, p.174). Des Forges, the author of Human Rights Watch's 1999 review of the genocide, strongly criticized the United Nations for 'having failed to provide adequate information and guidance to members of the Security Council' (1999). Additionally, according to Barnett, UN Secretary-General Boutros Boutros-Ghali 'emanated indecision to the point of paralysis, if not complacency' (1997, p.559).

The reluctance to act on the information provided to the DPKO by the force commander of UNAMIR was a product of a fear among UN officials that a poorly executed mission would 'fatally harm the legitimacy of the whole organization', and yet the failure to act had precisely this effect (Cronin and Hurd, 2008, p.11). Barnett argues that the United Nations calculated that it had more to lose by taking action and being associated with another failure than it did by not taking action and allowing the genocide in Rwanda to occur (1997, p.561–2). Geoffrey Robertson went so far as to accuse the United Nations of 'assisting with genocide' and being 'complicit in a crime against humanity' (2002, p.73).

This led to calls for reform of the United Nations and specifically initiatives to increase the United Nations' early warning capacity (Barnett, 2003, p.175; Jones, 1995, p.232). Additionally the UN policy of neutrality in its peacekeeping operations was questioned. If, as ostensibly was the case in

Rwanda, there was an obvious aggressor, what was the point of maintaining a non-partisan approach? According to Clapham, 'to remain "neutral", in the way that a UN force was bound to do, was to be condemned, as eventually happened, to impotence' (1998, p.206).

Despite the provisions of the Genocide Convention, the United Nations failed to respond to the most aggressive act of genocide since the Holocaust, and the utility of the Convention itself was questioned (Klinghoffer, 1998, p.105). The lack of a military response derived in no small part from the fact that the United Nations lacked the capacity to launch an intervention without the support of the Security Council and the will of member-states to supply troops. Calls for intervention made by states with modest military capacity in 1994 were, therefore, essentially calls for states with the necessary military capacity to take action (Wheeler, 2002, p.227). This paradox is succinctly captured by Barnett, who notes caustically that 'the international community seemed willing to fight down to the last U.S. citizen' (1997, p.572). Even if smaller states such as New Zealand and the Czech Republic had been willing to volunteer troops, as indeed Ghana and Senegal eventually were, these states lacked the capacity to actually deploy their troops, and were reliant on major states to provide the finances and logistical support. Thus, in light of this failing radical reforms were proposed involving a standing UN army or rapid reaction force (Johansen, 2006). No concrete steps have been taken to implement these proposals, although in the wake of the crisis in Darfur (see Chapter 13) such proposals have regained some currency (Hehir, 2008a, p.130).

Critiquing intervention

The genocide in Rwanda also led to a questioning of the very efficacy of both peacekeeping and humanitarian intervention. While, as noted in the second section of this chapter, many lamented the international community's 'failure to act' and the United Nations' inadequate preventative capacity (Evans, 2008, p.79), others argued that the lesson of Rwanda was actually that international intervention, in the form of peacekeeping, mediation or military intervention, often had deleterious consequences (Kuperman, 2001, pp.109–10).

Uvin notes that following the genocide scholars, policy makers and journalists engaged in 'collective self-flagellation'. In addition to lamenting their own, and the international community's, failure to act, they cried out for action to strengthen the capability of the international community to intervene before and during humanitarian crises. He argues, however, that there has been little public criticism of this position although it 'may well be incorrect' (Uvin, 2001, p.89). Anne Orford notes that Rwanda has become emblematic of the 'need for early action', yet she argues that 'surprisingly little attention has been paid to the presence and activity of

international institutions and agencies ... prior to the outbreak of violence' (2003, p.85). The idea that the genocide occurred because of a lack
of international involvement is thus questioned, with certain authors
arguing that international involvement was in fact pronounced, and most
damningly, a causal factor in the eventual slaughter. The fact that the
genocide was sparked by a number of external factors, such as the legacy
of colonial rule, the structural adjustment programmes of the World Bank
and the IMF, the pressure put upon Habyarimana in the early 1990s to
democratize and the externally brokered Arusha Accords, suggested to
some that international intervention was part of the problem, and thus
calls for greater international involvement were counter-intuitive (Collins,
2002; Williams, 2005, p.113).

The genocide was blamed by many observers on the unwillingness of the
international community to get involved in Africa. Clapham argues, however, 'This claim can scarcely be made in the case of the Rwandan conflict,
where the international community, led by regional states and the
Organisation of African Unity, took an active role in attempting to nego-
tiate a solution from a very early stage' (1998, p.200). James Mayall notes,
'In many ways the pre-genocide Rwanda peace process was exemplary'
(2006, p.136), while Wheeler argues:

> It has become an accepted truism to claim that preventative diplomacy
> is always better than a belated intervention when things start to go
> wrong. However, the lesson of the Arusha process is that outside inter-
> vention aimed at averting a civil war can have unintended conse-
> quences that produce human wrongs on an unimaginable scale. (2002,
> 214)

Jones similarly points to the fact that for at least three years prior to the
genocide the international community was deeply involved in Rwanda.
'The ultimately catastrophic failure of those efforts,' he suggests, 'should
give pause for thought to those who believe that the appropriate response
to Rwanda is to fashion an intrusive international regime of preventive
intervention' (Jones, 1995, p.226).

There thus began to emerge a view, namely that 'the liberal bias in
peacemaking (in Rwanda) ... not only fails to alleviate human insecurity
or promote emancipation but may even help create the conditions for further violence' (Bellamy, 2005c, p.32). Thus preventive diplomacy, as
clearly practised in Rwanda from 1990–4, is not universally heralded as a
necessity (Clapham, 1998, pp.203–4). The eventual French intervention, as
previously noted, had mixed, if not in fact ultimately negative results, and
thus served to further tarnish the image of international intervention.
While few argued that a policy of non-intervention should be maintained
in the face of genocide, some concluded that it was perhaps best to stay out

of intra-state conflicts as such disputes, like the American Civil War, can only be resolved by the parties themselves and probably through the defeat of one side by the other (Luttwak, 1999).

Conclusion

Speaking at a conference to mark the ten-year anniversary of the genocide, Dallaire claimed:

> I still believe that if an organisation decided to wipe out the 320 mountain gorillas there would be still more of a reaction by the international community to curtail or to stop that than there would be still today in attempting to protect thousands of human beings being slaughtered in the same country. (BBC News, 2004)

The international reaction to the crisis in Darfur is perhaps evidence that, as Dallaire suggests, little has changed since 1994 despite the general acceptance that more should have been done.

Hindsight, of course, provides crystal clarity. It seems obvious today that the genocide was years in the planning and immediately obvious from 6 April onwards. Uvin, however, cautions that 'predicting an actual genocide was much more difficult than usually suggested' (2001, p.90). Hitler infamously, though arguably accurately, remarked that no one remembered the Armenians despite their wholesale slaughter at the hands of the Turks in 1915. International reaction to the Turkish actions was minimal, and the event was soon consigned to the dark recesses of the historical record. Unlike the Armenian genocide, however, the Rwandan genocide took place during the post-Cold War era of unprecedented global communication, when international cooperation against oppression was ostensibly more practicable. Thanks to the new globalized media we now know the gruesome details of what happened in 1994, and Rwanda will therefore not suffer the same fate as Armenia. This is surely cold comfort, however, for the 800,000 victims of the slaughter and the many more who continue to live with the scars.

Rwanda shattered any tentative conviction that the post-Cold War era had catalyzed an attitudinal sea-change amongst Western states. The inaction seemed evidence that narrowly conceived national interests continued to dominate. Wheeler claims that President Clinton 'squandered a golden opportunity to make the case that the moral obligation to protect human rights in Rwanda was in conformity with an enlightened view of US national interests' (2002, p.240). Whether Rwanda altered states' view of their national interest is a matter of some contention, although lamentably, the evidence against this view is compelling.

Questions

- What do you consider to have been the primary causes of the genocide in Rwanda?
- Could more have been done to prevent or halt the genocide?
- What lessons does the genocide in Rwanda have for the international community?
- To what extent does Rwanda demonstrate the dangers inherent in international intervention in intra-state conflicts?

Further reading

Barnett, M. (2002) *Eyewitness to Genocide: The United Nations and Rwanda* (Ithaca, N.Y.: Cornell University Press).

Dallaire, R. (2004) *Shake Hands with the Devil: The Failure of Humanity in Rwanda* (London: Arrow).

Des Forges, A. (1999) *Leave None to Tell the Story: Genocide in Rwanda*, Human Rights Watch [online] http://www.hrw.org/legacy/reports/1999/rwanda/index. htm#TopOfPage (accessed 2 May 2009).

Gourevitch, P. (1998) *We Wish to Inform You that Tomorrow we will be Killed with Our Families* (London: Picador).

Klinghoffer, J. (1998) *The International Dimension of Genocide in Rwanda* (Basingstoke and New York: Palgrave Macmillan).

Kroslak, D. (2007) *The Role of France in the Rwandan Genocide* (London: Hurst).

Kuperman, A. (2001) *The Limits of Humanitarian Intervention: Genocide in Rwanda* (Washington DC: Brookings Institution Press).

Mandani, M. (2001) *When Victims Become Killers: Colonialism, Nativism and the Genocide in Rwanda* (Princeton, N.J.: Princeton University Press).

Melvern, L. (2004) *Conspiracy to Murder: The Rwandan Genocide* (London: Verso).

United Nations (UN) (1999) 'Report of the Independent Inquiry into the Actions of the United Nations During the 1994 Genocide in Rwanda', S/1999/1257, 15 December [online] http://www.un.org/News/dh/latest/rwanda.htm (accessed 2 May 2009).

Uvin, P. (1998) *Aiding Violence: The Development Enterprise in Rwanda* (West Hartford, Conn.: Kumarian Press).

Wheeler, N. (2002) *Saving Strangers* (Oxford: Oxford University Press).

Chapter 11

Kosovo

NATO's intervention in Kosovo in 1999 constitutes one of the defining moments in post-Cold War International Relations (IR). The significance of the campaign is described by Nicholas Wheeler as 'immense' (2002, p.242). The fusion of many major IR themes generated great interest in the intervention, its origins and possible repercussions, and a subsequent plethora of academic investigations. NATO's intervention in Kosovo constitutes a decisive juncture in the history of humanitarian intervention with which all serious scholars of this issue must engage.

Significant disagreements exist over NATO's 'true' motivation, the nature of the conflict between the Serbs and the Kosovar Albanians, and the diplomacy that led to the launch of Operation Allied Force. This chapter engages with these questions but seeks to address in greater detail those aspects of the campaign that had implications beyond Kosovo and which influenced the trajectory of the debate on humanitarian intervention.

This chapter initially provides an overview of the crisis in Kosovo, highlighting those factors that led to the crisis in 1998–9. The second section assesses the diplomatic role played by the international community in the ten years before the initiation of the air-strikes and the nature of the intervention itself. The final section analyses the impact Operation Allied Force had on the debate about humanitarian intervention and the differing perspectives on its merits.

Nature of the crisis

The history of the conflict in Kosovo is arguably as divisive an issue as NATO's intervention. Much of the violence in the Balkans in the 1990s was attributed to 'ancient ethnic hatreds', thereby suggesting the different ethnic groups were irreconcilably driven by past grievances (Kaplan, 1993). While in Kosovo 'history is war by other means' (Judah, 2000, p.1), it is an exaggeration to attribute the violent implosion of the Socialist Federal Republic of Yugoslavia (SFRY) exclusively to historical legacies. According to Mark Mazower, a 'less jaundiced' understanding requires us to situate the Balkans in a broader European context which highlights that events there have been driven by 'more sweeping narratives of the development of European identity and civilisation' (2003, pp.14–15). The crisis in Kosovo in 1999 did have deep historical roots, but as the Independent International Commission on Kosovo (IICK) asserted 'the latest round of violence cannot be explained merely by reference to this history' (2000, p. 33).

A number of events in the early 1980s – the death of Tito in 1980, the global economic crisis, and ongoing dissatisfaction with the provisions of the 1974 constitution – led to tensions among SFRY's constituent republics (Serbia, Croatia, Bosnia, Macedonia, Montenegro and Slovenia). In 1981, Albanian students at the University of Pristina protested at their poor facilities, and within weeks this had developed into a pro-independence rally. The Kosovo Serbs were shocked that the ethnic Albanians, who had seemingly benefited so much from the 1974 constitution, would protest so fiercely. The police launched a crackdown and the Kosovo Communist Party was purged. Nonetheless many Serbs still felt that Albanians dominated the political system in Kosovo, and many left the province with (often unsubstantiated) tales of oppression, Albanian-inspired ethnic violence and the widespread rape of Serbian women (Mertus, 1999). The new post-Tito political climate was more tolerant of the public airing of grievances, although nationalism was still officially condemned as counter-revolutionary. In 1986 a Memorandum of the Serbian Academy of Sciences and Arts was published outlining the plight of the Serbs in Kosovo. There then began a spiral of allegations and counter-allegations proffered by the Serbs and the Albanians in Kosovo. The public disagreements soon embroiled other nations, and the issue of Kosovo became a catalyst for the emergence of nationalism throughout the SFRY in the mid-1980s (Horton, 1992; Pesic, 1996, pp.33–4).

In 1989 Slobodan Milosevic, the then President of Serbia, repealed Kosovo's autonomy within Serbia. Previously Kosovo, like the northern province Vojvodina, was an autonomous province within Serbia enjoying significant political independence. In response the majority of the members of the Kosovo Assembly met and declared independence for Kosovo. The change in Kosovo's legal status in 1989 and Belgrade's implementation of certain discriminatory laws between 1989 and 1991 are widely acknowledged as the starting points of the phase in Kosovo's history that culminated in NATO's intervention. The changes in 1989 are portrayed by supporters of NATO's later intervention as indicative of Milosevic's long-held bias against the Kosovar Albanians (Gow, 2003), while those who opposed NATO's intervention either downplay the significance of 1989 or suggest that the lack of Western action at the time shows how little the West really cared about the Kosovar Albanians, thereby contradicting the concern voiced over their plight ten years later (Jatras, 2000, p.23).

From 1990 to 1995, in stark contrast to the violence elsewhere in the Balkans, an uneasy peace existed in Kosovo. The Kosovo Albanian majority operated a 'phantom state' whereby schools, hospitals and taxes were administrated by the unrecognized local regime, while Serbs continued to adhere to rule from Belgrade. In 1995 the Dayton Peace Accords were signed primarily to end the conflict in Bosnia. The lack of any provision relating to Kosovo in the Accords is widely regarded as having inflamed the Kosovar Albanians (Hedges, 1999, p.31). Dayton was 'an extraordinary trauma for the Kosovar Albanians', who were dismayed that their policy of peaceful civil resistance had been ignored (Judah, 2000, p.124). The Accords are regarded by some as having sounded the death knell for the pacifist politics pursued by the largest Kosovo Albanian party, the Democratic League of Kosovo, led by Ibrahim Rugova, as the Kosovo Liberation Army (KLA) exploited the widespread dissatisfaction and began to step up its armed campaign (see Box 11.1). As Carl Hodge states, 'In effect Dayton told autonomists in Kosovo that the metal in Kosovo was not hot enough to bring about political change. The KLA decided to make it glow' (2000, p.26). There followed an escalating cycle of retaliatory violence between the KLA and the Federal Republic of Yugoslavia's (FRY's) police and military, resulting in thousands of deaths, hundreds of thousands of internally displaced persons and thousands of refugees leaving Kosovo for Albanian and Macedonia. The KLA adopted a strategy of provoking Belgrade into launching excessive counter-attacks in order to generate domestic support, and more importantly, force the international

---

Box 11.1 The rise of the KLA

In January 1982 the Gërvalla brothers established the Popular Movement for the Republic of Kosovo (LPRK). In 1993 the LPRK split into two factions, the Popular Movement for Kosovo (LPK) and the National Movement for the Liberation of Kosovo (LKCK). Those in the LKCK were Marxist-Leninists who sought to provoke a mass uprising. The LPK, the forerunners of the KLA, were committed to guerrilla tactics and were not ideologically homogeneous (Hedges, 1999, p.58). In May 1993 the KLA claimed their first victims when two Serb policemen were shot in Glogovác. The KLA were a fringe group throughout much of the 1990s, and by 1997 their membership, mainly comprising families and local tribes, was about 150. In 1997 a 'Ponzi' pyramid scheme collapsed in Albania and the country descended into chaos. The KLA poured across the border and looted the abandoned army barracks. The KLA was soon well armed and financed but their numbers, though on the increase, remained small. By late 1997, the cycle of reprisal killings between the KLA and the Serb authorities was gaining momentum and, exploiting the high levels of disenchantment with peaceful politics, the Serbian crackdown and the 70 per cent unemployment rate in Kosovo, the KLA grew exponentially in size.

community to condemn the Milosevic regime and ultimately intervene on the side of the Kosovar Albanians (Gow, 2003, p.256; Kuperman, 2006).

By autumn 1998 Kosovo was at the top of the international agenda, with Security Council Resolution 1199 describing the situation as a threat to peace and stability in the region and empowering the Council to act under Chapter VII of the UN Charter. The number of deaths in the year prior to NATO's intervention is estimated at 500, with some 400,000 people displaced (Wheeler, 2002, p.269). The death toll is low compared with say Rwanda, but it was routinely stated at the time that without international action Milosevic would increase his oppression of the Kosovo Albanians and ultimately the death toll would rise drastically. The situation was often said to be analogous to that of the early stages of the war in Bosnia, and the eventual carnage in 1995 was proffered as the likely consequences of inaction (Hehir, 2006). The scale of the suffering in the region was a source of debate. According to Gordon Bardos 'there was no humanitarian crisis in Kosovo in 1997, or in 1998, or in 1999 in any conventionally understood sense of the term' (2003, p.57), whereas Timothy Garton-Ash claims, 'Anyone who was in Kosovo, as I was, in the winter of 1998–1999 could see that there was a humanitarian disaster' (2000, p.2).

International response

The international response to Kosovo culminated in the 1999 military intervention. International engagement with the region was not always this direct, however. The following sections outline the various phases of international engagement.

1989–98: distracted superpowers

The crisis in Kosovo had been brewing since at least 1981, and many observers and fact-finding groups had warned that the situation was liable to explode. According to the IICK:

> From the 1980's onwards, Kosovo exhibited all the signs of a catastrophe waiting to happen . . . the failure to respond adequately at an early stage of the evolution of the conflict created difficulties in later stages. At each stage of the conflict, the diplomatic options narrowed. (2000, 62)

While the break-up of SFRY was unquestionably a cause of great international concern, Kosovo was sidelined by the more violent conflicts between Serbia, Croatia and Bosnia. Before March 1998 the response of the international community to the situation in Kosovo was limited and reactive (Gow, 1994; Bellamy, 2002, p.37). A number of non-governmental organizations (NGOs) had reported on the situation in the region, but official international political engagement was extremely limited, and a number of opportunities for constructive engagement were missed (IICK, 2000, p.51).

Given that Kosovo's explosive potentiality was so widely discussed, it is paradoxical that it never received the attention its reputation should have commanded. Whereas in Macedonia from 1993 to 1999 a coordinated international conflict prevention mission was largely successful, Kosovo was ignored. Marc Weller writes of the 'schizophrenic' nature of the international response which acknowledged Kosovo's explosive potentiality but acted according to 'a hope that the situation would go away if ignored for a sufficiently long time' (1999, p.33). On Christmas Eve 1992 the outgoing Bush administration issued the so-called 'Christmas warning'. Lawrence Eagleburger, acting US secretary of state, sent a cable to the US chargé d'affaires in Belgrade with the instruction that the contents be read to Milosevic in person. The message stated, 'In the event of conflict in Kosovo caused by Serbian action, the US will be prepared to employ military force against Serbians in Kosovo and Serbia proper.' This warning was endorsed by the Clinton administration. As the situation in Kosovo degenerated, especially after 1995, this commitment increasingly became an embarrassment as inaction prevailed (IICK, 2000, p.344; Bellamy, 2002, p.50).

Alex Bellamy suggests three reasons why Kosovo was so marginalized in the various international diplomatic processes (2002, pp.24–6). First, prior to 1998 there was not an alarming level of violence in Kosovo. While allegations of oppression were made by NGOs such as Amnesty, Save the Children and Oxfam, and particularly by Tadeusz Mazowiecki, the UN special rapporteur on human rights in the former Yugoslavia, it seems that the only statistics that would prompt an international response were those relating to deaths, and these did not become significant until 1998 (Daalder and O'Hanlon, 2000, p.9). The second reason was that it was felt that to engage with the secessionists in Kosovo would have sparked a similar cry for secession from the Serbs in Croatia and Bosnia and further destabilize the region. The final reason is that those seeking independence were not in control of the territory they sought independence for. Had the Kosovars been in positions of political, judicial and military power in Kosovo, as the Croats and Slovenes were, then the international community may have countenanced the separation.

October 1998–March 1999: diplomatic failure

By mid-1998 the number of internally displaced persons and refugees fleeing to Albania and Macedonia ensured that Kosovo could no longer be ignored. According to the World Refugee Survey, Kosovo ranked in the top five globally for the number of refugees and internally displaced people, with the total figure an estimated 300,000. The credibility of the West, and NATO in particular, diminished as the conflict escalated without resolution. The more NATO threatened action and yet failed to subsequently do anything, the more the Milosevic regime appears to have concluded that nothing would ever happen (Weller, 1999, p.398; Bellamy, 2002, p.124).

A settlement was negotiated in October 1998 but failed to hold in large part because the chief US negotiator, Richard Holbrooke, gave personal assurances that the KLA would comply with the agreement, assurances later described by the IICK as 'ill founded' (2000, p.149). The KLA did not abide by the agreement, and by the end of the year the cycle of retaliatory violence resumed. On 15 January 1999 Serb forces moved into the town of Racak in central Kosovo. The following day, media from around the world broadcast images of 45 dead ethnic Albanians, all purported to be civilians. International opinion turned sharply against Milosevic and the momentum in favour of more robust international involvement grew.

At the end of January the Contact Group (the United States, United Kingdom, France, Russia, Germany and Italy) summoned all relevant parties to attend negotiations at Rambouillet, France on 6 February. The next day NATO issued a statement threatening to use force against any party which did not attend and to any group which was the cause of a breakdown in the forthcoming negotiations. According to Weller, this 'remarkable' summons involved NATO, 'acting as it were as the enforcement agent of the Security Council, albeit a self-appointed one'. Weller describes the NATO threat as 'entirely unprecedented in post UN Charter history and somewhat reminiscent of an exercise of Great Power diplomacy in the classical balance of power system of the post Napoleonic Concert of Europe' (1999, p.397). NATO's threat did not merely suggest that the parties had to attend Rambouillet, it stipulated that they must reach an agreement there, based on a plan drawn up by the Contact Group. Indeed, Holbrooke described Rambouillet as 'a very legitimate attempt to bring the parties together to force them to agree' (Frontline, 2000).

Ultimately the Rambouillet negotiations broke down when the representatives from the FRY rejected an agreement which the Kosovar Albanian delegation signed. Whether the negotiations were conducted fairly is a matter of some controversy. Some argue that the NATO powers contrived a situation whereby the FRY would be cast as spoiler, thereby clearing the way for a bombing campaign. The provisions of Appendix B(8) (see Box 11.2) in particular have been cited as consciously unpalatable to Belgrade (Gowan, 2000, p.8; Hagen, 1999, p.59). Rambouillet is variously described as 'Albright's charade to get a bombing campaign', 'a textbook example of how not to practice diplomacy' and as having constituted 'an inherently unstable' agreement (Jatras, 2000, p.24, Layne, 2000, p.15; Bandow, 2000, p.33). Noam Chomsky argues that there was in fact no

Box 11.2 The Rambouillet Accords

Appendix B(8): NATO personnel shall enjoy, together with their vehicles, vessels, aircraft, and equipment, free and unrestricted passage and unimpeded access throughout the FRY including associated airspace and territorial waters. This shall include, but not be limited to, the right of bivouac, maneuver, billet, and utilization of any areas or facilities as required for support, training, and operations.

'failure' at Rambouillet, but rather what happened 'was the rationally chosen course that led to a predictable victory for the values that mattered, with the fate of the populations as an incidental concern' (1999, p.108).

The counter-perspective suggests that, while certain mistakes were made, Rambouillet was a genuine attempt to broker an agreement. Bellamy, while outlining a number of Western diplomatic errors during the negotiations, ultimately suggests that the Yugoslavs had a 'lack of interest in the diplomatic process' and that 'Milosevic had already decided that he would test NATO's resolve and go to war' (2002, pp.147, 150). Although he describes Rambouillet as 'more a shambles then a grand design', Weller concludes that Rambouillet was 'a heroic failure' given the earnest attempts made to reconcile the parties (1999, p.392). He dismisses the argument that the contentious provisions of Appendix B were responsible for the Serb unwillingness to sign as 'conspiracy theories' (ibid., p.397). The IICK detailed many of the flaws in both the deal proposed at Rambouillet and the manner in which the negotiations were pursued, particularly in relation to NATO's intransigence on the issue of Appendix B. While they argued that compromising on this aspect of the deal was 'an obvious negotiating opening that might have broken the impasse' they ultimately conclude, 'The minimum goals of the Kosovar Albanians and of Belgrade were irreconcilable' (IICK, 2000, pp.157, 161). Either way the breakdown of the negotiations led directly to the initiation of NATO's air strikes.

24 March 1999–10 June 1999: intervention

On 24 March NATO began air-strikes against FRY. Support for the strikes was strong among the NATO states with the exception of Greece. Within the Security Council both China and Russia strongly opposed NATO's actions, as did India. The Russian foreign minister claimed the bombing constituted 'a strike against Russia' (Bellamy, 2002, p.166). Additionally the West's tradition allies, such as Japan, Indonesia and South Korea, far from being supportive of NATO, were 'mute in their response' (ibid., p.167). The provisions of the *Uniting for Peace* resolution (see Chapter 5) which enable the General Assembly to act when the Security Council is unable unanimously to sanction action, were, according to Nigel White, 'conveniently forgotten in the case of the Kosovo crisis' (2000, p.41). Prior to NATO's intervention it was suggested to the UK Foreign Office that NATO could use the *Uniting for Peace* provision but this was rejected because officials felt it was highly unlikely that two-thirds of the General Assembly would vote in favour of NATO's actions (Chesterman, 2003, p.57).

The international response to NATO's action was thus mixed if not negative. Critics of this assertion point to Russia's failed attempt to have Operation Allied Force condemned by the Security Council, and the support afforded to the operation by the Organisation for Islamic Conference (OIC) (Caplan, 2000: 24). While the 12–3 Security Council vote against Russia's draft resolution appears conclusive, Wheeler has noted that the result was less emphatic then it appears. He points to the fact that five of the 12 who voted against the resolution were members of NATO and only three of the remaining seven spoke in support of the intervention (2002, p.291). Additionally White notes that 'lack of condemnation by the Security Council cannot be seen as an authorization to use force' (2000, p.33). The OIC's support for the intervention was largely the consequence of an expression of solidarity with Kosovo's predominantly Muslim population rather than support for the idea of humanitarian intervention per se. Indeed, 50 of the 57 members of the OIC were among the 133 states in the G-77 that voted twice to condemn unconditionally the notion of unilateral humanitarian intervention.

Military advice stated categorically that the campaign would not be a short one (Clark, 2001, p.185). This advice appears to have been ignored by NATO's political hierarchy, who continued to claim that Milosevic would quickly capitulate. The day the air strikes began, US secretary of state Madeleine Albright stated, 'I don't see this as a long term operation. I think that this is something . . . that is achievable within a relatively short period of time' (Daalder and O'Hanlon, 2000, p.91). However, Albright later stated that when President Clinton said to her on 25 March, 'This is not going to be over quickly,' she replied, 'I feel the same way. Nobody should ever think that we had gone into this without our eyes wide open' (Sciolino and Bronner, 1999, p.3). Similarly, two weeks into the campaign she proclaimed, 'We never expected this to be over quickly' (Layne, 2000, p.11). The campaign itself lasted 78 days, resulting in 10,000 deaths, including those Kosovars killed by Yugoslav forces. NATO flew 38,400 sorties and released 26,614 air munitions. The US flew over 60 per cent of all sorties and carried out over 80 per cent of all strike sorties.

In his televised address on the first day of bombing President Clinton stated, 'I do not intend to put our troops in Kosovo to fight a war' (*New York Times*, 1999, p.15). This categorical pledge is seen by many as an error as it informed the FRY army that they would not have to plan for a NATO ground intervention. To avoid Serbian anti-aircraft fire NATO planes flew above 15,000 feet, and this had three major consequences for the campaign. First, this made the targeting of FRY infantry, tanks and police units much more difficult. These components of the FRY military were most responsible for the ground operation within Kosovo yet they escaped the bombing relatively unharmed. Second, targeting from such a height depended on clement weather conditions, and when there was cloud cover the air strikes had to be halted, prolonging the campaign and negating the impact on the FRY military. Third, bombing from these heights increased the instances of 'collateral damage'. The IICK estimates that NATO bombs killed 495 civilians while Human Rights Watch puts the figure at 527 (IICK, 2000, p.94). Certain targets were harder to identify, and this resulted in the bombing of civilian convoys and trains and the widespread bombing of decoy targets.

The enduring images of the NATO intervention are of Kosovar refugees huddling in makeshift camps in Macedonia. The unity of resolve among NATO members held in large part because of this refugee flow, and Ivo Daalder and Michael O'Hanlon speculate that had Milosevic's forces not embarked upon this course of action, 'NATO could have lost the war' (2000, p.6). NATO's resolve was severely tested at times, particularly early on in the campaign. After the first night the Italian Communist Party threatened to pull out of the coalition government, while 98 per cent of the population in Greece opposed the initiation of the military campaign (ibid., p.167).

The activities of certain elements of the FRY military and police forces were used as a central justification for the bombing. According to the IICK over 90 per cent of the Kosovar population was displaced during Operation Allied Force (2000, p. 90). Advocates of NATO's intervention argue that the intervention was necessary because of the actions of the FRY after the intervention began, and claim that Milosevic always planned to 'cleanse' Kosovo of its Albanian population (Robertson, 2002, p.441). In defence of this argument certain observers have claimed the existence of 'Operation Horseshoe' – a military plan to forcibly expel the Kosovo Albanians, allegedly uncovered by Bulgarian intelligence and passed on to the German army prior to Operation Allied Force. While some doubt exists as to the authenticity of this plan (Judah, 2000, pp.240–1; Chomsky, 1999, pp.35–6), even if it is accepted that it was real this begs the question posed by Bellamy; 'If Operation Horseshoe was known about, why was so little done to prepare the UNHCR and other agencies to receive refugees in Albania and Macedonia?' (2002, p.165).

NATO's intervention unquestionably led to a dramatic increase in ethnic cleansing, with Misha Glenny accusing NATO of having 'contributed to a flood of biblical proportions' (1999, p.658). Despite numerous warnings, and the predictions of senior military figures like General Clark, few preparations were made for the refugee crises that erupted. In a 6 March meeting, Madeleine Albright had asked General Clark, 'If we commence the strikes will the Serbs attack the population?' He replied, 'Almost certainly' (Clark, 2001, p.173). Yet General Clark later noted that 'one of the most obvious features of the conflict was the West's lack of preparedness when the conflict actually began' (ibid., p.423).

This lack of preparedness was strongly criticized by human rights organizations, and particularly by Macedonia, which felt the brunt of the refugee exodus. A UN High Commissioner for Refugees (UNHCR) report following the campaign noted that 'UNHCR received no advance warning from any government or other source', and asserted that prior to Operation Allied Force NATO governments had in fact been urging the organization to prepare for the implementation of the Rambouillet Accords (Judah, 2000, p.240). The longer the campaign went on without halting the ethnic cleanings, the more NATO's strategy and capacity were called into question. Defeating the FRY military and stemming the tide of refugees thus became a matter of enormous political importance for NATO's member states, and the very credibility of the organization itself (see Box 11.3).

The termination of the NATO air strikes came on 10 June, when the FRY army and NATO signed the Military Technical Agreement. Though heralded in some quarters as a capitulation by Milosevic, the provisions of the peace plan were considerably less draconian than those presented at Rambouillet, leading Simon Chesterman to ask, 'why were the terms presented to Serbia at Rambouillet more onerous than those offered after a 78 day bombing campaign?' (2003, p.54). Significantly Appendix B had been removed from the Military Technical Agreement and the deployment of NATO was no longer a *sine qua non*. The IICK noted, 'The final agreement did contain some gains from the FRY point of view' (2000, p.96), and Security Council Resolution 1244 which endorsed this agreement recognized FRY's territorial integrity and Belgrade's jurisdiction over Kosovo. Of course, all FRY military did have to leave Kosovo, and they have not returned.

Box 11.3 NATO credibility?

[W]hat Milosevic never really understood was this wasn't a conflict strictly about Kosovo. It wasn't even a conflict ultimately about ethnic cleansing. It was a battle about the future of NATO, about the credibility of the United States as a force in world affairs. And the longer it went on the more clearly the nations of the West could see those issues.

General Clark, quoted in Prokopijevic (2004, p.187).

Impact on the debate

Operation Allied Force catalyzed intense international debate about the merits of NATO's intervention and also about the broader issue of humanitarian intervention. Opinion was sharply divided on a number of key issues, and the intervention propelled the issue of humanitarian intervention to the top of the international political agenda.

A war fought for values

While many humanitarian NGOs, such as Amnesty and Human Rights Watch, were critical of the manner in which Operation Allied Force was executed (see pages 216 to 218), the intervention was favourably received by many global civil society activists (see Chapter 6) and those keen to enable the enforcement of human rights. NATO's action was seen to 'represent the wave of the future' (Fuller, 1999, p.12) and many heralded the dawn of a new age of human rights. Geoffrey Robertson described Operation Allied Force as 'the first war waged for ethical principles alone', and but one of many 'hopeful signs that we are indeed entering the third age of the human rights revolution: the era of enforcement' (2002, pp.451, 387).

The intervention, supporters argued, highlighted the changed attitudes of Western states and the power of global civil society to influence foreign policy. Constituting 'the first war of humanitarian intervention ever carried out by the Western military powers' (Coll, 2001, p.128) the extensive humanitarian rationale espoused by the intervening states – such as Tony Blair's statement that this was a war fought for 'values' (Chatterjee and Scheid, 2003, p.7) – suggested that the pressure exerted by proponents of human security had effected change. Bellamy argues that the intervention pointed to 'a heightened degree of liberal institutionalism in global politics', and illustrated the 'extent to which international values and interests have begun to come together during the 1990s' (2002, pp.211–14). Wheeler and Dunne highlighted the United Kingdom's particularly important role in pushing for the intervention, and hailed the Blair government as a 'norm entrepreneur' (1998, p.177). Operation Allied Force thus was held to illustrate the capacity of the human rights movement and global civil society to compel Western states to alter their priorities from narrow national interests towards a universal concern with human security (Thomas and Tow, 2002, p.178).

This apparent new concern with morality, and specifically human rights, amongst the West was correctly deemed of major significance. Traditionally states had demonstrated a pronounced unwillingness to act in defence of others where there were no national interests involved (see Chapter 9). The attitudinal sea-change ostensibly highlighted by Operation

Allied Force created the prospect of greater humanitarian activism, increased coercive enforcement of human rights norms and the development of Western foreign policy based on universal values rather than national interests. In the wake of Operation Allied Force, therefore, significant optimism prevailed amongst those eager to prioritize human security that Western states were finally prepared to act on their humanitarian commitments and forge a new international system based on human rights (see Chapter 6). Human Rights Watch described the 1999 interventions in Kosovo and East Timor as indicative of a new era for human rights in which Western states would use their military to come to the aid of victims of atrocities (2000).

'The new military humanism'

Those opposed to the intervention argued that Kosovo highlighted a disturbing trend towards greater Western interventionism and the unwarranted expansion of Western interests. The moral arguments were considered either entirely hypocritical or foolhardy. This perspective is manifest in (broadly) two forms, a left-wing and a realist critique.

Left-wing critics argued that NATO's action was inspired by the desire to proliferate capitalism and project power into Eastern Europe. The argument that NATO was compelled by moral concern was deemed implausible given the West's history of oppression (Chomsky, 1999, p.74). The edited collection *Masters of the Universe* presented the intervention as a purely self-interested exercise in great power domination with humanitarianism serving as a consumer friendly veneer; Operation Allied Force was 'all about US global hegemony' (Wood, 2000, p.190). Diana Johnstone similarly argued that NATO, far from being driven by a sense of moral duty, was motivated 'quite simply by the desire to demonstrate NATO's new mission in time for its fiftieth anniversary' (2000, p.8). This new mission constituted an effort by American liberals and European social democrats to maintain the illusion that they are determined to pursue social justice. Maya Chadda asserted that the real motive behind the intervention was 'to establish hegemonic influence enabling [NATO] to structure interstate relations in the region and be able to punish and reward states that deny the contour of political/ideological order advantageous to the hegemonic state' (2003, p.321). David Chandler argued that Operation Allied Force constituted an escalation of an already prevalent Western disposition towards legitimizing greater influence in international affairs though the discourse of human rights and the establishment of a compliant international community subordinate to Western cultural and political values (2002, p.17). NATO's action was thus seen by many on the left as the precursor to greater Western expansionism and an attempt to subvert the existing norms in international relations.

Many realists argued that the intervention set a dangerous precedent which would destabilize the international system. Stanley Kober argued that NATO's illegal action would anger other countries, lead to the rapid degradation of international law and culminate with the world 'primed for major conflict' (2000, p.117). Douglas Bandow suggested that the intervention 'deepened European dependence on America for defence of European interests that have little relevance to America' and 'put US military personnel at risk without any serious, let alone vital, US interest at stake' (2000, p.31). Michael Mandelbaum argued that the intervention severely strained relations with Russia and China and also destabilized the wider Balkans (1999).

Realists are inherently sceptical, if not actively hostile towards, the influence of morality in international relations, and the idea of rejecting formal legal authority in favour of moral authority is deemed undesirable (see Chapter 4). As explored in Chapter 7, the question 'who decides' is of paramount importance; international law comprises a hierarchical structure which provides an answer to this question, whereas morality is, by definition, subjective and devoid of formal authoritative structure. Thus the move to moral authority seemingly signalled by NATO's intervention disrupted the existing authoritative structure with potentially destabilizing effects.

So while the left-wing and realist critiques shared a scepticism about the moral imperative cited by NATO, and both viewed the intervention as a strategy of expansion, they differed in their views on this expansionism, with the left seeing it as capitalist oppression and the realists decrying unsustainable over-extension.

International law after Kosovo

The dominant rationale advanced by NATO in 1999 was the moral imperative to aid the Kosovar Albanians (Guicherd, 1999, p.19). Certain NATO states also advanced a legal justification in tandem with the more prominent humanitarian argument. The three NATO states on the Security Council argued that their actions were consistent with Security Council Resolutions 1160, 1199 and 1203. While these resolutions did empower the Security Council to act under Chapter VII, there is no obvious provision in any of the three that could be said to constitute a trigger for collective, let alone unilateral, military intervention. The then UK defence minister George Robertson stated, 'We are in no doubt that NATO is acting within international law. Our legal justification rests upon the accepted principle that force may be used in extreme circumstances to avert a humanitarian catastrophe' (Holbrook, 2002, p.141). This principle permitting the use of force in extreme circumstances to prevent a humanitarian crisis was certainly not 'accepted', as the legal debate which followed testified. The UK House of Commons Foreign Affairs Select

Committee concluded that NATO's military action was 'of dubious legality in the current state of international law' (House of Commons, 2000: para. 1138) and this is the dominant view, although NATO still officially maintains that its action was in accordance with international law (Hehir, 2008b, 2009a).

While NATO did not gain Security Council approval for its actions, the intervention was justified by its supporters on the grounds that positive law, and especially the Security Council veto, had to be subverted by the moral need to intervene. Jane Stromseth argued that the intervention demonstrated that deviation from international law could be legitimate in 'exceptional circumstances' (2005). The majority of the supporters of the intervention did not rejoice in the fact that the United Nations was ignored but rather used this case to highlight the ostensibly anachronistic nature of existing international law. Many turned to natural or moral law in preference to positive law as a means by which to justify this 'illegal' action (see Chapters 2 and 5).

The controversy surrounding the legality of NATO's actions thus led to increased speculation about the key tenets of international law and its very utility. David Armstrong and Theo Farrell note that Kosovo revelled the tension between law and legitimacy more starkly than even the later intervention in Iraq (2005, p.13). The legality of NATO's actions, and unilateral humanitarian intervention more generally, became a subject of intense debate amongst scholars of IR and international law. As was discussed in detail in Chapter 5, the majority view was that international law did not permit humanitarian intervention of the kind prosecuted by NATO, although perhaps it should and one day might (Ambos, 1999; Cassese, 1999, Simma, 1999). This debate catalyzed a comprehensive review of the existing tenets of international law and especially the process of customary law formation (Hehir, 2009b).

The debate reignited the issue of authority and legitimacy in international relations (see Chapter 7). The Security Council may well have formal legal authority but many felt it lacked legitimacy. The refusal of China and Russia to support measures to forcibly halt the oppression of the Kosovo Albanians was deemed to be indicative of both states' general reluctance to look beyond narrow national interests when deliberating at the Security Council (Bellamy, 2002, p.212). If authority is distinguishable from power by the perceived legitimacy of the formally authoritative actor (Hurrell, 2005, p.16) then the Security Council, by virtue of China and Russia's membership, had lost its legitimacy although it retained its formal legal authority.

The IICK found that Operation Allied Force was 'illegal but legitimate', and noted that this disjuncture required action (2000, p.10) a view later supported by the ICISS (2001, p.3). Thus many argued that rather than viewing Operation Allied Force as indicative of NATO's disregard for legal norms, it should be seen as the catalyst for much-needed amendments to international law and the UN Charter in particular (Simma, 1999, p.6; Guicherd, 1999, p.20). The call for reform also came from critics of NATO's intervention, who argued that the existing provisions governing the use of force for human protection were inadequate and widely perceived as such, and therefore constituted a potential pretext for unilateral action. States could justify bypassing the United Nations by pointing to its anachronistic provisions, thereby potentially legitimizing any illegal use of force and undermining the very basis of international law (Hehir, 2008a, pp.121–30).

Finally, more broadly, the legal controversy led many to question the utility of international law. Certain observers argued that given the veto powers of the P5 and the attitudes of both China and Russia, acting without Security Council authorization was inevitable and often just (Daalder and O'Hanlon, 2000, p.218). Bellamy posed the question, 'Why . . . should undemocratic states with poor human rights records prevent a group of democratic states from protecting people in foreign countries?' (2002, p.212). It was claimed that as both Russia and China so obviously remained wedded to narrow geopolitical worldviews and retained a stranglehold over international law, the utility of law was diminished. International law was therefore deemed by some as subordinate to morality and natural law, and they argued that certain ostensibly more ethically advanced states should not be bound by provisions that enable genocide and human rights violations (Cooper, 2002; Linklater, 2000; Nardin, 2003; Robertson, 2002).

Conversely critics of the invasion argued that NATO's actions graphically highlighted the West's, and especially the United States', disregard for international law (Bowring, 2008, pp.49–54; Chomsky, 1999, p.150). The flouting of international law was further evidence, some argued, of the West's determination to disregard all legal constraints in its quest for global dominance. The intervention illustrated the extent to which the United States acts as 'an all powerful Monarch' in an international system 'where the justice system becomes subordinated to personal whims and self-interests' (Thomas, 2003, p.171). The manner in which the intervention was prosecuted showed 'A disturbing disregard for the principles of humanitarianism that should guide any such action' (Hayden, 2003, p.276).

In light of the legal controversy generated by the intervention, Kofi Annan called for new thinking on the issue. In response the Canadian Government established the ICISS, which released its report – *The Responsibility to Protect* – in December 2001. The report outlined a means by which the terms of the debate surrounding humanitarian intervention could be altered to put the onus on the host state's responsibilities rather than the legal right of the intervening states (see Chapter 6). Bellamy argues that while the debate regarding NATO's intervention was divisive, it did highlight an emerging global consensus over the responsibility states have towards their citizens. The 'widespread acknowledgement of sovereign responsibility that accompanied the Kosovo war,' he claims, 'provided a catalyst for new thinking about the use of armed force for humanitarian purposes,' and led directly to the incorporation of the idea of a 'responsibility to protect' in the 2005 World Summit outcome document (Bellamy, 2009b, p.164).

Force protection and international humanitarian law

NATO's tactics, particularly its decision to bomb from 15,000 feet, drew criticism from many human rights organizations which argued that this was a contradictory, if not counter-productive, means of protecting human life. With the commencement of military action NATO's main priority appeared to be the safety of its own soldiers rather than the Kosovar Albanians. Despite the rhetoric of the politicians advocating air strikes, the military were clear about their objectives and did not attempt to portray the campaign as anything other than a targeted military strike. While Tony Blair said that the objective was 'to avert a humanitarian catastrophe' (Bellamy, 2002, p.157), General Clark suggested that the goal was not humanitarian, stating:

> [Operation Allied Force] was not designed as a means of blocking Serb ethnic cleansing. It was not designed as a means of waging war against the Serb and MUP forces in Kosovo. Not in any way. There was never any intent to do that. That was not the idea. (Chomsky, 1999, p.36)

According to Michael Ignatieff, NATO 'talked the language of ultimate commitment and practiced the warfare of minimal risk' (2000, p.111). Flying at high altitudes meant that NATO was largely unable to prevent the Yugoslav forces on the ground from attacking the KLA and the civilian population, and thus NATO's tactics had the effect of 'exporting virtually all the risk of harm or death to non-combatants' (Lucas, 2003, p.79). General Clark admitted during the campaign that 'air power alone cannot stop paramilitary action' (Wheeler, 2002, p.270).

At the initiation of the air strikes General Clark outlined three 'Measures of Merit' that would determine the prosecution of the campaign and the analysis of its success or failure. They were first, not to lose aircraft; second, 'impact the Yugoslavian military and police activities on the ground as rapidly and as effectively as possible'; and third, 'protect our ground forces' (Clark, 2001, p.185). As is clear, two of the three measures directly related to the safety of NATO personnel. The second measure was conditional on accommodating the other two, and its realization was, as such, dependent on NATO's assessment of the risk involved. As Bellamy notes, 'Interesting omissions were the protection of the Kosovar Albanian victims . . . the wholesale ethnic cleansing and mass murder of Kosovar Albanians did not alter Clark's understanding of success or failure' (2002, p.160). As the war progressed it became clear that NATO was prepared to do very little that would impact on the Yugoslav activities on the ground because of the dangers involved. Ground troops were ruled out by President Clinton from the beginning, and the strategy employed remained bombing from the safe distance of 15,000 feet.

The majority of bombs dropped were aimed at non-military infrastructure, and thus the aim of the campaign appeared to be to intimidate the population and make living conditions as difficult for them as possible so as to compel them to pressurize Milosevic to concede (Coll, 2001, p.144; Shue 2003, p.99). During the campaign Kenneth Roth, executive director of Human Rights Watch, wrote, 'We are concerned that NATO bombed the civilian infrastructure not because it was making a significant contribution to the Yugoslav military effort but because its destruction would squeeze Serb civilians to put pressure on Milosevic to withdraw from Kosovo' (2000).

NATO General Mike Jackson was open about the strategy, stating, 'Just focusing on fielded forces is not enough. . . . The people have got to get the point that their lights are turned off, their bridges are blocked so they can't get to work' (Hayden, 2003, p.264). This strategy of intentionally increasing hardship amongst civilians is certainly both illegal and contrary to the Just War tradition (see Chapter 2).

The US Defense Department admitted dropping over 1100 cluster bomb canisters with 220,000 'bomblets' over Kosovo, while the United Kingdom dropped approximately 500 bombs, each with 147 'bomblets' (Hayden, 2003, p.262). Human Rights Watch, describing cluster bombs as 'grave violations of humanitarian law', estimates that up to 150 civilians were killed in Kosovo by these devices, and notes that the Red Cross found that more than 150 more died in the 12 months after Operation Allied Force because unexploded cluster bombs detonated (2001). Amnesty International's assessment of NATO's campaign concluded, 'civilian deaths could have been significantly reduced if NATO forces had fully adhered to the laws of war. . . . NATO did not always meet its legal obligations in selecting targets and in choosing means and methods of attack (2000).

In March 2000 NATO admitted that it had dropped 31,000 rounds of depleted uranium throughout Kosovo. A report issued by the Balkan Task Force, established by the United Nations in 1999 to assess the environmental impact of the air strikes, noted that NATO had not supplied it with sufficient information about the nature of these devices (Sulyok, 2003, p.154).

Thus the methods employed led to a debate about the morality of 'bombing for humanity' (Brown, 2000, McCoubrey, 2000, Miller, 2000a;

Young, 2000). The IICK argued that the NATO's priorities somewhat undermined the mission they sought to achieve (2000, p.181). NATO's overall record was described by the IICK, however, as 'unprecedented to the extent that it avoided civilian damage through the accuracy of its targeting' (2000, p.181). This strategy of bombing designed to ensure zero casualties led Ignatieff to coin the phrase 'virtual war'. Ignatieff worried that the manner in which the campaign was prosecuted could inure Western citizens and political leaders to the consequences of military action. He warned, 'If war becomes virtual and without risk, democratic electorates may be more willing to fight especially if the cause is justified in the language of human rights and even democracy itself' (2000, pp.179–80).

The concern regarding a future of 'virtual war' has been somewhat negated by the interventions in Afghanistan and Iraq, where ground forces were deployed and heavy losses endured. The Just War tradition (see Chapter 2) contends that the use of force is just only when the provisions of both *jus ad bellum* and *jus in bello* are met, and many argued that Operation Allied Force failed in terms of the latter. Of course, as dealt with in Chapter 8, it is perhaps to be expected that states will deploy their troops in a way that minimizes their exposure to risk and this is arguably likely to be more pronounced if the use of force is carried out in defence of others (Miller, 2000a). Whether this reality therefore undermines the very idea of bombing for humanity is an ongoing matter of debate. Additionally, as noted in Chapter 8, certain observers hold that it is not valid to preclude an intervention from being considered humanitarian if we discern an element of self-interest on the part of the intervening forces (Brown, 2001, p.23; Weiss, 2007, p.7; Wheeler, 2002, p.38).

Conclusion

Many cases in the 1990s catalyzed intense debate about humanitarian intervention, and Kosovo constituted the high water mark of this discussion. While the intervention sparked intense controversy and was criticized on a number of grounds, the support for Operation Allied Force was unprecedented, and it constitutes the most widely acclaimed act of military humanitarian intervention in the contemporary era. In light of the widespread international outcry at the attempt to portray the invasion of Iraq in 2003 as an act of humanitarian intervention (see Chapter 13), Kosovo has increasingly come to be used as a example of a 'genuine' humanitarian intervention by those eager to counter the claim that such action is always hypocritical and a function of geopolitics.

Interest in this issue remains enormous, and Kosovo's place in the history of humanitarian intervention is surely secure. The details of the conflict between the Serbs and Kosovo Albanians will doubtless remain contested, and Kosovo's declaration of independence in February 2008 renewed the controversy surrounding the relationship between these two polarized groups. Milosevic's indictment for crimes against humanity in the midst of NATO's campaign and subsequent trial at The Hague, cut short by his death in 2006, constituted a new, if highly controversial, departure for international law. The ICISS report commissioned in the wake of Operation Allied Force continues to generate debate, and the role of international law, seemingly exposed as limited by NATO's actions, remains a seminal political issue.

It is perhaps to be regretted, though perhaps it is not surprising, that the enormous interest in humanitarian intervention generated by Operation Allied Force has not resulted in a resolution of the penumbra that is humanitarian intervention. The primary sources of dissonance exposed by Operation Allied Force remain despite the many efforts since to generate consensus.

Questions

- To what extent did the lack of violence in Kosovo from 1989–95 impact on international engagement with the issue? What are the implications of this?
- Did NATO's tactics during Operation Allied Force fundamentally undermine the humanitarian credentials of its intervention?
- Did Operation Allied Force constitute evidence of the West's new moral dispensation?
- How convincing are the critiques of Operation Allied Force?

Further reading

On the history of the crisis in Kosovo

Glenny, M. (1999) *The Balkans, 1804–1999* (London: Grant).

Judah, T. (2000) *Kosovo, War and Revenge* (New Haven and London: Yale University Press).

Malcolm, N. (1998) *Kosovo, A Short History* (London: Papermac).

Mazower, M. (2003) *The Balkans* (London: Phoenix).

Mertus, J. (1999) *Kosovo: How Myths and Truths Started a War* (London: University of California Press).

Positive perspectives on Operation Allied Force

Bellamy, A. (2002) *Kosovo and International Society* (Basingstoke and New York: Palgrave Macmillan).

Daalder, I. and O'Hanlon, M. (2000) *Winning Ugly* (Washington DC: Brookings Institution Press).

Gow, J. (2003) *The Serbian Project and its Adversaries: A Strategy of War Crimes* (Montreal: McGill-Queens University Press).

Robertson, G. (2002) *Crimes Against Humanity: The Struggle for Global Justice* (London: Penguin).

Weller, M. (1999) *The Crisis in Kosovo 1989–1999: International Documents and Analysis* (Cambridge: Documents and Analysis Publishing).

Critical perspectives on Operation Allied Force

Ali, T. (ed.) (2000) *Masters of the Universe? NATO's Balkan Crusade* (London: Verso).

Carpenter, T.G. (ed.) (2000) *NATO's Empty Victory* (Washington: Cato Institute).

Chandler, D. (2002) *From Kosovo to Kabul: Human Rights and International Intervention* (London: Pluto).

Chomsky, N. (1999) *The New Military Humanism: Lessons from Kosovo* (London: Pluto.

Hammond, P. and Herman, E. (eds.) (2000) *Degraded Capability: The Media and the Kosovo Crisis* (London: Pluto).

Johnstone, D. (2002) *Fools' Crusade: Yugoslavia, NATO and Western Delusions* (London: Pluto).

Thomas, R. (ed.) (2003) *Yugoslavia Unraveled: Sovereignty, Self Determination, Intervention* (Oxford: Lexington).

On the legacy of Operation Allied Force

Booth, K. (ed.) (2000) *The Kosovo Tragedy: The Human Rights Dimension* (London: Routledge).

Bowring, B. (2008) *The Degradation of the International Legal Order?: The Rehabilitation of Law and the Possibility of Politics* (Oxon: Routledge-Cavendish).

Chesterman, S. (2002) *Just War or Just Peace?* (Oxford: Oxford University Press).

Hehir, A. (2008) *Humanitarian Intervention after Kosovo: Iraq, Darfur and the Record of Global Civil Society* (Basingstoke and New York: Palgrave Macmillan).

Jokic, A. (ed.) (2004) *Lessons of Kosovo: The Dangers of Humanitarian Intervention* (Toronto: Broadview Press).

Weiss, T. (2007) *Humanitarian Intervention* (London: Polity).

Wheeler, N. (2002) *Saving Strangers* (Oxford: Oxford University Press).

Chapter 12

Iraq

The invasion and occupation of Iraq generated unprecedented controversy and caused a deep division within the international community. After the invasion the United States was cast as a global pariah, in stark contrast to the international solidarity shown after 11 September 2001 (Singh, 2006, p.14). In his resignation speech to the UK House of Commons former foreign secretary Robin Cook stated:

> Only a year ago, we and the United States were part of a coalition against terrorism that was wider and more diverse than I would ever have imagined possible. History will be astonished at the diplomatic miscalculations that led so quickly to the disintegration of that powerful coalition. (BBC News, 2003)

Indeed by 2006 a poll found that 69 per cent of British respondents believed US policies since 2001 had made the world less safe, 75 per cent considered President Bush a threat to world peace and 71 per cent stated that the war in Iraq was unjustified (Glover, 2006).

Had the US-led coalition justified their actions solely on the basis of the threat posed by Saddam Hussein's regime, then Operation Iraqi Freedom would have little importance for the humanitarian intervention debate. The fact is, however, that in tandem with the security rationale, a robust humanitarian justification was proffered, particularly when weapons of mass destruction (WMD) failed to materialize. As a consequence the invasion of Iraq, Fernando Tesón notes, 'reignited the passionate humanitarian intervention debate' (2005b, p.1).

This chapter begins with an overview of the international policy towards Iraq prior to the 11 September 2001 attacks. The subsequent section outlines the key events in the 2002–03 period, demonstrating how Iraq rapidly became the target of ever more bellicose threats from the United States and United Kingdom and consequently the paramount international political issue. The final section analyses the impact of Operation Iraqi Freedom, highlighting those aspects of the contentious debate on the intervention which have influenced the contemporary debate on humanitarian intervention.

221

Nature of the crisis

Iraq is often referred to as the 'cradle of civilization' in reference to the fact that the Sumerian culture established there in the late sixth millennium BC exported mathematics, writing, law and philosophy across the region and the wider world. Iraq's strategic location has been much coveted and its history is characterized by invasion and occupation. From 1831 to 1918 the region was part of the Ottoman Empire, and following the dissolution of the Empire in 1918 the League of Nations granted the territory to the United Kingdom as a mandate. In 1932 the United Kingdom approved Iraq's independence, recognizing the Hashemite King Faisal as head of state. In 1941 the United Kingdom invaded Iraq again, amidst fears that the government would cut off oil supplies to the Allies. The occupation lasted until 1948 when the Hashemite monarchy was restored. The monarchy was overthrown in 1958 by a military coup and in 1968 the pan-Arab socialist Ba'ath Party assumed power.

According to Toby Dodge, even before Iraq gained independence in 1932 politics there has been dominated by 'the deployment of extreme levels of organized violence by the state to dominate and shape society'. Dodge argues that the state, throughout the various changes in leadership, has functioned on the basis of bribery and oil revenues which have enabled the state to 'increase its autonomy from society' (2003, p.169). The ruling elite, and in particular the Ba'thist regime, were thus able to act independently of their people and maintain power through oppression and externally generated wealth. The Ba'ath Party often brutally suppressed opposition and played on ethnic prejudices; fearful of the Shia community's support for the Iranian regime, the Ba'thists largely privileged the Sunni community and consistently opposed the Kurdish community's calls for greater autonomy and independence.

The ideologically driven Ba'thist movement, which had parties in other states in the region, attempted to impose itself on the wider Middle East in the late 1970s, particularly when Saddam Hussein assumed power in 1978. Hussein sought to assume the position of leader of the Arab world, and undertook a highly confrontational foreign policy particularly towards Iran and Israel. Given the United States' extreme hostility towards the Iranian regime of Ayatollah Khomeini, during the 1980s Hussein and the Ba'thist regime were 'the toasts of much of Washington' (Malone, 2006, p.7). In September 1980 Iraq invaded Iran, sparking a war that would last until 1988 and claim over 500,000 lives.

The 'muted international outcry' in response to Iraq's invasion and conduct of the war appears to have emboldened Hussein (Sutterlin, 2003, p.105). The United Nations' response to Iraq's attacks, according to David Malone, 'doubtless contributed to Saddam Hussein's contempt for the United Nations with fateful consequences ten years later' (2006, p.22). In

August 1990 Iraq invaded Kuwait, claiming it was historically part of Iraq. Based on the reaction to his invasion of Iran, Hussein had concluded 'that the Security Council would ... again take no early action' (Sutterlin, 2003, p.17). Gorbachev's *perestroika* reforms in the Soviet Union and the greatly improved relations between East and West, however, meant that the Security Council was far less polarized and hence paralyzed in 1990 than in had been ten years earlier. In November 1990 the Security Council passed Resolution 678 demanding that Iraq withdraw from Kuwait or be forced to do so. Following the expiry of the deadline for withdrawal, the United States led a coalition, mandated by the United Nations, against Iraq in Kuwait on 17 January 1991 which pushed the Iraqi army out. Combat operations officially ended on 6 April.

During the Gulf War in 1991 the US Government encouraged the Iraqis to 'take measures into their own hands' and overthrow Saddam Hussein. When the Kurds and the Shiites did rise up against the regime, however, 'the USA stood idly by' (Crawford, 2006, p.36). As the suppression of the Kurds in particular grew more extreme and international media reports more frequent, momentum in favour of action increased and ultimately prevailed. Resolution 688, passed by the Security Council on 5 April 1991, mandated the deployment of UN troops to Northern Iraq and also provided for no-fly zones over northern and later southern Iraq. Apart from earlier resolutions on Rhodesia and South Africa, Resolution 688 was the first time the Security Council had described a humanitarian crisis as a threat to international peace and stability (see Chapter 9). The initial reaction of the Soviet Union – soon to be replaced by the Russian Federation – and China to Resolution 688 stressed the territorial integrity and sovereignty of Iraq. Malone notes, however, that throughout the 1990s 688 was used by the United States, United Kingdom and to a lesser extent France as a pretext for attacking Iraq, and Russia and China largely acquiesced (2006, p.88).

Following the invasion of Kuwait, Iraq was the subject of what came to be a highly controversial sanctions regime. The sanctions were exploited by Hussein, and the impact was borne by the civilian population, especially children. Air strikes against Iraq were conducted by the United States and the United Kingdom throughout the 1990s, allegedly in retaliation for breaches of international law. In August 1998 the US Congress passed the Iraqi Liberation Act calling for regime change in Iraq.

The election of George W. Bush in 2000 led to a more belligerent US policy toward Iraq. The Bush Administration included a number of neo-conservatives who had long called for the overthrow of Hussein and had been vocal critics of President George H. W. Bush's decision in 1991 not to invade Iraq following the liberation of Kuwait. In 1991 President Bush defended his decision, warning that the occupation of Iraq would 'turn the whole Arab world against us . . . [and] plunge that part of the world into even greater instability (Ryan, 2007, p.131). Such caution was, however, routinely dismissed by the neo-conservative group Project for a New American Century, which called for action against Iraq throughout the 1990s.

Malone suggests four reasons why the neo-conservatives were 'itching to take on Iraq' (2006, p.188). First, many harboured an inherent appetite for military action, believing that the US military was a tool to be used regularly. Second, they were conscious of the threat posed to oil reserves in the Middle East by the unpredictable and patently aggressive Hussein regime. Third, many felt that Hussein was an active sponsor of terrorist groups and could only be prevented from doing so by decisive military force. Fourth, neo-conservativism is based on a vision of universal morality, proactive international engagement and the validity of the democratic peace theory, and hence the overthrow of tyranny is a fundamental goal.

Following the 11 September 2001 attacks the influence of this group appears to have increased dramatically, and while the clear links between al-Qaeda and Afghanistan led to an initial focus on the Taliban, attention soon shifted to Saddam Hussein's Iraq.

International response

By 2002 the United States and the United Kingdom had dramatically increased their warnings about the dangers posed by Iraq, and the world was consumed by the debate about Iraq's alleged stockpile of WMDs.

The Bush doctrine and Iraq

The US 2002 National Security Strategy (NSS) outlined the Bush administration's post-11 September worldview and constituted a coherent expression of what has become known as the Bush doctrine. According to Jean-Marc Coicaud, the NSS was 'based on and expresses a rather dark vision of the world,' and constituted 'a significant depreciation of international rules, treaties and security partnerships as they had previously been conceived' (2006, pp.427–8). The NSS refers to pre-emptive force, the dangers of failed states and rogue regimes, and the apocalyptic threat posed by global terrorism. In January 2002 President Bush identified Iraq as part of an 'Axis of Evil' and accused it of sponsoring terrorism and stockpiling WMDs. Throughout 2002 the United States and United Kingdom increasingly accused Iraq of violating the terms of Security Council Resolution 678 and of supporting international terrorism. The leaders of the key states calling for an intervention in 2002–03 each outlined the moral imperative of acting to halt Saddam Hussein's tyranny. In a speech to the United Nations in late 2002, President Bush outlined a litany of humanitarian abuses being committed in Iraq, and warned of the 'horrors concealed from the world by the apparatus of a totalitarian state' (Bush, 2002). On 17 March 2003 Bush, in addition to highlighting the threat posed by Iraq's arsenal of WMDs, emphasized the humanitarian aspect of the looming intervention:

> We will tear down the apparatus of terror and we will help you to build a new Iraq that is prosperous and free. In a free Iraq, there will be no more wars of aggression against your neighbors, no more poison factories, no more executions of dissidents, no more torture chambers and rape rooms. The tyrant will soon be gone. The day of your liberation is near. (White House, 2003a)

Prior to the invasion John Howard, prime minister of Australia, stated, 'the end of Saddam Hussein's regime would provide an opportunity to lessen the suffering of the Iraqi people,' and he warned of 'the enormous humanitarian cost ... to the people of Iraq, of Saddam Hussein remaining in charge'. Howard described in explicit detail the abuses carried out by Iraq, such as the mutilation of children and the systematic amputation of tongues, and noted, 'the removal of Saddam Hussein's regime would produce a better life and less suffering for the people of Iraq than its continuation (Howard, 2003). Tony Blair stated, 'Riding the world of Saddam will be an act of humanity. It is leaving him there that is in truth inhumane' (Hinsliff, 2003).

The United States and United Kingdom demanded that Iraq allow weapons inspectors unfettered access, and on 8 November 2002 the Security Council passed Resolution 1441 which asserted, 'Iraq's non-compliance with Council resolutions and proliferation of weapons of mass destruction and long-range missiles poses to international peace and security'. The Council agreed to give Iraq one last chance to comply with its disarmament obligations. Thereafter the world eagerly awaited the reports of the UN Monitoring, Verification and Inspection Commission (UNMOVIC), which set about trying to verify Hussein's claims that he had destroyed his arsenal of chemical weapons.

From December 2002 to February 2003 Hans Blix, the head of UNMOVIC, reported his teams findings, noting that Iraqi compliance with the inspections was often lacking and that more time would be required to search the country and verify the regimes claims. Following a 7 March report by Blix, where he again noted Iraq's often uncooperative stance, but also stated that there was no evidence of WMDs, the United States determined that Iraq was in material breach of Resolution 1441 and hence more robust measures were required. There then began a frantic round of diplomacy whereby the United Kingdom in particular attempted to secure a second UN Security Council resolution sanctioning military action. France,

China and Russia all refused to support such a resolution, and the matter was never put to a vote. On 19 March the US-led 'Coalition of the Willing' launched Operation Iraqi Freedom.

Operation Iraqi Freedom

The military campaign against Iraqi was relatively short and hugely successful. After the rout of the Iraqi army the intervening coalition briefly appeared militarily and morally victorious, as Iraqis clamoured to dismantle the iconography of the old regime. On 1 May 2003 President Bush declared 'Mission Accomplished' aboard the USS *Abraham Lincoln*. The scale of the ensuing insurgency and the exposé of the enormous intelligence failure regarding the non-existent WMDs and the lack of any link between Hussein and al-Qaeda quickly undermined support for the invasion.

It soon became clear that the intervening coalition had grossly underestimated the scale of the task involved in stabilizing Iraq and suppressing the insurgency. Soon after he declared major combat operations to be over, President Bush was asked about the escalating insurgent attacks. He responded, 'Bring 'em on' (Malone, 2006, p.204). Insufficient troops were deployed to post-invasion Iraq largely as a result of a mistaken belief that the coalition would be greeted as liberators. US vice-president Dick Cheney stated in September 2002, 'after liberation the streets in Basra and Baghdad are sure to erupt in joy in the same way the throngs in Kabul greeted the Americans' (Herring and Rangwala, 2006, p.11).

Eric Herring and Glen Rangwala note that the State Department and the Pentagon both outlined competing strategies for the invasion and post-conflict reconstruction of Iraq. The Bush administration came down on the side of the Pentagon, whose strategy involved 'a high degree of trust in the assurances of supportive exiled groups' (ibid., p. 12). Ahmad Chalabi of the Iraqi National Congress was central to the Pentagon's planning, and it was he who claimed that the regime had WMDs, that US forces would be welcomed as liberators, and that his organization would be able to provide security after the invasion. Each claim proved false.

A litany of excessive violence ostensibly aimed at routing insurgents – such as the destruction of Fallujah – and systematic human rights violations perpetrated by the coalition troops – in particular the prisoner abuse scandal in Abu Ghraib – soon undermined what little goodwill existed amongst the Iraqi population (Ryan, 2007, p.130). Malone argues that the fierce insurgency which erupted after the invasion 'should have occasioned little surprise,' as the sanctions regime had produced a 'ruralized, radicalized, increasingly undereducated, unemployed mass of young men with hatred of the West in their hearts' (2006, p.136). Certain policies implemented by the US Administration in Baghdad exacerbated the problem. The policy of de-ba'athification, whereby some 30,000 individuals purportedly linked to the previous regime were fired, had disastrous results, creating an enormous administrative black hole resulting in severe breakdown in the country's infrastructure, power supply and internal economy (Herring and Rangwala, 2006, p.73). Additionally the decision to disband the Iraqi army had the effect of 'instantly creating some 500,000 unemployed, highly trained, armed enemies of occupation, most of them Sunni' (Malone, 2006, p.203). Despite an enormous public relations campaign, the US-led coalition failed to project an image of benign liberators; a poll conducted as early as September 2003 found only 5 per cent of respondents believed the invasion to have been motivated by a desire to help the Iraqi people, while nearly half said the motivation was Iraq's oil (Tyner, 2006, p.107).

Most destructive to the coalition's cause was the realization that the stockpile of WMDs did not exist and Hussein's Iraq did not constitute the threat alleged prior to the invasion. According to Hans Blix, Iraq was 'not an imminent or even a remote threat to the United States or to Iraq's neighbors' (2004). In July 2004 the US Senate Intelligence Committee confirmed that many of the claims made by the Bush administration were 'either substantially or completely wrong' (Malone, 2006, p.235).

Lies?

It has since been alleged that the intervening coalition, particularly the Bush Administration, manipulated intelligence to support their determination to go to war. Richard Clark, chief counter-terrorism adviser on the US National Security Council, noted that immediately after the 11 September attacks President Bush 'wanted me to come back with a report that said "Iraq did this"' (Malone, 2006, p.187). Within months of 9/11 the Bush administration began to contradict many of its own earlier declarations which suggested Saddam's military capability had been crippled by the sanctions regime (see Box 12.1). In February 2001 Colin Powell had praised the effectiveness of the sanctions regime in containing Saddam's military capability, declaring, 'He has not developed any significant capability with respect to weapons of mass destruction'. Only 18 months later Condoleezza Rice warned, 'we don't want the smoking gun to be a mushroom cloud' (Gardner, 2007, pp.16, 19).

By July 2002 the UK government was convinced that the United States was committed to invading Iraq regardless of what the weapons inspectors found. Jack Straw, then UK foreign secretary, stated that following a meeting with US officials, 'It seemed clear that Bush had made up his mind to take military action, even if the timing was not yet decided' (Malone, 2006, p.191). According to Paul Wolfowitz, then US deputy secretary of defense, 'The truth is that for reasons that have a lot to do with US government bureaucracy we settled on the one issue that everyone could agree on,

Box 12.1 'WMDs? It's a slam dunk!'

In a December 2002 Oval Office meeting, the President had sought the firmest commitment from [George] Tenet that the DCI [Director of Central Intelligence for the CIA] would stand behind the WMD intelligence. 'George, how confident are you?' Rising from one of the couches, Tenet, an avid Georgetown fan, threw his arms in the air, 'Don't worry, it's a slam dunk!'
(Gardner, 2007, p. 23)

[T]here is no doubt that Saddam Hussein now has weapons of mass destruction. There is no doubt he is amassing them against our friends, against our allies, against us . . . . Many of us are convinced that Saddam will acquire nuclear weapons fairly soon.
Dick Cheney, 26 August 2002 (quoted in White House, 2002b)

Intelligence gathered by this and other governments leaves no doubt that the Iraq regime continues to possess and conceal some of the most lethal weapons ever devised.
George Bush, 17 March 2003 (quoted in White House, 2003a)

which was weapons of mass destruction as the core reason' (Cortright, 2006, p.89). The Bush Administration thus appears to have chosen to focus primarily on WMDs because this offered the greatest potential for garnering support, rather than because it was an accurate assessment of Iraq's military capability. According to Malone, 'In retrospect the fear of WMD seems to have been instrumentalized to sell a decision to go to war that had already been made in Washington' (2006, p.212).

By the end of 2008 the number of civilian deaths in Iraq was at least 100,000, over 4000 coalition troops had been killed, while some 4.4 million Iraqis remained displaced (Human Rights Watch, 2008, p.478). The International Crisis Group's assessment of Iraq since 2003 is bleak: 'Iraq has plunged into a crisis of governance, with a popularly elected but weak government, unremitting insurgency, growing sectarian strife and rule by militia' (2008).

Impact on the debate

The invasion of Iraq has proved to be a hugely divisive issue, one that will doubtless continue to incite passions for decades. Regardless of how well Iraq functions in the coming years, questions will always remain about the decision to intervene and the humanitarian claims made by the US-led coalition.

The abuse of humanitarian intervention

Operation Iraqi Freedom is considered by many to have dealt a significant blow to the status of humanitarian intervention. As Alex Bellamy notes:

> rightly or wrongly, a large majority of the world's state's believe that the coalition abused humanitarian justifications to suit their own purposes. This will set back attempts to galvanize a global consensus on the necessity of action when basic human rights are violated on a massive scale. (2006b, p. 221)

The humanitarian intent advanced by the US-led coalition both before and particularly after the invasion has been deemed evidence of the extent to which claims of a 'humanitarian intervention' are invariably cynical.

The primary rationale advanced for the intervention was the security threat posed by Hussein's regime: that is, his alleged stockpile of WMDs, links to al-Qaeda and attempts to import uranium from Niger. A robust humanitarian rationale was additionally proffered, however. President Bush stated that one of the United States' key goals of the invasion was 'to free the Iraqi people' (White House, 2003b), and the name of the military operation – 'Iraqi Freedom' – attests to the emphasis sought for this humanitarian aspect of the intervention. Bellamy notes that when it became clear that the Security Council was not going to sanction the invasion, the rationale for the intervention increasingly focused on the humanitarian justifications. Bellamy therefore concludes, 'it appears that humanitarian justifications were abused to justify a war that could not be justified by either positive international law or reasons of the state' (2004, p.145).

Nicholas Wheeler and Justin Morris suggest that Blair's moral instincts, more than his security concerns, pushed him to support the invasion, and that he assented to the security arguments because he knew a humanitarian intervention would have been illegal. Both security *and* humanitarian considerations, they argue, were crucial to Blair, but legitimating the war could only be done by reliance on the Security Council, and hence the argument that Iraq was in breach of successive UN resolutions (2006, p.454).

When the WMDs were not found and the links to Al Qaeda lost credibility, renewed emphasis was placed on the moral aspect of the intervention which, it was claimed, meant that even though the security-oriented rationale proved largely false, the invasion was still justifiable on humanitarian grounds. Tony Blair stated:

> I can apologise for the information that turned out to be wrong, but I can't, sincerely at least, apologise for removing Saddam. The world is a better place with Saddam in prison not in power . . . success for us in Iraq is not success for America or Britain or even Iraq itself but for the values and way of life that democracy represents. (2004b)

As the credibility of the security rationale eroded, Blair declared in a key speech to his constituency party, 'we surely have a responsibility to act when a nation's people are subjected to a regime such as Saddam's' (2004a). This speech drew parallels between Kosovo and Operation Iraqi Freedom, and Blair emphatically reiterated his belief in the 'Doctrine of the International Community' speech he made during the intervention in Kosovo (see Chapter 11).

Bush similarly focused more on the humanitarian side of the invasion as the reality of Saddam's military capability came to light. In April 2004 Bush spoke of 'America's commitment to freedom in Iraq,' and claimed, 'free Iraq will confirm to a watching world that America's word, once given, can be relied upon, even in the toughest times (White House, 2004a). Richard Melanson argues that the heightened emphasis placed on the humanitarian aspect of the intervention initially worked, as the American public seemed willing to forgive the WMDs 'mistakes' because the invasion seemed to have brought such rich humanitarian benefits (2007, p.59). This was a short-lived view as the revelations of extensive atrocities perpetrated by coalition forces, the rising death toll of coalition troops and the obvious resistance amongst the citizens of Iraq to the 'liberators' clearly undermined the purported 'humanitarian' inclinations and effects.

Tesón, however, argues that the invasion 'was morally justified as humanitarian intervention' (2005b, p.2). He distinguishes between intention and motive: intention relates to 'the willed act and the consequences of the willed act,' whereas motive 'is a further goal that one wishes to accomplish with the intended act' (ibid., p.5). Thus Tesón argues that it is entirely appropriate to criticize the governments for erring or lying about the weapons of mass destruction, and yet also praise the act of intervention which brought an end to a reign of terror (ibid., p.6). Additionally, he argues that it is simply wrong to argue that the intervening coalition was not significantly motivated by humanitarian aims; 'the removal of Hussein,' he argues, 'was central in the minds of political leaders throughout the whole exercise,' and part of the US-led drive to promote international democracy and liberalism as a means to achieving international peace (ibid., p.10). Terry Nardin, writing in response to Tesón's article, argues that even if the collation was significantly motivated by the desire to overthrow Saddam Hussein, regime change of this type does not necessarily constitute humanitarian intervention (2005, p.21). It is not the character of a regime but its crimes that determine whether humanitarian intervention is warranted. Additionally, Nardin challenges Tesón's endorsement of the US-led global democratization project. This radical challenge to the status quo posed by the United States and its allies is justified on the basis that the overthrow of tyranny worldwide will be good not just for those suffering directly at the hands of tyrants but also for the global community. Tesón's endorsement of action 'in the name of humanity', Nardin argues, is 'a contribution to the literature of empire' and not related to the accepted understanding of humanitarian intervention (2005, p.25).

The 'true' motives of the intervening coalition are difficult to discern, and will doubtless be a source of controversy for some time. Less subjective is the situation in Iraq prior to the intervention. As Bellamy notes, 'The problem of viewing Iraq as a humanitarian intervention is not so much the interveners motives as the difficulty of arguing that humanitarian conditions in early 2003 were so bad as to warrant unauthorised intervention' (2006b, p.220). Material conditions within Iraq were certainly extremely poor, but arguably this was a function of the sanctions regime. While the Hussein regime certainly had a record of extreme brutality, in 2002–03, there was no sudden upsurge in oppression. The time of greatest humanitarian need was arguably during the Al-Anfal campaign against the Kurds between 1986 and 1989, when some 100–200,000 Kurds were killed, including more than 3000 when chemical weapons were used against the citizens of Halabja. At this time, however, Iraq was fighting Iran and hence in the United States' favour, and the international reaction was limited (Hiltermann, 2007). Gareth Evans notes the irony that since the 2003 invasion Iraq has become a humanitarian catastrophe (2008, p.71).

The humanitarian rationale used to justify the invasion of Iraq 'broke the Kosovo liberal intervention consensus' (Clark, 2003) and burst the bubble of optimism that had been tentatively building after Kosovo, East Timor and to some extent Afghanistan. The seemingly cynical misuse of humanitarian rhetoric undermined the arguments of those who believed a new moral dispensation had evolved amongst Western states, and confirmed the worst fears of the many states in the developing world who viewed NATO's intervention in Kosovo in 1999 with alarm. The acrimony caused by the invasion created a 'poisonous' atmosphere within the General Assembly, which had definite implications for attempts to forge consensus on new rules governing the use of force, and the 2005 World Summit in particular (Weiss, 2007, p.125).

The role of international law

The invasion of Iraq polarized the international community on a number of issues, not least its legality. Many argued that the intervening coalition had not only broken international law, they had in fact conducted 'a multiple assault on the foundations and rules of the existing UN-centred world order' (Thakur and Sidhu, 2006, pp.3–4).

The cause of much of the dissonance at the Security Council in 2002–03 centred, to a large extent, on the relevance of Resolution 678 and the meaning of the term 'serious consequences' as used in Resolution 1441. The United States and United Kingdom noted that Resolution 678 in 1990 authorized the use of all necessary measures to restore international peace in the region, and was the basis for the use of force to expel Iraq from Kuwait. Resolution 687 was linked to 678, and obliged Iraq to disarm certain weapons and cease the production and development of these weapons. Provided Iraq complied with 687, the threat contained within 678 was suspended. Resolution 1441, however, ostensibly reactivated 678 as it found Iraq to have failed to comply with 687. Resolution 1441 noted that Iraq had failed to comply with its disarmament obligations as per Resolution 687, and stated, 'the Council has repeatedly warned Iraq that it will face serious consequences as a result of its continued violations of its obligations'. Lord Goldsmith, the UK attorney general, outlined this position in his legal advice to the UK government:

> Authority to use force against Iraq exists from the combined effect of resolutions 678, 687 and 1441. All of these resolutions were adopted under Chapter VII of the UN Charter which allows the use of force for the express purpose of restoring international peace and security . . . all that resolution 1441 requires is reporting to and discussion by the Security Council of Iraq's failures, but not an express further decision to authorise force. (Number 10, 2003)

Ruth Wedgewood described Resolution 687 as 'the mother of all resolutions, setting out the requirements for post-Gulf-war Iraq. This 1991 resolution requires, in perpetuity, that Iraq give up its weapons of mass destruction and permit verification' (2003). Wedgewood later argued, 'There is nothing in the text of resolution 678 that limits its duration or suggests expiry,' and she maintained that 1441 did not rescind 678 but gave Saddam Hussein one last opportunity to comply with its provisions. Hussein was found to have breached 678 by the weapons inspectors, and thus the threat inherent in 678 could be acted on. Following the overthrow of Hussein's regime, Wedgewood notes that the Iraq Survey Group *did* find evidence that Iraq had developed a 'clandestine network of laboratories and facilities' for the production of biological weapons (ibid., p.422). Blair also maintained that the post-invasion inspections demonstrated 'that Iraq was indeed in breach of UN Resolution 1441' (Blair, 2004 b).

Of course this is not a universally endorsed view. Kofi Annan described the war as illegal (Kreiger, 2006, p.386), while Richard Falk noted that it is always possible to find some lawyer to contrive a legal defence for any action, although this does not constitute a objective or accurate legal appraisal (2005a, p.48). In a letter to the *Guardian* newspaper, 19 experts on international law wrote, 'there is no justification under international law for the use of military force against Iraq' (Guardian, 2003). Similarly David Kreiger claimed that the argument that Resolution 678 provided a legal justification 'is basically . . . sophistry in relation to the 2003 attack'

(2006, p.385). It has additionally been seen as curious that the United States, and especially the United Kingdom, would expend so much time and energy seeking to secure another Security Council resolution before launching their invasion if ultimately these same states later maintained that another resolution was unnecessary. As noted by former UK foreign secretary Robin Cook in his resignation speech on the eve of the invasion, 'the very intensity of those attempts [to secure a second resolution] under-lines how important it was to succeed. Now that those attempts have failed, we cannot pretend that getting a second resolution was of no impor-tance' (BBC News, 2003). Prior to the invasion President Bush asked, 'Will the United Nations serve the purpose of its founding, or will it be irrele-vant?' (Malone, 2006, p.192). Failure on the part of the Security Council to support the United States was therefore portrayed, somewhat ironically, as a dereliction of duty and a blow to the UN-centred system of international law (see Chapter 7).

The invasion was seen by some as a part of a broader post-Cold War trend in Western policy towards international law. According to Nigel White:

> In many ways the Iraq crisis of 2003 was the culmination of a decade of pressure by the United States and United Kingdom directed at changing the legal framework governing the use of force contained in the UN Charter, in a concerted effort to widen both exceptions to the ban on the threat or use of force. (2004, p.660)

The intervention in Kosovo – itself of questionable legality – was cited by certain supporters of the invasion of Iraq, who pointed out that the Operation Allied Force had also been 'illegal but legitimate'. Ann-Marie Slaughter made the comparison, noting, 'the Bush administration has started on a course that could be called "illegal but legitimate" a course that could end up, paradoxically, winning United Nations approval for a military campaign in Iraq' (2003). Clearly, it would be an exaggeration to claim that Operation Iraqi Freedom was a consequence of Operation Allied Force, although the continuities between the two interventions are strong. Opponents of the invasion of Iraq argued that NATO's actions in 1999 contributed to the erosion of the status of the United Nations and interna-tional law (Orford, 2003, p.5). This loss of faith in international law and the attendant acceptance that the United Nations was not the world's only legitimate authority was a central aspect of the pro-invasion perspective in 2003, although many supporters of the NATO action in 1999 rejected this claim and were the most vociferous opponents of the invasion of Iraq (Clark, 2003).

While the intervening coalition did proffer a robust legal justification, this was rejected by the majority of observers. In tandem with the legal rationale, many of those supportive of the invasion expressed a desire to change the rules governing the use of force, thereby suggesting in effect that while the invasion may not have been strictly legal, international law, and the UN system itself, had to change to meet the demands of the modern era. James Gow argued that the invasion 'was neither a breach of international law, nor the end of the United Nations,' but rather 'an important incident in the continuing evolution of international affairs, and particularly with regard to the laws governing the use of force' (2005, p.122). Similarly Tony Blair stated:

> It may well be that under international law as presently constituted, a regime can systematically brutalise and oppress its people and there is nothing anyone can do, when dialogue, diplomacy and even sanctions fail, unless it comes within the definition of a humanitarian catastrophe (though the 300,000 remains in mass graves already found in Iraq might be thought by some to be something of a catastrophe). This may be the law, but should it be? (2004b)

Wheeler and Morris argue that Blair felt he had to frame his justifications for the use of force in the more traditional language of Chapter VII rather than humanitarianism, and they note 'the attempts he has made since the war both to justify Iraq as a humanitarian intervention and to change international law so that armed intervention would be permissible against tyrants such as Saddam' (2006, p.454).

Others argued that the rejection of international law was born less from conviction and more from expediency (see Chapter 5). According to Michael Byers, the UN system has functioned relatively well given the constraints it faces, and can only continue to function and increase its effectiveness if the most powerful states adhere to its most important provisions. He notes, however, that since 2001 the United States has demonstrated 'contempt' for international law (Byers, 2005, p.67). Falk claimed after the invasion that the United Nations had been relegated to the role of 'a debating society' (2005a, p.42), while Malone similarly lamented, 'Above all, the UN was the loser, not in terms of compromise to its principles, but in perceptions of its effectiveness and centrality' (2006, p.247). Yet, the fact that the Security Council 'stood up to the United States' and refused to support the invasion is heralded by some as evidence of the United Nations' vitality. Ian Hurd argues, 'Far from undermining the Council the spectacular diplomatic confrontations and failures pre-and postwar enhanced the Council by reinforcing its basis of legitimization' (2007, p.190). In this respect the United Nations faced a dilemma; to support the invasion could have been read either as the maintenance of the principle that Security Council authorization for the use of force was an accepted principle of international law or the capitulation of the P-5 in response to US bullying. Conversely the refusal to endorse the invasion has been cast as both the death knell of the organization and the affirmation of its continued utility.

The utility of the Just War criteria

NATO's intervention in Kosovo appeared to signify a new dispensation on the part of certain liberal democracies to act to preserve basic human rights even if this action was not strictly legal (see Chapter 11). While extensive human rights legislation had been codified since the Second World War, the enforcement of this legislation was heavily dependent on states voluntarily abiding by the new codes, or failing this, coercive action by the Security Council (se Chapter 5). The record in both respects, however, had been quite poor: states evidently felt able to assent to human rights legislation without actually adhering to it, while the Security Council remained paralyzed by politically motivated decision making (see Chapter 6). NATO's intervention suggested that Western states were prepared to fill this enforcement vacuum and act, in effect, as the guardians of universal human rights.

So as to retain some framework of constraint and appraisal for 'illegal but legitimate' action, many looked to the tenets of the Just War theory (see Chapter 2). The Danish Institute of International Affairs (DIIA) proffered a list of criteria specifically drawing on the Just War theory, noting, 'Such a list could be used to justify one's own interventions and to criticise those of others.' They suggest that equipped with this criteria, 'the international community . . . may choose on a case by case basis not to condemn if the intervention is truly humanitarian and morally justifiable' (DIIA, 1999, pp.104–05). States that claimed to be acting in the interests of humanity could therefore be tested on their adherence to the Just War theory, thereby ensuring that in the absence of positive law some framework of constraint could be maintained. Mark Evans described Operation Iraqi Freedom 'as a laboratory in which the [Just War] theory may be put to the most exacting tests' (2005, p.71).

Determining the legality of an act, though not without the potential for genuine dispute, is largely a matter of facts. The morality of an action, however, is clearly much more subjective. Thus many argued that a fundamental proviso for any state wishing to appeal to the 'moral' or 'natural' law was that this state be democratic (Shaw, 1994, pp.180–1). Democratic states, it was argued, were inherently less likely to make false claims, and if false claims were made, they were easier to expose given the openness and accountability of these regimes. Additionally, democratic states were considered more likely to act in accordance with the Just War tradition's tenets given their inherent desire to win broad domestic and foreign support (Wheeler, 1997b, p.22).

The invasion of Iraq dealt a blow to this conception in two key respects. First there is evidence that the intervening coalition falsified intelligence and knowingly contrived a bogus legal argument prior to the intervention, and thus effectively lied to both their domestic public and the international community. Second it seems that while many utilized the Just War tradition as a means by which to critique the invasion, the effectiveness of this critique has been minimal.

One of the main reasons that the debate about the invasion of Iraq proved so divisive was the allegation that the intervening coalition was creative with the truth if not complicit in massive international deception. Both the legal defence and the claims that Iraq possessed WMD are alleged by many to have been fabricated. In January 2003 the UK Attorney General Lord Goldsmith advised the Foreign Office on the legality of an invasion of Iraq, and while he did not unequivocally state that such action would be legal or illegal, he certainly did not advise that this would be legal. His advice on 17 March 2003, however, was that action would be legal under Resolution 1441. This new more definite legal advice has been portrayed as dubious, and according to Philippe Sands QC, the attorney general was pressurized by legal advisors from the United States to fabricate a legal justification for the invasion (2006, p.196). This is an allegation the attorney general has strongly refuted (see Box 12.2).

There is clearly no doubt that the allegation regarding Iraq's WMD have proved to have been greatly exaggerated. This could of course have been the function of faulty intelligence rather than a nefarious plot, and Prime Minister Blair has since apologized for 'the intelligence which turned out to have been wrong' (2004b). Others have suggested that the intelligence was not mistaken but rather falsified (Bellamy, 2004, p.145; Malone, 2006, p.212). At a meeting of key UK ministers and intelligence chiefs on 23 July 2002, Sir Richard Dearlove, the chief of MI6, stated that 'the intelligence and the facts were being fixed around policy' (Sands, 2006, p.184). The UK government warned in a dossier in September 2002 – the now infamous 'dodgy dossier' – that 'The Iraqi military are able to deploy these

Box 12.2 Operation Iraqi Freedom as legal

I stand by my conclusion that military action was lawful. That was a judgment I had to reach. I reached it and I stand by it. . . . And I want to reject the suggestions that I was leant on, or that this somehow was not my genuine opinion. These suggestions that this was not genuinely my view – these are fantasies and they need to be seen as such. . . . I would not have hesitated to give negative advice if that had been my conclusion.

Lord Goldsmith, UK attorney general, 26 May 2005 (quoted in Rengger, 2005, p.145)

weapons [of mass destruction] within 45 minutes of a decision to do so' (HM Government, 2002, p.17). This claim was later retracted when it was proven to lack any factual basis. The extent to which 'evidence' about Iraq's arsenal, links to al-Qaeda and attempts to import uranium from Niger began to surface with increasing frequency in 2002 is seen by many as suspicious when viewed in the context of the evident desire on the part of a number of officials within the United Kingdom and United States to attack Iraq. It seems clear that the least favourable evidence about Iraq was proffered as definitive with little substantive critical appraisal. Thus, given the increased evidence that both the legal and security rationale for the invasion were knowingly false, the idea of allowing Western democracies exceptional powers of intervention has lost some of its attraction.

Additionally, even leaving aside the suspicions regarding the coalition's claims it is clear that even amongst supporters of the idea of an international responsibility to protect, there was disagreement over whether the situation in Iraq warranted military intervention. Michael Ignatieff argued prior to the invasion that Iraq was a definite threat to international peace and security, and also a persistent violator of human rights. Iraq was thus indicative of those situations 'when war is the only real remedy for regimes that live by terror' (Ignatieff, 2003). Gareth Evans, conversely, argues that while the human rights situation in Iraq prior to the invasion in 2003 was a cause for concern, it was 'not much worse than a score or two of other countries' and certainly not a situation that demanded coercive military intervention (2008, p.71).

The effectiveness of the Just War tradition as a means by which the actions of states can be constrained is premised on the receptiveness of states to critical council (Bellamy, 2004, p.134). 'Normative pressure' was indeed exercised prior to, during and after the invasion of Iraq, although the effectiveness of this pressure appears to have been limited. The coalition that invaded Iraq did make a case to have adhered to the criteria, and perhaps more damningly, were not significantly influenced by the rejection of the veracity of their humanitarian claims. If the humanitarian justifications for the invasion were prompted by a desire to present a sectional intervention as an act of altruism, then, as evidenced by the now routine rejection of these claims, this strategy has failed. The fact that the case for intervention was rejected but intervention occurred anyway, however, potentially suggests that the power of the Just War tradition to constrain the actions of states is limited.

The invasion of Iraq also suggests that massive domestic pressure can be resisted by Western democracies. The scale of the opposition to the invasion was unprecedented: on 15 February 2003 up to one million people marched in each of London, Rome and Madrid in what David Cortright described as 'the largest-scale single day of anti-war protest in human history' (2006, p.75). Patrick Tyler wrote that the demonstrations highlighted that the United States now faced a 'rival superpower' – world public opinion – and that 'politicians and leaders are unlikely to ignore it' (2003). Yet the global demonstrations were ignored when the United States led the invasion of Iraq. This highlights, at the very least, a breakdown in communication between the government and the public within these democracies. At worst it suggests that governments – even democratic ones – determined to pursue what they believe to be a necessary foreign policy will do so regardless of whether there is support for this policy within their domestic constituency. Cortright, however, rejects this negative diagnosis, arguing that the anti-war movement exerted 'considerable international influence'. He suggests, 'the strength of worldwide anti-war sentiment prevented the Bush administration from gaining UN support for its planned invasion and forced the administration to abandon efforts to win UN endorsement' (2006, p.75). While it is difficult to determine definitively exactly why France, Russia and China refused to support the United States and the United Kingdom, it is hard to believe that government officials in Moscow and Beijing in particular were influenced in their deliberations by anti-war demonstrations in Western cities.

Taylor Seybolt writes with respect to the claim that the invasion was a humanitarian intervention, 'Human rights organizations . . . forced the US administration of President George W. Bush to back away from the claim when they exposed its absurdity' (2007, p.2). Thus while the United States may have claimed to have adhered to moral guidelines, objective observers were able to use these guidelines to expose the United States' many failings. Thomas Weiss employs the Just War tradition's criteria as a means by which the invasion can be critiqued, and argues that this framework bolstered the anti-war case (2007, p.126–7). Indeed, as noted in Chapter 2, the utility of the Just War theory is not necessarily evident in its capacity to prevent spurious 'just wars' or 'humanitarian interventions'. Rather it is a means by which the morality of a particular conflict can be assessed and judged (Rengger, 2002). In the same way that states may appeal to international law to justify an act and be judged according to the tenets of positive law, states may assert that their actions adhere to the principles of the Just War tradition, and in doing so, they must accept critical judgement on this basis. A finding that a supposedly 'just war' failed to meet the Just War criteria cannot, many argue, be deemed a failing of the tradition.

Conclusion

In his now infamous 'Mission Accomplished' speech aboard the USS *Abraham Lincoln* on 1 May 2003, President Bush stated, 'In the Battle of Iraq, the United States and our allies have prevailed. And now our coalition is engaged in securing and reconstructing that country' (White

House, 2003b). The 'securing and reconstructing' of Iraq proved more costly and bloody than President Bush and indeed many others could have imagined. According to Vittorio Parsi, a vociferous supporter of US foreign policy, since the invasion Iraq has become 'a never ending nightmare' (2006, p.79). Indeed, by 2006 it seemed that nearly everyone in Iraq was unhappy.

The invasion of Iraq has proved to be the most divisive issue of the post-Cold War era, plunging the United Nations into a crisis of confidence and deeply dividing the international community. Old fissures between Russia and the West have re-emerged while relations between the Islamic world and the West have plummeted. On the day the invasion UN secretary-general Kofi Annan stated, 'we must all feel that this is a sad day for the UN and the international community' (Malone, 2006, p.204).

The fact that the intervening coalition portrayed their intervention as motivated to a significant extent by a desire to aid suffering Iraqis has significantly undermined the status of 'humanitarian intervention'. The term has been so tarnished by association with Iraq that it appears unlikely that any consensus on this emotive issue will be reached in the near future.

Clearly the invasion was not motivated primarily by humanitarian intent, and the intervening coalition did not attempt to justify their invasion solely on this basis. As the security rationale evaporated, however, 'the human rights argument was the only one left with a shred of credibility and was embraced accordingly' (Evans, 2008, p.70). By this stage, however, the coalition had arguably lost all credibility given the exposé of the WMD debacle and the other clearly false – though not necessarily contrived – threats posed by the Hussein regime. Had the post-invasion insurgency not occurred, however, and the coalition been greeted – as indeed they expected to be – as liberators, then perhaps the invasion of Iraq might well have left a more positive legacy for the humanitarian intervention debate. Indeed, perhaps as the years go by and Iraq stabilizes, such a conclusion could yet be reached. As Wheeler and Morris note:

> If Iraq evolves in the next few years into a tolerant rights-respecting society, then this will provide support to those who seek to represent the Iraq war as a justifiable humanitarian intervention. . . . The final conclusions that one should draw from this complex balancing act are yet to be determined. (2006, pp.450–1)

'Iraq' much like 'Vietnam' is destined to be utilized by critics of humanitarian intervention and US foreign policy for the foreseeable future. What exactly we mean by 'Iraq' is liable to change, however, and it is not inconceivable that someday 'Iraq' may well be a by-word for success. At present this seems far-fetched of course but given that the consequences of the invasion are evolving, so is history's judgement.

Questions

- How convincing are the legal arguments put forward by the coalition that invaded Iraq in 2003?
- Has the invasion of Iraq demonstrated international law's weaknesses and the impotence of the United Nations?
- To what extent were the humanitarian justifications offered for the invasion convincing?
- Has the invasion of Iraq irrevocably tarnished the status of humanitarian intervention?

Further reading

Blair, T. (2004b) 'Speech to the Labour Party Conference', 28 September [online] http://www.labour.org.uk/ac2004news?ux_news_id=ac04tb (accessed 2 May 2009).

Buckley, M. and Singh, R. (eds) (2006) *The Bush Doctrine and the War on Terrorism* (London: Routledge).

Dodge, T. (2003) *Inventing Iraq: The Failure of Nation-Building and a History Denied* (New York: Colombia University Press).

Dumbrell, J. and Ryan, D. (eds) (2007) *Vietnam in Iraq* (London: Routledge).

Heazle, M. and Islam, I. (2006) *Beyond the Iraq War: The Promises, Pitfalls and Perils of External Interventionism* (Cheltenham: Edward Elgar).

Herring, E. and Rangwala, G. (2006) *Iraq in Fragments: The Occupation and its Legacy* (London: Hurst).

Malone, D. (2006) *The International Struggle Over Iraq: Politics in the UN Security Council 1980–2005* (Oxford: Oxford University Press).

Parsi, V. E. (2006) *The Inevitable Alliance: Europe and the United States Beyond Iraq* (Basingstoke and New York: Palgrave Macmillan).

Thakur, R. and Sidhu, W. P. S. (eds), (2006) *The Iraq Crisis and World Order: Structural, Institutional and Normative Challenges* (New York: United Nations University Press).

Weiss, T. (2007) *Humanitarian Intervention* (London: Polity).

Chapter 13

Darfur

Many hoped at the end of the Cold War that the international community, and the United States in particular, would engage more with Africa on issues such as human rights. Given that the Soviet threat no longer existed it was hoped that the United States could begin to distance itself from those pro-Western dictators it had previously supported. In reality 'geostrategic imperatives of national interest continued to hold sway over suggestions to move toward new foreign policy approaches' (Docking, 2008, p.208). Many have argued that the crisis in Darfur is evidence of this prioritization.

The situation in Darfur deteriorated rapidly in 2003 and by 2004 was arguably the worst humanitarian crisis in the world. The international community has certainly not ignored the issue: non-governmental organizations (NGOs) have devoted enormous resources to publicising the crisis and many Security Council resolutions have been passed. Yet, the response to the crisis has been roundly criticized as ineffective and timid (Lu, 2006, p.2). Many have argued that the situation demanded a humanitarian intervention as the Sudanese government were actively involved in the killings and displacement. Although UN troops have been deployed to Darfur they have had limited impact and have been deployed with the consent of the Sudanese government.

This chapter begins with an overview of the crisis in Darfur, highlighting those factors that led to the crisis in 2003. The second section assesses the international reaction to the crisis and in particular the role played by the Security Council from 2003–08. The final section analyses the impact the crisis in Darfur has had on the debate about humanitarian intervention.

Nature of the crisis

The contemporary borders of Sudan owe more to the legacy of the British occupation (1899–1956) than to any demographic trends or topography. Indeed, Stuart Kaufman describes Sudan as 'one of the less sensible results of map-making by colonial powers in Africa' (2008, p.208). Sudan has rarely enjoyed national unity and since independence in 1956 there have been only 11 years of peace, with the northern and southern regions in a near perennial state of conflict (Straus, 2005). A civil war between the

Islamic north – which has generally controlled the government in Khartoum – and the Christian/animist south erupted in 1983, claiming some 2 million lives, although the world largely ignored it (Fisher, 2007, p.102). This broader conflict has been simmering in parallel throughout the course of the recent crisis in Darfur in western Sudan. The Comprehensive Peace Agreement signed in January 2005 formally ended the north–south war, and many have suggested that the Sudanese government used this agreement as a bargaining chip during the crisis in Darfur (Mayroz, 2008, p.365).

The roots of the conflict in Darfur can arguably be traced back hundreds of years although it is clearly unfeasible to engage in such historical detail here (O'Reilly, 2004; de Waal, 2007b). Darfur is a region with a large number of different ethnic groups although the vast majority are Islamic. The region is divided primarily between two groups: the 'Africans' whose livelihood is based around sedentary agriculture, and the 'Arabs' who are predominantly semi-nomadic livestock herders (Straus, 2005). The conflict in Darfur has regularly been portrayed as one between the Arab and African groups, although this conceptualization has been criticized as over-simplistic (de Waal, 2004; Hoile, 2005, pp.93–111).

The UN High-Level Mission to Darfur in 2006 noted that administrative changes made by the Sudanese government in the 1970s eroded the system of tribal dispute settlement mechanisms (UN Human Rights Council, 2007, p.11). This system had previously reduced conflict between the various groups competing for food, land and water in Darfur. When drought and desertification hit the region in the late 1970s competition for resources intensified, and without the old dispute settlement mechanisms groups lacked legitimate institutional means by which to channel their concerns and ultimately mediate conflicts. Alex de Waal argues that complex relationships between competing elites in Khartoum and local powers in the periphery, such as in Darfur, have resulted in a dysfunctional Sudanese leadership, largely incapable of negotiating effective peace agreements (2007c, pp.23–4). Additionally the people of Darfur have traditionally felt disenfranchised from the national political system and the Khartoum regime, and as tensions escalated, many began to form village defence groups and militias. In 2001 the Sudanese Liberation Army (SLA) and the Justice and Equality Movement (JEM) were formed from these village militias.

In February 2003 the SLA launched attacks against government military installations, and they were soon joined by the JEM. While the rebel forces initially achieved some success, the central government launched a fierce counter-attack in April. The Sudanese Air Force was deployed and a large number of civilians were killed. The mobilization of the Janjaweed militia proved most destructive, however, and the violence perpetrated by this group has become the iconic image of the conflict's brutality. The Janjaweed – which roughly translates as 'evil men on horseback' – are far from a homogenous organization, and it has been asserted that the term is a catch-all with little empirical quality (Hoile, 2005, pp.112–25).

Many of the militias in Darfur acted in concert with the Sudanese government and appear to have received funding and logistical support from Khartoum. According to Human Rights Watch, 'government forces waged a systematic campaign of "ethnic cleansing" against the civilian population,' noting further, 'Sudanese government forces and the Janjaweed militias burned and destroyed hundreds of villages, caused tens of thousands of civilian deaths, displaced millions of people, and raped and assaulted thousands of women and girls' (2007). The sheer scale and barbarity of the violence soon generated international attention. Negotiations and ceasefires followed but none succeeded in stemming the violence. By April 2004 the counter-insurgency had killed 30,000 people, mostly civilians. This figure rose to 70,000 by September, by which time some 1.2 million people had fled their homes, with 200,000 entering Chad. By mid-2004 the World Health Organization estimated that between 240 and 440 people were dying every day, and Darfur was by this stage, 'commonly described within the UN system and Western states as "the most serious humanitarian emergency in the world today"' (Williams and Bellamy, 2005, p.30).

International response

The primary focus of academic enquiry into the crisis in Darfur has been on the response of the international community rather than the dynamics of the situation itself. In general, appraisals of this response have been negative, and many have drawn parallels between the response to Darfur and the reaction to the Rwandan genocide in 1994.

2003–05

The first Security Council resolution to mention the situation in Darfur was passed on 11 June 2004, 16 months after the conflict began. Resolution 1547 contained one sentence on Darfur, noting, '[The Security Council] calls upon the parties to use their influence to bring an immediate halt to the fighting in the Darfur region.' The resolution did not blame any one of the 'parties' for the humanitarian crisis, and contained no threats of further action. Resolution 1556, passed on 30 July 2004, went further although again it lacked real substance. 1556 recognized the territorial integrity of Sudan and called on the Sudanese government to protect its civilians from the Janjaweed and 'establish credible security conditions for the protection of the civilian population'. The Security Council threatened further action if the government did not disarm the Janjaweed in 30 days. Given that there was widespread evidence that the government was actually working with, if not effectively employing, the militias, it was somewhat paradoxical to call on Khartoum to disarm, apprehend and bring to justice the Janjaweed.

In April 2004 the UN High Commissioner for Refugees (UNHCR) blamed the government of Sudan for the crisis and stated, 'It is clear there is a reign of terror in Darfur ... [our] mission identified disturbing patterns of massive human rights violations in Darfur perpetrated by the Government of the Sudan and its proxy militia' (UNHCHR, 2004, pp.6, 3, 22). Additionally, even if the will existed within the government disarming the militia within 30 days was a tall order, with de Waal describing it as 'frankly impossible' (2004). None of the states that voted for Resolution 1556 asserted that the Security Council had a right or duty to intervene in Darfur, with the onus instead placed on the Sudanese government, and failing that, the African Union (AU). In June 2004 Russia, China and Pakistan noted at a meeting of the Security Council that they believed the government of Sudan should deal with the crisis, as the scale was insufficient to warrant external interference (Bellamy, 2006b, p.223).

When the Security Council passed Resolution 1556 the US ambassador to the United Nations, John Danforth acknowledged that the resolution did not go as far as many wished, and noting the calls for a declaration of genocide, stated, 'it is important that we not become bogged down over words. It is essential that the Security Council act quickly, decisively and with unity. We need to fix this humanitarian problem now' (UN Security Council, 2004, p.4). Danforth stated that the resolution guaranteed that Darfur would be on the Security Council's agenda 'for as long as it takes to ensure that the people of Darfur can live in peace' (ibid., p.5). As with all other states supportive of the resolution, however, the United States threatened only to impose further sanctions if the government of Sudan did not cooperate. Resolution 1556 did mandate the deployment of a contingent of AU troops – the African Union Mission in Darfur (AMIS) – in August 2004. AMIS was under-resourced and understaffed, however, and it soon became clear that the African Union was unable to deploy the 3000 troops required. In December 2004 Kofi Annan stated that AMIS was 'not working' (Bellamy, 2006b, p.224).

Security Council Resolution 1564 in September 2004 recognized that the Sudanese government had failed to honour Resolution 1556. This resolution did not impose any punitive measures, however, stating only that the Council 'shall consider taking additional measures' should Sudan's non-compliance continue. Humanitarian organizations had been hoping for a stronger resolution (Hoge, 2004). Resolution 1564 established the International Commission of Enquiry on Darfur (ICED), and in January 2005 ICED published its report which detailed a litany of extreme violence and widespread sexual cruelty. The report found that 'The Government of Sudan and the Janjaweed are responsible for serious violations of international human rights and humanitarian law amounting to crimes under international law' (2005, p.3).

In September 2004 the Bush Administration accused the government of Sudan of genocide. This was not a universally endorsed view; the African Union and reputable humanitarian organizations such as Médecins Sans Frontières (MSF), disagreed (Assembly of the African Union, 2004, para 2; MSF, 2005). Indeed, throughout 2004 the African Union continued to assert that the situation in Darfur was improving, in contrast to the many UN reports stating precisely the opposite.

2005–08

Seven resolutions were passed by the Security Council in 2005, and while each constituted strongly worded condemnations, none implemented significant punitive action. AMIS's mandate was extended and a 'Panel of Experts' was established to oversee and report on the crisis. Resolution 1593 in March 2005 referred the situation to the International Criminal Court (see Box 13.1). In April 2006 the Security Council agreed to impose targeted sanctions against four individuals. This constituted the most forceful action taken by the Council to that point; according to Thomas Weiss, 'the chasm between the magnitude of the suffering and the international response could hardly have been greater' (2007, p.55). Security Council Resolution 1706 in August 2006 finally authorized the deployment of 17,300 troops and 3300 civilian police to replace the 7000-strong AMIS contingent. Once again, however, this action was taken with the consent of the Sudanese Government.

The situation improved somewhat in late 2006, although conditions in the region remain extremely poor. The Report of the UN High-Level Mission in March 2007 advised that the steps taken by the international community in response to the crisis in Darfur 'have not proven adequate' (UN Human Rights Council, 2007: 22). According to Human Rights Watch:

> As of September 2007, approximately 2.2 million displaced people live in camps in Darfur and more than 200,000 people have fled to neighbouring Chad, where they live in refugee camps. In addition to the people displaced by the conflict, at least 2 million additional people are considered 'conflict-affected' by the United Nations and many need some form of food assistance because the conflict has damaged the local economy, markets, and trade in Darfur. (2007)

Estimates of the number of deaths range from 300,000 to 400,000 (SaveDarfur, 2007, p.1). A report drafted by 15 humanitarian NGOs found that in the first ten months of 2008 some 290,000 people had been displaced – 40,000 in September alone – while some 4 million are in

Box 13.1   Sudan and the ICC

In April 2007 the ICC issued warrants for government minister Ahmad Harun and Janjaweed leader Ali Kushayb. The Sudanese Government is not a party to the Rome Statute and has consistently refused to cooperate with the ICC. Indeed, subsequent to the ICC's issuing a warrant Ahmad Harun was promoted to minister for humanitarian affairs. On 4 March 2009 Luis Moreno-Ocampo, the ICC prosecutor, issued an arrest warrant for the Sudanese President Omar al Bashir for war crimes, crimes against humanity and genocide.

need of humanitarian assistance (Coalition of NGOs on Darfur, 2008, pp.7–8). The UN special rapporteur on Sudan, Sima Samar, reported in September 2008 that 'violence and sexual abuse of women and children . . . continue almost unabated throughout Darfur' (UN General Assembly, 2008, p.12).

Impact on the debate

Three explanations have been frequently cited for the lack of military inter-vention (Mayroz, 2008, pp.362–4). First the sheer size of Sudan – the largest state in Africa – and its infrastructural limitations, in particular the poor roads, railways, and lack of modern air bases, made it logistically dif-ficult to intervene. Second, it was feared that an intervention would disrupt aid supplies to those already suffering in Darfur. Third, it was claimed that such an intervention would be poorly received in the Arab world. Sending troops into Sudan would be seen as 'one more incursion of a Christian army into and Islamic land' (Rieff, 2006). Eyal Mayroz additionally sug-gests a fourth reason, 'the defensive campaign against external intervention carried out by the regime in Khartoum' (2008, p.365). The Sudanese Government exploited the disunity within the Security Council and the African Union and variously portrayed itself as the victim of Western aggression, an honest broker eager to resolve an internal dispute and an impoverished state in need of assistance. Mayroz argues that Sudan's repeated success in delaying, watering down and disrupting the implemen-tation of many Security Council resolutions has set a precedent likely to undermine the Council's authority and credibility in dealing with future crises (2008, p.366). Whichever factor or combination thereof is respon-sible for the response to the crisis, Darfur has become synonymous with inaction and failure, much like Rwanda ten years earlier (see Chapter 10).

Back to Rwanda?

The nature and scale of the crisis in Darfur have evoked memories of the genocide in Rwanda in 1994. The international community's seemingly wilful paralysis in the face of the death of some 800,000 people is arguably the most frequently decried episode in contemporary international politics (see Chapter 10). Following that genocide, 'never again' became a frequent refrain of political leaders, and the intervention in Kosovo five years later suggested that this commitment was finally being realized (see Chapter 11). Hugo Slim highlighted the legacy of Rwanda when he described Darfur as the 'test case by which to judge whether the international community has got any better at responding to genocide and crimes against humanity' (2004, p.811).

In March 2004 the UN humanitarian coordinator in Khartoum, Mukesh Kapila, publicly drew parallels between the crisis in Darfur and the early stages of the genocide in Rwanda (Slim, 2004, p.815). The coverage of the unfolding disaster in Darfur by the media, NGOs and UN fact-finding missions in 2003 surpassed that of the initial stage of the genocide in Rwanda, and the violence which followed was therefore not an unexpected eruption. Regarding the response to Darfur, Roméo Dallaire, force commander for the UN Assistance Mission in Rwanda in 1994, wrote:

> Although the early stages of the Darfur situation received more news coverage than the Rwanda genocide did, at some level the Western governments are still approaching it with the same lack of priority. In the end, it receives the same intuitive reaction: 'What's in it for us? Is it in our "national" interest?'

Dallaire described the reaction to Darfur bluntly as 'not nearly enough' (2004b). Instead, according to John Mueller, 'the international community, after ten years of mea culpa breast beating over its failure to intervene in Rwanda, responded with little more than huffing and puffing' (2005, pp.122–3).

As noted in Chapter 10, in 1994 ever more creative ways to describe the carnage in Rwanda were employed in an effort to avoid using the term 'genocide' and somehow downplay the extent of the violence. In September 2004, however, US secretary of state Colin Powell announced before the US Senate Foreign Relations Committee, 'genocide has been committed in Darfur and . . . the Government of Sudan and the Jingaweit (*sic*) bear responsibility' (US Department of State, 2004). This constituted the first time that any state had officially accused another of genocide while it was allegedly occurring (Mayroz, 2008, p.367). Yet Powell subsequently stated:

> no new action is dictated by this determination . . . let us not be too preoccupied with this designation. . . . Call it civil war; call it ethnic

cleansing; call it genocide; call it 'none of the above'. The reality is the same. There are people in Darfur who desperately need the help of the international community. (US Department of State, 2004)

President Bush endorsed Powell's view on 21 September (White House, 2004b). Powell's plea 'not be too preoccupied with this designation' was a clear attempt to distance the United States from any obligation to intervene. The Clinton Administration had feared in 1994 that to describe the violence in Rwanda as 'genocide' would have obliged it to take action under the 1948 Genocide Convention. Evidently the legal advice received by the Bush Administration in 2004 was that using the term 'genocide' 'would not obligate the US to anything beyond – in the words of the Genocide Convention – calling "upon the competent organs of the United Nations to take such action"' (Mayroz, 2008, p.367).

From a strict legal perspective the US administration were quite possibly correct that a finding of genocide only compelled it to refer the matter to the Security Council – which it did – rather than to take action. As Yoram Dinstein notes, the Genocide Convention does not contain any provision that triggers military action once the 'g-word' is used (2005, pp.72–3). Yet articulating a legal defence for a seemingly ineffective response to what you acknowledge as being genocide certainly undermines the 'never again' declarations routinely made after 1994. As Weiss laments, 'If we recognize the existence of genocide and do nothing besides ask the ICC to split genocidal hairs, the 1948 Convention on the Prevention and Punishment of the Crime of Genocide is literally not worth the paper on which it is reproduced' (2007, p.54).

John Danforth, US ambassador to the United Nations in 2004, stated, after he stepped down in 2005, that the finding of genocide was made for 'internal consumption within the US' and never intended as an act that would alter US policy (Mayroz, 2008, p.371). David Hoile argues that the term was 'transparent political opportunism' designed to deflect public attention from Iraq during the 2004 US Presidential elections (2005, p.95).

Scott Straus notes that the case of Darfur has 'made it clear that "genocide" is not a magic word that triggers intervention'. While the term provokes attention, and in the case of Darfur ensured the situation would be at the top of the international political agenda, the subsequent inaction 'showed that the Genocide Convention does not provide nearly the impetus that many thought it would'. He notes that previously, most notably in the case of Rwanda in 1994, governments avoided using the term genocide, yet the crisis in Darfur 'shows that the definitional dance may not have mattered' (Straus, 2005, p.132). The parallels between Darfur and the Rwandan genocide, itself evocative of the Holocaust, were clear in terms of both the violence and the ineffective international response. According to Weiss, 'The collective yawn in the face of Darfur's disaster could be even more destructive of the fabric of international law than the 800,000 deaths in Rwanda' (2007, p.54). Kofi Annan's appraisal of the reaction to Darfur concluded, 'We were slow, hesitant, uncaring and we had learnt nothing from Rwanda' (Fisher, 2007, p.103).

R2P RIP?

Following NATO's intervention in Kosovo in 1999 the International Commission on Intervention and State Sovereignty (ICISS) was established to find a means by which human rights and sovereignty could be reconciled and the efficacy of international responses to mass atrocities improved (see Chapter 6). The ICISS's main argument was that states had the primary responsibility for the welfare of their people, and if they failed in this respect the responsibility transferred to the international community which could, if necessary, intervene militarily without the host state's consent. These provisions were endorsed by all the world's states in 2005 at the World Summit, albeit in a somewhat diluted form (Wheeler, 2005; Bellamy, 2006a).

The reaction of the international community to Darfur suggests that the latter responsibility – that of the international community to those suffering at the hands of oppressive or incompetent regimes – has not readily been assumed. Clearly the Security Council was unwilling to take military action, and the legal wrangling and habitual calls for more information by the Council in the face of evident tragedy stands as an unedifying portrait of its effectiveness and the priorities of its members. The Security Council has remained 'seized of the matter' since Resolution 1547 in June 2004 and has passed many resolutions since criticising the Khartoum government. Yet a consistent feature of Security Council action has been the expressed desire to operate in concert with the Sudanese Government. Indicatively Resolution 1706 which finally authorized the deployment of a robust military force 'invites the consent of the Government of National Unity' and requests their involvement in the decision regarding the deployment of the new force. This therefore possibly constituted a regression from the proposals put forward by *The Responsibility to Protect*, which explicitly stated that consent was not required. The Khartoum government has been accused by reputable international humanitarian organizations and the United Nations itself of intentionally preserving conditions of poor sanitation and famine (Mayroz, 2008, p.361) and conducting 'genocide by attrition', leaving the non-Arab population 'in the throes of a slow, remorseless destruction' (Reeves, 2005). The expressed desire for an invitation from the very perpetrators of the crime which necessitated action, according to Weiss, 'mocks the values of the emerging R2P norm' (2007, p.58).

The ICISS report stated that the Security Council remained the primary international arbiter of when it was right to intervene, and outlined its commitment to make the Council work better rather than to find alternatives to its authority. Nonetheless the ICISS did state that it could not accept that failure by the Security Council to act must be the last port of call, and warned that it was unreasonable to expect that inaction by the Council in the face of mass atrocities would be tolerated by concerned states (2001, pp.53–5). This therefore appeared to allow for the possibility of 'illegal but legitimate' action such as that ostensibly undertaken by NATO in 1999 in Kosovo, and clearly suggested that certain states were unwilling to tolerate the systematic violation of human rights by others. The scale of the tragedy in Darfur was, as many have suggested, of sufficient magnitude to legitimately warrant external intervention regardless of the Security Council's position or the views of the Sudanese Government, as the situation had clearly passed any 'just cause threshold' (Bellamy, 2006b, p.223).

As Slim states, 'Whatever the right legal label, such extreme policies operated by the Sudanese government demanded a concerted, immediate and assertive international political and humanitarian response. No such response emerged' (2004, p.815). The 'Somalia syndrome', derived from the United States' bad experiences in Somalia in 1993 (see Chapter 9), appears to have influenced the decision not to intervene in Darfur in 2004, as it had in Rwanda ten years earlier (see Chapter 10). This syndrome suggests that interventions in Africa are doomed to fail given the endemic ethnic hatreds and violent opposition towards external interference prevalent in the region. Additionally, as Weiss notes, the United States was 'disinclined to commit significant political and military resources to human protection' (2007, p.119) given its enormous military commitments in Afghanistan and Iraq.

While the explanations for the response of the international community, and the West in particular, may be accurate, they do suggest that massive human rights violations in themselves are insufficient to compel states to intervene to protect suffering masses abroad. As with Rwanda in 1994, it seems that despite the scale of the 'genocide' in Darfur the costs of intervention was deemed too high and the benefits too low. This need not necessarily lead us to conclude that states are hypocritical or amoral; it suggests rather that any 'responsibility to protect' foreign citizens is very much secondary to national responsibilities and domestic exigencies. According to de Waal, the fixation with coercive action against the Sudanese Government and military intervention diverted attention from the only viable solution to the crisis, the deployment of UN peacekeepers and the simultaneous provision of emergency humanitarian aid. He dismisses R2P as 'a slogan', and argues that in light of the response to Darfur we must conclude 'RIP R2P' (2008). One consequence of the emergence of 'the responsibility to protect' doctrine not anticipated by either its proponents or critics was the extent to which this normative prescription actually facilitated inaction, and as noted in Chapter 6, this use of R2P to justify inaction has been a feature of the international response to Darfur (Bellamy, 2006a, p.33).

While Darfur has been deemed by many to have crossed the threshold for military intervention, others have argued that this in itself is not sufficient grounds for launching such action. According to Gareth Evans there is a difference between a necessary and a sufficient condition for intervention; while the scale of the crisis in Darfur was certainly grave enough to potentially warrant military intervention, this is not the only factor to be considered when deciding whether or not to intervene militarily. According to Evans, 'a nonconsensual military intervention ... would almost certainly be disastrously counterproductive, in terms of its impact on current humanitarian relief operations and the very fragile north–south peace process' (2008, p.61). In this situation the international community's response had to 'take other forms', in particular earlier and more robust deployment of UN and AU peacekeepers, and therefore the reaction to the crisis, though flawed on many levels, was not an 'R2P failure' (Evans, 2008, p.61). De Waal similarly cautioned against the clamour for military intervention, noting that 'providing physical protection for Darfurians with international troops is not feasible' (2007a).

The argument that military intervention was impractical is rejected by Bellamy, who argued that it would have been possible to use air power and light infantry to protect those huddled in camps and ensure the safe passage of humanitarian aid (2006b, p. 225). Susan Rice also criticizes the 'excuses' offered for the lack of what she believes was a duty to intervene, with or without the assent of Khartoum or the UN Security Council (2005). Similarly a report by the US National Defense University found that a military intervention prosecuted in a certain way would have achieved success (see Box 13.2).

It is, of course, impossible to determine what effects a non-consensual military intervention would have had in 2003–04. Any such move would doubtless have been fiercely resisted by the Sudanese army and the various militias, and the impact of the intervention would have been dependent on the military tactics employed. Given the localized nature of the killings on the ground, and the tactics of the militias, one could reasonably argue that an intervention prosecuted exclusively from the air, in the style of Operation Allied Force, would have potentially caused an escalation in the terror tactics of the militias. A ground offensive, if sufficiently robust, might well have constituted the only viable means by which a military intervention could have had a positive humanitarian impact.

Many critics of R2P argued that it paved the way for increased Western interventionism based on subjective claims of humanitarian need (Chandler, 2004a). The crisis in Darfur has arguably shown that the age-old problem of 'inhumanitarian non-intervention' remains the norm. 'Overzealous military action for insufficient humanitarian reasons,' notes

Box 13.2 Would military intervention have been effective?

[A]n intervening combat force would have had little trouble stopping killings by the Janjaweed if it could have tracked and engaged them. The killers lack skill, strong motivation, and capabilities, and with decent intelligence it is not very difficult to distinguish them from their civilian targets...On balance, it seems reasonable to expect that a fast, light, lethal, well-trained, and well-led African combat force, operating in distributed, interconnected, and collaborative fashion, could have been more forward deployed and dispersed to strategic points throughout Darfur, better able to obtain intelligence on Janjaweed movements and intentions, mobile enough to move quickly to areas of potential or ongoing killings, and stop or deter mass killing, provided the force could get deep into Darfur, receive ample intelligence, and be backed up by precision air-strikes if trapped, ambushed, or confronted by Sudanese military units. Western support would be indispensable; with it, decisive success would be feasible.

(Gompert et al., 2005, p.26)

Weiss in light of Darfur, 'certainly is no danger. Rather the real threat to international society comes from doing nothing while condoning massive suffering' (2007, p.52). Darfur shows that even if agreement on the criteria justifying humanitarian intervention can be reached, disagreement over whether these criteria have been met is still possible, and this has implications for the effectiveness of R2P. Indeed Bellamy (2009a) argues that the disagreement over the merits of intervention in Darfur highlights the need for those concerned about the utility of R2P to abandon the search for criteria for decision making about the use of force in favour of using the R2P framework to identify and neutralize potential moral hazards and highlight alternatives to coercive military intervention.

The limits of global civil society?

Many argued that NATO's intervention in Kosovo in 1999 demonstrated the power of global civil society and the so-called 'boomerang effect' (see Chapter 6). The Kosovo Albanians had alerted the world to their plight by appealing to international human rights organizations and their overseas diaspora. Humanitarian NGOs publicized the situation and attracted increased media attention, which combined to create a momentum amongst domestic publics in the West for action against Milosevic's regime. NATO's eventual intervention, though certainly criticized by many global civil society activists for the manner in which it was executed (see Chapter 11), thus seemed to demonstrate the power of this new international actor. Clearly, if foreign policy was now, to some significant extent, an internationalized bottom-up process, then the nature of international relations would have changed markedly.

The conflict in Darfur since 2003 evidences a contrast between enormous international publicity of the crisis and timid and equivocal action on the part of the UN Security Council and Western states. The international media, NGOs and many UN reports consistently highlighted the suffering occurring in Darfur since 2003. Additionally many, though by no means all, states have acknowledged the extent of the violence, with the United States going so far as to use the term genocide. While, in contrast to China and Russia, Western states have vocally condemned the Sudanese government, the practical steps taken to stop the killings have been, from the perspective of respected international observers, a 'dismal failure' (Wheeler and Morris, 2006, p.457).

Médecins Sans Frontières note, 'The media attention and political involvement means that everyone knows about the conflict here, but in the last four years the situation has not improved. In fact, for most people things have got worse' (Huig, 2007). NGOs such as Human Rights Watch, the International Crisis Group and Amnesty International have regularly criticized the response of the international community and appealed for more direct engagement. Certain activists, frustrated with the United Nations' response, have called on Western powers to take unilateral action. Indicatively John O'Shea, head of the charity GOAL, declared, 'The US as the superpower should take the action on its own .... There is nothing that the UN has done since day one that has saved the life of a single person in Darfur' (De Bréadún, 2004). The United Nations' capacity to act is of course dependent on the Security Council, which is itself reliant on its permanent members, including the United States, and thus 'the United Nations' cannot reasonably be criticized for not taking military action as it does not have the independent capacity to do so. Appealing to Western states to extricate themselves from the restrictive embrace of the United Nations is of questionable utility given that the Western powers, and the United States in particular, have maintained a very close adherence to the deliberations and rulings of the Security Council in contrast to their behaviour over Kosovo in 1999 and Iraq in 2003.

SaveDarfur, an NGO umbrella group comprising 114 different NGOs and some 48 regional groups, has been to the fore in highlighting the issue of Darfur within the United States. SaveDarfur's strategy is based on the fundamental assumptions behind the project of global civil society; 'We utilize media outreach, public education, targeted coalition building and grassroots mobilization to pressure policymakers and other decision-makers in the United States and abroad to help the people of Darfur' (SaveDarfur, 2007). The group launched the 'Million Voices for Darfur' campaign in January 2006, and by the end of June it had collected 1 million signatures from people in the United States urging the Bush Administration to support the deployment of a large military force to the region. On 30 April 2006 hundreds of thousands of people attended approximately 20 separate rallies across the United States calling on President Bush to do more to stop the conflict in Darfur, and a second rally was held on 17 September.

The campaign to raise awareness has been a success; according to SaveDarfur, 'just about everyone who's heard of Darfur believes that more should be done to help Darfur'. Yet despite the massive public outcry, SaveDarfur described its campaign as 'complex, grinding, and profoundly frustrating'. It credited the African Union with taking a proactive approach, contrasting this with 'the rest of the international community [who] stood by and watched' (Meixner, 2007). This record does not complement the notion that sustained and widespread pressure will compel democratic states to act abroad. In this case, despite the widespread mobilization of domestic and global civil society in favour of robust military intervention, the United States, and the West generally, have successfully resisted popular moral outrage. Three years after the killings began and the appeals for action were made, Weiss notes that the only country to respond unequivocally to the United Nations' calls for peacekeeping troops was the United States, which 'categorically said "no"' (2007, p.55).

Clearly such a response not just to the crisis itself but to the international campaign for action challenges the assumptions that global civil society is a key actor in contemporary international relations and that Western states are receptive to calls for intervention. Of course, the widely heralded interventions in Kosovo and East Timor in 1999 took place during the tenure of President Clinton, and thus the character of the US administration had changed by the time the crisis in Darfur began. Additionally Darfur occurred after 11 September 2001, by which time the United States and wider Western world had adopted a foreign policy characterized by 'the prioritization of strategic concerns to the virtual exclusion of humanitarian ones' (Weiss, 2007, p.55). In this respect the context in which the response to Darfur occurred differed greatly from that of Kosovo in 1999. Nonetheless, while these differences perhaps explain why the responses to Kosovo and Darfur were so different, they do not alter the fact that the power of global civil society appears to have waned.

In its defence global civil society has never claimed to have an irresistible impact on Western foreign policy, and it obviously has no independent military capacity. The movement is based on the assumption that crises abroad will be highlighted by NGOs, which will put pressure on governments to take action. This action need not necessarily take the form of military intervention, and therefore the lack of military intervention is not indicative of global civil society's failings. Mayroz (2008) argues that the United States' response to the crisis in Darfur, though certainly not as robust as many

would have wished, evidences a new willingness to act on the recommendations of global civil society and pressurize the Sudanese government despite
the fact that Sudan was an important ally in the war on terror. Additionally
Adam Jones highlights a 'truly encouraging sign' that attitudes to foreign
policy have changed thanks to global civil society: the actions of students in
high schools and universities across the United States who called for action
and urged boycotts of companies linked to Sudan (2008, p.194). Thanks to
the campaign waged by global civil society, public awareness was quite
high, groups were effectively mobilized and Darfur became a key domestic
political issue, even impacting on the 2004 US presidential elections. If proponents of global civil society asserted that global civil society would
always force states to act and that this action would take the form of military intervention, then clearly the response to Darfur undermines these
ideals. Global civil society did not make these claims, however, and this
must temper any appraisal of global civil society's capacity. Many humanitarian organizations cautioned against military intervention, and therefore
the response to Darfur, though arguably ineffective, may well tally with
that advocated by global civil society.

Conclusion

On 11 September 2006 Kofi Annan, by this stage 'at the end of his tether',
posed three questions:

> Can we, in conscience, leave the people of Darfur to such a fate? Can
> the international community, having done not enough for the people of
> Rwanda in their time of need, just watch as this tragedy deepens?
> Having finally agreed just one year ago that there is a responsibility to
> protect, can we contemplate failing yet another test? (Weiss, 2007,
> p.57)

Weiss laments that each of these questions 'actually received affirmative
responses' (2007, p.57). Perhaps the most disappointing if not disturbing
aspect of the crisis in Darfur has been that while the situation has received
enormous international publicity, and few states have denied the scale of
the tragedy, the response has been certainly ineffective and arguably weak.
According to Bellamy, 'the concern with Darfur is not so much that the US
and UK have not intervened but that neither these states nor their allies
seem to have accepted their duty to protect Darfurians' (2006b, p.226). He
further argues, 'States that invoked a broad right of intervention in the
Kosovo and/or Iraq cases cannot avoid a duty to act in a case like Darfur
without undermining future claims for a permissive right of intervention'
(ibid., p.226). Thus Darfur has seemingly exposed in tragic clarity the

selective approach to humanitarian crises and the continuing dominance of national interests.

Whatever one's perspective on humanitarian intervention, the response to Darfur can only be seen in a negative light. Unquestionably millions of people have suffered terrible hardship, with thousands killed, raped, starved, and many more displaced. Darfur shows that the international community of states has yet to find an effective means by which such humanitarian disasters can effectively be halted. Whether a humanitarian intervention would have been an effective solution is debatable, but clearly something more should have been done. Many imagined that the Rwandan genocide so shocked the conscience of humankind that no such atrocity would be permitted to take place again. As Weiss notes, however, while 'never again' was the mantra espoused post-Rwanda, the crisis in Darfur and the attendant international inaction means that '"here we go again" is closer to the truth' (2007, p.154).

Questions

- What does the use of the term 'genocide' in the context of Darfur tell us about the effectiveness of the Genocide Convention?
- What options were available to the Security Council that it did not take advantage of? Why do you think this was the case?
- Has the crisis in Darfur demonstrated the limitations of global civil society?
- Kofi Annan claims that Darfur demonstrates that 'we had learnt nothing from Rwanda'. Do you agree?

Further reading

On the history of the crisis in Darfur

Daly, M. W. (2007) *Darfur's Sorrow: A History of Destruction and Genocide* (New York: Cambridge University Press).
De Waal, A. (2006) *Darfur: A Short History of a Long War* (New York: Zed).
O'Fahe, R. S. (2008) *The Darfur Sultanate: A History* (London: Hurst).
Prunier, G. (2005) *Darfur: The Ambiguous Genocide* (Ithaca, N.Y.: Cornell University Press).

On the international response to the crisis

Chedle, D. and Prendergast, J. (2007) *Not on our Watch: The Mission to End Genocide in Darfur and Beyond* (Meath: Maverick House).

De Waal, A. (ed.) (2007) *War in Darfur and the Search for Peace* (Cambridge: Global Equity Initiative, Harvard University).

Hoile, D. (2005) *Darfur in Perspective* (London: European-Sudanese Public Affairs Council).

International Commission of Enquiry on Darfur (ICED) (2005) 'Report of the International Commission of Inquiry on Darfur to the United Nations Secretary-General', 25 January [online] http://www.un.org/news/dh/sudan/com_inq_darfur.pdf (accessed 21 December 2008).

Mandani, M. (2009) *Saviours and Survivors: Darfur, Politics, and the War on Terror* (London: Pantheon).

Weiss, T. (2007) *Humanitarian Intervention* (London: Polity).

The Future of Humanitarian Intervention?

Humanitarian intervention is very much a live issue. As you read this book it is highly likely that there is a crisis somewhere in the world which has generated heated debate about the need to intervene. If history is a guide then it is likely that international relations will continue to be periodically punctuated by humanitarian crises; as has been noted, 'Mass starvation, rape and suffering will reappear as global security threats, and humanitarian intervention will continue to smolder on the public policy agenda' (Macfarlane, Thielking and Weiss, 2004, p.986). The controversies explored in this book are therefore likely to re-emerge.

Unlike some issues in International Relations (IR), humanitarian intervention is an aspect of international politics that generates intense popular concern. The question of how, or indeed whether, to 'save strangers' interrogates humanity's moral calculus and necessarily provokes emotive reactions. A scepticism towards, and even a rejection of, humanitarian intervention does not necessarily constitute an immoral or even amoral outlook; genuine concerns remain about the effects that such action has, with many arguing that humanitarian intervention does more harm then good. As Alan Kuperman rightly notes, 'no policy of humanitarian military intervention should be implemented without a sober consideration of its unintended consequences' (2000a, p.118).

This final chapter highlights potential future trajectories for the status of humanitarian intervention and the arguments for and against each. Security Council use of Chapter VII in the 1990s has meant that we can now affirm with at least some confidence that the Council has the power to sanction humanitarian intervention, even if the basis for this competency is somewhat ambiguous (Chesterman, 2002, p.48; DIIA, 1999, p.62). The focus in this chapter, therefore, is on the status of unilateral humanitarian intervention: that is, intervention not explicitly sanctioned by the Security Council (see Chapter 1).

Three scenarios

As the contentious debate about humanitarian intervention has raged, certain academics and policy makers have advanced prescriptions in an effort to resolve the dispute. The following sections assess the pros and cons of three such approaches, beginning with the argument for the maintenance of the status quo, then the perspective in favour of legal and political reform, and finally, most radically and controversially, the argument that the current foundational norms and practices of international law are no longer apposite and should be disregarded.

In defence of the status quo

Despite the fact that the current status of humanitarian intervention is clearly problematic, many support the maintenance of the status quo. Advocates of this perspective argue that any change in favour of humanitarian intervention would necessarily undermine the principle of sovereign inviolability and negatively impact on international peace and stability.

As the tenets of sovereignty constitute a bulwark, albeit a normative one, against great-power interference in the affairs of smaller states, the principle of non-intervention, it is argued, is a norm that should be maintained (Ayoob, 2002, pp.82–3). Sovereignty has acted as an ordering principle in international relations, and diminishing its provisions, even for ostensibly altruistic reasons, would have a destabilizing effect on the international system, as states would subjectively judge each other's moral rectitude, leading to a proliferation of interventions and wars (Holbrook, 2002, p.148). Since 1945 the principle of non-intervention has, it is claimed, been responsible for the reduction in inter-state wars, and this progressive trend will be jeopardized if sovereignty is diluted (Reus-Smit, 2005, pp.72–5). Therefore, a new law regarding humanitarian intervention may have positive effects on the willingness of states to adhere to international human rights legislation but would certainly lead to more wars between states, the negative consequences of which would outweigh any related positives (Jackson, 2000, pp.291–2).

It is argued that moves to facilitate humanitarian intervention, far from protecting the weak from the strong, will actually further empower the existing international hierarchy, which will abuse this new doctrine (Chandler, 2002, pp.190–1; Whitman, 2005, p.266). Adherents to this view are inherently sceptical of the willingness of states to act morally, and fear that any increase in the scope of legitimate intervention would be abused. Many point to the inaction in the face of the genocide in Rwanda to support their claim that interests must be involved when states intervene, and thus humanitarian intervention is illusory (Burke, 2004, pp.77–8; Whitman, 2005, pp.261–3).

Clearly, therefore, one school of thought on the need to maintain the status quo derives its conviction from an inherent suspicion of humanitarian intervention; to paraphrase Robert Cox, intervention is always for someone and some purpose (see Chapter 4). Not all adherents to the idea of maintaining the status quo, however, base their prescriptions on this view. Many agree that changing international law to accommodate humanitarian intervention would have negative effects, but do not discount the possibility that a genuine humanitarian intervention may well have positive consequences. Certain writers have argued, therefore, that the current tenets of international law should be maintained but that humanitarian interventions, though always illegal, should be tolerated provided they are judged to have been genuinely humanitarian.

In contrast to those who are inherently critical of humanitarian intervention, proponents of the 'mitigation' perspective seek to enable interventions with positive humanitarian consequences without adversely affecting sovereignty's status as the foundation of the international system (Wheeler, 2002, p.129). Simon Chesterman argues, 'In the event of an intervention alleged to be on humanitarian grounds, the better view is that such an intervention is illegal but that the international community may, in extreme circumstances, tolerate the delict' (2002, pp.231–2). Rather than excluding the possibility that humanitarian intervention could ever be justified, or contriving a new legal doctrine of intervention, this perspective advocates maintaining the present illegality of such action but suggests that judgements should be made on a case-by-case basis. If a particular act is deemed to have had a positive humanitarian outcome, it could be deemed illegal but judged leniently (Byers and Chesterman, 2003, pp.198–203; Rengger, 2005, pp.159–61; Stromseth, 2003, pp.243–4). Thomas Franck argues that this idea of mitigation has precedents in the national legal systems of most countries. He cites those cases where illegal acts have undeniably been committed and yet, though a guilty verdict is returned, the judge takes account of the circumstances and motivations behind the act and the punishment is mitigated accordingly. 'Law' he argues, 'does not thrive when its implementation produces *reductio ad absurdum*: when it grossly offends most person's common moral sense of what is right' (Franck, 2005, p.212). Humanitarian intervention could therefore conceivably be excused as an extraordinary remedy to a great wrong (Simma, 1999, p.22).

While this idea of mitigation is certainly attractive, proponents are somewhat vague about who the jury would be and how exactly their opinion could be gauged (Byers and Chesterman, 2003, pp.198–203; Falk, 2005a, p.48). Additionally how sanctions might be imposed against those states that fail to have their plea of mitigation accepted is problematic: the Security Council certainly has the power to impose sanctions but requires the assent of the P5 to do so. Therefore, the rejection of a state's claim of mitigation could very well have no adverse consequences for that state if it convinced a member of the P5 to block any censure. Additionally, while the idea of not creating a potentially destabilizing precedent is proffered as a means to close the floodgates to intervention, there is no way to guarantee that instances when mitigation is granted will not be cited in the future. A number of NATO states, particularly Germany, expressly stated in 1999 that they did not want Operation Allied Force to become a precedent, yet it has been cited since, most recently by Russia during its 2008 intervention in Georgia. Without clear guidelines about what constitutes a legitimate humanitarian intervention, determining when mitigation should be afforded is inherently subjective. Formally codifying the basis for legitimate humanitarian intervention is a solution to this particular concern, but this necessarily involves initiating legal change which constitutes a change to the status quo.

The need for legal reform

In the wake of NATO's intervention in Kosovo in 1999, a number of major international commissions argued that legal change to the status of humanitarian intervention is a pressing requirement (IICK, 2000, p.186; ICISS, 2001, p.3). As the Security Council constitutes the only viable means by which humanitarian intervention can legally be sanctioned, and because the Council is so obviously partisan, it has been suggested that reform of the international legal and political system is a necessity (Simma, 1999, p.6; Guicherd, 1999, p.20).

There are many aspects of international law that require reform, but humanitarian intervention is presented as uniquely important. As Andrew Hurrell argues, 'The degree to which international society is affected morally and practically by humanitarian catastrophe means that we need new rules on humanitarian intervention' (2005, p.30). Unlike the status quo/mitigation perspective, advocates of legal reform are uncomfortable with a legal system that criminalizes legitimate action. As Paul Christopher states, 'surely in those cases where we find our legal and moral rules at odds, we should endeavor to reconcile these differences' (2004, p.248). Clearer rules would serve to remove the subjectivity currently inherent in the legality of humanitarian intervention, as detailed in Chapter 5, and enable more consistent and regulated action in defense of the oppressed.

Differing perspectives exist regarding precisely what this legal reform should involve. Proposals suggested thus far include a new treaty of unilateral humanitarian intervention (Burton, 1996); the creation of a new military force exclusively at the disposal of the United Nations (Johansen, 2006); the establishment of new international bodies empowered to deploy troops when situations deteriorate to certain levels (Woodhouse and Ramsbotham, 2005, p.152; Held, 2005, p.25; Hehir, 2008a, p.130); and reforming the membership and powers of the Security Council (UN High-Level Panel on Threats, Challenges and Change, 2004, pp.77–83). Changing the law to permit unilateral humanitarian intervention is clearly the proposal that most directly addresses the dilemma posed by humanitarian intervention, and it is, perhaps unsurprisingly, also the most controversial.

A rationale for advocating reform of the existing political/legal structure is that this structure currently prevents genuine humanitarian interventions from taking place. This premise is rejected by those who argue that the reason interventions do not take place has little to do with the legal prescriptions against such action, and much more to do with the lack of will for such action (Chesterman, 2002, p.54). Reform, therefore, is a solution to a problem which does not exist. Additionally many are concerned that permitting unilateral intervention 'would encourage more frequent resort to the practice in less compelling circumstances than at present by creating an additional doctrinal basis for justifying the use of force' (Stromseth, 2005, p.257). Advocates of new rules have countered that this concern lacks credibility given that it assumes that international law is currently free from potential abuse, which is patently not the case (Chopra and Weiss, 1992). Additionally Michael Burton notes:

> While no legal norm is entirely free from potential abuse . . . the use of codified criteria will diminish rather than exacerbate the problem of pre-textual interventions. A codified rule of intervention is less prone to abuse than is the current 'sublegal' status accorded unilateral humanitarian intervention. (1996, p. 422)

The concern expressed by those who support the status quo lest reform undermine sovereignty is potentially assuaged if reform is initiated with the consent of the international community of states. Indeed, as Hedley Bull, one of the most vocal proponents of the principle of sovereignty, stated, 'the idea of sovereign rights existing apart from the rules laid down by international society itself and enjoyed without qualification has to be rejected in principle' (1984a, pp.11–12). The status of sovereignty at any given time should therefore reflect the general will of states, and changes in this status can occur if the international community agrees that these changes are required. Amendments to the law governing humanitarian intervention, derived from an inclusive process and with the assent of all states, would potentially constitute a diminution of the status of sovereignty but would be based on general agreement rather than the initiative of a powerful elite (Burton, 1996, pp.233–6).

Beyond current international law

Reforming international law is notoriously difficult; the lack of enthusiasm and subsequent action that greeted the publication in 2004 of the recommendations of the UN High-Level Panel on Threats, Challenges and Change, and the negligible reforms implemented at the 2005 World Summit are indicative of the difficulties inherent in achieving international consensus (Weiss, 2007, p.112; Evans, 2008, p.47). This difficulty is particularly pronounced when it comes to issues as sensitive as intervention and sovereignty.

Frustrated by the often glacial pace of reform and not least the developing world's seemingly intransigent adherence to ostensibly anachronistic legal doctrine, many have argued that the necessary reforms cannot be achieved through consensus. The opposition voiced by states to changes to the status of sovereignty, and the willingness of China and Russia to veto any substantial reform in the status of humanitarian intervention, are portrayed as self-interested spoiling by illiberal governments that reflect neither the wishes of their own citizens or world opinion (Pattison, 2007, pp.307–8; Reisman, 2000, pp.13–15). It is argued, therefore, that change must be forced through by those 'enlightened states' that embody progressive moral rectitude (Glennon, 1999, p.2).

Geoffrey Robertson has argued that 'the struggle for global justice' is a struggle against sovereignty. He suggests that a state's right to sovereignty must be conditioned on its record, and in this respect, 'The reality is that states are not equal' (2002, p.372). Increased intervention is championed by those who believe the West has a duty to engage in 'a new kind of imperialism, one acceptable to a world of human rights and cosmopolitan values' (Cooper, 2002). A new legal asymmetry between Western states and 'old fashioned kinds of states outside the post-modern continent of Europe [and America]' is legitimized on the basis that the West is a positive trailblazing force in international affairs (ibid.). It is argued that as long as international law lags behind the evolution of moral values and facilitates the perpetuation of human suffering, it is legitimate to bypass its tenets.

This strain of thought has led to the idea of assigning unique powers to democracies. Democracies would be granted special dispensation to act when morally necessary for the good of humankind (Elshtain, 2003b). A new right of humanitarian intervention would therefore be created, but this right would be conditional on the democratic credentials of the intervening state, and subject to the judgement of other ostensibly 'morally reliable' actors, namely liberal democracies (Buchanan and Keohane, 2004; Ikenberry and Slaughter, 2006, pp.25–6). The fear that a new right of intervention reserved for a select few constitutes a regression is rejected; intervention would still be constrained by the normative pressure exercised by other democracies which would ensure that the new privilege was not abused (Glennon, 1999; Gow, 2005, pp.13–14, 123; Reisman, 2000, pp.16–17). This idea was espoused during the 2008 US presidential elections by Republican nominee Senator John McCain, who spoke of his belief in the need to create a 'league of democracies' (McCain, 2007).

It is claimed that the rationale for creating a new conditional right of unilateral humanitarian intervention is further enhanced by the additional assertion that the use of force by liberal democracies will necessarily benefit the world through the spread of liberal values and the expansion of the community of democratic states. The spread of democracy is good not only for the people within these newly liberated states but also for the global community, due to the fact that democracies do not go to war with other democracies, so the zone of peace will expand. Hence democratic interventionism will bring positive benefits to the oppressed who are saved, to the global community which will enjoy a reduction in warfare, and to the intervening state itself which benefits from increased global stability and security (Gow, 2005).

As noted in Chapter 5, the evolution of international law and the increased preference for codification as the source of international law since 1945 have been driven to a large extent by a perceived need to create a more egalitarian international regime, though the extent of this democratization of international law should not be exaggerated (Simpson, 2004). The rehierarchization of the international sphere into liberal and illiberal states clearly challenges this trajectory, and is therefore considered by some to constitute regression rather than progress (Reus-Smit, 2005).

More generally, the presumption that democratic states are uniquely reliable actors in international relations is contested (Alvarez, 2001). This presumption has undeniably been tarnished by the Bush Administration's foreign policy. Prior to becoming US secretary of state, Condoleezza Rice argued that 'America's pursuit of the national interest will create conditions that promote freedom, markets and peace. . . . American values are universal' (2000, p.47), while President G. W. Bush continually stressed the need for the United States to unilaterally assume a leadership role in defending civilization and spreading democratic values. Proponents of the view that international law must be superseded by a new normative framework would certainly recoil at an association with Bush's more bellicose statements, such as 'I don't care what the international lawyers say; we are going to kick some ass' (Coicaud, 2006, p.426). The record of the United States since 2001 in terms of defending freedom, spreading liberal values and increasing international security is mixed to say the least (Singh, 2006). Moves to unilaterally alter the rules governing the use of force and the status of sovereignty are additionally likely to ferment further tensions in international relations, as the so-called unenlightened states will resist such moves (Falk, 2004, p.41).

Conclusion

The prescriptions assessed in this chapter constitute three potential scenarios for the future status of humanitarian intervention. As is clear, none is without contention and each holds the potential to contribute to, rather than reduce, instability and violence. Over the course of the next decade it will be interesting to see which – if indeed any – achieves ascendancy.

In the past 20 years alone views on humanitarian intervention have fluctuated widely, from being portrayed generally as either inconceivable or highly dangerous during the Cold War, to being touted as a global panacea in the 1990s, to once again being deemed misplaced, and indeed dangerous, utopianism in the wake of 11 September 2001. One constant during this period has been that at any given time somewhere in the world people have been systematically persecuted by their own state and they have cried out to the nebulous 'international community' for help. While some lucky souls have indeed been rescued many, many more have not. During the bloody 20th century far more people were killed at the hands of their own government than by foreign forces, and instances of intra-state violence have continued to degrade international relations in the new millennium.

Violence has been a perennial feature of human history. We can think not only of the organized violence of the industrialized state or the mechanized slaughter of the Holocaust; evidence from the pre-modern world suggests that humanity has always found a rationale for the use of force. The eminent historian Ronald Wright has pointed to troubling evidence that our disposition to violence may well be a genetic function of our ancestral evolution, and specifically the struggle between our ancestors the Cro-Magnons and the Neanderthals:

> If it turns out that the Neanderthals disappeared because they were an evolutionary dead end, we can merely shrug and blame natural selection for their fate. But if they were in fact a variant or race of modern man, then we must admit to ourselves that their death may have been the first genocide. Or, worse, not the first – merely the first of which evidence survives. It may follow from this that we are descended from a million years of ruthless victories, genetically predisposed by the sins of our fathers to do likewise again and again. (2006, p.25)

Wright's thesis highlights that despite the often self-congratulatory talk of 'progress', contemporary civilization faces a number of challenges which bear striking similarities to those our ancestors confronted, and if anything we appear to be failing to meet them more spectacularly than ever before. Indeed, despite the enormous changes that have occurred in the last 200 years in both domestic and international politics, it is sobering that the dilemma posed by humanitarian intervention remains unresolved.

The concepts 'human rights' and 'humanitarian intervention' are certainly (relatively) new, but debates about the morality of war and the more vexed question of coming to the aid of the suffering certainly are not. There is no reason to suspect that in the future these debates, central to the issue of humanitarian intervention, will somehow resolve themselves, or that some international accord will emerge with such normative or legal force that intra-state violence will cease. It is safe to say, therefore, that intra-state atrocities will occur periodically, and thus the issue of humanitarian intervention will continue to exercise the minds of academics, complicate the agenda of international statesmen and women and outrage the moral sensibilities of the general public.

One of our most exalted human characteristics is our capacity for empathy and perennial predisposition towards the avowal of, if not always the adherence to, moral norms. Yet, we have failed to find a way to resolve these traits with our preferred unit of political order, the state. The emergence of the state as the dominant unit of currency in IR has facilitated some of the worst atrocities in human history. Unless we conclude that, on this basis, the state has lost its utility we must find some way to accommodate the state with human rights. The significance of the relationship between sovereignty and human rights is immense, and as Chris Brown notes, 'has plenty of life left in it as a focus for study' (2006, p.4). Humanitarian intervention is interesting, depressing and hugely important. I hope this book has stimulated interest in this subject and that it will serve as the basis for much-needed further research.

Bibliography

Alvarez, J. (2001) 'Do Liberal States Behave Better? A Critique of Slaughter's Liberal Theory', *European Journal of International Law*, 12:2, 183–246.

Ambos, K. (1999) 'Comment – NATO, the UN and the Use of Force: Legal Aspects', *European Journal of International Law*, 10:1, 1–22.

Amnesty International (2000) 'NATO/Federal Republic of Yugoslavia: "Collateral Damage" or Unlawful Killings?' [online] http://web.amnesty.org/library/index/ENGEUR700182000 (accessed 2 May 2009).

Anderson, B. (1991) *Imagined Communities: Reflections on the Origins and Spread of Nationalism* (London: Verso).

Anderson, M. S. (1998) *The Origins of the Modern European State System, 1494–1618* (London: Longmans).

Anheier, H., Glasius, M. and Kaldor, M. (2001) 'Introducing Global Civil Society', in H. Anheier, M. Glasius and M. Kaldor (eds), *Global Civil Society 2001* (Oxford: Oxford University Press).

Annan, K. (1999a) *The Question of Intervention* (New York: United Nations University Press).

Annan, K. (1999b) 'Two Concepts of Sovereignty', *Economist*, 18 September, 49–50.

Annan, K. (1999c) 'Secretary-General Presents his Annual Report to General Assembly', UN document SG/SM/7136-GA/9596, 20 September [online] http://www.un.org/News/Press/docs/1999/19990920.sgsm7136.html (accessed 2 May 2009).

Annan, K. (2000) 'Annex 1: Opening Remarks', in J. Sherman (rapporteur), *'Humanitarian Action: A Symposium Summary'*, International Peace Academy, International Policy Conference, 20 November [online] http://www.ciaonet.org/wps/shj04/ (accessed 2 May 2009).

Annan, K. (2005a) *In Larger Freedom: Towards Development, Security and Human Rights for All*, UN document A/59/2005, 21 March [online] http://www.un.org/largerfreedom/ (accessed 2 May 2009).

Annan, K. (2005b) 'In Larger Freedom: Decision Time at the UN', *Foreign Affairs*, 84:3, 63–70.

Archibugi, D. (2003) 'Cosmopolitical Democracy', in D. Archibugi (ed.), *Debating Cosmopolitics* (London: Verso).

Arend, A. and Beck, R. (1993) *International Law and the Use of Force* (London: Routledge).

Armstrong, D. and Farrell, T. (2005) 'Introduction: Force and Legitimacy in World Politics', in D. Armstrong and T. Farrell (eds), *Force and Legitimacy in World Politics* (Cambridge: Cambridge University Press).

Armstrong, D., Farrell, T. and Lambert, H. (2007) *International Law and International Relations* (Cambridge: Cambridge University Press).

Armstrong, D., Farrell, T. and Maiguashca, B. (eds) (2005) *Force and Legitimacy in World Politics* (Cambridge: Cambridge University Press).

Assembly of the African Union (2004) 'Decision on Darfur', Third Ordinary Session, 6–8 July, Addis Ababa, Ethiopia [online] http://www.africa-union.org/DARFUR/homedar.htm# (accessed 30 November 2007).

Ayoob, M. (2002) 'Humanitarian Intervention and State Sovereignty', *International Journal of Human Rights*, 6:1, 81–102.

Bain, W. (2003a) *Between Anarchy and Society* (Oxford: Oxford University Press).

Bain, W. (2003b) 'The Political Theory of Trusteeship and the Twilight of International Equality', *International Relations*, 17:1, 59–77.

Bain, W. (ed.) (2006) *The Empire of Security and the Safety of the Peoples* (London: Routledge).

Bain, W. (2007) 'In Praise of Folly: International Administration and the Corruption of Humanity', in A. Hehir and N. Robinson (eds), *State-Building: Theory and Practice* (London: Routledge).

Bainton, R. (1986) *Christian Attitudes Towards War and Peace* (Nashville, Tenn.: Abingdon Press).

Bandow, D. (1999) 'Europe's Welfare Queens', Cato Institute, 30 March [online] http://www.cato.org/pub_display.php?pub_id=5502 (accessed 2 May 2009).

Bandow, D. (2000) 'NATO's Hypocritical Humanitarianism', in T. G. Carpenter (ed.), *NATO's Empty Victory* (Washington DC: Cato Institute).

Bardos, G. (2003) 'International Policy in Southeast Europe: A Diagnosis', in R. Thomas (ed.), *Yugoslavia Unraveled: Sovereignty, Self Determination, Intervention* (Oxford: Lexington).

Barnett, M. (1997) 'The UN Security Council, Indifference, and Genocide in Rwanda', *Cultural Anthropology*, 12:4, 551–78.

Barnett, M. (2002) *Eyewitness to Genocide: The United Nations and Rwanda* (Ithaca, N.Y.: Cornell University Press).

Barnett, M. (2003) 'Bureaucratizing the Duty to Aid: The United Nations and the Rwandan Genocide', in A. Lang (ed.), *Just Intervention* (Washington DC: Georgetown University Press).

Baylis, J. and Smith, S. (eds) (2007) *The Globalization of World Politics* (Oxford: Oxford University Press).

BBC News (2003) 'Cook's Resignation Speech', 18 March [online] http://news.bbc.co.uk/1/hi/uk_politics/2859431.stm (accessed 2 May 2009).

BBC News (2004) 'UN Chief's Rwanda Genocide Regret', 26 March [online] http://news.bbc.co.uk/2/hi/africa/3573229.stm (accessed 2 May 2009).

Beetham, D. (1991) *The Legitimisation of Power* (Basingstoke and New York: Palgrave Macmillan).

Beitz, C. (1992) 'Cosmopolitanism and Sovereignty', *Ethics*, 103, 48–75.

Bellamy, A. (2002) *Kosovo and International Society* (Basingstoke and New York: Palgrave Macmillan).

Bellamy, A. (2003) 'Humanitarian Intervention and the Three Traditions', *Global Society*, 17:1, 3–20l.

Bellamy, A. (2004) 'Ethics and Intervention; The "Humanitarian Exception" and the problem of Abuse in the Case of Iraq', *Journal of Peace Research*, 41:2, 131–47.

Bellamy, A. (2005a) 'Responsibility to Protect or Trojan Horse? The Crisis in Darfur and Humanitarian Intervention after Iraq', *Ethics and International Affairs*, 19:2, 31–54.

Bellamy, A. (2005b) 'Introduction'. in A. Bellamy (ed.), *International Society and its Critics* (Oxford: Oxford University Press).

Bellamy, A. (2005c) 'The "Next Stage" in Peace Operations Theory', in P. Williams and A. Bellamy (eds), *Peace Operations and the Global Order* (Oxon: Routledge).

Bellamy, A. (2006a) 'Whither the Responsibility to Protect? Humanitarian Intervention and the 2005 World Summit', *Ethics and International Affairs*, 20:2, 143–69.

Bellamy, A. (2006b) *Just Wars: From Cicero to Iraq* (London: Polity).

Bellamy, A. (2009a) *Responsibility to Protect* (London: Polity).

Bellamy, A. (2009b) 'The Responsibility to Protect and the Problem of Military Intervention', *International Affairs*, 84:4, 615–39.

Bellamy, A. (2009c) 'Kosovo and the Advent of Sovereignty as Responsibility', *Journal of Intervention and Statebuilding*, 3:2, 163–84.

Bellamy, A. and Wheeler, N (2008) 'Humanitarian Intervention in International Society', in J. Baylis and S. Smith (eds), *The Globalization of World Politics* (Oxford: Oxford University Press).

Bennett, W. (2000) 'Morality Character and American Foreign Policy', in I. Kristol and R. Kagan (eds), *Present Dangers* (San Francisco: Encounter).

Berman, F. (2007) 'Moral Versus Legal Legitimacy', in C. Reed and D. Ryall (eds), *The Price of Peace* (Cambridge: Cambridge University Press).

Bickerton, C., Cunliffe, P. and Gourevitch, A. (eds) (2006) *Politics without Sovereignty: A Critique of Contemporary International Relations* (London: Routledge).

Blair, T. (1999) 'Doctrine of the International Community', Speech at the Economic Club, Chicago, 24 April [online] http://www.number-10.gov.uk/output/Page1297.asp (accessed 2 May 2009).

Blair, T. (2004a) 'Full Text – Tony Blair's Speech', *Guardian*, 5 March [online] http://www.guardian.co.uk/politics/2004/mar/05/iraq.iraq (accessed 2 May 2009).

Blair, T. (2004b) 'Speech to the Labour Party Conference', 28 September [online] http://www.labour.org.uk/ac2004news?ux_news_id=ac04tb (accessed 2 May 2009).

Blix, H. (2004) 'The Importance of Inspections', Carnegie Endowment for International Peace, Proliferation Brief 7, No. 11 [online] http://www.carnegieendowment.org/publications/index.cfm?fa=viewandid=1591 (accessed 4 October 2007).

Bloom, W. (1990) *Personal Identity, National Identity and International Relations* (Cambridge: Cambridge University Press).

Bolton, J. (2005) 'Letter to President Ping', 30 August [online] http://www.responsibilitytoprotect.org/index.php/government_statements/554?theme=alt1 (accessed 2 May 2009).

Booth, K. (2001) 'Three Tyrannies', in T. Dunne and N. Wheeler (eds), *Human Rights in Global Politics* (Cambridge: Cambridge University Press).

Booth, K. (ed.) (2000) *The Kosovo Tragedy: The Human Rights Dimension* (London: Routledge).

Boucher, D. (1998) *Political Theories of International Relations* (Oxford: Oxford University Press).

Boucher, D. and Kelly, P. (2003) *Political Thinkers: From Socrates to the Present*, (Oxford: Oxford University Press).

Boutros-Ghali, B. (1992) 'An Agenda for Peace', Report of the Secretary-General, UN document A/47/277-S/24111), 17 June [online] http://www.un.org/docs/SG/agpeace.html (accessed 2 May 2009).

Bowring, B. (2008) *The Degradation of the International Legal Order? The Rehabilitation of Law and the Possibility of Politics* (Oxford: Routledge-Cavendish).

Boyle, J. (2006) 'Traditional Just War Theory and Humanitarian Intervention', in T. Nardin and M. Williams (eds), *Humanitarian Intervention: NOMOS XLVII* (New York: New York University Press).

Brown, C. (1992) *International Relations Theory: New Normative Approaches* (Hemel Hempstead: Harvester Wheatsheaf).

Brown, C. (2000) 'A Qualified Defense of the Use of Force for Humanitarian Reasons', in K. Booth (ed.), *The Kosovo Tragedy: The Human Rights Dimension* (London: Routledge).

Brown, C. (2001) 'Ethics Interests, and Foreign Policy', in K. E. Smith and M. Light (eds), *Ethics and Foreign Policy* (Cambridge: Cambridge University Press).

Brown, C. (2002) 'Marxism and International Ethics', in T. Nardin and D. Mapel (eds), *Traditions of International Ethics* (Cambridge: Cambridge University Press).

Brown, C. (2006) *Sovereignty, Rights and Justice: International Political Theory Today* (London: Polity).

Brown, C. and Ainley, K. (2005) *Understanding International Relations* (Basingstoke and New York: Palgrave Macmillan).

Brown, C., Nardin, T. and Rengger, N. (eds) (2002) *International Relations in Political Thought* (Cambridge: Cambridge University Press).

Brownlie, I. (1973) 'Thoughts on Kind-Hearted Gunmen', in R. B. Lillich (ed.), *Humanitarian Intervention and the United Nations* (Charlottesville, Va.: University Press of Virginia).

Brownlie, I. (1974) 'Humanitarian Intervention', in J. Moore (ed.), *Law and Civil War in the Modern World* (Baltimore, Md.: Johns Hopkins University Press).

Buchanan, A. and Keohane, R. O. (2004) 'The Preventive Use of Force: A Cosmopolitan Institutional Proposal', *Ethics and International Affairs*, 18:1, 1–22.

Buckley, M. and Singh, R. (eds) (2006) *The Bush Doctrine and the War on Terrorism* (London, Routledge).

Bull, H. (1984a) *Justice in International Relations: Hagey Lectures*, (Ontario: University Publications Distribution Service).

Bull, H. (1984b) 'Conclusion', in H. Bull (ed.), *Intervention in World Politics* (Oxford: Oxford University Press).

Bull, H. (2002) *The Anarchical Society: A Study of Order in World Politics* (Basingstoke: Palgrave Macmillan and New York: Columbia University Press).

Burchill, S. (2005) 'Liberalism', in S. Burchill, R. Devetak, A. Linklater, M. Paterson, C. Reus-Smit and J. True (eds), *Theories of International Relations* (Basingstoke and New York: Palgrave Macmillan).

Burchill, S., Devetak, R., Linklater, A., Paterson, M., Reus-Smit, C. and True, J. (2005) *Theories of International Relations* (Basingstoke and New York: Palgrave Macmillan).

Burchill, S. and Linklater, A. (2005) 'Introduction', in S. Burchill, R. Devetak, A.

Linklater, M. Paterson, C. Reus-Smit and J. True (eds), *Theories of International Relations* (Basingstoke and New York: Palgrave Macmillan).

Burke, A. (2004) 'Just War or Ethical Peace? Moral Discourses of Strategic Violence after 9/11', *International Affairs*, 80:2, 329–53.

Burton, M. (1996) 'Legalising the Sublegal', *Georgetown Law Journal*, 85, 417–54.

Bush, G. (2002) 'Transcript: Bush's Speech to the UN on Iraq', *New York Times*, 12 September.

Buzan, B. (1991) *People, States and Fear: An Agenda for International Security Studies in the Post-Cold War Era* (London: Harvester Wheatsheaf).

Byers, M. (2005) 'Not Yet Havoc: Geopolitical Change and the International Rules on Military Force', in D. Armstrong, T. Farrell and B. Maiguashca (eds), *Force and Legitimacy in World Politics* (Cambridge: Cambridge University Press).

Byers, M. and Chesterman, S. (2003) 'Changing the Rules About Rules?' in J. Holzgrefe and R. Keohane (eds), *Humanitarian Intervention: Ethical, Legal and Political Dilemmas* (Cambridge: Cambridge University Press).

Callinicos, A. (2000) 'The Ideology of Humanitarian Intervention', in T. Ali (ed.), *Masters of the Universe? NATO's Balkan Crusade* (London: Verso).

Camilleri, J. A. and Falk, J. (1992) *The End of Sovereignty* (London: Elgar).

Campbell, D. (1994) 'The Deterritorialization of Responsibility: Levinas, Derrida, and Ethics After the End of Philosophy', *Alternatives*, 19:4, 455–84.

Campbell, D. (1998a) *National Deconstruction: Violence, Identity and Justice in Bosnia* (Minneapolis, Minn.: University of Minnesota Press).

Campbell, D. (1998b) 'Why Fight: Humanitarianism, Principles, and Post-structuralism', *Millennium*, 27:3, 497–521.

Canning, J. (2003) 'Aquinas', in D. Boucher and P. Kelly (eds), *Political Thinkers: From Socrates to the Present* (Oxford: Oxford University Press).

Capital and Class (2003) 'Editorial Comment on the War in Iraq', *Capital and Class*, 22 June.

Caplan, R. (2000) 'Humanitarian Intervention: Which Way Forward?' *Ethics and International Affairs*, 14, 23–38.

Carnegie Commission on Preventing Deadly Conflict (CCPDC) (1997) 'Preventing Deadly Conflict: Final Report with Executive Summary', December [online] http://www.wilsoncenter.org/subsites/ccpdc/pubs/rept97/finfr.htm (accessed 2 May 2009).

Carr, E. H. (2001) *The Twenty Years Crisis* (Basingstoke: Palgrave Macmillan).

Carroll, R. (2004) 'US Chose to Ignore Rwandan Genocide', *Guardian*, 31 March.

Cassese, A. (1999) '*Ex iniuria ius oritur*: Are we Moving Towards International Legitimisation of Forcible Humanitarian Countermeasures in the World Community?', *European Journal of International Law*, 10:1, 23–30.

Cassese, A. (2005) *International Law* (Oxford: Oxford University Press).

Chadda, M. (2003) 'Intervention in Ethnic and Civil Wars', in R. Thomas (ed.), *Yugoslavia Unraveled: Sovereignty, Self Determination, Intervention* (Oxford: Lexington).

Chandler, D. (2000a) 'International Justice', *New Left Review*, 6, Nov/Dec, 55–66.

Chandler, D. (2000b) *Bosnia: Faking Democracy after Dayton* (London: Pluto).

Chandler, D. (2002) *From Kosovo to Kabul* (London: Pluto).

Chandler, D. (2004a) 'The Responsibility to Protect? Imposing the "Liberal Peace"', *International Peacekeeping*, 11:1, 59–81.

Chandler, D. (2004b) *Constructing Global Civil Society: Morality and Power in International Relations* (Basingstoke and New York: Palgrave Macmillan).

Chatterjee, D. and Scheid, D. (2003) 'Introduction', in D. Chatterjee and D. Scheid (eds), *Ethics and Foreign Intervention* (Cambridge: Cambridge University Press).

Chavez, H. (2005) Speech Given by President Hugo Chavez at 60th UN General Assembly, New York, 15 September [online] http://www.embavenez-us.org/news.php?nid=1745 (accessed 15 January 2008).

Chedle, D. and Prendergast, J. (2007) *Not on our Watch: The Mission to End Genocide in Darfur and Beyond* (Meath: Maverick House).

Chesterman, S. (2002) *Just War or Just Peace?* (Oxford: Oxford University Press).

Chesterman, S. (2003) 'Hard Cases Make Bad Law', in A. Lang (ed.), *Just Intervention* (Washington DC: Georgetown University Press).

Chesterman, S. (2006) 'Humanitarian Intervention and Afghanistan', in J. Welsh (ed.), *Humanitarian Intervention and International Relations* (Oxford: Oxford University Press).

Chesterman, S. and Byers, M. (1999) 'Has US Power Destroyed the UN?' *London Review of Books*, 29 April, 21.

Chomsky, N. (1999) *The New Military Humanism: Lessons from Kosovo* (London: Pluto).

Chopra, J. and Weiss, T. (1992) 'Sovereignty is No Longer Sacrosanct', *Ethics and International Affairs*, 6, 95–117.

Christopher, P. (2004) *The Ethics of War and Peace* (Upper Saddle River, N.J.: Prentice Hall).

Clapham, C. (1998) 'Rwanda: The Perils of Peacemaking', *Journal of Peace Research*, 35:2, 193–210.

Clapham, C. (1999) 'Sovereignty and the Third World State', *Political Studies*, 47:3, 522–37.

Clark, D. (2003) 'Iraq Has Wrecked Our Case for Humanitarian Wars', *Guardian*, 12 August, 20.

Clark, I. (2005) *Legitimacy in International Society* (Oxford: Oxford University Press).

Clark, W. (2001) *Waging Modern War* (Oxford: Public Affairs).

Coalition of NGOs on Darfur (2008) 'Rhetoric vs. Reality: The Situation in Darfur' [online] http://www.hrw.org/sites/default/files/related_material/darfur1208.pdf (accessed 2 May 2009).

Coates, A. J. (1997) *The Ethics of War* (Manchester: Manchester University Press).

Coates, A. J. (2006) 'Humanitarian Intervention: A Conflict of Traditions', in T. Nardin and M. Williams (eds), *Humanitarian Intervention: NOMOS XLVII* (New York: New York University Press).

Cockayne, J. and Samii, C. (2006) 'Structural and Normative Challenges', in R. Thakur and W. P. S. Sidhu (eds), *The Iraq Crisis and World Order: Structural, Institutional and Normative Challenges* (New York: United Nations University Press).

Cohen, J. (2004) 'Whose Sovereignty? Empire Versus International Law', *Ethics and International Affairs*, 18:3, 1–24.

Cohen, M. (1984) 'Moral Skepticism and International Relations', *Philosophy and Public Affairs*, 13:4, 299–346.

Coicaud, J. M. (2006) 'Iraq and the Social Logic of International Security', in R.

Thakur and W. P. S. Sidhu (eds), *The Iraq Crisis and World Order: Structural, Institutional and Normative Challenges* (New York: United Nations University Press).

Coicaud, J. M. and Wheeler, N. (2008) 'Introduction: The Changing Ethics of Power Beyond Borders', in J. M. Coicaud and N. Wheeler (eds), *National Interests and International Solidarity* (New York: United Nations University Press).

Coleman, W. and Wayland, S. (2006) 'The Origins of Global Civil Society and Nonterritorial Governance', *Global Governance*, 12, 242–5.

Coll, A. (2001) 'Kosovo and the Moral Burdens of Power', in A. Bacevich and E. Cohen (eds), *War Over Kosovo* (New York: Columbia University Press).

Collins, B. (2002) 'New Wars and Old Wars? The Lessons of Rwanda', in D. Chandler (ed.), *Rethinking Human Rights* (Basingstoke and New York: Palgrave Macmillan).

Convention on the Rights and Duties of States (1933) *Convention signed at Montevideo December 26, 1933* [online] http://avalon.law.yale.edu/20th_century/intam03.asp (accessed 1 February 2009).

Cook, M. (2003) '"Immaculate War": Constraints on Humanitarian Intervention', in A. Lang (ed.), *Just Intervention* (Washington DC: Georgetown University Press).

Cooper, R. (2002) 'The New Liberal Imperialism', *Observer*, 7 April.

Cooper, R. (2004) *The Breaking of Nations* (London: Atlantic).

Cortright, D. (2006) 'The World Says No: The Global Movement Against War', in R. Thakur and W. P. S. Sidhu (eds), *The Iraq Crisis and World Order: Structural, Institutional and Normative Challenges* (New York: United Nations University Press).

Cox, R. (1981) 'Social Forces, States and World Orders', *Millennium*, 10:2, 127–55.

Cox, R. (1986) 'Social Forces, States and World Orders', in R. Keohane (ed.), *Neorealism and its Critics* (New York: Colombia University Press).

Cox, R. (1996) *Approaches to World Order* (Cambridge: Cambridge University Press).

Crawford, T. (2006) 'Moral Hazard, Intervention and Internal War', in T. Crawford and A. Kuperman (eds), *Gambling on Humanitarian Intervention* (London: Routledge).

Crawford, J. and Olleson, S. (2006) 'The Nature and Forms of International Responsibility', in M. Evans (ed.), *International Law* (Oxford: Oxford University Press).

Cronin, B (2008) 'International Consensus and the Changing Legal Authority of the UN Security Council', in B. Cronin and I. Hurd (eds), *The UN Security Council and the Politics of International Authority* (London: Routledge).

Cronin, B. and Hurd, I. (2008) *The UN Security Council and the Politics of International Authority* (London: Routledge).

Daalder, I. and O'Hanlon, M. (2000) *Winning Ugly* (Washington DC: Brookings Institution Press).

Daillaire, R. (1994) 'Request for Protection of Informant: 11 January', PBS Frontline – "The Triumph of Evil" [online] http://www.pbs.org/wgbh/pages/frontline/shows/evil/warning/cable.html (accessed 2 May 2009).

Dallaire, R. (2004a) *Shake Hands with the Devil: The Failure of Humanity in Rwanda* (London: Arrow).

Dallaire, R. (2004b) 'Looking at Darfur, Seeing Rwanda', *New York Times*, 4 October.

Dallmayr, F. (2003) 'Cosmopolitanism: Moral and Political', *Political Theory*, 31:3, 421–42.

Daly, M. W. (2007) *Darfur's Sorrow: A History of Destruction and Genocide* (New York: Cambridge University Press).

Danish Institute of International Affairs (DIIA) (1999) *Humanitarian Intervention: Legal and Political Aspects* (Copenhagen: Danish Institute of International Affairs).

De Bréadún, D. (2004) 'A Defiant Bush Defends Iraq Strategy Before the UN', *Irish Times*, 22 September, 11.

De Brichambaut, M. P. (2000) 'The Role of the UN Security Council in the International Legal System', in M. Byers (ed.), *The Role of Law in International Politics* (Oxford: Oxford University Press).

De Waal, A. (1994) 'Genocide in Rwanda', *Anthropology Today*, 10:3, 1–2.

De Waal, A. (2004) 'Darfur's Deep Grievances Defy All Hopes for a Fast Solution', *Observer*, 25 July.

De Waal, A. (2007a) 'No Such Thing as Humanitarian Intervention', *Harvard International Review*, 21 March [online] http://www.harvardir.org/articles/1482/3/ (accessed 2 May 2009).

De Waal, A. (ed.) (2007b) *War in Darfur and the Search for Peace* (Cambridge, Mass.: Harvard University Press).

De Waal, A. (2007c) 'Sudan: The Turbulent State', in A. de Waal (ed.), *War in Darfur and the Search for Peace* (Cambridge: Global Equity Initiative, Harvard University).

De Waal, A. (2008) 'Why Darfur Intervention is a Mistake', BBC World News, 21 May [online] http://news.bbc.co.uk/2/hi/africa/7411087.stm (accessed 2 May 2009).

Deane, H. (1963) *The Political and Social Ideas of St Augustine* (New York: Colombia University Press).

Deng, F. M., Kimaro, S., Lyons, T., Rothchild, D. and Zartman, I. W. (1996) *Sovreignty and Responsibility: Conflict Managment in Africa* (Wsahington DC: Brookings Institution).

Der Derian, J. and Shapiro, M. J. (eds) (1989) *International/Intertextual Relations: Postmodern Readings of World Politics* (Lexington, Ky: Lexington Books).

Des Forges, A. (1999) *Leave None to Tell the Story: Genocide in Rwanda*, Human Rights Watch [online] http://www.hrw.org/legacy/reports/1999/rwanda/index.htm#TopOfPage (accessed 2 May 2009).

Des Forges, A. (2000) 'Shame – Rationalizing Western Apathy on Rwanda: Alas we Knew', *Foreign Affairs*, 79:3, 141–2.

Destexhe, A. (1995) *Rwanda and Genocide in the Twentieth Century* (London: Pluto).

Devetak, R. (2009) 'Post-structuralism' in S. Burchill, A. Linklater, R. Devetak, J. Donnelly, T. Nardin, M. Paterson, C. Reus-Smit and J. True, *Theories of International Relations* (Basingstoke and New York: Palgrave Macmillan).

Dinstein, Y. (2005) *War, Aggression and Self-Defence* (Cambridge: Cambridge University Press).

Dixon, M. (2007) *Textbook on International Law* (Oxford: Oxford University Press).

Docking, T. (2008) 'US Foreign Policy Towards Africa', in J. M. Coicaud and N. Wheeler (eds), *National Interests and International Solidarity* (New York: United Nations University Press).

Dodge, T. (2003) *Inventing Iraq: The Failure of Nation-Building and a History Denied* (New York: Colombia University Press).

Donnelly, J. (1989) *Universal Human Rights in Theory and Practice* (Ithaca, N.Y.: Cornell University Press).

Donnelly, J. (2002) 'Twentieth Century Realism', in T. Nardin and D. Mapel (eds), *Traditions of International Ethics* (Cambridge: Cambridge University Press).

Douzinas, C. (2000) *The End of Human Rights* (Oxford: Oxford University Press).

Doyle. M. (1986) 'Liberalism and World Politics', *American Political Science Review*, 80:4, 1151–69.

Dryzek, J. and Dunleavy, P. (2009) *Theories of the Democratic State* (Basingstoke and New York: Palgrave Macmillan).

Duffield, M. (2005) 'Getting Barbarians to Fight Savages: Development, Security and the Colonial Present', *Conflict, Security and Development*, 5:2, 141–59.

Duffield, M. (2006) *Global Governance and the New Wars: The Merging of Development and Security* (London: Zed).

Duffield, M. and Waddell, N. (2006) 'Securing Humans in a Dangerous World', *International Politics*, 43:1, 1–23.

Dumbrell, J. and Ryan, D. (2007) 'Introduction', in J. Dumbrell and D. Ryan (eds), *Vietnam in Iraq* (London: Routledge).

Dunleavy, P. and O'Leary, B. (1987) *Theories of the State* (London: Macmillan).

Dunne, T. (1998) *Inventing International Society* (Basingstoke: Palgrave Macmillan).

Dunne, T. Kurki, M. and Smith, S. (2007) *International Relations Theories: Discipline and Diversity* (Oxford: Oxford University Press).

Edkins, J. (2000) *Whose Hunger? Concepts of Famine, Practices of Aid* (Minneapolis, Minn.: University of Minneapolis Press).

Edkins, J. (2003) 'Humanitarianism, Humanity, Human', *Journal of Human Rights*, 2:2, 253–8.

Edkins, J. (2005a) *Poststructuralism and International Relations: Bringing the Political Back In* (Boulder, Colo.: Lynne Rienner).

Edkins, J. (2005b) 'Ethics and Practices of Engagement: Intellectuals as Experts', *International Relations*, 19:1, 64–9.

Edkins, J. and Pin-Fat, V. (1998) 'The Subject of the Political', in J. Edkins, N. Persram and V. Pin-Fat (eds), *Sovereignty and Subjectivity* (Boulder, Colo.: Lynne Rienner).

Elshtain, J. B. (ed.) (1992) *Just War Theory* (New York: New York University Press).

Elshtain, J. B. (2003a) 'St Augustine', in D. Boucher and P. Kelly (eds), *Political Thinkers: From Socrates to the Present* (Oxford: Oxford University Press).

Elshtain, J. B. (2003b) 'International Justice as Equal Regard and the Use of Force', *Ethics and International Affairs*, 17:2, 63–75.

Evans, G. (2008) *The Responsibility to Protect: Ending Mass Atrocity Crimes Once and For All* (Washington DC: Brookings Institution Press).

Evans, M. (2005) *Just War Theory: A Reappraisal* (Edinburgh: Edinburgh University Press).

Falk, R. (1995) *On Humane Governance* (Cambridge: Polity).

Falk, R. (2004) 'Humanitarian Intervention After Kosovo', in A. Jokic (ed.), *Lessons of Kosovo: The Dangers of Humanitarian Intervention* (Toronto: Broadview Press).

Falk, R. (2005a) 'Legality and Legitimacy: The Quest for Principled Flexibility and Restraint', in D. Armstrong, T. Farrell and B. Maiguashca (eds), *Force and Legitimacy in World Politics* (Cambridge: Cambridge University Press).

Falk, R. (2005b) '(Re)Imagining the Governance of Globalization', in A. Bellamy (ed.), *International Society and its Critics* (Oxford: Oxford University Press).

Farer, T. (2003) 'The Ethics of Intervention in Self Determination Struggles', in D. Chatterjee and D. Scheid (eds), *Ethics and Foreign Intervention* (Cambridge: Cambridge University Press).

Finnemore, M. and Sikkink, K. (1998) 'International Norm Dynamics and Political Change', *International Organization*, 52:4, 887–917.

Finnis, J. (1998) *Aquinas: Moral, Political and Legal Theory* (Oxford: Oxford University Press).

Fisher, D. (2007) 'Humanitarian Intervention', in C. Reed and D. Ryall (eds), *The Price of Peace* (Cambridge: Cambridge University Press).

Fitzmaurice, M. (2006) 'The Practical Working of the Law of Treaties', in M. Evans (ed.), *International Law* (Oxford: Oxford University Press).

Foucault, M. (1980) 'Truth and Power', in M. Foucault and C. Gordon (eds), *Power/Knowledge: Selected Interviews and Other Writings 1972–1977* (London: Longman).

Foucault, M. (1991) *Discipline and Punish* (London: Penguin).

Fox, F. (2002) 'Conditioning the Right to Humanitarian Aid? Human Rights and the "New Humanitarians"', in D. Chandler (ed.), *Rethinking Human Rights: Critical Approaches to International Politics* (Basingstoke: Palgrave Macmillan).

Franck, T. (1999) 'Lessons of Kosovo', *American Journal of International Law*, 93:4, October, 857–60.

Franck, T. (2005) 'Interpretation and Change in the Law of Humanitarian Intervention', in J. L. Holzgrefe and R. O. Keohane (eds), *Humanitarian Intervention: Ethical, Legal and Political Dilemmas* (Cambridge: Cambridge University Press).

Franck, T. and Rodley, N. (1973) 'After Bangladesh: The Law of Humanitarian Intervention by Military Force', *American Journal of International Law*, 67, 275–305.

Freedman, L. (2005) 'The Age of Liberal Wars', in, D. Armstrong, T. Farrell and B. Maiguashca (eds), *Force and Legitimacy in World Politics* (Cambridge: Cambridge University Press).

Frontline (2000) 'War in Europe Interview with Richard Holbrooke' [online] www.pbs.org/wgbh/pages/frontline/shows/kosovo/interviews/holbrooke.html (accessed 2 November 2008).

Frontline (2004) 'Ghosts of Rwanda – Transcript' [online] http://www.pbs.org/wgbh/pages/frontline/shows/ghosts/etc/script.html (accessed 2 November 2008).

Frost, M. (2001) 'The Ethics of Humanitarian Intervention', in K. E. Smith and M. Light (eds), *Ethics and Foreign Policy* (Cambridge: Cambridge University Press).

Fukuyama, F. (1992) *The End of History and the Last Man* (New York: Avon).

Fukuyama, F. (2006) 'Nation-building and the Failure of International Memory', in F. Fukuyama (ed.), *Nation-Building: Beyond Afghanistan and Iraq* (New York: Johns Hopkins University Press).

Fuller, G. (1999) 'Two, Three, Many Kosovars', *New Perspectives Quarterly*, 16, 4.

Gardner, J. (2007) 'The Final Chapter?' in J. Dumbrell and D. Ryan (eds), *Vietnam in Iraq* (London: Routledge).

Garton-Ash, T. (2000) 'The War We Almost Lost', *Guardian*, 4 September.

Gellner, E. (1994) *The Conditions of Liberty* (London: Hamish Hamilton).

Glennon, M. (1999) 'The New Interventionism', *Foreign Affairs*, 78:3, 2–7.

Glenny, M. (1999) *The Balkans, 1804–1999* (London: Granta Books).

Glover, J. (2006) 'British believe Bush is more dangerous than Kim Jong-il', *Guardian*, 3 November.

Gompert, D. C., Richardson, C., Kugler, R. L. and Bernath, C. H. (2005) 'Learning from Darfur: Building a Net-Capable African Force to Stop Mass Killing', Centre for Technology and National Security Policy, National Defense University [online] http://www.ndu.edu/CTNSP/Def_Tech/DTP%2015%20Darfur.pdf (accessed 26 February 2009).

Gourevitch, P. (1998) *We Wish to Inform You that Tomorrow We Will be Killed with Our Families* (London: Picador).

Gow, J. (1994) 'Nervous Bunnies: The International Community and the Yugoslav War of Dissolution, the Politics of Military Intervention in a Time of Change', in L. Freedman (ed.), *Military Intervention in European Conflicts* (Oxford: Blackwell).

Gow, J. (1997) *Triumph of the Lack of Will: International Diplomacy and the Yugoslav War* (New York: Colombia University Press).

Gow, J. (2000) 'A Revolution In International Affairs?' *Security Dialogue*, 31:3, 293–306.

Gow, J. (2003) *The Serbian Project and its Adversaries* (Montreal: McGill-Queens University Press).

Gow, J. (2005) *Defending the West* (Cambridge: Polity).

Gowan, P. (2000) 'The Euro-Atlantic Origins of NATO's Attack on Yugoslavia', in T. Ali (ed.), *Masters of the Universe?* (London: Verso).

Gowan, P. (2003) 'The New Liberal Cosmopolitanism', in D. Archibugi (ed.), *Debating Cosmopolitics* (London: Verso).

Gowlland-Debbas, V. (2000) 'Functions of the United Nations Security Council in the International Legal System', in M. Byers (ed.), *The Role of International Law in International Politics* (Oxford: Oxford University Press).

Graubart, J. (2008) 'NGOs and the Security Council', in B. Cronin and I. Hurd (eds), *The UN Security Council and the Politics of International Authority* (London: Routledge).

Gray, C. (2001) 'No Good Deed Shall Go Unpunished', in K. Booth (ed.), *The Kosovo Tragedy* (London: Frank Cass).

Green, L. (1988) *The Authority of the State* (Oxford: Clarendon).

Greenwood, C. (1993) 'Is There a Right of Humanitarian Intervention?' *World Today*, 49:2, 34–40.

Griffins, M. (2007) *International Relations Theory for the 21st Century* (London: Routledge).

Group of 77 (G-77) (2000) 'Declaration of the South Summit', Havana, Cuba, 10–14 April, article 54 [online] http://www.g77.org/summit/Declaration_ G77Summit.htm (accessed 6 June 2008).

Guardian (2003) 'War would be illegal', letter, *Guardian*, 7 March.

Guichord, C. (1999) 'International Law and the War in Kosovo', *Survival*, 41:2, 19–34.

Hagen, W. (1999) 'The Balkans Lethal Nationalisms', *Foreign Affairs*, 78/4, 52–64.

Hammond, P. (2002) 'Moral Combat', in D. Chandler (ed.), *Rethinking Human Rights* (Basingstoke and New York: Palgrave Macmillan).

Harrison, G. (2004) *The World Bank in Africa: The Construction of Governance States* (London: Routledge).

Hayden, P. (2005) *Cosmopolitan Global Politics* (Aldershot: Ashgate).

Hayden, R. (2003) 'Biased Justice', in R. Thomas (ed.), *Yugoslavia Unraveled: Sovereignty, Self Determination, Intervention* (Oxford: Lexington).

Heazle, M. and Islam, I. (2006) *Beyond the Iraq War: The Promises, Pitfalls and Perils of External Interventionism* (Cheltenham: Edward Elgar).

Hedges, C. (1999) 'Kosovo's Next Masters', *Foreign Affairs*, 78:3, 24–42.

Hehir, A. (2006) 'The Impact of Analogical Reasoning on US Foreign Policy Towards Kosovo', *Journal of Peace Research*, 43:1, 67–81.

Hehir, A. (2008a) *Humanitarian Intervention after Kosovo: Iraq, Darfur and the Record of Global Civil Society* (Basingstoke and New York: Palgrave Macmillan).

Hehir, A. (2008b) 'Interview with Jamie Shea: NATO's Role in Statebuilding', *Journal of Intervention and Statebuilding*, 2:2, 227–41.

Hehir, A. (2008c) 'The Changing Conception of Self-Defense', in I. Wilson and J. Forest (eds), *Defence Politics: International and Comparative Perspectives* (London: Routledge).

Hehir, A. (2009a) 'Interview with Lord Robertson', *Journal of Intervention and Statebuilding*, 3:2, 259–75.

Hehir, A. (2009b) 'NATO's Humanitarian Intervention in Kosovo: Precedent or Aberration?' *Journal of Human Rights*, 8:3, 1–20.

Hehir, A. and Robinson, N. (eds) (2007) *State-building: Theory and Practice* (London: Routledge).

Held, D. (1995) *Democracy and the Global Order* (London: Polity).

Held, D. (2004) *A Globalizing World?* (London: Routledge).

Held, D. (2005) 'Globalization: The Dangers and the Answers', in D. Held (ed.), *Debating Globalization* (London: Polity).

Heller, T. and Sofaer, A. (2001) 'Sovereignty: The Practitioners' Perspective', in S. Krasner (ed.), *Problematic Sovereignty: Contested Rules and Political Possibilities* (New York: Colombia University Press).

Hendrickson, D. (1997) 'In Defense of Realism: A Commentary on Just and Unjust Wars', *Ethics and International Affairs*, 11, 19–55.

Henkin, L. (1990) 'Compliance with International Law in an Inter-State System', *Academie de droit international, Recueil des cours 1989* (Dordrecht: Martinus Nijhoff).

Hensel, H. (2004) 'Introduction', in H. Hensel (ed.), *Sovereignty and the Global Community* (Aldershot: Ashgate).

HM Government (2002) 'Iraq's Weapons of Mass Destruction: The Assessment of the British Government', September [online] http://www.archive2.official-documents.co.uk/document/reps/iraq/iraqdossier.pdf (accessed 2 May 2009).

Herbst, J. (1989) 'The Creation and Maintenance of National Boundaries in Africa', *International Organization*, 43:4, 673–92.

Herring, E. and Rangwala, G. (2006) *Iraq in Fragments: The Occupation and its Legacy* (London: Hurst).

Herz, J. (1957) 'Rise and Demise of the Territorial State', *World Politics*, 9:4, 473–93.

Heuser, B. (1997) 'Sovereignty, Self-Determination and Security', in S. Hashmi (ed.), *State Sovereignty: Change and Persistence in International Relations* (Pennsylvania Pa.: Pennsylvania State University Press).

Hilpold, P. (2001) 'Humanitarian Intervention: Is There a Need for a Legal Reappraisal?' *European Journal of International Law*, 12:3, 437–67.

Hiltermann, J. (2007) *A Poisonous Affair: America, Iraq and the Gassings of Halabja* (Cambridge: Cambridge University Press).

Hinsliff, G. (2003) 'Blair Stakes His Political Future on Beating Iraq', *Observer*, 16 February.

Hintjens, H. M. (1999) 'Explaining the 1994 Genocide in Rwanda', *Journal of Modern African Studies*, 37:2, 241–86.

Hobbes, T. (1968) *Leviathan*, ed. C. B. Macpherson (London: Penguin).

Hobson, J. (2000) *The State and International Relations* (Cambridge: Cambridge University Press).

Hodge, C. (2000) 'Casual War: NATO's Intervention in Kosovo', *Ethics and International Affairs*, 14, 39–54.

Hoffmann, S. (2003) 'Intervention: Should It Go On? Can It Go On?' in D. Chatterjee and D. Scheid (eds), *Ethics and Foreign Intervention* (Cambridge: Cambridge University Press).

Hoge, W. (2004) 'U.N. Council Threatens to Punish Sudan Over Militia Killings', *New York Times*, 31 July.

Hoile, D. (2005) *Darfur in Perspective* (London: European-Sudanese Public Affairs Council).

Holbrook, J. (2002) 'Humanitarian Intervention', in D. Chandler (ed.), *Rethinking Human Rights* (Basingstoke and New York: Palgrave Macmillan).

Hollis, M. and Smith, S. (1991) *Explaining and Understanding International Relations* (Oxford: Clarendon Press).

Holmes, R. (1992) 'Can War be Morally Justified?' in J. B. Elshtain (ed.), *Just War Theory* (Oxford: Blackwell).

Holmes, R. L. (1989) *On War and Morality* (Princeton, N.J.: Princeton University Press).

Holzgrefe, J. L. (2005) 'The Humanitarian Intervention Debate', in J. L. Holzgrefe and R. Keohane (eds), *Humanitarian Intervention: Ethical, Legal and Political Dilemmas* (Cambridge: Cambridge University Press).

Horton, J. (1992) 'The National Question', in J. Allcock, J. Horton and M. Milivojevic (eds), *Yugoslavia in Transition* (Oxford: Berg).

House of Commons (UK) (2000) *Foreign Affairs – Fourth Report*, No. HC 28-1 of 7 June 2000, paragraph 1138 [online] www.publications.parliament.uk/pa/cm199900/cmselect/cmfaff/28/2802.htm (accessed 12 June 2007).

Howard, J. (2003) 'Transcript of the Prime Minister's Address to the National

Press Club', 14 March [online] http://www.pm.gov.au/media/Speech/2003/speech74.cfm (accessed 4 October 2007).

Howard, M. (2000) *The Invention of Peace* (London: Profile).

Huig, A. (2007) 'Darfur has Become an Even Greater Challenge for Humanitarian Action', Médecins Sans Frontières, 26 October [online] http://www.msf.org.uk/articledetail.aspx?fId=Darfur_has_become_an_even_greater_challenge_for_humanitarian_action (accessed 4 June 2009).

Human Rights Watch (2000) 'Introduction', *World Report 2000* [online] http://www.hrw.org/wr2k/Front.htm#TopOfPage (accessed 2 November 2007).

Human Rights Watch (2001) 'Cluster Bombs in Afghanistan: A Human Rights Watch Backrounder', October [online] http://www.hrw.org/backgrounder/arms/cluster-bck1031.pdf (accessed 2 November 2007).

Human Rights Watch (2007) 'Human Rights News: Crisis in Darfur', 18 September [online] http://www.hrw.org/english/docs/2004/05/05/darfur8536.htm (accessed 8 October 2007).

Human Rights Watch (2008) *2008 World Report* [online] http://www.hrw.org/sites/default/files/reports/wr2k8_web.pdf (accessed 2 November 2007).

Hurd, I. (2007) *After Anarchy: Legitimacy and Power in the United Nations Security Council* (Princeton, N.J.: Princeton University Press).

Hurd, I. (2008) 'Theories and Tests of International Authority', in B. Cronin and I. Hurd (eds), *The UN Security Council and the Politics of International Authority* (London: Routledge).

Hurrell, A. (2005) 'Legitimacy and the Use of Force: Can the Circle be Squared?' in D. Armstrong, T. Farrell and B. Maiguashca (eds), *Force and Legitimacy in World Politics* (Cambridge: Cambridge University Press).

Hutchings, K. (1999) *International Political Theory* (London: Sage).

Ignatieff, M. (2000) *Virtual War: Kosovo and Beyond* (New York: Picador).

Ignatieff, M. (2003) 'The American Empire: The Burden', *New York Times Magazine*, 5 January.

Ikenberry, J. and Slaughter, A. M. (2006) 'Forging A World of Liberty under Law: U.S. National Security in the 21st Century', *Princeton Project Papers*, 27 September.

Independent International Commission on Kosovo (IICK) (2000) *Kosovo Report* (Oxford: Oxford University Press).

International Commission of Enquiry on Darfur (ICED) (2005) 'Report of the International Commission of Inquiry on Darfur to the United Nations Secretary-General', 25 January [online] http://www.un.org/news/dh/sudan/com_inq_darfur.pdf (accessed 21 December 2008).

International Commission on Intervention and State Sovereignty (ICISS) (2001) *The Responsibility to Protect* (Ottawa: International Development Research Centre).

International Criminal Tribunal for the Former Yugoslavia (ICTY) (1996) *Prosecutor v. Tadic*, Judgement, ICTY Case No. IT-94-1-AR72 (Jurisdiction), Appeals Chamber, 1995, 35 ILM 35.

International Crisis Group (2008) *Iraq Country Report* [online] http://www.crisis-group.org/home/index.cfm?id=2436andl=1 (accessed 21 December 2008).

Jackson, R. (1996) *Quasi-States: Sovereignty, International Relations and the Third World* (Cambridge: Cambridge University Press).

Jackson, R. (2000) *The Global Covenant: Human Conduct in a World of States* (Oxford: Oxford University Press).

Jackson, R. (2006) 'The Safety of the People is the Supreme Law: Beyond Hobbes but not as far as Kant', in W. Bain (ed.), *The Empire of Security and the Safety of the People* (London: Routledge).

Jackson, R. (2007) *Sovereignty: Evolution of an Idea* (London: Polity).

Jackson, R. and Sørensen, G. (2003) *Introduction to International Relations* (Oxford: Oxford University Press).

James, A. (1986) *Sovereign Statehood* (London, Allen & Unwin).

Janzekovic, J. (2006) *The Use of Force in Humanitarian Intervention: Morality and Practicalities* (Hampshire: Ashgate).

Jatras, J. (2000) 'NATO's Myths and Bogus Justifications for Intervention', in T. G. Carpenter (ed.), *NATO's Empty Victory* (Washington DC: Cato Institute).

Job, B. (2006) 'International Peace and Security and State Sovereignty: Contesting Norms and Norm Entrepreneurs', in R. Thakur and W. P. S. Sidhu (eds), *The Iraq Crisis and World Order: Structural, Institutional and Normative Challenges* (New York: United Nations University Press).

Johansen, R. (ed.) (2006) *A United Nations Emergency Peace Service to Prevent Crimes Against Humanity* (New York: World Federalist Movement).

Johnson, J. T. (1987) *The Quest for Peace: Three Moral Traditions in Western Cultural History* (Princeton, N.J.: Princeton University Press).

Johnston, J. T. (2005) 'Just War, as it was and is', *First Things*, 149, 14–24.

Johnstone, D. (2000) 'NATO and the New World Order', in P. Hammond and E. Herman (eds), *Degraded Capability: The Media and the Kosovo Crisis* (London: Pluto).

Jones, A. (2008) 'Genocide and Mass Killing', in P. Williams (ed.), *Security Studies: An Introduction* (London: Routledge).

Jones, B. D. (1995) '"Intervention without Borders": Humanitarian Intervention in Rwanda 1990–94', *Millennium*, 24:2, 225–49.

Joras, U. and Schetter, C. (2004) 'Hidden Ties: Similarities Between Research and Policy Approaches to Ethnic Conflicts', in A. Wimmer, R. Goldstone, D. Horowitz, U. Joras and C. Schetter (eds), *Facing Ethnic Conflicts: Towards a New Realism* (Oxford: Rowman & Littlefield).

Joyner, D. H. (2002) 'The Kosovo Intervention: Legal Analysis and a more Persuasive Paradigm', *European Journal of International Law*, 13:3, 597–619.

Judah, T. (2000) *Kosovo: War and Revenge* (New Haven, Conn.: Yale University Press).

Kaldor, M. (1999) *New and Old Wars* (London: Polity).

Kaldor, M. (2003) *Global Civil Society: An Answer to War* (London: Polity).

Kaldor, M. (2005) 'What is Human Security?', in D. Held (ed.), *Debating Globalization* (London: Polity).

Kaplan, R. (1993) *Balkan Ghosts: A Journey Through History* (New York: St Martins Press).

Kaplan, R. (2003) *Warrior Politics: Why Leadership Demands a Pagan Ethos* (New York: Random House).

Kaufman, S. (2008) 'Ethnic Conflict' in P. Williams (ed.), *Security Studies: An Introduction* (London: Routledge).

Kaul, I. (1995) 'Peace Needs no Weapons', *Ecumenical Review*, 47:3, 313–19.

Keane, J. (2003) *Global Civil Society?* (Cambridge: Cambridge University Press).

Keck, M. and Sikkink, K. (1998) *Activists Beyond Borders: Advocacy Networks in International Politics* (Ithaca, N.Y.: Cornell University Press).

Kedourie, E. (1971) *Nationalism* (London: Hutching University Library).

Keen, D. (2001) 'War and Peace: What's the Difference?', *International Peacekeeping*, 7:4, 1–22.

Kennan, G. (1985) 'Morality and Foreign Policy', *Foreign Affairs*, 64:2, 205–18.

Kennedy, D. (2006) *The Dark Sides of Virtue: Reassessing International Humanitarianism* (Princeton, N.J.: Princeton University Press).

Kennedy, P. (1987) *The Rise and Fall of the Great Powers* (New York: Random House).

Kennedy, P. (2006) *The Parliament of Man: The Past, Present and Future of the United Nations* (New York: Random House).

Keohane, R. and Nye, J. (1977) *Power and Interdependence: World Politics in Transition* (Boston, Mass.: Little, Brown).

Khong, Y. F. (1992) *Analogies At War* (Princeton, N.J.: Princeton University Press).

Kinsella, H. (2005) 'Discourses of Difference: Civilians, Combatants, and Compliance with the Laws of War', in D. Armstrong and T. Farrell (eds), *Force and Legitimacy in World Politics* (Cambridge: Cambridge University Press).

Kissinger, H. (1992) 'Humanitarian Intervention has its Hazards', *International Herald Tribune*, 14 December.

Klein, B. S. (1994) *Strategic Studies and World Order* (Cambridge: Cambridge University Press).

Klinghoffer, J. (1998) *The International Dimension of Genocide in Rwanda* (Basingstoke and New York: Palgrave Macmillan).

Kober, S. (2000) 'Setting Dangerous International Precedents', in T. G. Carpenter (ed.), *NATO's Empty Victory* (Washington DC: Cato Institute).

Kouchner, B. (1999) 'The Right to Intervention: Codified in Kosovo', *New Perspectives Quarterly*, 16, Summer, 4.

Kratochwil, F. (1995) 'Sovereignty as Dominium', in G. Lyons and M. Mastanduno (eds), *Beyond Westphalia: State Sovereignty and International Intervention* (Baltimore: Johns Hopkins University Press).

Krasner, S. (1999) *Sovereignty: Organized Hypocrisy* (Princeton, N.J.: Princeton University Press).

Krasno, J. and Das, M. (2008) 'The Uniting for Peace Resolution and other ways of Circumventing the Authority of the Security Council', in B. Cronin and I. Hurd (eds), *The UN Security Council and the Politics of International Authority* (London: Routledge).

Kreiger, D. (2006) 'The War in Iraq as Illegal and Illegitimate', in R. Thakur and W. P. S. Sidhu (eds), *The Iraq Crisis and World Order: Structural, Institutional and Normative Challenges* (New York: United Nations University Press).

Kristol, W. and Brooks, D. (1997) 'What Ails Conservatism', *Wall Street Journal*, 15 September.

Kroslak, D. (2007) *The Role of France in the Rwandan Genocide* (London: Hurst).

Krygier, M. (1986) 'Law as Tradition', *Law and Philosophy*, 5, 237–62.

Küng, H. (1991) *Global Responsibility* (New York: Crossroad).

Kum, J. (1990) 'African Interstate Conflict: A Perceptual Approach', *Journal of Peace Research*, 27:4, 445–60.

Kuperman, A. (2000a) 'Rwanda in Retrospect', *Foreign Affairs*, 79:1, 94–118.

Kuperman, A. (2000b) 'Shame – Rationalizing Western Apathy on Rwanda: Kuperman Replies', *Foreign Affairs*, 79:3, 142–4.

Kuperman, A. (2001) *The Limits of Humanitarian Intervention: Genocide in Rwanda* (Washington DC: Brookings Institution Press).

Kuperman, A. (2003) 'Transnational Causes of Genocide', in R. Thomas (ed.), *Yugoslavia Unraveled: Sovereignty, Self Determination, Intervention* (Oxford: Lexington).

Kuperman, A. (2006) 'Suicidal Rebellions and the Moral Hazard of Humanitarian Intervention', in T. Crawford and A. Kuperman (eds), *Gambling on Humanitarian Intervention* (London: Routledge).

Landman, T. (2005) *Studying Human Rights* (London: Routledge).

Lang, A. (2003) 'Humanitarian Intervention: Definition and Debates', in A. Lang (ed.), *Just Intervention* (Washington DC: Georgetown University Press).

Laughland, J. (2002) 'Human Rights and the Rule of Law: Achieving Universal Justice?' in D. Chandler (ed.), *Rethinking Human Rights* (Basingstoke and New York: Palgrave Macmillan).

Lauterpacht, H. (1952) 'The Problem of the Revision of the Law of War', *British Yearbook of International Law*, 29.

Layne, C. (1993) 'The Unipolar Illusion: Why new Great Powers Will Rise', *International Security*, 17:4, 5–51.

Layne, C. (1994) 'Kant or Cant: The Myth of the Democratic Peace', *International Security*, 19:2, 5–49.

Layne, C. (2000) 'Miscalculations and Blunders Lead to War', in T. G. Carpenter (ed.), *NATO's Empty Victory* (Washington DC: Cato Institute).

Lenin, V. I. (1964) *Collected Works* (Moscow: Progress).

Levy, J. (1989) 'Domestic Politics and War', in R. Rotberg and T. Rabb (eds). *The Origin and Prevention of Major Wars* (Cambridge: Cambridge University Press).

Levy, M. A., Young, O. R. and Zürn, M. (1995) 'The Study of International Regimes', *European Journal of International Relations*, 1:3, 267–330.

Lillich, R. (1967) 'Forcible Self-Help by States to Protect Human Rights', *Iowa Law Review*, 53, 290–314.

Linklater, A. (1998) *The Transformation of Political Community* (Oxford: Polity).

Linklater, A. (2000) 'The Good International Citizen and the Crisis in Kosovo', in A. Schnabel and R. Thakur (eds), *Kosovo and the Challenge of Humanitarian Intervention* (New York: United Nations University Press).

Linklater, A. (2005) 'The English School', in S. Burchill, R. Devetak A. Linklater, M. Paterson, C. Reus-Smit and J. True (eds), *Theories of International Relations* (Basingstoke: Palgrave Macmillan).

Linklater, A. (2006) 'The Achievements of Critical Theory', in S. Smith, K. Booth and M. Zalewski (eds), *International Theory: Positivism and Beyond* (Cambridge: Cambridge University Press).

Lu, C. (2006) *Just and Unjust Interventions in World Politics: Public and Private* (Basingstoke and New York: Palgrave Macmillan).

Lucas, G. R. (2003) 'From *jus ad bellum* to *jus ad pacem*: Re-thinking Just-war Criteria for the Use of Military Force for Humanitarian Ends', in D. K. Chatterjee and D. E. Scheid (eds), *Ethics and Foreign Intervention* (Cambridge: Cambridge University Press).

Luttwak, E. (1999) 'Give War a Chance', *Foreign Affairs*, 78:4, 36–44.

Lyons, G. and Mastanduno, M. (1995) 'Introduction', in G. Lyons and M. Mastanduno (eds), *Beyond Westphalia: State Sovereignty and International Intervention* (Baltimore: Johns Hopkins University Press).

Macfarlane, N., Thielking, C. and Weiss, T. (2004) 'The Responsibility to Protect: Is Anyone Interested in Humanitarian Intervention?', *Third World Quarterly*, 25:5, 977–92.

MacMahon, J. (2005) 'Just Cause for War', *Ethics and International Affairs* 19:3, 1–21.

Malanczuk, P. (2006) *Akehurst's Modern Introduction to International Law* (London: Routledge).

Malcolm, N. (2002) *Aspects of Hobbes* (Oxford: Oxford University Press).

Malone, D. (2006) *The International Struggle Over Iraq: Politics in the UN Security Council 1980–2005* (Oxford: Oxford University Press).

Malmvig, H. (2001) 'The Reproduction of Sovereignties: Between Man and State During Practices of Intervention', *Cooperation and Conflict*, 36:3, 251–72.

Mamdani, M. (2009) *Saviors and Survivors: Darfur, Politics, and the War on Terror* (London: Pantheon).

Mandani, M. (2001) *When Victims Become Killers: Colonialism, Nativism and the Genocide in Rwanda* (Princeton, N.J.: Princeton University Press).

Mandel, M. (2003) 'Illegal Wars, Collateral Damage and International Criminal Law', in R. Thomas (ed.), *Yugoslavia Unraveled: Sovereignty, Self Determination, Intervention* (Oxford: Lexington).

Mandelbaum, M. (1999) 'A Perfect Failure; NATO's War Against Yugoslavia', *Foreign Affairs*, 78:5, 2–8.

Marx, K. (2006) *Capital: Critique of Political Economy, III*, trans. D. Fernbach (London: Penguin).

Mayall, J. (2006) 'Humanitarian Intervention and International Society: Lessons From Africa', in J. Welsh (ed.), *Humanitarian Intervention and International Relations* (Oxford: Oxford University Press).

Mayroz, E. (2008) 'Ever Again? The United States, Genocide Suppression, and the Crisis in Darfur', *Journal of Genocide Research*, 10:3, 359–88.

Mazower, M. (2003) *The Balkans* (London: Phoenix).

McCain, J. (2007) 'An Enduring Peace Built on Freedom', *Foreign Affairs*, 86:6, 19–34.

McCoubrey, H. (2000) 'International Humanitarian Law and the Kosovo Crisis', in K. Booth (ed.), *The Kosovo Tragedy: The Human Rights Dimension* (London: Routledge).

Mearsheimer, J. (1990) 'Back to the Future', *International Security*, 15:4, 5–56.

Mearsheimer, J. (1994) 'The False Promise of International Institutions', *International Security*, 19:3, 5–49.

Médecins Sans Frontières (MSF) (2005) 'MSF Condemns Violence in Darfur', 8 April [online] http://www.msf.org/msfinternational/invoke.cfm?component=articleandobjectid=2260FE2B-E018-0C72-09DACE85BB3176F8andmethod=full_html (accessed 2 November 2007).

MSF (2008) 'About Us: What is Doctors Without Borders/Médecins Sans Frontières?' [online] http://www.doctorswithoutborders.org/aboutus/ (accessed 2 November 2007).

Meixner, A. (2007) 'Darfur: A Problem Worth Solving', SaveDarfur, 1 November [online] http://www.savedarfur.org/blog/entries/darfur_a_problem_worth_solving/ (accessed 2 November 2007).

Melanson, R. (2007) 'Unraveling the Domestic Foreign Policy Consensus', in J. Dumbrell and D. Ryan (eds), *Vietnam in Iraq* (London: Routledge).

Melvern, L. (2004) *Conspiracy to Murder: The Rwandan Genocide* (London: Verso).

Mertus, J. (1999) *Kosovo: How Myths and Truths Started A War* (London: University of California Press).

Miller, R. (2000a) 'Humanitarian Intervention Altruism, and the Limits of Casuistry' *Journal of Religious Ethics*, 28:1, 3–35.

Miller, R. (2000b) 'Respectable Oppressors, Hypocritical Liberators: Morality, Intervention and Reality', in D. Chatterjee and D. Scheid (eds), *Ethics and Foreign Intervention* (Cambridge: Cambridge University Press).

Molloy, S. (2006) *The Hidden History of Realism* (Basingstoke and New York: Palgrave Macmillan).

Morgenthau, H. J. (1951) *In Defense of the National Interest: A Critical Examination of American Foreign Policy* (New York: Alfred Knopf).

Morgenthau, H. J. (1954) *Politics Among Nations: The Struggle for Power and Peace* (New York: Alfred Knopf).

Moxon-Browne, E. (1998) 'A Future for Peacekeeping?', in E. Moxon-Browne (ed.), *A Future for Peacekeeping?* (New York: St Martin's Press).

Mueller, J. (2000) 'The Banality of "Ethnic War"' *International Security*, 25:1, 42–70.

Mueller, J. (2005) 'Force, Legitimacy, Success, and Iraq', in D. Armstrong, T. Farrell and B. Maiguashca (eds), *Force and Legitimacy in World Politics* (Cambridge: Cambridge University Press).

Mueller, J. (2006) 'Vietnam and Iraq', in J. Dumbrell and D. Ryan (eds), *Vietnam in Iraq*, (London: Routledge).

Myers, R. J. (1996) 'Notes on the Just War Theory: Whose Justice, Which Wars?', *Ethics and International Affairs*, 116–30.

Nardin, T. (ed.) (1998) *The Ethics of War and Peace: Religious and Secular Perspectives* (Princeton: Princeton University Press).

Nardin, T. (2002) 'Ethical Traditions in International Affairs', in T. Nardin and D. R. Mapel (eds), *Traditions of International Ethics* (Cambridge: Cambridge University Press).

Nardin, T. (2003) 'The Moral Basis for Humanitarian Intervention', in A. Lang (ed.), *Just Intervention* (Washington DC: Georgetown University Press).

Nardin, T. (2005) 'Response to "Ending Tyranny in Iraq": Humanitarian Imperialism', *Ethics and International Affairs*, 19:2, 21–6.

New York Times (1998) 'Clinton in Africa; Clinton's Painful Words of Sorrow and Chagrin', *New York Times*, 26 March.

New York Times (1999) 'Conflict in the Balkans', Foreign Desk, *New York Times*, 25 March.

NATO (1999) 'Statement by the North Atlantic Council on Kosovo', press release 99(12), 30 January [online] http://www.nato.int/docu/pr/1999/p99-012e.htm (accessed 26 February 2009).

Niebuhr, R. (1932) *Moral Man and Immoral Society: A Study in Ethics and Politics* (New York: Charles Scribners).

Number 10 (2003) 'Legal basis for the use of force against Iraq', Number 10.Gov.UK, 17 March [online] http://www.number10.gov.uk/Page3287 (accessed 26 February 2009).

O'Donovan, O. (2003) *The Just War Revisited* (Cambridge: Cambridge University Press).

O'Fahey, R. S. (2008) *The Darfur Sultanate: A History* (London: Hurst).

O'Reilly, F. (2004) 'Environmental Degradation as a Cause of Conflict in Darfur', Conference Proceeding, Khatoum, December, University for Peace [online] http://www.unsudanig.org/darfurjam/trackII/data/cluster/development/Environm ental%20Degradation%20as%20a%20cause%20of%20conflict%20in%20Darf ur%20(.pdf#page=23 (accessed 26 February 2009).

O'Tuathail, G. (1996) 'An Anti-Geopolitical Eye: Maggie O'Kane in Bosnia, 1992–93', *Gender, Place an Culture*, 3:2, 171–85.

Oppenheim, L. (2006) *International Law: A Treatise* (London: Lawbook Exchange).

Orend, B. (2000) 'Jus Post Bellum', *Journal of Social Philosophy*, 31, 1, 117–37.

Orford, A. (2003) *Reading Humanitarian Intervention* (Cambridge: Cambridge University Press).

Osiander, A. (1994) *The State System of Europe, 1640–1990* (Oxford: Oxford University Press).

Owens, P. (2004) 'Xenophilia, Gender and Sentimental Humanitarianism', *Alternatives*, 29, 285–304.

Pangle, T. and Ahrensdorf, P. (1999) *Justice Among Nations: On the Moral Basis of Power and Peace* (Kansas: University Press of Kansas).

Parsi, V. E. (2006) *The Inevitable Alliance: Europe and the United States Beyond Iraq* (Basingstoke and New York: Palgrave Macmillan).

Pasic, A. and Weiss, T. (2003) 'The Politics of Rescue: Yugoslavia's Wars and the Humanitarian Impulse', in A. Lang (ed.), *Just Intervention* (Washington DC: Georgetown University Press).

Pattison, J. (2007) 'Humanitarian Intervention and International Law: The Moral Importance of an Intervener's Legal Status', *Critical Review of International Social and Political Philosophy*, 10:3, 301–19.

Pavkovic, A. (2003) 'Humanitarian Intervention in Nationalist Conflicts', in A. Jokic (ed.), *Lessons of Kosovo: The Dangers of Humanitarian Intervention* (Ontario: Broadview Press).

Pesic, V. (1996) 'The War for Ethnic States', in N. Popov (ed.), *The Road to War in Serbia* (New York: CEU Press).

Pogge, T. (1994) 'Cosmopolitanism and Sovereignty', in C. Brown (ed.), *Political Restructuring in Europe: Ethical Perspectives* (London: Routledge).

Power, S. (2001) 'By-standers to Genocide', *Atlantic*, September [online] http://www.theatlantic.com/doc/200109/power-genocide (accessed 2 May 2009).

Project for a New American Century (1998) 'Open Letter to President William J. Clinton', 26 January [online] http://www.newamericancentury.org/iraqclinton-letter.htm (accessed 2 May 2009).

Prokopijevic, M. (2004) 'Humanitarian Intervention', in G. Meggle (ed.), *Ethics of Humanitarian Intervention* (Frankfurt: Ontas).

Prunier, G. (1997) *The Rwanda Crisis: History of a Genocide* (New York: Colombia University Press).

Prunier, G. (2005) *Darfur: The Ambiguous Genocide* (Ithaca, N.Y.: Cornell University Press).

Rabinow, P. (ed.) (1984) *The Foucault Reader* (New York: Pantheon).

Reed, C. and Ryall, D. (2007) 'Introduction', in C. Reed and D. Ryall (eds), *The Price of Peace* (Cambridge: Cambridge University Press).

Reeves, E. (2005) 'Genocide by Attrition: Agony in Darfur', *Dissent*, Winter.

Reisman, M. (2000) 'Unilateral Action and the Transformations of the World Constitutive Process: The Special Problem of Humanitarian Intervention', *European Journal of International Law*, 11:1, 3–18.

Rengger, N. (2002) 'On the Just War Tradition in the Twenty First Century', *International Affairs*, 78:2, 353–63.

Rengger, N. (2005) 'The Judgment of War: On the Idea of Legitimate Force in World Politics', in D. Armstrong, T. Farrell and B. Maiguashca (eds), *Force and Legitimacy in World Politics* (Cambridge: Cambridge University Press).

Reus-Smit, C. (2005) 'Liberal Hierarchy and the License to Use Force', in D. Armstrong, T. Farrell and B. Maiguashca (eds), *Force and Legitimacy in World Politics* (Cambridge: Cambridge University Press).

Rice, C. (2000) 'Promoting the National Interest', *Foreign Affairs*, 79:1, 45–78.

Rice, S. (2005) 'Why Darfur Can't be Left to Africa', *Washington Post*, 7 August [online] http://www.brookings.edu/articles/2005/0807africa_rice.aspx (accessed February 2009).

Richmond, O. (2005) 'UN Peacebuilding Operations and the Dilemma of the Peacebuilding Consensus', in A. Bellamy and P. Williams (eds), *Peace Operations and the Global Order* (London: Routledge).

Rieff, D. (2004) 'Kosovo: The End of an Era?' in F. Weissman (ed.), *In the Shadow of 'Just Wars': Violence, Politics and Humanitarian Action* (London: Hurst).

Rieff, D. (2006) 'A Nation of Pre-emptors?', *New York Times Magazine*, 15 January.

Roberts, A. (1999) 'NATO's "Humanitarian War" over Kosovo', *Survival*, 41, 102–23.

Roberts, A. (2002) 'The So-Called "Right" of Humanitarian Intervention', in *Yearbook of International Humanitarian Law 2000*, 3 (The Hague: T.M.C. Asser).

Roberts, A. (2006) 'The United Nations and Humanitarian Intervention', in J. Welsh (ed.), *Humanitarian Intervention and International Relations* (Oxford: Oxford University Press).

Robertson, G. (2002) *Crimes Against Humanity* (London: Penguin).

Rodin, D. (2002) *War and Self-Defence* (Oxford: Clarendon Press).

Rodley, N. and Cah, B. (2007) 'Kosovo Revisited: Humanitarian Intervention on the Fault Lines of International Law', *Human Rights Law Review*, 7: 2, 275–97.

Roper, J. (2006) 'Europe's Vietnam Syndrome: America and the Quagmire of Iraq', in J. Dumbrell and D. Ryan (eds), *Vietnam in Iraq* (London: Routledge).

Rosenberg, J. (1994) *Empire of Civil Society* (London: Verso).

Rosenthal, J. H. (1995) 'Biography, Ethics and Statecraft', in C. J. Nolan (ed.), *Ethics and Statecraft: The Moral Dimensions of International Affairs* (Westport, Conn.: Praeger).

Roth, K. (2000) 'Bombs Report off Target', *Guardian*, 12 January, 21.

Rupert, M. (2007) 'Marxism and Critical Theory', in T. Dunne, M. Kurki and S. Smith (eds), *International Relations Theories: Discipline and Diversity* (Oxford: Oxford University Press).

Russett, B. Starr, H. and Kinsella, D. (2000) *World Politics: The Menu for Choice* (New York: St Martins Press).

Ryan, D. (2007) '"Vietnam", Victory Culture and Iraq', in J. Dumbrell and D. Ryan (eds), *Vietnam in Iraq* (London: Routledge).

Said, E. (1993) *Culture and Imperialism* (London, Chatto & Windus).

Sands, P. (2006) *Lawless World* (London: Penguin).

SaveDarfur (2007) 'About US: Frequently Asked Questions' [online] http://www.savedarfur.org/pages/faq/#1 (accessed 2 November 2007).

Schabas, W. (2000) *Genocide in International Law: The Crimes of Crimes* (Cambridge: Cambridge University Press).

Schachter, O. (1991) *International Law in Theory and Practice* (London: Martinus Nijhoff).

Schmitt, C. (1996) *The Concept of the Political*, trans. G. Schwab (Chicago: University of Chicago Press).

Sciolino, E. and Bronner, E. (1999) 'Crisis in the Balkans', *New York Times*, 18 April, 3.

Sciolino, E. (2007) 'A Surprising Choice for France's Foreign Minister', *New York Times*, 18 May.

Seybolt, T. (2007) *Humanitarian Military Intervention: The Conditions for Success and Failure* (Oxford: Oxford University Press).

Shaw, M. (1994) *Global Civil Society and International Relations* (London: Polity).

Shawcross, W. (2001) *Deliver Us From Evil* (London: Bloomsbury).

Shue, H. (2003) 'Bombing to Rescue? NATO's 1999 bombing of Serbia', in D. Chatterjee and D. Scheid (eds), *Ethics and Foreign Intervention* (Cambridge: Cambridge University Press).

Simma, B. (1999) 'NATO, the UN and the Use of Force', *European Journal of International Law*, 10:1, 1–22.

Simpson, G. (2004) *Great Powers and Outlaw States* (Cambridge: Cambridge University Press).

Singh, R. (2006) 'The Bush Doctrine', in M. Buckley and R. Singh (eds), *The Bush Doctrine and the War on Terrorism* (London, Routledge).

Slaughter, A. M. (2003) 'Good Reasons for Going Around the UN', *New York Times*, 18 March.

Slim, H. (2004) 'Dithering over Darfur?', *International Affairs*, 80:5, 811–28.

Smith, M. (1998) 'Humanitarian Intervention: An Overview of Ethical Issues', *Ethics and International Affairs*, 12:1, 63–79.

Sørensen, G. (2001) *Changes in Statehood: The Transformation of International Relations* (Basingstoke and New York: Palgrave Macmillan).

Spykman, N. (1942) *America's Strategy in World Politics* (New York: Harcourt, Brace).

Starr, H. (1995) 'International Law and International Order', in C. Kegley (ed.), *Controversies in International Relations Theory* (New York: St Martins Press).

Steans, J. and Pettiford, L. (2005) *Introduction to International Relations* (London: Pearson Longmans).

Straus, S. (2005) 'Darfur and the Genocide Debate', *Foreign Affairs*, 81:4, 123–33.

Stromseth, J. (2005) 'Rethinking Humanitarian Intervention', in J. L. Holzgrefe and R. Keohane (eds), *Humanitarian Intervention* (Cambridge: Cambridge University Press).

Sulyok, G. (2003) 'The Theory of Humanitarian Intervention with Special Regard to NATO's Kosovo Mission', in F. Bieber and Z. Daskalovski (eds), *Understanding the War in Kosovo* (London: Frank Cass).

Sutterlin, J. (2003) *The United Nations and the Maintenance of International Security* (Westport, Conn.: Praeger).

Tanguy, J. (2003) 'Redefining Sovereignty and Intervention', *Ethics and International Affairs*, 17:1, 141–8.

Tesón, F. (1988) *Humanitarian Intervention: An Enquiry into Law and Morality* (New York: Transnational).

Tesón, F. (1996) 'Collective Humanitarian Intervention', *Michigan Journal of International Law*, 17, 323–71.

Tesón, F. (2005a) 'The Liberal Case for Humanitarian Intervention', in L May, E. Rove and S. Viner (eds), *The Morality of War: Classical and Contemporary Readings* (Upper Saddle River, N.J.: Pearson).

Tesón, F. (2005b) 'Ending Tyranny in Iraq', *Ethics and International Affairs*, 19:2, 1–20.

Thakur, R. (2006) 'The Responsibility to Protect', in R. Thakur and W. P. S. Sidhu (eds), *The Iraq Crisis and World Order: Structural, Institutional and Normative Challenges* (New York: United Nations University Press).

Thakur, R. and Sidhu, W. P. S. (2006) 'Iraq's Challenge to World Order', in R. Thakur and W. P. S. Sidhu (eds), *The Iraq Crisis and World Order: Structural, Institutional and Normative Challenges* (New York: United Nations University Press).

Thomas, N. and Tow, W. (2002) 'The Utility of Human Security: Sovereignty and Humanitarian Intervention', *Security Dialogue*, 33:2, 127–40.

Thomas, R. (2003) 'Wars, Humanitarian Intervention and International Law', in R. Thomas (ed.), *Yugoslavia Unraveled: Sovereignty, Self Determination, Intervention* (Oxford: Lexington).

Thompson, J. (1992) *Justice and World Order: A Philosophical Enquiry* (London: Routledge).

Thucydides (1972) *History of the Peloponnesian War*, trans. R. Warner (London: Penguin).

Tilly, C. (1990) *Coercion, Capital and European States* (Oxford: Blackwell).

Tooke, J. (1965) *The Just War in Aquinas and Grotius* (London: S.P.C.K).

Tucker, R. (1960) *The Just War: A Study on Contemporary Doctrine* (Baltimore, Md.: Johns Hopkins University Press).

Tyler, P. (2003) 'Threats and Responses: News Analysis; A New Power in the Streets', *New York Times*, 17 February.

Tyner, J. (2006) *The Business of War* (Aldershot: Ashgate).

United Nations (UN) (1999) 'Report of the Independent Inquiry into the Actions of the United Nations During the 1994 Genocide in Rwanda', S/1999/1257, 15 December [online] http://www.un.org/News/dh/latest/rwanda.htm (accessed 2 May 2009).

UN Commission on Global Governance (1995) *Our Global Neighbourhood* (Oxford: Oxford University Press).

UN General Assembly (1993) 'Vienna Declaration and Programme of Action', A/CONF.157/23, 12 July [online] http://www.unhchr.ch/huridocda/huridoca.nsf/(Symbol)/A.CONF.157.23.En (accessed 26 February 2009).

UN General Assembly (2000) 'United Nations Millennium Declaration', 55/2, 8 September [online] http://www.un.org/millennium/declaration/ares552e.htm (accessed 26 February 2009).

UN General Assembly (2005) *Outcome Document* for 2005 World Summit, A/60/L.1, 15 September [online] http://www.who.int/hiv/universalaccess2010/worldsummit.pdf (accessed 26 February 2009).

UN General Assembly (2008) 'Human Rights Situations that Require the Council's Attention: Report of the Special Rapporteur on the Situation of Human Rights in the Sudan, Sima Samar', A/HRC/9/13, 2 September [online] http://www. reliefweb.int/rw/RWFiles2008.nsf/FilesByRWDocUnidFilename/EGUA-7JJNR2-full_report.pdf/$File/full_report.pdf (accessed 24 September, 2008).

UN High Commissioner for Human Rights (UNHCHR) (2004) 'Report of the United Nations High Commissioner for Human Rights and Follow-Up to the World Conference on Human Rights: Situation of Human Rights in the Darfur region of Sudan', E/CN.4/2005/3, 7 May [online] http://www.unhchr.ch/ huridocda/huridoca.nsf/AllSymbols/863D14602AA82CAEC1256EA80038E268/ $File/G0414221.doc?OpenElement (accessed 12 October 2007).

UN High-Level Panel on Threats, Challenges and Change (2004) *A More Secure World: Our Shared Responsibility*, 2 December [online] http://www.un.org/ secureworld/report.pdf (accessed 2 May 2009).

UN Human Rights Council (2007) 'Report of the High-Level Mission on the Situation of Human Rights in Darfur pursuant to Human Rights Council decision S-4/101', A/HRC/4/80, 9 March.

UN Security Council (1994) 'Letter Dated 15 April 1994 from the Permanent Representative of Belgium to the United Nations Addressed to the President of the Security Council', S/1994/446, 15 April.

UN Security Council (2004) 5015th Meeting, 30 July, S/PV.5015 [online] http://daccessdds.un.org/doc/UNDOC/PRO/N04/445/15/PDF/N0444515.pdf? OpenElement (accessed 2 November 2007).

United States Department of State (2004) 'The Crisis in Darfur: Secretary Colin Powell, Testimony before the Senate Foreign Relations Committee', 9 September [online] http://www.state.gov/secretary/former/powell/remarks/36042.htm (accessed 11 October 2007).

Uvin, P. (1998) *Aiding Violence: The Development Enterprise in Rwanda* (West Hartford, Conn.: Kumarian).

Uvin, P. (1999) 'Ethnicity and Power in Burundi and Rwanda: Different Paths to Mass Violence', *Comparative Politics*, 31:3, 253–71.

Uvin, P. (2001) 'Reading the Rwandan Genocide', *International Studies Review*, 3:3, 75–99.

Vincent, J. (1974) *Non Intervention and International Order* (Princeton, N.J.: Princeton University Press).

Vincent, J. (1986) *Human Rights and International Relations* (Cambridge: Cambridge University Press).

Voeten, E. (2008) 'Delegation and the Nature of Security Council Authority', in B. Cronin and I. Hurd (eds), *The UN Security Council and the Politics of International Authority* (London: Routledge).

Walker, R. B. J. (2003) 'Polis, Cosmopolis, Politics', *Alternatives*, 28, 267–86.

Wall Street Journal (1992) 'Everybody's Business', editorial, *Wall Street Journal*, 24 August.

Wallerstein, I. (1974) *The Modern World System* (New York: Academic Press).

Waltz, K. (1979) *Theory of International Politics* (Toronto: McGraw-Hill).

Waltz, K. (1981) 'The Spread of Nuclear Weapons: More May Be Better', *Adelphi Papers*, 171 (London: International Institute for Strategic Studies).

Waltz, K. (1991) 'Realist Thought and Neo-realist Theory', in R. L. Rothstein (ed.),

The Evolution of Theory in International Relations (Columbia, S.C.: University of South Carolina Press).

Walzer, M. (1992b) 'The Argument about Humanitarian Intervention', in N. Mills and K. Brunner (eds), *The New Killing Fields* (New York: Basic Books).

Walzer, M. (1992) *Just and Unjust Wars* (New York: Basic Books).

Walzer, M. (2006) *Just and Unjust Wars*, rev. edn (New York: Basic Books).

Watts, A. (2001) 'The Importance of International Law', in M. Byers (ed.), *The Role of International Law in International Politics* (Oxford: Oxford University Press).

Weber, C. (1995) *Simulating Sovereignty: Intervention, the State and Symbolic Exchange* (Cambridge: Cambridge University Press).

Wedgewood, R. (2003) 'Legal Authority Exists for Strike on Iraq', *Financial Times*, 14 March.

Wedgewood, R. (2006) 'The Multinational Action in Iraq and International Law', in R. Thakur and W. P. S. Sidhu (eds), *The Iraq Crisis and World Order: Structural, Institutional and Normative Challenges* (New York: United Nations University Press).

Weigel, G. (2007) 'The Development of Just War Thinking in the post-Cold War World', in C. Reed and D. Ryall (eds), *The Price of Peace* (Cambridge: Cambridge University Press).

Weiss, T. (1999) 'Principles, Politics and Humanitarian Action' *Ethics and International Affairs*, 13, 1–22.

Weiss, T. (2007) *Humanitarian Intervention* (London: Polity).

Weller, M. (1999) *The Crisis in Kosovo 1989–1999* (Cambridge: Documents and Analysis Publishing).

Welsh, J. (ed.) (2006) *Humanitarian Intervention and International Relations* (Oxford: Oxford University Press).

Wesley, M. (2006) 'The New Interventionism and the Invasion of Iraq', in M. Heazle and I. Islam (eds), *Beyond the Iraq War: The Promises, Pitfalls and Perils of External Interventionism* (Cheltenham: Edward Elgar).

Wheeler, N. (1992) 'Pluralist or Solidarist Conceptions of International Society: Bull and Vincent on Humanitarian Intervention', *Millennium*, 21:3, 463–87.

Wheeler, N. (1997a) 'Guardian Angel or Global Gangster?' *Political Studies*, 44:1, 123–35.

Wheeler, N. (1997b) 'Agency, Humanitarianism and Intervention', *International Political Science Review*, 18, 1, 9–25.

Wheeler, N. (2002) *Saving Strangers: Humanitarian Intervention in International Society* (Oxford: Oxford University Press).

Wheeler, N. (2003) 'Humanitarian Intervention after September 11, 2001', in A. Lang (ed.), *Just Intervention* (Washington DC: Georgetown University Press).

Wheeler, N. (2005) 'A Victory for Common Humanity? The Responsibility to Protect after the 2005 World Summit', *Journal of International Law and International Relations*, 2:1, 95–106.

Wheeler, N. (2006) 'The Humanitarian Responsibilities of Sovereignty', in J. Welsh (ed.), *Humanitarian Intervention and International Relations* (Oxford: Oxford University Press).

Wheeler, N. and Dunne, T. (1998) 'Good International Citizenship: A Third Way for British Foreign Policy', *International Affairs*, 74:4, 847–70.

Wheeler, N. and Dunne, T. (2001) 'East Timor and the New Humanitarian Interventionism', *International Affairs*, 77/4, 805–27.

Wheeler, N. and Morris, J. (2007) 'Justifying the Iraq War as a Humanitarian Intervention: The Cure is Worse then the Disease' in R. Thakur and W. P. S. Sidhu (eds), *The Iraq Crisis and World Order: Structural, Institutional and Normative Challenges* (New York: United Nations University Press).

White, N. (2000) 'The Legality of Bombing in the Name of Humanity', *Journal of Conflict and Security Law*, 5:1, 27–43.

White, N. (2004) 'The Will and Authority of the Security Council after Iraq', *Leiden Journal of International Law*, 17: 4, 645–72.

White House (2002a) 'President Delivers State of the Union Address', 29 January [online]   http://www.whitehouse.gov/news/releases/2002/01/20020129-11.html (accessed 15 June 2008).

White House (2002b) 'Vice President speaks at VFW 103rd National Convention', 26 August [online] http://www.whitehouse.gov/news/releases/2002/08/20020826.html (accessed 15 June 2008).

White House (2003a) 'President Says Saddam Hussein Must Leave Iraq Within 48 Hours: Remarks by the President in Address to the Nation', 17 March [online] www.whitehouse.gov/news/releases/2003/03/20030317-7.html (accessed 15 June 2008).

White House (2003b) 'President Discusses Beginning of Operation Iraqi Freedom', White House press release, 22 March [online] http://www.whitehouse.gov/news/releases/2003/03/20030322.html (accessed 4 October 2007).

White House (2003c) 'President Announces End to Major Combat Operations', 1 May [online] http://www.whitehouse.gov/news/releases/2003/05/20030501-15.html (accessed 15 June 2008).

White House (2004a) 'President Addresses the Nation in Prime Time Press Conference', 13 April [online] http://www.whitehouse.gov/news/releases/2004/04/20040413-20.html (accessed 4 October 2007).

White House (2004b) 'President Speaks to the United Nations General Assembly', White House press release, 21 September [online] http://www.whitehouse.gov/news/releases/2004/09/20040921-3.html (accessed 12 December 2008).

White House (2004c) 'President and Prime Minister Blair Discussed Iraq, Middle East', press release, 12 November [online] http://www.whitehouse.gov/news/releases/2004/11/20041112-5.html (accessed 15 June 2008).

Whitman, J. (2005) 'Humanitarian Intervention in an Era of Pre-emptive Self-defence', *Security Dialogue*, 36:3, 259–74.

Wight, M. (1966a) 'Why Is There no International Theory?' in H. Butterfield and M. Wight (eds), *Diplomatic Investigations: Essays in the Theory of International Politics* (Cambridge, Mass.: Harvard University Press).

Wight, M. (1966b) 'Western Values in International Relations', in H. Butterfield and M. Wight (eds), *Diplomatic Investigations: Essays in the Theory of International Politics* (Cambridge, Mass.: Harvard University Press).

Wight , M. (1979a) *Power Politics* (Harmondsworth: Penguin).

Wight, M. (1979b) *International Theory: The Three Traditions*, ed. G. Wight and B. Porter (Leicester: Leicester University Press).

Williams, M. (2005) 'What is the National Interest? The Neoconservative Challenge in IR Theory', *European Journal of International Relations*, 11:3, 307–33.

Williams, M. (2007) *Realism Reconsidered* (Oxford: Oxford University Press).

Williams, P. (2005) 'Peace Operations and the International Financial Institutions: Insights from Rwanda and Sierra Leone', in P. Williams and A. Bellamy (eds), *Peace Operations and the Global Order* (Oxford: Routledge).

Williams, P. (ed.) (2008) *Security Studies: An Introduction* (London: Routledge).

Williams, P. and Bellamy, A. (2005) 'The Responsibility to Protect and the Crisis in Darfur', *Security Dialogue*, 36:1, 27–47.

Wood, E. M. (2000) 'Kosovo and the New Imperialism', in T. Ali (ed.), *Masters of the Universe? NATO's Balkan Crusade* (London: Verso).

Woodhouse, T. and Ramsbotham, O. (2005) 'Cosmopolitan Peacekeeping and the Global Order', *International Peacekeeping*, 12:2, 139–56.

Wolf, M. (2005) 'The Case for Optimism: A Response', in D. Held (ed.), *Debating Globalization* (London: Polity).

Wright, R. (2006) *A Short History of Progress* (Edinburgh: Canongate).

Young, I. (2000) 'Violence Against Power: Critical Thoughts on Humanitarian Intervention', in D. Chatterjee and D. Scheid (eds), *Ethics and Foreign Intervention* (Cambridge: Cambridge University Press).

Young, M. B. (2006) 'The Vietnam Laughter Track', in J. Dumbrell and D. Ryan (eds) *Vietnam in Iraq* (London: Routledge).

Zakaria, F. (1992) 'Is Realism Finished?' *The National Interest*, Winter, 30.

Zaum, D. (2007) *The Sovereignty Paradox: The Norms and Politics of International Statebuilding* (Oxford: Oxford University Press).

Zolo, D. (1997) *Cosmopolis* (Cambridge: Polity Press).

Index